Debunking
History

Debunking
History

152 Popular Myths Exploded

Ed Rayner & Ron Stapley

SUTTON PUBLISHING

This book was first published in 2002 by
Sutton Publishing Limited · Phoenix Mill
Thrupp · Stroud · Gloucestershire · GL5 2BU

This new paperback edition first published in 2006

Reprinted 2006

British Library Cataloguing in Publication Data
A catalogue record for this book is available from the British
Library.

ISBN 0 7509 4151 0

Typeset in 10/12.5pt Iowan.
Typesetting and origination by
Sutton Publishing Limited.
Printed and bound in Great Britain by
J.H. Haynes & Co. Ltd, Sparkford.

CONTENTS

Contents

Contents

PREFACE

It is sometimes said that there can be no such thing as an error in history, since history is concerned with what has already happened, and what has happened is forever fixed and unalterable. Only in the present is there any choice about what we do, and certainly here it is possible to make an error. What has happened in the past is settled and done with, and there is no way that we in the present can change that. But history is not solely *what happened* in the past; it is also the *study* of what happened in the past. Here it is certainly possible to make mistakes.

Errors. Either accidentally through ignorance, or deliberately through misrepresentation, we can get the facts of history wrong. If we said that Nelson was killed at the battle of Waterloo, such a statement would plainly be an error, as it would if we stated that the Allies dropped the first atomic bombs on Japan in 1941. Such errors are brought about by ignorance of the facts of history. Misrepresentation of the facts, say for purposes of propaganda – the view, for example, that during the First World War the British fleet secured an overwhelming victory at Jutland over the Germans in 1916 – would also be an error, even though it achieved wide acceptance at the time and afterwards. This was the British propaganda view of the battle, and differed significantly from the truth.

Myths. Misrepresentations also include myths and legends in history, for the borderline between error and deliberate misrepresentation is uncertain and often blurred. Sometimes what originated as a simple error has achieved a certain permanence in people's minds because it seems appropriate – a *myth* perhaps even more appropriate than the truth – and therefore lives on, even after efforts have been made to correct it. This was the case with Marie Antoinette's reported advice to the hungry Parisians in the French Revolution: 'Let them eat cake!' While this version of events was not true, it seemed to characterise the heartlessness and stupidity of the young Queen at that time, and in a way was actually *better than the truth*.

A *legend*, too, is something that people choose to believe whether it is true or not. The historical reputations of Davy Crockett, John Brown or General Custer in nineteenth-century American history have something of this legendary quality, or, closer to home, the reputations of people such as Florence Nightingale or Lawrence of Arabia. In all these cases the historical truth, itself already fascinating, has been elaborated upon by admirers or hagiographers, who have less regard for what *actually* happened and more for what *should have* happened, until the historical figure achieves unquestioned greatness in the popular imagination and performs the function of some moral fable or parable. A truthful account is pedestrian by comparison.

Historical controversies. These occur when historians, looking separately at sets of events that have occurred in the past, enter into a debate about the significance of these facts, arguing that their real importance is perhaps different from their surface appearance. Historians often construct *different theories* to explain what they believe to be the most likely course of these events, or the most likely explanation for whatever may have happened.

There was a time, for example, when historians, looking at the events which led to the political unification of Italy in the 1860s, used the facts at their disposal to argue that Cavour, the Prime Minister of Piedmont, deliberately fostered the creation of a united Italian state. Later, looking at the same facts, but this time in the light of new documentary evidence resulting from the opening up of the archives of the Gregorian University in Rome in the later 1940s and 1950s, they concluded that unification was not actually his objective at all; indeed, in a number of ways, he actually was opposed to it. This particular controversy now seems to have been settled, but no matter how apparently firm are historians' conclusions there is no guarantee that later finds of fresh evidence – or new ways found of looking at the old evidence – will not radically alter things.

To those who argue that such controversies are purely speculative the answer should be that in history *all* theories and *all* controversies are necessarily speculative. For the facts of history do not wear labels indicating their real significance; this has to be worked out through the deductions of individual historians. Unlike science, where facts can be experimentally tested and proven, the facts of history are *past facts* and lie beyond experimentation. Only cosmology, where it has also so far proved impossible to manipulate the available facts, bears some resemblance to history (at least at present); here, too, widely different theories have been advanced to explain the origins of the universe.

Controversies may occur over the true significance of a character in history, or of a historical event. Was Abraham Lincoln really the champion of slave emancipation? Does the existence of the Hossbach Memorandum really prove that Hitler was planning to start the Second World War? Such views have been seriously advanced, but are they true? They are in fact no more than theories, and their reliability must be assessed. The *best* theory remains the theory which most simply and most comprehensively explains the facts available at the time. As theories change, however, they frequently leave behind a backlog of unadjusted thinking which this book aims to examine.

For the purpose of this book, the errors, the myths and legends and the controversies have been divided into thirteen categories, each arranged in roughly chronological order. This division may be regarded as rather arbitrary, and the distinctions between them rather fine, since some of the entries may be thought to fit into other categories, but reference to the table of contents will enable the reader to locate the entry he is looking for. The categories are:

1. *Ancient Grievances.* These include old grievances still rankling at the present time, though grounded on evidence which is often disputed.

2. *Conspiracies and Plots*. Here the argument is about what really happened in the past, and whether it involved any kind of conspiracy.

3. *Heroes and Villains*. Here the question revolves round some historical character, and whether our view of him as a 'hero' or a 'villain' is the right one.

4. *Historical Debates*. These include matters apparently already settled in agreement, but which perhaps deserve further discussion.

5. *Historical Revisions*. These challenge the accuracy of established historical views, providing a different view of characters or episodes in history.

6. *Historical Re-evaluations*. These give perhaps a new slant on characters or episodes in history, with a view to their being seen in a rather different light.

7. *Political Re-evaluations*. These provide a new slant on events and characters in more recent political history, with a view to re-assessing their true importance.

8. *International Re-evaluations*. These offer a new take on developments in recent international events, with a view to re-assessing their true importance.

9. *Long-standing Puzzles*. These offer different and perhaps novel interpretations of what have been perplexing features of past events.

10. *On-going Controversies*. These offer further thoughts on what have been, and continue to be, disputed verdicts on past events and people.

11. *Popular Misconceptions*. These deal with the kernel from which this book sprang, namely the 'silly mistakes' which people make in history.

12. *Persistent Misrepresentations*. These identify people or events in the past which have commonly been misjudged, and tries to set the record straight.

13. *Unresolved Problems*. These are historical questions where the 'jury is still out' and where satisfactory answers to important questions are still being sought.

Preface

The authors apologise in advance to any reader who feels cheated that his or her favourite error or controversy has been omitted. They do not claim either infallibility in detecting errors, or omniscience in correcting them. Nor do they claim always to be able to distinguish unfailingly an error from a misrepresentation, or a myth from a legend. Each of the authors has a lifetime's experience as a college teacher and a chief examiner of history, and they have the red-ink stains to prove it; but while they hope that their observations may be enlightening (and even amusing), their comments have necessarily had to be limited both from the point of view of geographical and of chronological coverage. Hence this book concentrates on the historical period from the later eighteenth century – the era of the American and French Revolutions – and focuses mainly on Britain and Europe, though it contains also some material relating to the United States and the rest of the world.

ANCIENT GRIEVANCES

The Boston Tea Party: Did it Spark the War of American Independence?

The story of the so-called Boston Tea Party provides one of the most colourful and enduring legends relating to the War of American Independence. But its significance and importance have often been misinterpreted, and its role in bringing war to the American colonies has often been misunderstood.

By the beginning of 1773 the main issues between Britain and its American colonies were already clear. Apart from the major question of taxation, whether for revenue or trade regulation (the factor which lay at the root of the Boston Tea Party) there was also the relationship between colonial legislatures and colonial governors, the question of billeting and martial law, and whether British justice was superior to colonial justice. The whole relationship between Britain and the colonies was under challenge, and no effective compromise had yet been found. But since the Boston Massacre of March 1770 American agitation had died down, and the colonies had resumed their former practice of quarrelling with each other: there were bitter boundary disputes between New York and New Hampshire, and between New York and Pennsylvania. In the Carolinas, 6,000 frontiersmen rebelled against the coastal colonial aristocracy, and were put down with the loss of 15 lives. The British government, at the same time, thought it opportune to revive the fortunes of the East India Company by encouraging more sales of its tea in America. The Tea Act allowed the importation of tea directly into America (i.e. without having to be taken to Britain first), and removed the burdensome English duty on the tea, but retained the American duty. To avoid smuggling, the Company was to deal with named official agents. This outraged those American merchants, particularly in New York and Philadelphia, who made fortunes out of smuggling tea and other goods into America: they were now to be excluded from legitimate trading and the low duty would make smuggling unprofitable. Reviving the non-importation agreements would be very difficult – after all, most of these had broken down. The patriots in Boston concluded that the Company would have no difficulty in recruiting agents there, and that they would have no difficulty in selling the tea. In desperation, therefore, some of them dressed as Mohawk Indians, boarded the two tea ships in Boston Harbour, and discharged the contents of 298 tea chests, worth £11,000, into the sea.

Did this event cause the Revolution? Not immediately and not directly. The British government could have ignored the event as it had done the pillaging of the *Gaspée* the year before. But with the *Gaspée* the main damage done was to persons rather than property, and in the eighteenth century injury to property was always regarded as much more reprehensible than injury to persons. The British government could have left it to the Massachusetts authorities to seek out and bring to justice the perpetrators. But although it was well known in Boston who the ring-leaders were, it was highly unlikely that there was enough evidence to convince a Boston jury. Throughout most of the rest of the colonies the Tea Party was a cause of shock rather than rejoicing. Even moderate patriots thought that things in Boston had gone too far.

And there it might have rested, with both British and Americans concentrating on what united rather than what divided them. But the British government somewhat mistakenly felt that even in America some punitive action was expected, and in Britain merchants and the East India Company clamoured for retribution. Having decided that the event could not go unpunished, the British government secured the passage through parliament, not without some strenuous opposition, of a series of Acts known to all patriotic Americans as the Retaliatory Acts, and these were to form the basis of the most tangible of the American grievances as listed in the American Declaration of Independence. The closing of the port of Boston was an arbitrary collective punishment. It aroused widespread resentment, even among those who would not have objected to the punishment of the perpetrators. Merchants and ordinary citizens in other ports along the eastern seaboard were alarmed that their prosperity depended on the whim of a government 3,000 miles away. The tampering with the charter of Massachusetts was an implied threat to the constitution of every other colony. The transferring of trials to England and the Quartering Act, which provided for an increased British military presence in Boston, revived earlier grievances which had been allowed to lie dormant.

Radical elements were able to persuade most Americans that the Quebec Act, which the British had been preparing some months before the Tea Party, was, in fact, an instrument for their further enslavement. New England, where conservative elements were strong outside the Massachusetts trouble centre, was predominantly Puritan. It viewed with alarm the religious freedoms confirmed to the Roman Catholics in Quebec, and regarded them incredibly as the first steps by the Church of England in alliance with the papacy (!) to destroy Puritanism. The more materialist of them objected to the extension of the Canadian frontier to the Ohio. Overall, the combined effect of the Retaliatory Acts and the Quebec Act was to play into the hands of those who wanted to revive the anti-British agitation. They were able to persuade even the moderates that it was deliberate British policy to subjugate and enslave the Americans.

It was the moderates who, fighting off proposals for a solemn league and covenant, successfully promoted the idea of an all-American Congress to meet at Philadelphia in 1774. It was soon taken over by the radicals. Without the Boston Tea Party it would probably never have met. Without the Boston Tea Party its main proposals – to pay no taxes to Britain, and to arm in self-defence – would never have been agreed. The First Continental Congress might just have avoided the breach with Britain if the British had been prepared to negotiate with it. But the British government regarded the Congress as an illegal assembly. It continued to pour troops into Boston; Massachusetts continued to arm its militia. Conflict was the inevitable result; it was not inevitable that there would be a bloody skirmish at Lexington on 19 April 1775, but it was inevitable that fighting would break out somewhere in Massachusetts during the spring of that year. The Boston Tea Party was the catalyst that helped to bring this about.

1:2

The United Empire Loyalists: Abandoned by Both Sides?

The American Revolution was the work of a vociferous minority. The passive majority, especially outside the major towns, had little interest in and less understanding of the struggle; and, unless British troops had actually plundered in their neighbourhood, little interest in the war's outcome. But there was an active minority, called Tories by the American patriots, and Loyalists (or United Empire Loyalists) by the British, who argued and sometimes fought for the British cause. During the war those Loyalists living in areas under the control of Congress suffered at best ostracism, and at worst tarring and feathering, loss of property and even loss of life. At the end of the war both sides made promises concerning the Loyalists, but whether or not they kept them has long been a matter of considerable controversy.

When Britain confirmed American independence in the peace negotiations, the problem of the Loyalists loomed large. Britain was particularly concerned that Loyalists with homes in the thirteen colonies should be allowed to return, and their properties restored. Thus the Treaty of Versailles (1783) which ended the war recommended 'to the states the payment of all debts due to British merchants and the passing of relief Acts for the restoration of the property and protection of the persons of the Loyalists'. It was difficult for the states to carry out this promise even if they had wanted to. The divisions of war were too recent and too deep. Returning Loyalists were often subjected to violence, and even when the war was over confiscations of Loyalist property continued. Only South Carolina attempted to carry out the letter of the Treaty; the other states ignored it.

Obviously treatment of the Loyalists in the thirteen states depended much on how strong the area had been for the patriotic cause. Thus some Loyalists returned quietly to their homes, and resumed their businesses without the need for state intervention in the form of relief Acts. But in areas where American patriotism had been strong, life for the Loyalists was intolerable. The British had promised that such people were free to settle in Canada. It was implied that there would be some material assistance in providing the resettlement. In the event there was nothing immediately. It is estimated that 50,000 Loyalists crossed into Canada, and that 50,000 more would have followed if the distances had not been so great. The new Canadians found nothing to succour them. Some dispersed into Nova Scotia and Quebec provinces, found employment and started to rebuild their lives without help. Others, fed by British promises, waited patiently for Britain to honour them. It took a long time, but eventually £12 million was spent in parliamentary grants to Loyalists 'of all classes and conditions'. To the British parliament, used to low taxation and minimal revenue, this seemed a very large sum; to the many Loyalists in great need it seemed little enough. Despairing of having to wait for spasmodic handouts from parliament, a small but determined group established the port of Halifax on the coast of Nova Scotia in 1791. Its subsequent prosperity was due mainly to the hard work of its inhabitants, and little enough to any generosity on the part of the British government.

It is possible to excuse the new America for its intolerance of the Loyalists, but Britain was slow to show gratitude to those who had risked so much in their defence of British interests. Perhaps anything for them was better than independence, and that is why Loyalists were in the vanguard of those who successfully defended Canada during the 1812–14 War.

1:3

The Irish Famine: Did the English Intend the Irish to Starve?

England is often given the blame for the Irish famine of 1846, and is accused of callously ignoring that country's plight, while deliberately failing to take the steps necessary to remedy the disaster. The view that British statesmen intentionally left Irishmen to starve is an unjustified slur on men of high probity like Peel and Russell. They were faced with an enormous economic and social disaster. This disaster had its roots in the English conquest of Ireland some centuries earlier, and from the alien system of land tenure resulting from it. But could the famine have been at least as much due to the primitive agricultural methods of the Irish peasantry, the backward state of their whole economy, their innate resistance to change and to the gross over-population from which Ireland was at that time suffering?

The Irish famine had become a disaster of unprecedented magnitude by the summer of 1846, and its after-effects, in terms of epidemics and destitution, continued long after the good harvests of 1847 and 1848. During the worst years over a million died. The famine embittered further the relations between the English and the Irish, and it was an important factor in the Irish demand for self-rule. It was generally believed in Ireland that an Irish government would have handled the famine better than the British government had done – surely it could have done no worse. So arose the widely held belief that the British government had failed to deal effectively with the famine; worse, that the British government had deliberately allowed the famine to rage in order to weaken Ireland and bring it to heel. And it passed into legend that the governments of Sir Robert Peel and Lord John Russell were so influenced by Malthus's views on population that they regarded a decline in Ireland's population as inevitable and even desirable, and did little to prevent it. The British government gave credence to these views by publicly apologising in 1998 for the British handling of the famine – an apology based more on political expediency than historical accuracy. How much truth is there in these indictments against the governments of Peel and Russell?

It could be argued that in one sense England *was* responsible for the famine. England had imposed upon Ireland an alien system of land tenure. Two and a half centuries earlier the English had dispossessed the ruling Irish chieftains and had replaced Irish landholding with a modified form of the landholding practised in England. But whereas in England most tenant farmers held long leases, in Ireland care was taken that tenants held land on short leases, or, as tenants-at-will, on no leases at all. Thus when tenants on short leases improved their land it gave their landlords the incentive to rack up the rents. After all, improved land was in demand and would command much higher returns. While the main crop was grain it was necessary for tenants to keep their land in full cultivation, but the introduction of the potato brought a dramatic change. It was a crop which could feed a family for a year on 20 per cent of the acreage necessary for a family dependent on oats or wheat. So a tenant farmer could leave much of his land uncultivated, allow his outbuildings to fall into rack and ruin, and keep a few animals to sell to pay the rent. This would be kept low by the poor and neglected state of his holding. Landless labourers would still work for the landowner, growing corn largely for export to England, but the tenant farmer would subsist virtually entirely on the potato which could provide almost all his nutritional needs. The potato came into widespread use in the second half of the eighteenth century. By 1845 it is reliably estimated that half of Ireland's eight million population was totally dependent upon it.

There had been partial failures of the potato crop before

1845, and these had necessitated widespread relief measures. But no one anticipated a disaster of the magnitude of 1845–6. Peel's Conservative government became alarmed when potato blight appeared in England in August 1845. Two experts, Dr Lyon Playfair and Professor Lindley, reported in late October that the situation was very serious, and that Ireland's potato harvest would be less than half of normal. They recommended drying potatoes in kilns, and applying chemical preservatives. These remedies were useless, but time was wasted in trying them. Since Peel received the report in late October there was some complacency in that most of the potatoes had already been harvested and were in store. So at first there was scepticism about the gravity of the situation. But potatoes taken from store were often found to be rotten, and Peel's public utterances showed from the beginning that he recognised not only the extreme seriousness of the situation, but also that it was the government's responsibility to deal with the famine, regardless of the *laisser-faire* notions current at the time. Peel decided to suspend the Corn Laws as early as November, but some of his aristocratic allies thought the Corn Law crisis had been drummed up for political reasons and that the rotten potato had become a political vegetable. One royal duke went so far as to assert that rotten potatoes mixed with grass made a very nutritious meal.

But this callous indifference did not represent the policy of the government. The Irish clamoured for a ban on corn exports. The English corn harvest had failed, while the Irish one was only a little below normal. Wagons taking corn to the ports while the Irish countryside starved necessitated the use of troops to guard them. But Peel thought that banning corn exports would solve nothing. It would ruin the landowners, some of whom were trying to help their tenants, and its retention for sale in Ireland would avail little as the Irish could not afford to buy it. Moreover, to aggravate the corn shortage in England by banning Irish corn imports would have been politically suicidal and in Peel's view unhelpful. He proposed other measures. He scoured Southern Europe to buy disease-free seed potatoes for the spring sowing. Even so, 75 per cent of the 1846 potato harvest was lost. Soup kitchens were set up in Irish towns and accessible Irish villages. These had the double motive of bringing succour to the starving and attempting to wean the Irish off their dependence on the potato. He secretly ordered maize to the value of £160,000 from the USA and sold it openly to the Irish peasantry at 1*d* per pound. To the peasant brought up on potato, maize savoured of animal feed and was unpleasant to the taste – it was nicknamed 'Peel's brimstone'. But the Irish were soon glad enough to eat it. To help the destitute pay for the maize and other available foods, Peel set up, through the Board of Works, a programme of relief works, such as drainage, railway construction and road improvements. Over £½ million was spent on this in 1846, but it was ineffective. Starving men could not cope with heavy labour. The officials in charge had no experience of dealing with famine; the few that had experienced it in India were still there. Some 15,000 officials were required in a matter of a few weeks, and many unsatisfactory appointments were made. There was much jobbery and corruption.

Even more was spent on relief works in 1847, but in March, rather tardily, Russell's government gave the Irish Boards of Guardians permission to grant outdoor relief. Ireland's workhouses were being swamped. The harvest of 1847 was good and showed little sign of blight, yet in many ways 1847 was the worst famine year. Infectious disease was always endemic in Ireland, and after nearly two years of deprivation diseases such as typhus took a heavy toll. It is impossible to state with accuracy how many died of disease and how many of starvation. It was not usual Irish practice to carry out post-mortems on bodies that had been lying undiscovered for weeks in remote districts. The lack of railways and the poor state of Irish roads meant that some areas were virtually untouched by relief efforts. But it is estimated that typhus killed 350,000 in 1847 alone, and tuberculosis resulting from the famine was still killing its victims into the 1850s. The best estimates suggest that, during the years 1845–51, ¼ million died of starvation, 1 million died of disease and 300,000 emigrated. At its height in the spring of 1847 3 million of

Ireland's 8 million were in receipt of some form of public relief. Of the one-third of Irish landlords who were ruined by the famine, many had lost everything by showing a duty to their tenants. They were soon to be replaced by absentee landlords interested only in maximising their rent rolls.

England was not indifferent to Ireland's plight. £7 million of public funds was spent on government relief efforts. Public subscription and private charities substantially supplemented the government's contribution. With annual British government expenditure in excess of £50 million an allocation of a little more than 2 per cent to Ireland at the height of famine seems inadequate. Yet the Irish famine could not easily have been solved by throwing more money at it. Distribution of relief suffered from inadequate roads and the absence of railways. It lacked honest and experienced officials. Attempts to distribute relief were often met by sullen resentment, suspicion and hostility from those the goverment was trying to help. Time was wasted on useless measures to deal with and prevent the spread of blight. And in the mid-1840s there were no magic bullets for the prevention and cure of epidemic disease. It is thus somewhat churlish to question the humanitarian motives of Peel's and Russell's governments. Neither government would have wanted so many deaths on their conscience. They floundered, and they possibly did too little, too late, but the famine was more the result of natural agents than human ones.

1:4

President Jackson and the Indians: Peaceful Emigration or Bloody Removal?

President Jackson, the tough, wiry frontiersman who was elected President in 1828, is often credited with ending the Indian threat to the supremacy of the white man by peacefully moving thousands of native tribesmen westwards over the Mississippi river. Does he deserve his heroic reputation?

Nearly 20,000 members of the Tsalagi tribe (known to English-speaking Americans as the 'Cherokee') had been guaranteed ownership of their tribal lands, first by George Washington in 1794, and later by a series of more than ninety treaties with their chiefs, the most important of which was agreed in 1798. They were among the most enlightened groups of native Americans in the south-east: they cultivated gardens and orchards, they engaged in trade and manufacture, they had a written language with which nearly all of them were conversant, and they developed schools, a newspaper and even a written constitution of their own. The area of land they were allowed, chiefly in Georgia, but also in nearby Alabama and Mississippi, was steadily whittled down by White encroachment from nearly 50,000 square miles to a mere 15,000 by 1828, when the state legislature of Georgia extended its remit over the whole area, thus effectively ending Cherokee independence. Jackson, now President, had as his main political constituency the rough, tough pioneers of the West and South, and was known to them already as the man who had repulsed the landing of the English at New Orleans in 1815. He agreed with the settlers' intention to expel the Indians from Federal territory, and had already fought against the Indians in the battle of Horseshoe Creek in Alabama in 1814. He promised a peaceful removal, but those who knew him recognised that his description of their movement as an 'emigration' was a euphemistic way of describing their harsh and often bloody removal.

In 1830, Jackson passed a Removal Bill through Congress, and began to use state militiamen to force the Cherokee from their homes. Opinion in the Eastern states was distinctly critical of Jackson's policy, and this gave the Cherokee some offer of hope. Their chief attempted to bring their plight to the attention of the Supreme Court, only to have his action disbarred on the grounds that the Indians were a 'domestic dependent nation' and therefore not able to plead. A second action, brought by a Vermont missionary against the State of Georgia, was more successful. It declared the Removal Law unconstitutional, an action which infuriated Jackson and Southern opinion generally, and which both of them effectively ignored. Martial law was proclaimed, and the Cherokee continued to be expelled. Pressure on them mounted until their leaders were forced to sign another treaty in 1835 agreeing to cede to the Federal government the last of their lands and to move to what is now Oklahoma. The US Senate debated this treaty long and hard, and eventually ratified it by a majority of one. By 1838, fewer than 2,000 Cherokee still remained in Georgia, and Martin van Buren, Jackson's successor, declared to Congress that 'the measures authorised by Congress in the last session . . . have had the happiest effect' and that 'the Cherokees have migrated without apparent reluctance' to their new homes.

A punitive expedition some years earlier against the Seminole Indians of Florida had produced an even more serious outcome, and resulted in the destruction of their homes, the deaths or migration of thousands of them, and the capture by the Whites of their chief, Osceola, while bearing a flag of truce.

Jackson's actions in Florida were murderous, and the enforced moving of nearly 20,000 native American people over a distance of some 800 miles on foot or by wagons and teams, though achieved in a relatively short time and without a great deal of bloodshed, hardly conformed to the notion of a voluntary national emigration, and certainly did not reflect the credit on Jackson that he claimed.

2

CONSPIRACIES AND PLOTS

Did the Dauphin Perish in the French Revolution?

The idea that during the Revolution, the son of Louis XVI escaped the clutches of the Revolutionaries and survived into manhood exercised compelling influence on many nineteenth-century minds.

In the years after the Terror the story developed that the young Dauphin, who automatically became King Louis XVII of France on the execution of his father in 1793, had somehow managed to survive the dank filth of the Temple and the crude ministrations of the Paris cobbler and his wife who were his jailers, and had made his escape to freedom. The story was sometimes elaborated with the suggestion that Robespierre himself had taken pity on the boy and connived at his flight. The boy was supposed to have been brought up in obscurity in the French countryside and only later found out that he was the rightful king. After 1815 a number of royal claimants, including a stable boy and a Prussian clockmaker, came forward as pretenders. The latter was so convincing that he was recognised by the now rather elderly Versailles maid who had attended the young prince, secured acceptance by King Louis Philippe and received a small pension from him, though he later died in obscurity and was buried in 1840 at Delft in Holland beneath the epitaph 'Here Lies Louis XVII, Duke of Normandy, King of France and of Navarre.' The idea of a dramatic escape from his jailers was later taken up by Baroness d'Orczy, who described the episode in the *Scarlet Pimpernel* stories, where she alleged that the boy had been whisked away to his relatives in Austria.

The truth is less exciting, though scarcely less incredible. The royal prince, always a delicate child, had succumbed to tuberculosis in the damp conditions of his cell at the age of ten, in 1795, and was buried under the name of Louis Charles Capet in a mass grave. Before the interment there had been an inquest, and the doctor in question, a man by the name of Pelletan, a royalist, had filched the heart at the autopsy, concealed it in his handkerchief and later passed it to the then Archbishop of Paris, who kept it in a jar until his cathedral was attacked and looted in the 1830 Revolution. The jar was smashed, Pelletan's son picked up the mummified remains of the heart, and himself kept it in a crystal urn. It was subjected to DNA tests in 1999, and samples compared with his mother's hair, that of two of her sisters, and the hair of two of the family's living relatives.

The tests proved beyond all reasonable doubt that the Dauphin had in fact died in 1795, and the heart was his. There had been in the previous century two different excavations of the grave in which his remains had been placed, and on both occasions the bones were said to have belonged to a much older boy of about seventeen. The DNA tests, however, are now accepted by nearly everybody as being definitive.

2:2

The Carbonari: Patriots or Brigands?

The story of Italian Unification has long lent itself to romanticisation. Mazzini, Cavour, Victor Emmanuel, Garibaldi, even Pius IX have been subjected to literary treatment which would make them unrecognisable even to themselves. And the Carbonari, long regarded as the founding fathers of Italian nationalism have not been spared. The oft-repeated picture is of intellectuals and liberals persecuted for their beliefs, taking shelter against the cold of Italy's winter nights with the charcoal burners in their mountain huts. There, with the purest of motives, they could dream of an Italy freed from foreign domination. An eminent historian could write, in 1939, that (in the 1820s) 'secret societies, chief of them that of the Carbonari, were formed everywhere to work for the union of Italy'. And in explaining the failure of the Carbonari such historians would point out that their weakness was their very idealism; they lacked the practical skills and organisation to bring their aims to fulfilment. This idealised picture of the Carbonari and their aims needs considerable modification.

In the first place it is wrong to suppose that the Italian revolutionary movements of the 1820s were all led by Carbonari. Such societies were not formed everywhere. The main area in which they operated was in the Kingdom of Naples with some overspill into the central Duchies and the Romagna. The early insurgents in Piedmont were not Carbonari but *'federati'* and lacked even the most tenuous links with them. Moreover, the Carbonari of Naples were by no means all liberal and nationalist idealists. There were, of course, numbers of middle-class intellectuals in their ranks, but in origin the Carbonari were members of secret societies, taking their inspiration (and sometimes their secret signs and passwords) from freemasonry. Such societies attracted not only idealists, but also adventurers, who were in it not for the cause but for the excitement. And it was not surprising that, especially in Naples where banditry and organised crime were rife, there should be some leavening of those who used the Carbonari as a cover for their kidnappings, robberies and murders. But it does not follow that the Neapolitan bandits were all members of or supporters of the Carbonari; banditry and revolutionary fervour were usually distinctly separate, even in Naples. Of course all revolutionaries who resort to arms are regarded by the authorities as terrorists, and the Neapolitan authorities knew how to exploit the unsavoury backgrounds and activities of some of the local Carbonari. Had they all been bandits they most certainly would not have been able to bring the Neapolitan government to its knees in 1820. In contrast, a few of the lower clergy sometimes became involved with the Carbonari; even Pius IX was rumoured to have belonged to a Carbonarist group in his youth.

Were the Carbonari patriots? In the sense that one of their most consistent aims was to remove foreign influence and the domination of Austria, then they were. In Naples this took the form of a desire to undermine the power of the Spanish Bourbon ruler. But the Neapolitan revolt of 1820 was more concerned to extract a liberal constitution, and one based on the Spanish constitution of 1812, rather than the overthrow of Ferdinand I himself. In the Duchies where the rulers were Austrian, imposed by the Treaty of Vienna, the Carbonari did aim to expel their foreign rulers. So the patriotism of most Carbonari extended to supporting and maintaining the independence of the existing Italian states; they were fierce in their patriotic loyalty to an independent Tuscany, or a restored Lombardy or Venice. But there is no evidence that the Carbonari aimed at a united Italy. Each Carbonarist group had its own limited and local aims. They all wanted an end to political repression. They all wanted a share in political power and an end to absolutism. And they all wanted the foreigners out. But what would remain would be the old mosaic of Italian states which had been Italy's lot since the Middle Ages. It was not their purpose to redraw the map of Italy, or to hand it over to Piedmontese domination. For the vast majority of groups the pursuit of limited local aims more often than not took precedence over the more profitable pursuit of felony, but Mazzini saw their weakness, and when he founded his 'Young Italy' in 1831 he was not trying to carry on the work of the Carbonari; he was attempting very different aims with much more sophisticated methods.

2:3

The Maine: Who Blew it Up?

One of the great legends of American history is that America's war against Spain in 1898 was justified because the Spaniards had deliberately blown up an American warship. From this interpretation it follows that the Americans went to war with reluctance but they had no choice in view of the provocation and that American annexations after the war were not examples of American imperialism in action but just recompense for Spain's infamy. All this is legendary nonsense, but was current at the time, and lingers on even now in a few popular texts.

On 15 February 1898 the American battleship, the *Maine*, blew up in Havana harbour with the loss of 2 officers and 258 men. The ship had been at Havana for three weeks, where it had been keeping a close eye on the Cuban insurrection against Spain, and was also intended to give reassurance to American citizens still in Cuba. The sinking revived war fever in America which had subsided after the recall of General Weyler, notorious for his harsh treatment of Cuban rebels. The American press blamed Spain for this sinking, and raised the cry of 'Remember the *Maine*'. On 25 April the USA declared war upon Spain: almost all America believed that the sinking justified the war declaration. But was Spain responsible for the sinking?

It seems most unlikely that the Spaniards would have deliberately provoked the Americans into war in this way. What could they have possibly hoped to gain by it? Their whole purpose had been to avoid antagonising the USA. Indeed only six days before the sinking the Spanish ambassador in Washington had been recalled to Madrid after an American outcry over some incautious anti-American remarks he had made in a private letter. Even if the Spaniards had regarded American intervention as inevitable, sinking the *Maine* would have had little military justification and in any case could have been postponed until war was actually declared. Cuban insurgents might have had a better reason for blowing up the *Maine*. In this way they could have ensured American entry into the war, and thus made Cuban independence a near certainty: but there is no evidence to support this contention.

At the time of the disaster the captain of the *Maine* warned against jumping to hasty conclusions. But an immediate American court of naval inquiry found that the *Maine* had been blown up as a result of an *external* explosion, thus implicating either the Spaniards, whom the Americans naturally regarded as the villains, or the Cubans. The Spanish court of inquiry found that the ship had blown up as a result of an *internal* explosion, thus exonerating both the Spaniards, and the Cubans, whom it might have been in Spanish interests to implicate.

Little was made of the suggestion that Cuban insurgents in the guise of dock labourers might have smuggled the explosives on board. The *Maine* was raised in 1911 and the original American findings were said to have been corroborated, thus giving a new lease of life to the legend without offering any substantial proof. It still seems most likely that the explosion was caused by faulty ammunition in the ship's magazine, or by an explosive mixture of air and coal dust in the fuel hold. But the sinking had served its purpose in justifying an American expansionist war, and even today the legend of the sinking, while moribund, still stubbornly refuses to die.

2:4

The Boer War: Was it an Imperialist Plot?

The Boer War, between the formerly Dutch settlers of the Cape of South Africa, and British and Empire troops fighting for the British government, has aroused popular feelings on both sides throughout the twentieth century. Though much of the indignation the war generated has mellowed with the passing of time, widely different views are still held about it.

The official attitude of the British government towards the war was studiously moderate, though there was background clamour in the press and elsewhere of a raucous and rather unpleasant imperialism. The views of Chamberlain and his cabinet colleagues such as Lord Lansdowne were undoubtedly imperialist, but were generally cloaked in civilised and moderate language. These were seemingly in harmony with those of Sir Alfred (later Viscount) Milner, appointed in 1897 as High Commissioner for South Africa, who, while he was somewhat lacking in diplomatic finesse, had an acute and finely tuned legal mind. They were all of the view that, though the formal mention of the contentious word 'suzerainty' agreed by the Pretoria Convention of 1881 to describe British authority over the Boer republics had been withdrawn in the London Convention of 1884, the material details of British overlordship were exactly the same as before, so that Britain had not only the right but even the duty to act as final arbiter in Boer affairs. In a number of ways the conduct of Paul Kruger, the elderly President of the Transvaal (and known to his loyal people by the affectionate name of 'Uncle Paul'), was genuinely believed to be unacceptable: he mistreated his substantial minority of foreign immigrants, or *Uitlanders*, including over 30,000 British subjects, whom he overtaxed and disfranchised; he held his black native peoples in absolute contempt; and he seemed determined to arm himself to the teeth with war material imported via Delagoa Bay in Portuguese East Africa. The flow of these armaments rocketed from little more than £60,000 per annum in 1895 to over £250,000 in 1897; he spent £1.5 million on the building of forts and on heavy artillery; and, most sinister of all, undertook the engagement of German military specialists as advisers.

Kruger refused to supply any satisfactory explanation for his armament drive, and failed to remedy the grievances of the Uitlanders. Hence, when the Uitlander Petition of March 1899 appealed to Queen Victoria to relieve the plight of British immigrants, the British government felt obliged to take up their case. Tedious negotiations in Bloemfontein in the first week of

May revealed Milner at his most precise and pedantic, and Kruger at his most devious and obstructive. Repeated efforts were made between July and September to avoid conflict, but all of them broke down. The notion began to grow that Kruger was merely playing for time until the South African campaigning season began.

After the outbreak of war, the British government speedily discovered the practical difficulties of conducting a war with little more than 50,000 unseasoned troops at a range of over 6,000 miles and against an agile and determined enemy. Britain suffered a number of disastrous reverses, culminating in 'Black Week' in early December 1899, when three senior British generals, Gatacre, Methuen and Buller, were defeated in the field and Boer sieges of the towns of Kimberley, Ladysmith and Mafeking, recently undertaken, were intensified to force them into an early surrender. The Kaiser disrespectfully wired his grandmother, Queen Victoria, advising her to take these defeats in the 'same spirit of fortitude' as England had taken the 'recent defeats in the Test series'. Once again, the Queen was not amused.

The appointment of Lord Roberts as British commander-in-chief, however, led to a swift change of fortune. In the spring and early summer of 1900, the beleaguered towns were relieved and British forces, substantially reinforced by several contingents of empire troops, entered Bloemfontein, Johannesburg and Pretoria. By August the war was as good as over, and in September Kruger fled into Portuguese territory. Only the stubbornness of the Boer volunteers enabled them to continue fighting. The final phase of the war, which went on from mid-1900 until peace was finally signed at Vereeniging in May 1902, was a guerrilla war, and proved to be the most costly and contentious. Popping up here and there unexpectedly, guerrilla bands, or 'commandos' as they were called, with powerful but mobile armament and with the sympathy of the bulk of the civilian population, harassed the thinly spread occupying army, carrying off substantial booty and damaging railways and other communications. The only way to counter this threat was to clear the countryside by 'concentrating' the population into temporary camps and carrying out wide sweeps of large areas to isolate, pin down and defeat the guerrilla forces. Sadly these 'concentration camps' (a name deriving from the Spanish-American War and later to be attached to the notorious camps in which twentieth-century dictators punished political opponents and annihilated minority groups) soon got themselves a bad name. As sometimes happens when the military are given a job outside their normal competence, the management of the camps was grossly inefficient. Food was poor and scanty, sanitation was primitive, and disease was rife. Of about 120,000 inmates of the camps, nearly 30,000 died, about 22,000 of them under sixteen years old. Of the total of inmates nearly 100,000 detainees were black Africans who were shut up in eighteen separate camps. Before the end of the war, about 18,000 of these were dead, and were buried clandestinely in unmarked graves. It took the work of an Englishwoman, Emily Hobhouse, and an influential committee of relief, to draw the attention of Chamberlain and the government to the abuses of the camps, and to install civilian instead of military supervision there. Only after ten years of hostility did relations between Boers and British begin to improve.

It should be observed that not all the outrages were perpetrated by the British side. Much of the Boer shelling of the beleaguered towns was indiscriminate and was intended to terrorise and destroy the civilian populations; while, during the guerrilla phase, the attacks of one of their leaders, de Wet, on the waterworks at Sennaspos was intended to promote the spread of enteric fever among the citizens of Bloemfontein. The most savage of the fury of the Boers was saved for the so-called 'Joiners', Boers who fought on the British side. But neither side saw fit to criticise this conduct at the time; indeed both seemed to find it quite acceptable.

Public attitudes in Britain were widely varied. The more extreme and jingoistic of the imperialists, whose attitudes were mirrored in the popular press, breathed fire against the Boers. To them the empire was sacred, and the affronts against it in

South Africa intolerable. People sang lewd songs about Kruger (whose name was given a soft 'g' and made to rhyme with 'screwed yer') and went into wild transports of delight at the relief of Mafeking. On the other hand there was a substantial body of opinion resolutely opposed to the war. Gladstone was now dead, but radical Liberals, including his biographer John Morley and Lloyd George, continued with his anti-empire policy in the face of Lord Rosebery and the 'Liberal-imperialist' wing, and soon became known as 'pro-Boers'. Even the subtle Chamberlain knew he could not safely fly in the face of such a body of opinion, and with Balfour, Hicks Beach and even Salisbury himself consciously moderated his anti-Boer tone. The 'pro-Boers' agreed (though for quite different reasons) with the Marxist belief that the war arose from an expansionist desire to acquire overseas lands and to exploit their natural resources to boost Britain's own economy. It was Rhodes's South Africa Company, in their view, and its drive for gold and diamonds that had led to Kruger's suspicions of Britain and his desire to protect himself and his people against encroachment. Rhodes himself was regarded with some ambivalence as an enthusiastic flag-waver and a ruthless tycoon who was preferable as an ally rather than as an enemy. Liberals' mistrust of militarism soon combined with their anti-imperialism in their criticisms of the campaigns in South Africa, and these were later reinforced by their humanitarian instincts when the horrors of the concentration camps were revealed to the public. All this helps to explain the determination of the Liberals after 1906 to deal fairly with the vanquished South Africa – to the point when many said that South Africa had lost the war but in the first years of the twentieth century were able to win the peace.

Boer opinion was very much aggrieved by the war. They had tried earlier to escape from British domination, but without success. At the time of the Great Trek in 1836, like the American pioneers, they had migrated in their covered wagons determined not so much to cross the great prairies as to escape from Cape Colony to form new settlements not under British authority. Later, they had established their freedom from British control by the Sand River Convention of 1852, only to find it whittled away after the Zulu War by the Pretoria Convention in 1881. When the British authorities dropped the dreaded word 'suzerainty' from the convention in 1884, the Boers imagined that at last they were free.

But Britain had by no means surrendered its imperial plans. When diamonds were found in Griqualand West in 1867, and gold discovered in the Transvaal in 1886, colonialist greed had again raised its ugly head. Imperialist ambitions had revived. Unwelcome prospectors and miners, many of them in the Boer view the scum of the earth, had poured in and set about mining in their country. The Boers, whose simple, rural, backward-looking way of life was disrupted by these events, regretted the new strains put upon them. They hated the new capitalist pressures and blamed all their evils on them.

In the Boers, xenophobia combined with latent anti-semitism to focus on 'Guggenheim', the greasy foreign Jewish capitalist portrayed in cartoons, symbolising greed and commercialism. Kruger, a boy of eleven at the time of the Great Trek, epitomised their feelings when he swore to have no truck with the Uitlanders and to keep the blacks in their proper place. He feared and mistrusted Rhodes's plans, first to take over Mashonaland and Matabeleland in the north and then Bechuanaland in the west. It seemed to him that the imperialists were trying to surround him. Kruger was once asked how he would kill a tortoise, and he replied in his guttural farmer's voice, 'I'd wait for him to put his head out – and then I'd chop it off!' Hence the Boers moved swiftly and effectively against Jameson at the time of his luckless Raid. And, as far as Kruger was concerned, the need for preparedness was the whole reason for his drive for armaments. A stubborn refusal to cooperate with the British and a profound mistrust of their intentions underlies the whole of his protracted negotiations with them in 1899, and his preference for war instead of surrender.

During the war, the enduring Afrikaner image is of the noble Boer, armed only with rifle, biltong and slouch hat, fighting against a brutal invader who pillaged his farmstead and starved his wife and family to death behind barbed wire, until necessity forced him to give in. Finally, however, overwhelming military might won the day and, after Vereeniging, the Boer leadership sought by guile what they had been unable to achieve by armed force. That same Milner who had jostled the Boer republics into war set himself the task after 1902 of rehabilitating them. He envisaged a line of self-governing settler communities stretching from the Cape to the Zambesi, federated together and leavened by a large injection of British immigration and British capital, the Whites living in peace among the mass of African natives, who were fairly treated. The Boers went along with this, while retaining their private opinions of the 'Kaffirs'. They suspected that instead of superior British practice in handling natives shaming the Boers into improving their own treatment of them, with *good* driving out *bad*, as Milner hoped, *bad* would drive out *good*. The emergence of systematic apartheid in the middle years of the twentieth century shows that this is very much what in fact took place. Only the permissiveness of the Treaty of Vereeniging and the generosity of the British South Africa Act in 1909–10 allowed this to happen, and allowed native rights, under the new South African constitution, to remain inadequately entrenched.

Black South African opinion generally tried to stand aloof from the conflict between Briton and Boer. They created the popular myth that the Boer War was a conflict between the two White tribes in which the coloured population had little other than spectator interest. From the beginning the British and the Boers had a tacit understanding that armed Black auxiliaries should not be used in what they regarded as a 'White Man's War'. However, it was never true that the war did not concern the native Africans. British colonial policy was always more enlightened towards the natives (perhaps because it was further away from them) than were the Boers, and Britain never had any intention to bar them from political enfranchisement in the way the Boers did. During the war, too, the British had less hesitation in arming the natives than the Boers. Whatever their seniors may have said, junior officers in the field employed them in numerous ways. Black troops formed part of the defensive garrisons of the beleaguered towns, even though their rations were only a fraction of those of the Whites – perhaps they were supposed to get food in ways unknown to their White comrades. Relying on their local knowledge, too, the British employed numbers of native scouts. But once the Boer commandos began castrating and killing Black captives, the British had no option but to arm them. By the end of the war there were 30,000 armed Black auxiliaries in the British forces. Furthermore, the Boers themselves placed great reliance on their natives, both in combatant and non-combatant roles. Some South African historians now estimate that up to 10,000 natives were willing to fight for their Boer masters, however little they were promised at the end of the war. But at the end of the war in the negotiations at Vereeniging, the Blacks were denied any voice. Those who thought the British would restore lands to them earlier taken by the Boers were disappointed. The Blacks got no more from the British than from the Boers. Thus to say that the natives were merely neutral onlookers in the war, or recognised at the end of it, is at best a simplification of the truth.

On balance, it seems likely that the commonly held view that the war was the outcome of a British imperialist plot to take over, by force if necessary, the gold and diamonds found in South Africa is not the full story, any more than is the traditional patriotic view that the war sprang from Kruger's stubborn refusal to play his allotted role in Britain's plans for a South African empire. On the other side of the picture, the myth of the noble Briton, inspired by a disinterested concern for the advance of the human race, is somewhat tarnished by the recollection of the concentration camps, just as the myth of the noble Boer, fighting for survival and to escape from tyranny, is tarnished by the carefully concealed atrocities for which he was responsible, and by the world's later experience of the brutal excesses of apartheid. Nor can the war any longer be regarded as of no consequence for the African peoples themselves. In fact, in its causes and events, the war was a product of the aspirations and the mistakes of both sides; and involved the deaths of many thousands of Africans. And while some Africans may have felt themselves uninvolved in it, the effects of the war were to weigh heavy on the whole of the Black population of South Africa for the greater part of the ensuing century.

2:5

The Sarajevo Assassination: Did Serbia Aim to Bring About War?

The murders of the Archduke Francis Ferdinand and his wife Sophie, shot in Sarajevo, the capital of Bosnia, on 28 June 1914, by Gavrilo Princip, a Serbian activist, were reputedly the cause of the outbreak of the First World War, and gave rise to the legend that Serbian provocation lay at the root of the war. Superficially there was something to be said for such a view. Princip, a nineteen-year-old Bosnian-Serb student, was a member of the secret nationalist movement Young Bosnia (Mlada Bosna), *and had used a pistol in the assassination supplied by the Serbian terrorist body known as the Black Hand (whose motto was* Ujedinjenje ili Smrt – *'Unity or death'), which was recruited from radical young Serbian army officers intent on uniting their co-nationals living in the Austrian and Turkish empires with those in Serbia itself. The Austrians, believing that the Serbian government had instigated the plot, sought the consent and approval of their allies, the Germans, for their actions, and after the lapse of a month sent a swingeing ultimatum to Belgrade on 23 July. When this was rejected they declared war on Serbia on 28 July, so setting in train the sequence of events that led to the outbreak of the First World War.*

None of the above facts is actually wrong, but nevertheless taken together they gave rise to an entirely misleading picture of the coming of the war. The Austrians saw the war not as the outcome of a series of events set into logical motion by a chance accident; they believed it to have been brought about by a deliberate plot. This 'Austrian interpretation' appeared to be reinforced by Serbia's recent aggressive wars in the Balkans, 1912–14, and by the often violent and turbulent character of Serbian politics. This view served to shift the main burden of responsibility for the war away from Vienna and Berlin and onto the shoulders of Serbia, now branded as the most militant of the minor powers in the Balkans. In reality the truth was not so simple.

Princip, hot-headed and painfully young, was hardly the stuff from which either heroes or international wars are made – indeed, he was too young for the death penalty, but languished for four years in an Austrian fortress before his death in April 1918 at the age of twenty-three. Neither were the many secret societies with which the Balkans were teeming at this time much of a threat to anybody, except – through their rashness – possibly to themselves. Nor was any shred of evidence later produced to justify the Austrian assertion that the Serbian government was behind the plot, even though a most rigorous investigation under close Austrian supervision was afterwards made. Indeed, quite the contrary. The Serbian government had been quite exhausted by its recent wars and had not yet completed its army reorganisation after their conclusion. Hence it was simply unready for war, and made genuine efforts to warn the Austrians against the Archduke's visit before it occurred. In early June they informed Bilinski, the Austrian minister in charge of the imperial administration of Bosnia, of the risks that the Archduke was taking: his visit would be deeply offensive to Serbian national feelings and might even result in an attempt being made on his life – an admission later interpreted by the Austrians as evidence of their foreknowledge. The Serbian government, furthermore, though it was innocent of the charges of complicity brought against it by the Austrians, returned the meekest and most submissive of responses to the outrageous ultimatum fired off at it by Vienna, accepting eight out of ten of its points and offering to negotiate about the remaining two, even though they involved the complete surrender of Serbia's position as a proud and independent nation. And finally it placed no obstacles in the way of a judicial inquiry into the affair afterwards, even though this inquiry was conducted largely by Austrian officials. In short, it swallowed its pride and did all it could do to avert war.

On the other hand, the Austrians were not the hapless victims they claimed to be. Dynastic considerations were pushing the Habsburgs towards the Balkans. For a time, in the decade after the murder, the notion prevailed that the imperial court had deliberately exposed Francis Ferdinand to the risk of assassination because he continued to stand by the unpopular idea of a 'Trialist Monarchy', a system of government conceding a voice to the Slav inhabitants of the empire, as well as to the Germans and the Magyars of the 'Dual Monarchy'. This idea was perhaps countenanced because of the widespread fatalistic notion that the members of the imperial royal family were cursed by a fate which brought a number of them to early graves. In truth there was nothing in this idea. However, it is certainly true that dynastic considerations lay behind the state visit to Sarajevo. The Archduke had earlier concluded a morganatic marriage with Countess Sophie Chotek, a Czech, and it was only by reason of Francis's military uniform as imperial Field Marshal that she could travel at his side in his car at Sarajevo, instead of being relegated far down the order of precedence on the occasion of a state visit. But for the Austrian royal family to flaunt its military supremacy as well as parading its Heir Apparent before the Serbians was deeply repugnant to them; added to which the visit was deliberately timed for Serbia's national day, the anniversary of the battle of Kossovo in 1389, a fact of which none of the organisers could have been unaware.

Indeed, senior officers of the imperial General Staff and senior officials of the Austrian government were both anxious for a showdown with Serbia. Count Conrad von Hötzendorff, Chief of the General Staff, had warned as early as 1912 of the growth of Serbia's military might and the threat this might pose to Austria: he declared that by 1914 the Serbian army would prove difficult to defeat, and by 1917 would be able themselves to defeat Austria, unless steps were taken before then to challenge them. The military men were divided as to what should be done with Serbia: some thought a short punitive expedition would be enough, followed by a financial indemnity; some favoured the annexation of part of Serbia's land; some wanted a partition of Serbian lands between Austria and Bulgaria. There was even a group which favoured the complete incorporation of Serbia as a dependent kingdom into the empire's territories (the final relic of the Archduke's suggestion of 'trialism'). What was certain was that independent Serbia was to be destroyed. The Foreign Minister Count Berchtold was also determined to force war on Serbia at the first opportunity, in alliance with Bulgaria, and urged close consultation with the Kaiser in Berlin, blaming Russian and Balkan 'Panslavism' for the crisis. In his letter to Berlin he declared that 'Serbia must be eliminated as a political factor in the Balkans . . . a friendly settlement is no longer to be thought of.' Kaiser Wilhelm – rather surprisingly in view of Austria's unexpected initiatives over the Buchlau crisis only a few years earlier – made no serious effort to hold the Austrians back, but came out quite enthusiastically in their favour, declaring that 'Action against Serbia should not be delayed. . . . Even if it should come to war, we are convinced Germany would stand by our side with her accustomed faithfulness as an ally.' So the fatal relentless fuse leading to war was lit, but the hands that lit it were at least as much Austrian as they were Bosnian Serb. The whole affair was an accident waiting to happen.

Britain, however, was characteristically unprepared for the catastrophe. The summer had been hot and long, the nation was on the beaches on holiday and the only cloud on the national horizon was the Irish affair, where King George V had recently encouraged the meeting of the Buckingham Palace Conference to consider the future of Ulster. Of the operation of the secret wheels of diplomacy the ordinary people knew nothing. They may have heard of the murder of the Archduke in a faraway country, but were no longer surprised by nasty events in the Balkans and, in any case, after a month went by, had come to believe the whole thing had probably blown over. When Europe tumbled into war they were shocked and surprised. At first, it did not seem unreasonable to think that it was Serbia who had started it.

2:6

The Massacre at Katyn Wood, 1940: Who Was Responsible?

No wartime controversy was so long or so bitterly contested as the Massacre at Katyn Wood in 1940. Only recently has the real truth of the affair been revealed.

In May 1943, German military units disinterred over 4,000 corpses close to an internment camp at the so-called Hill of Goats in the Katyn Forest on the banks of the Dnieper near Smolensk. Most had their hands tied behind them and each had been shot in the back of the head. The Nazis claimed that they had been killed by the Russians; the Russians that they had been killed by the Nazis.

The German version of events was as follows. After the Russians had occupied the eastern part of Poland in September 1939, about 15,000 Poles, largely army officers, had been detained in the Soviet Ukraine for interrogation and 're-education'. This process, conducted by Brigadier 'Zombrig' Zarubin of the Soviet secret police, had been conspicuously unsuccessful, and the mass of prisoners had been broken up and sent to separate camps, one of which was at Kozelsk, close to Katyn. When the Germans invaded Poland in June 1941, the Poles unexpectedly became Soviet allies, and Winston Churchill even sought assurances from the Russians that the Poles had been properly treated. Smolensk fell to the Germans in July 1941, and in the early spring of 1942, acting on rumours from the local peasantry, Polish members of the Organization Todt (the German compulsory labour corps) found a small number of bodies in Katyn Wood, which they reburied with proper reverence, marking the graves with birch crosses. It was not until 1943 that further evidence came to light. German army officers had questioned a number of local residents, some of whom had produced graphic accounts of mass burials in the area, and in April 4,500 bodies were recovered from trenches in Katyn Wood. Over 10,000 bodies were never found. Documents on the bodies showed them to be from among the Polish detainees about whom Churchill had been concerned. The German investigating authorities concluded that all had been executed by the Russians.

The Soviet authorities stoutly denied the allegations. When they recovered Smolensk in September 1943, Soviet officials maintained that the executions had taken place at the end of 1941, and had been of Polish prisoners of war and political detainees who had been employed by the Germans on road repair work in the area. In alleging that the murders had been committed by the Russians, the Nazis were merely seeking to sow dissension between the Allies. The Russians maintained that the prisoners were still alive at the time the Germans occupied Smolensk, and that there were a host of eyewitnesses who had seen them working in the area. The Soviet version of events was that the investigations by the 'medical experts' appointed by the Germans had been hasty and superficial, that they had deliberately tied and executed the prisoners in a crude attempt to smear their opponents, and that, finally, the bullets found in the gunshot wounds were of a large calibre and were of German origin. After the war, the Soviet story gained some credibility when the horrific discoveries at Auschwitz, Buchenwald and Dachau starkly revealed the barbaric behaviour of the Nazis.

The Polish government in exile in London requested an independent inquiry by the Swiss Red Cross at the end of 1943, and the Germans agreed to this. But the Soviet response was in the nature of a bombshell. They rejected the request, broke off relations with their Polish allies for 'aiding and abetting Hitler', and shortly afterwards set up a puppet Polish government in

Moscow. The Soviets insisted that the matter should not be investigated further. Their version of events was repeated at the Nuremberg Tribunal, where it was not seriously challenged by the other Allies. It therefore was picked up in accounts that became current in the immediate postwar years. Only in 1989 did the Soviet authorities admit that the Russians had been responsible for executing all 15,000.

2:7

The Assassination of President Kennedy: Was it a Conspiracy?

The assassination of the American President in 1963 gave rise to a whole host of popular myths and legends explaining such a dramatic and world-shaking event. At a range of what is now nearly forty years it is perhaps time to reconsider the circumstances.

President Kennedy flew to Texas in November 1963 in the hope of healing rifts among Southern Democrats, many of whose conservative wing were critical of the tone of his presidency. Texas was a large state with an important bloc of electoral votes that Kennedy had won only narrowly in 1960. These he hoped to win again in 1964, with the assistance of his Vice-President, Lyndon Johnson, himself a Southern Democrat. Kennedy arrived at Dallas airport in Texas on the morning of 22 November, from where his motorcade proceeded into Dallas shortly after noon. It turned into Elm Street and drove past the Texas Book Depository Building, from which a number of shots rang out, fatally wounding the President in the neck and head. He was rushed to Parkland Hospital nearby, where he was pronounced dead.

Within an hour and a half, after a bizarre chase through the city, the police arrested Lee Harvey Oswald, a loner with a rather chequered background. He was interrogated; and, two days later, on his way to court, was confronted by Jack Ruby, a

Dallas nightclub owner, who shot him at point-blank range and killed him in front of the television cameras. Ruby was arrested and convicted of his murder in 1964, but his death sentence was quashed and another trial ordered; but before this took place he died of cancer in January 1967, still without giving any satisfactory explanation for his actions.

Since that time, conspiracy theories have raged in the USA, even after the clear findings of the Warren Commission, a body set up especially by the Federal government to investigate the circumstances of the murder. How do we now regard these investigations?

Kennedy's murder was greeted with horror and dismay not only in America, where people wept openly in the streets, but throughout the world. Newly appointed President Johnson, sworn in immediately aboard the presidential plane at the airport, took charge. He was anxious that the whole affair should be settled before the next presidential elections took place the following November, and appointed a Special Commission, headed by Chief Justice Earl Warren, to take statements, examine the evidence and report on the murder as soon as possible. It evaluated reports made to it by the FBI, the Secret Service, the Dallas police department, Federal departments and agencies and Congressional committees. It also took the sworn testimony of 552 witnesses. After ten months it released its findings in September 1964.

The Commission concluded that Oswald fired three shots from the Book Depository Building; that these shots killed President Kennedy, and that later Oswald shot and killed Police Patrolman J.D. Tippitt when he tried to arrest him. The report analysed the character of Oswald, pointing out his deep-seated hostility towards, and resentment of, authority. In spite of the fact that Oswald had recently defected to the Soviet Union for espionage training and had actually been involved in espionage on behalf of Cuba, the Commission insisted there had been no evidence of foreign involvement, nor of conspiracy. Neither did it connect the assassination of President Kennedy with Oswald's own murder shortly afterwards. It went on to make a number of criticisms of the FBI and the Secret Service, and made recommendations for the better protection of presidents in the future.

At first the Warren Report was received with acclaim for the speed and thoroughness with which it had been carried out. There were, however, a number of curious circumstances surrounding the whole episode, and these soon prompted speculation about it which has continued to the present time. Because Oswald could not be brought to trial and the evidence relating to his alleged offence examined in the usual way, doubts surfaced almost immediately about his guilt and about the possibility of a cover-up or a conspiracy.

How many shots were actually fired at the time of the assassination? The curious acoustics of Dealey Plaza meant that there was doubt about even that elementary fact. Was it physically possible for Oswald to have fired all of them with the weapon he used during the few seconds that he had had the President in his sights? Or did he perhaps have accomplices? Were shots fired from the so-called 'grassy knoll' alongside the road, and not from the rear of the motorcade as previously thought? Was Oswald perhaps not the real assassin at all? Could he have been 'framed', and then shot to keep him quiet? If indeed he had been involved in espionage training and activity, how could the Commission deny that there was foreign involvement in the affair? Was not perhaps the vast bulk of evidence that had been accumulated by the Commission a method of concealing the truth rather than revealing it?

There were even wilder suggestions. Some thought there was a Secret Service plot to eliminate the President; some suggested that Johnson himself was behind the plot for reasons of his own ambition, and pointed to the indecent haste with which the new President, dispensing with the normal protocol, was sworn in. It was even suggested that FBI chief J. Edgar Hoover knew more about it than he said, but that he remained silent because he was under pressure from the Mafia to say nothing – they having discovered that Hoover was a secret transvestite! There were also a number of strange events that took place at later dates, which no one has ever satisfactorily explained. Why, for example, was the elaborate brass casket in which Kennedy's body was placed later surreptitiously exchanged for a plain wooden one, and why, in 1999, was this brass coffin dumped several thousand fathoms deep by the US Air Force in the Atlantic? All these things seemed to be too bizarre to have a simple explanation.

However, nobody has ever produced hard evidence to refute the Warren Commission's findings. All the same, a number of films have been made, and over a thousand books have been written, to put forward explanations other than those advanced by the Commission. The American people seem to love a good mystery, and better still a good conspiracy.

The passage of time has perhaps clouded the original picture. It cannot be denied that there was considerable criticism of Kennedy, especially in the South. Contemporary observers noted the ugly tone of some of the placards displayed on the day of the presidential visit, comments such as 'Help Kennedy Stamp Out Democracy!' or 'You're a Traitor!' or, more circuitously, 'Mr President because of your socialist tendencies and because of your surrender to communism I hold you in complete contempt!' There were others, even respectable Southerners, who held that Kennedy was a windbag, or else considered that his electoral promises were hardly more than rhetoric. It is true that his programme had not yet progressed much beyond the blueprint stage. His Civil Rights Bill, for example, would not reach Congress until the following year, and other measures were still only a twinkle in the President's eye.

Whatever criticism of him there was, however, sprang always from political judgments about him. His role in the diplomatic world during the Berlin Crisis and conduct during the Cuban Missiles Crisis were generally admired, even by his opponents. His sexual promiscuity and his relentless womanising were not at the time common knowledge.

The Camelot legend, and Kennedy's secular beatification – themselves the product of the tide of articles in mawkish sentimentality that swept America in the wake of the assassination – may help to explain the uncritical admiration with which he was vested. In such a hothouse atmosphere it is not surprising that conspiracy theories should take root.

2:8

What is the Truth About the Hitler Diaries?

In 1983, The Times *announced its intention to publish the diaries of Adolf Hitler, which had been unearthed after a protracted search and duly authenticated, and which promised to be perhaps the most important single document relating to the period of the Second World War that had ever been published. Shortly after, the documents in question were discovered to be forgeries. What is the truth about this hoax?*

The German magazine *Stern* had for a number of years employed a news reporter called Heidemann, an ardent enthusiast for Nazi memorabilia, who for some time had imagined himself to be on the trail of documents purporting to be Hitler's personal diaries. He was prepared to offer the magazine's money to purchase them, and this offer tempted one Konrad Kujau, a compulsive liar and a Jack-of-all-trades with a criminal record, then living near Stuttgart, to embark upon an elaborate career of forgery more profitable than the small-time forgeries he had produced to date. Kujau elaborated the story that Hitler, in the final days of the Third Reich, had arranged for ten tin trunks of valuable archive material to be flown from Berlin to safety in the south, but that the Junkers 352 carrying them had crashed in the Heidenholz forest close to the Czech border, destroying its crew and most of its cargo in the fire that followed the crash. He pretended to have gained access to the diary material, but, because of the sensitive nature of his sources, which lay behind the Iron Curtain, refused to divulge the origins of the diaries. In fact he was industriously manufacturing them volume by volume, at something like 50,000 DM per volume. Since Heidemann had acquired the sum of 80,000 DM for each, as well as substantial additional payments, and was pocketing the difference, the two hushed up the whole endeavour, keeping the details secret from the management of the magazine until late in the day, and going along enthusiastically with their suggestion that the authentication of the diaries – indeed their very existence – should remain well out of the public gaze, for fear that someone else might stumble on the secret and be the first to publish the 'scoop'. This deception continued until 1983, the fiftieth anniversary of Hitler's coming to power, by which time no fewer than fifty-eight volumes of the 'diary' had been written by Kujau and purchased by Heidemann. Few people examined them, and of those who did even fewer could read them, since they were penned in the old Germanic script now no longer in use.

They were large exercise-book size (they *were* in fact exercise books) with stiff black covers, some of them bearing red wax seals in the shape of the German eagle, and others decorated with the initials 'AH' on the cover. Most of them bore typewritten labels signed by Martin Bormann declaring them to be the property of the Führer. They contained a small number of astonishing revelations, such as the admission that Hitler had been quite aware of Hess's peace mission to Britain in May 1941, but repudiated knowledge of it after it failed. Some of the details that Kujau had fabricated, such as the disclosure that Hitler much admired Chamberlain for his cool professionalism, were almost laughable. But for the most part the diary's contents were boring and trivial, the bulk of them extracted, sometimes word for word, from a two-volume edition of Hitler's *Speeches and Proclamations, 1932–45*, published in 1962 by the German historian Max Domarus.

Rupert Murdoch, proprietor of *The Times* and the *Sunday Times*, engaged in an unseemly battle with the US magazine *Newsweek* to secure the rights, but these negotiations fell through when the owners of *Stern* shamelessly jacked up the price to nearly $5 million. Besides, proper authentication was still lacking, and no one seemed anxious to put the diaries to the test. An effort had been made by a retired 'expert' to identify the handwriting, but since it was to be compared with 'genuine' Hitler handwriting that actually had also been forged by Kujau, it is not surprising that the diaries passed this simple test. No professional archivist and no forensic examination were called for until very late in the day. The eminent British historian Hugh Trevor-Roper said at first that they were genuine, persuaded by the enormous bulk of the forgery rather than by its contents, which he could neither read nor understand. The actual publication had already begun by *Stern* before the hoax was uncovered.

Apart from the textual errors, which were numerous, some resulting from Kujau's careless copying, some from errors contained in his source material and literally transcribed by him into the diaries, there were plainly other errors and inconsistencies in the text. Elderly survivors such as Hitler's former secretary, Christa Schroeder, confirmed that the Führer never wrote anything; his adjutant, von Below, that he often ate at about four o'clock in the morning before going to bed, and had no time to write a diary in the small hours. The diaries even showed he made an entry for the night when a bomb attack was made on his life in July 1944, although this was quite impossible, since his right arm was injured in the blast and photographs taken at the time showed him with his arm in a sling. The forensic evidence was even more damning. The paper was of inferior quality and contained a chemical paper whitener not invented until 1955; the binding, the glue and the thread were also of postwar manufacture; the red threads on the covers attaching the seals contained polyester, and the initials affixed were made of modern plastic. The typed labels had been done on an old machine, not over a period of years, between 1924 and 1937, but quite close together. Chemical analysis of the ink showed that the books had been written recently, not at the time they were supposed to have been written.

The hoax collapsed abruptly, leaving a number of the characters, like Trevor-Roper, with egg on their faces. The chief perpetrators, Heidemann and Kujau, were tried and sent to prison for substantial terms.

3

HEROES AND VILLAINS

Who was 'Ned Ludd'?

The original 'King Lud' was supposedly a king of Britain who, the legend goes, developed and improved the city of London sometime in the Medieval period. Though he could well have been a local official or wealthy merchant, and the 'royal' title purely honorific, there is no good evidence for his existence. He is popularly supposed to have been buried by Ludgate, one of the former gates of the city, named after him. Ludgate Hill and Circus survive as street names. Was he the model for 'Ned Ludd', the shadowy leader of the workers' sabotage against machines, that bore his name? Most likely it is just coincidence. But the later Ludd could hardly have been any more real, since he appears synchronistically in so many scattered locations during his brief 'reign' between 1810 and 1812.

The name Lud, or Ludd, seems to have been adopted as the symbol of the common man in his struggle to improve the quality of his life. The condition of industrial workers in the early nineteenth century had become rapidly worse as a result of the seemingly unstoppable advance of mechanisation in industry, creating widespread unemployment and low wages. They perhaps felt they needed such a champion from Britain's mythical past. 'Luddites', as they came to be known, appeared all over the North and Midlands at this time.

The Luddites of Lancashire were handloom weavers in the cotton industry, whose jobs were threatened by the spread of

Cartwright's power-loom after 1785, driven first by water and later by steam. The Lancashire men succeeded at the third attempt in burning the steam-loom factory at West Houghton in April 1812. Many of the miscreants were afterwards rounded up. Four of them were hanged and seventeen sentenced to transportation.

The Yorkshire Luddites were croppers or nappers, skilled shearmen who cut the nap off woollen cloth. They felt threatened by the introduction of the shearing frame, which could do the work of four men and was rapidly putting many of them out of work. They attacked Cartwight's mill at Liversedge, also in April 1812, but were able to do little damage, since Cartwright himself and a body of soldiers were waiting for them, and they were driven off after suffering casualties. Two of the captured later died of wounds but refused to betray the names of any of their associates. A later unsuccessful attempt was made on Cartwright's life; indeed, one of his fellow employers, William Horsfall of Marsden, was actually shot by Luddite rioters and killed.

In Nottingham, South Derbyshire and Leicestershire the Luddites turned their attention to the hand-frames which the local master hosiers had been introducing at a rent into the cottages of the stockingers as a means of increasing their output, an intrusion which many felt powerless to resist. The attack on local jobs was made worse by the introduction of 'cut-up' hosiery knitted on a wider frame, which simply unravelled when cut up, so undermining not only the wages of local employees but their trade reputation as well. In the year 1811–12 over a thousand stocking frames were smashed. The frames being in private houses it was easy to get at them, and there were usually sympathetic householders prepared to help the saboteurs escape. It is sometimes claimed, indeed, that it was from Leicestershire that the Luddite movement sprang. Local legend even today has it that 'Ned Ludd' came from the village of Anstey near Leicester. It was in his name that letters and proclamations were signed by the Luddites, some of them giving the home of 'King Lud' as Sherwood Forest (the home of an even more famous folk hero, Robin Hood), though in fact Sherwood Forest was well over twenty miles away.

In their efforts to stem Luddism the authorities used police, yeomanry, regular infantry and even cavalry, and in 1812 raised the penalty for machine-breaking by making it a capital offence. The activities of the Luddites were reminiscent of those of the equally legendary 'Captain Swing' who in 1830 challenged the power of the farmer and landlord by his attacks on agricultural machinery, and protested against the harsh treatment of the farmworkers by the poor law authorities. Both movements evinced the power of popular protest, and in both cases the government's answer was harsh repression. By such means the dangers of militant sabotage were gradually mastered and working-class discipline was maintained.

3:2

Talleyrand: Was He Guided by Principle or Personal Advantage?

The reputation of Talleyrand was that of a turncoat, trimming his principles to suit the ideas of the regime he was currently serving, whether it was a left-wing revolutionary regime, or a right-wing monarchist one. Thus he appeared to his contemporaries to have neither morals nor conscience. Indeed his former master the Emperor Napoleon, with characteristic frankness, said of him that he was 'merde dans un bas de soie' ('shit in silk stockings'). Is this the correct way to look at him?

Talleyrand was almost continuously employed in leading public capacities from 1789 until his death in 1834, a period of tempestuous change for France and for the whole of Europe. It is certainly true that to maintain his foothold in an age so dangerously slippery, he was obliged to be something of an acrobat. This gymnastic skill he demonstrated to perfection.

Charles Maurice de Talleyrand was born in 1754 of

aristocratic parentage, and though he had no particular religious calling secured office in the Church, becoming Bishop of Autun in 1789. He sided with the Third Estate in the Estates General, and supported the Civil Constitution of the Clergy and numerous other anti-clerical measures; but he kept his see until January 1791. He was sent to London as France's diplomatic representative in 1792, but fled to the United States when Louis XVI was executed, remaining in exile until the establishment of the Directory in 1795. He was Foreign Minister for the Directory from 1797 until 1799, when he resigned office and assisted Napoleon in his Brumaire coup d'état. Talleyrand served Napoleon as Foreign Minister from 1799 until 1807, playing an important role in France's policies in Germany. By 1808 he had come to the conclusion that Napoleon was riding rapidly for a fall, and therefore left office, awaiting a chance to offer his services to the Allies.

When Paris fell in 1814, Talleyrand negotiated with the Tsar and, having persuaded Louis XVIII to sign the Charter of Ghent, formally announced Napoleon's removal from power. He represented France at the Congress of Vienna in 1815, did everything he could to sow dissension among the Allies and to secure their acceptance of France as a Great Power at the negotiating table. He retired from career politics under the later Bourbons, but came back to play an important role in the removal of Charles X from the French throne at the time of his replacement by Louis Philippe. He returned to London as French Ambassador from 1830 to 1834, when he made his peace with the Church, and on his deathbed received the last rites as a bishop.

It is hardly surprising that such a widely varied career aroused considerable scepticism among contemporaries about the morals of the individual who figured in it. At the same time, the late eighteenth and early nineteenth centuries were an age where democracy and nationalism struggled against autocracy and legitimism. As a result, moral considerations were always uppermost in people's minds, and Talleyrand's failings seemed all the more glaring. He treated criticism with an easy cynicism that seemed almost as damning as a confession of guilt. Nevertheless his real motivation went much deeper than this.

He revealed beneath his fickleness and superficiality a clear streak of patriotism. Whatever the political complexion of the regime in power, whether it was right-wing or left-wing, he always kept what he saw as the interests of his country clearly in view. This could be seen, for example, at the Congress of Vienna when he played a weak hand with consummate skill. France, as the defeated power, might so easily have been treated harshly, but he used his position at the conference table to exploit the weaknesses and the mutual suspicions of the victors, and so achieved a moderate and acceptable settlement. Perhaps his observation in his memoirs, where he said that he never deserted a cause until it ceased to be advantageous to France, had more truth in it than has been usually conceded.

3:3

The Legend of John Brown: Hero and Martyr?

In 1859, John Brown struck a blow for the freedom of American slaves that has earned for him immortality in legend and popular song. The reputation which history has accorded to him, however, is not necessarily the correct one.

Brown was a lonely and fanatical man, one of those self-styled heroes feared and mistrusted by his friends almost as much as he was hated by his enemies in the Southern states. Earlier in the 1850s he had witnessed the encroachments being made on 'Free' America in the name of popular sovereignty by slave-owning immigrants to Kansas, and had been involved in skirmishes between parties of Northern (anti-slave) partisans and Southern (pro-slave) partisans. He had himself accounted for quite a number of 'border ruffians' in the so-called Pottawatomi massacres, though in fact he was clearly a bit of a ruffian himself. Brown was also one of the numerous abolitionists who helped to run what was known as the 'Underground Railway', whereby many slaves were assisted in their flight to free soil. These helpers took charge of such slaves, hiding and feeding them, disguising them, and passing them on from one farmstead to another until they were clear of their pursuers. Canada was the ultimate aim of their escape, for the Fugitive Slave Act which might lead to their recapture did not apply there.

In 1859, Brown devised a harebrained scheme for freeing the slaves by fomenting a slave rebellion in the South. His plan was to invade Virginia with a small army of supporters, seize the United States arsenal at Harper's Ferry, and summon the slaves to rise and join him in a national revolt. The whole idea was wildly impracticable. In October 1859, with only about twenty supporters, he seized the fire engine house at the ferry, where he was promptly surrounded by troops and besieged. The slaves did not move to help his hopeless cause. His two sons were killed at his side and the siege ended ignominiously after two days with all of his men dead or wounded except four. The Federal officer who captured him was Robert E. Lee. Brown was arrested and tried for treason, murder and criminal conspiracy. He was found guilty and hanged in December 1859.

Brown was that curiously modern American mixture of Christian love and Satanic hatred, of saintliness and violence; while he was genuinely deeply religious he would stop at nothing to inflict any brutality or cruelty on the slave-owners he so hated. The effect of his ill-conceived rising was to inflame feeling both among the Southerners, who thought he was the Devil incarnate, and the Northerners, who thought he was a hero and a martyr. R.W. Emerson was doing no more than voice the opinions of the bulk of Northerners when he said that John Brown was: 'That new saint, than whom nothing finer or more brave was ever led by love of men into conflict and death. . . . He will make the gallows glorious like the Cross.'

John Brown, in staging his desperate coup, was doing what his conscience demanded of him, whatever contemporaries may have thought. He did not aim to achieve fame and, if he had lived, he would have been astonished to get it. Nevertheless, history manufactures strange and often flawed heroes, and John Brown for all his faults was one of them.

3:4

Wyatt Earp: Hero of the Wild West?

Wyatt Earp, lawman of the Middle West states, has become a resounding legend for the American people. Is there any truth behind his story?

Born in 1849, Earp was later famed as Marshal of Dodge and Tombstone, whose streets he made safe for ordinary folk by his stern pursuit of wrongdoers and his belief in the rule of law. A Tombstone lawyer wrote of him in 1881: 'His conduct as a peace officer was above reproach. He was quiet, but absolutely fearless in the discharge of his duties. He usually went about in his shirtsleeves, without a coat and with no weapons in sight.' He was said to be a lean, athletic man, dour and unsmiling, his face adorned with a drooping moustache, and with a deep growling voice that could quell the resistance of his hearers. Of all the stories of the Wild West, his is probably the least accurate and the most enduring, the subject of a number of Hollywood epics, including the 1957 John Sturges classic, *Gunfight at the OK Corral*, starring Burt Lancaster.

Earp was never appointed Marshal of anywhere, and probably would never have been elected Sheriff. Peacekeeping as a deputy or as an assistant was easier for him, and was a part-time activity that did not impede Earp's business interests as a saloon keeper. It seems he preferred ice cream to hard liquor. He participated in only two shoot-outs, of which the more famous, against the Clanton brothers at the OK Corral, lasted less than thirty seconds. His skills as a gunman were chiefly confined to 'buffaloing', or pistol whipping, rowdy drovers in his saloon. If, as legend has it, he owned a twelve-inch Buntline Special, he probably used it as a side baton rather than as a side iron. He was known to fumble his draw: in fact, on one such occasion, his gun-belt slipped down and pinned his thighs together, making him look extremely foolish and preventing him from mounting his horse.

The fact that we have such inaccurate information on Wyatt Earp is largely due to inconsistencies in the story put about mainly by himself, but partly also by the romancings of his wife, Sadie. The drab truth is that, in reality, Earp was first a pioneer farmer engaged in taking land from the Indians, then a buffalo hunter, then a railroad worker, only finally a businessman. It was not his aim to clean up Tombstone, but merely to amass mining claims and land holdings. With a fifth share in a saloon's gambling concession, he presided over the dregs of humanity and was careful not to let his peace-keeping interfere with the flow of his profits. As for lawmen shooting it out with unindicted suspects, such action was disapproved of by Westerners even as early as 1880. Earp is branded a murderer by some old Arizona hands even today for killing a cowboy in such circumstances, and later for pursuing a vendetta against the murderers of his own youngest brother, Morgan. These critics said of him that he was 'little more than a tinhorn outlaw operating under the protection of a tin badge.'

A more interesting question is why the Americans have for so long needed this kind of idealised morality play to be a symbol of their culture. Wild West novels and films throughout this century have propagated the idea of goodness and truth challenged by villainy and finally victorious over it. But this notion of a knight on a white charger vanquishing evil without compromising his own virtue in fact disguises one of the least creditable episodes in American history – the virtual extermination of the aboriginal population and the theft of their land because of naked greed. In one way, therefore, it is a soothing substitute. Its origin is explained by the lure of the unknown and of the testing of manhood with the call to 'Go West, young man!' It is mixed with the adventure of travelling by wagon train to build a new life in unexplored lands, the challenge of the open air and of the hard, simple life where every man fought for himself and his family. It is evidence, too, of the strong grip over men's minds held by simple puritan religion, with its clear, uncomplicated distinction between good and evil. It has its equivalents in the legend of King Arthur and his Knights of the Round Table, or of Robin Hood and his Merry Men against the wicked Sheriff of Nottingham. For those who need the guidance of a moral example it is a cultural icon and perhaps still has validity.

3:5

Cecil Rhodes: Visionary or Villain?

Opinions of the character and achievements of Cecil Rhodes have come to vary widely in the course of the second half of the twentieth century. He was regarded by generations of schoolboys (of whom the present writer was one) as the great hero of imperial history, the main architect of the British Empire in southern Africa, the dreamer who conceived the idea of the Cape to Cairo railway, the founder of Rhodesia, and the idealist and philanthropist who conceived of the Rhodes scholarships at Oxford University. Others regarded him in a much less charitable light as an intriguer, a crook, a liar, a careerist who made his fortune in gold and diamonds, and the ruthless champion of doctrines of white supremacism. It now seems entirely possible that his character was a curious mix of all these things, and that he contrived to be good and bad at the same time.

Cecil John Rhodes was born the son of an Anglican parson in 1859, and brought up and educated at Bishop's Stortford. He had trouble with his chest, and in 1869 was sent to South Africa to stay with his brother in Natal for the sunshine and the fresh air. He moved on to Kimberley in 1871, and for the next two years lived the life of a pioneer, sleeping in a tent and sitting on an upturned bucket to sort through the dirt looking for diamonds. Later he claimed he had been earning £100 a week. During his stay he found time to make an eight-month journey by ox-cart into the Transvaal and Bechuanaland (present-day Botswana). What he saw gripped his imagination, confirming him in his determination to develop the area he came to call 'My North'. Later the diamond prospector became undergraduate when he embarked on his studies at Oriel College, Oxford in 1873. At university he listened to the stirring words of John Ruskin, who appealed to the youth of England to help their country '. . . found colonies as fast as she is able . . . seizing upon any piece of fruitful waste ground she can set her foot on and there teaching her colonists that their chief virtue is fidelity to their country'.

Returning to South Africa, he became chairman of a diamond company in 1880, and in the years that followed secured extensive interests in the gold mines of the Transvaal. In 1889, by the amalgamation of a number of such companies, he became chairman of the massive de Beers Consolidated Mines. In 1887 he had founded the British South Africa Company, and was granted a Royal Charter in 1889 to develop the region north of the Transvaal later known by his own name as Rhodesia. By what might be regarded now as sharp practice he obtained permission from Lobengula, king of the Matabele, to dig for precious metals in his country, and promised in turn to supply him with rifles for his warriors. These could at the time be bought freely in England for the sum of 12s 6d (62½p) each, though, happily, at such a price they were not very reliable. It was no easy task to get the first 200 settlers through hundreds of miles of trackless *veldt*, but eventually Rhodes established them at Fort Salisbury (present-day Harare), with permanent houses, a bank, a newspaper and even a telegraph office.

In the meantime, he had become in 1880 a member of the Cape Colony legislature, and was Premier of the Colony from 1890 to 1896, when he was forced to resign because of his connection with the Jameson Raid. This occurred when discontent among the numerous *Uitlander* population of the Transvaal led to the formation of a plot at Christmas, 1895, to overthrow the Boer government in Johannesburg, and Dr Starr Jameson, a close colleague of Rhodes, was encouraged to invade the country at the head of a band of 500 armed policemen to restore order there. Unfortunately the Uitlanders hesitated, and Jameson crossed the border before any rising occurred. He found himself pursued by Boer sharpshooters and was finally ignominiously arrested by the very forces he had been sent to discipline. The leaders were brought to trial in Johannesburg, four of them (including Rhodes's own brother) being convicted and sentenced to death, and fifty-nine others to various periods of imprisonment with fines of £2,000 each. Political pressure on the Boer government brought their release, and a number of the ringleaders were retried in London later. Rhodes paid the fines demanded by the Boers from his own pocket, but the episode marked the end of Rhodes's career, and he never returned to office. He died in 1902, just before the end of the Boer War, without ever recovering his former eminence in Cape Colony. He left a fortune of over £6 million, including a large sum for the endowment of scholarships tenable by men of high character from the British overseas empire, to instil in their minds 'the advantage to the Colonies as well as to England of the retention of the unity of the Empire'.

It is by no means sure that Rhodes would ever have qualified for one of his own scholarships, considering the flaws in his character. Though his reputation was one of maintaining friendly attitudes towards the coloured native workers, whose interests he was known on occasions to champion, he nevertheless could be ruthless with his rivals and authoritarian with his supporters. Both in business and in politics he knew the arts of fraud and skulduggery: the first he amply showed in his dealings with Lobengula; the second he demonstrated with the Jameson Raid. He moved in influential circles in Britain, where he was proud of his acquaintance with many contemporary political leaders, though some of them, like Joseph Chamberlain, were not too keen on knowing him. His views showed imagination and vision, but tarnished quickly and soon became unpopular. His values verged on being intolerant and triumphalist and in the world of the twentieth century rapidly came to be regarded as parochial. Throughout his life it remained his credo that: 'As God is manifestly fashioning the English-speaking race as the chosen instrument by which He may bring in a state of society based on justice, liberty and peace, He must obviously want me to give as much scope and power to that race as possible.'

From him, for a time, such words to the English seemed acceptable; but when put into the mouths of racist leaders of regimes in other countries they now can be seen as the dangerous nonsense they really are.

3:6

Was Marconi's 'Wireless' Triumph Based on a Stolen Invention?

The three short pips sent from his wireless on the beach at Poldhu in Cornwall in 1901 were effective in making Guglielmo Marconi's name almost synonymous with the invention of radio. His team had built a crude wireless transmitter in England from which they sent the Morse code letter 'S', while on the other side of the Atlantic, at Signal Hill, St Johns, in Newfoundland, Marconi and his helpers sat round an equally crude receiver, using an aerial flown by a kite. Now, however, a century later, Marconi's reputation as the father of modern radio has been shown to be based on an error.

An electronics specialist working for NASA in Houston has revealed that Marconi employed a discovery of Sir Jagadis Chandra Bose, a maverick scientist who worked from a one-room laboratory in Calcutta. A scientific paper published by Bose in 1899 describes the same device used by Marconi for the transmission he made two years afterwards. The device, called a *coherer*, consisted of a small glass tube containing a globule of mercury between two iron plugs. It was the vital element needed to transform the first radio signal beamed from

Cornwall into an audible sound at the listening station in Newfoundland. Enquiry proved that the device used by Marconi precisely matched the description of the iron-mercury coherer published by Bose. Perhaps this was why Marconi diverted attention from the true inventor of the coherer by claiming that the idea came from research undertaken by the Italian navy – indeed it became known as the 'Italian Navy coherer', even though Marconi eventually patented it under his own name.

Marconi moved to London from Bologna in 1896, the year after Bose left Britain to set up his laboratory in Calcutta. It seems unlikely that the two ever met, but they were probably familiar with each other's work. Marchese Luigi Solari, a wealthy Italian aristocrat from whom Marconi claimed to have taken the idea, said he first read of it in 'some English publication' he failed later to trace; and it may well be that it was an account of Bose's coherer, published obscurely in 1899 in the *Proceedings* of the Royal Society in London, that was the document he failed to find.

3:7

Was Roger Casement the Victim of a Smear Campaign?

Roger Casement was arrested in Ireland in 1916, brought to London, charged with high treason, tried and hanged. Still highly regarded by Irish nationalists as a patriot martyr, he has been systematically smeared by the British, who made use of a diary (not produced in court) containing sordid details of his private life and making him out to be a homosexual pervert. His case has given rise to a controversy that remains unresolved to this day.

Casement, born near Dublin in 1864, entered the British Consular Service in 1892, and gained distinction for himself by reporting on the harsh conditions prevailing in the rubber industries of the Congo and the Amazon. He resigned from the consular service in 1913 and became a fervent Irish Nationalist. In 1914 he was in the USA, trying to enlist American aid for Irish independence. Then he set off to recruit 'Irish Brigades' among Irish prisoners of war in Germany, but his efforts met with little success. Then he tried to organise German help for a rebellion in Ireland. In 1916 he was landed from a German U-boat on the coast of Kerry near Tralee on the eve of the Easter Rising, but was arrested within a few hours and so brought to trial.

Even after he was convicted there were many who considered that he was likely to be reprieved, since, although he had had treasonable intentions, Casement had hardly had time to make his treason effective. Such people thought that he had been made the victim of a deliberate smear campaign, encouraged by the authorities in order to stifle the demand for a reprieve.

The slur on Casement's moral character arose from the unscrupulous use of extracts from certain cash-ledgers and journals that came to be known as the 'black diaries' – to distinguish them from the so-called 'white diary' now in the National Library in Ireland, in which he gave details of his enquiries in South America. The 'white diary' was for a long time thought to be a cleaned-up version of the black diaries from which all the obscene material had been deleted. But recent detailed comparison of the two revealed not only differences of orthography, spelling and dates, but material variations that were thought to reveal the hand of the forger. On the other hand, there was scientific evidence declaring that the same person wrote both of them, and the disconcerting fact that, to produce them, the forger went to the immense trouble of producing lengthy and numerous volumes – a forgery on the scale of the so-called Hitler diaries (see page 36).

A new enquiry into the authenticity of the diaries, published in 2002 as part of an Anglo-Irish exercise in improving their relations, sought finally to establish that they were genuinely written by Casement himself. The 'black' diaries were written in pencil, while the 'white' diary was in a mixture of pen and crayon. Both diaries were borrowed for detailed forensic tests on the handwriting, the ink and on the paper used. There was even an enquiry whether the pollen from plants in Africa and Brazil, where Casement was supposed to have written the diaries, could be detected on the paper. The scientists conducting the enquiry established their authenticity beyond doubt, a decision gratifying Roger Sawyer, one of Casement's modern biographers. But not everybody was pleased. Historians living in Ireland, including the Scottish historian Angus Mitchell, persisted in thinking them fakes, saying: 'They were texts rewritten by British security from earlier versions.' In spite of all the proofs offered, therefore, the question even today remains disputed.

3:8

The Last Tsar: A Vicious Tyrant?

Looking back on Tsarist Russia in its later days from the perspective of the twentieth-century Soviet Union, there is a natural tendency to accept the Bolshevik version of history and condemn Tsar Nicholas II as a tyrant pitilessly repressing the Russian people, up to the point when, goaded beyond endurance, they rose up against their oppressor and swept him away. It is, however, a historical error to exaggerate the extent of the Tsar's tyranny – just as it is an error to overestimate the extent of the Revolutionaries' liberalism.

There can be no doubting that Russia, as a modern state, was different from France, Italy or Germany. In the first place, in spite of modernising efforts by rulers since Peter the Great, Russia was still in some ways backward. It joined western Europe relatively late, having emerged from subservience to the Mongols only in the sixteenth century. Hence the tradition of a wider medieval Christian community was lacking. As far as Russian traditionalists were concerned European culture was *foreign*, and Russia's distinct identity was to be found in its Slavonic roots and not in any craven imitations of the West. Secondly, though it was beginning to make quite rapid progress in the development of its industries, the Russian style of government was highly authoritarian. The separation of Church and state, the secularising of political power and the subordination of political government to some form of popular control had all passed Russia by. Even the impact of the French Revolution on Russian thinking had proved to be minimal. The Russian system depended solely on the Tsar, who was not merely the political head of the state, but the social and religious apex of all power. After the death of Alexander II in 1881 the impulse toward 'European' reform had withered and been replaced under Alexander III by the alternative – a policy of reaction with an emphasis on the anti-European features of society. Alexander's main helper was the Procurator of the Holy Synod, Konstantin Pobyedonostzev, who successfully eroded the power of the peasant commune and halted the slow and difficult process of change. The autocracy had become even more centralised, with the expanding bureaucracy tending to replace the traditional aristocracy, who retired to their estates to lead a life of effete rural splendour. Excluded from positions of trust, the aristocracy could block the policies of reforming ministers like Witte and Stolypin, but could no longer replace them. Instead they flirted with radicalism, or even revolution.

These backward, autocratic and over-centralised features of Russian political life were compounded by another – the desire, official after Alexander III's reign, to assimilate the whole of life to the standard Russian pattern. The pioneers of this policy were the new bureaucrats, who, blindly modelling themselves on the more illiberal features of the Prussian government, aimed at order and uniformity. In the Baltic provinces, Poland, the Ukraine, Bessarabia, Transcaucasia and in the Muslim provinces of Asia, a policy of ruthless Russification replaced traditional diversity of the empire. Among those who suffered the most were the Jews, subject to periodic 'pogroms', often quite spontaneous, but sometimes encouraged by the state, in which their property and lives were exposed to the crudest hatred and resentment. By 1900, therefore, Russia became a country not of quiet stability, but of seething discontents and frustrated hopes, where the traditional slogan, coined by Nicholas I's Minister of Education, Count Ovarov, 'Orthodoxy, Autocracy, Nationality', pleased hardly anybody.

The Tsar's government, though based on a semi-skilled professional bureaucracy, had by 1900 taken aboard a tremendous responsibility for the country's future. The Tsar himself, the centre of all power, was an amiable but quite limited individual, and strongly prejudiced in his opinions. Often he was quite unable to grasp the nature of the demands being made on him. With no free expression of public opinion being permitted, Tsar Nicholas lived in a political vacuum, beset by feelings of uncertainty and insecurity. The Third Section of his Chancellery, and the dreaded secret police, the Okhrana, were supposed to look out for foreigners, dissenters, agitators, criminals and all others who might prove dangerous to him, but this was an enormous task that proved quite beyond them. In 1905, advised by Count Witte, the reformist but not very liberal Finance Minister, and under pressure as a result of defeats during the Russo-Japanese War, Nicholas accepted the so-called October Manifesto, with the modest beginnings of a democratic form of government. But within weeks, as the result of the end of the Japanese war, he backtracked on its main concessions, withdrew a number of its key provisions and instead proclaimed martial law. None the less, the Manifesto did produce the first Duma, the stage from which, however limited it might be, the reformers could in future demand further concessions.

By 1907, however, the Tsar was back in full control of the situation. A wave of repression took place, with critics being sentenced to exile in Siberia, to prison or death; the second Duma, elected even more narrowly than the first, was dissolved on the Tsar's orders and even moderate Social Democrat deputies were arrested and deported. A new and sterner set of ministers came to office. Having dismissed Witte in 1906 because his ideas suddenly seemed too democratic, Nicholas appointed Stolypin as Prime Minister instead. He was no liberal either, but he continued with reforms, this time chiefly of the land. In 1909 he enabled the peasant to acquire land legally and effectively, thus laying the foundations of what might have been a modern commercial system of agriculture. But as the First World War approached the use of police repression, the courts, and the secret service, crushed political and labour opposition, driving leaders abroad or confining them to labour camps in Siberia. So successful was this repression that Lenin as late as 1917 seriously doubted whether he would ever live long enough to see the outbreak of a popular revolution.

But though it is impossible to deny that repression took place, it remained a systematic, legal form of repression, using the courts and the due processes of the law. It sprang from the stolid conservatism of the Tsar's government and was authoritarian without being capricious. The rules, unenlightened though they may have been, were set out in Russia's code of law, and the government enforced them without fear and certainly without favour. What the government did fear was the breakdown of law and order in revolution, when public order, property and lives would be equally at risk from the unpredictable surge of popular forces. By 1917, the Tsar's view was that any form of harshness was preferable to total breakdown in revolution; the revolutionaries on the other hand believed that even revolution was preferable to the continuance of Nicholas's tyranny.

3:9

How Did Rasputin Die?

Mystery surrounds the murder in 1916 of Grigori Rasputin, self-styled monk, a dirty and unkempt libertine given to orgies of sex and drink, yet friend of the Tsarina and chief adviser of Tsar Nicholas II, on the eve of the Russian Revolutions of 1917. What is the truth behind all these conflicting stories?

In the 1920s, an action was brought in London before Mr Justice Avory by Prince Yusupov, with Sir Patrick Hastings appearing for the plaintiff, against the Metro-Goldwyn-Mayer Corporation of America in respect of a film made by that company about Rasputin. In this film he was portrayed as the lover of Princess Yusupov, a claim which she and her husband strenuously denied. The story is told in Sir Patrick's memoirs, published in 1949 under the title of *Cases in Court*. Both the Princess and the Prince were impressive in the witness box, and were successful in winning damages from the film company for the (then) enormous sum of £25,000. Free from any threat of prosecution in Britain after the Russian Bolshevik revolution, Yusupov, asked the direct question by his counsel as he gave his evidence, said quite frankly: 'Yes, I killed Rasputin. It was my duty to kill him. So I killed him.'

He told how a group of Russian nobles, disturbed at Rasputin's hold over the Tsarina – who seems to have been convinced that he alone could alleviate her son's haemophilia – and anxious lest Rasputin's wild and irresponsible decisions in Russia should lead the country on the path to destruction, decided in December 1916 to assassinate him. The task would not be easy. Superstition claimed that the intended victim was impervious to poison, and that bullets could not harm him. In fact it was believed Rasputin could not die. All the same, he was invited to the Prince's own Moika Palace on the pretence of enjoying one of those drunken orgies in which Rasputin revelled.

When the victim arrived, music was playing supposedly for his entertainment, but really to prevent the outside world from hearing any noise from the struggle that followed. He was taken by his host to one of the lower rooms of the palace, where he was regaled with the sweet cakes which he so enjoyed. The cakes were soaked in enough cyanide to kill a dozen men, but Rasputin wolfed them one by one without apparent ill effect. Yusupov, unnerved, seized a revolver and emptied it into his victim, but Rasputin remained upright and charged about the room roaring like a bull. When he fell, Yusupov beat him to death with a loaded stick. Then his fellow conspirators helped him to dump the body into the ice-bound River Neva. But when the body was recovered, there was water in the lungs. Rasputin was discovered not to have been dead at all; he had drowned by immersion in the freezing river. Possibly because of the universal hatred in which Rasputin was held, the only action taken by the Tsar against Yusupov at the time was to exile him to a remote part of his estate in rural Russia.

Yusupov's testimony created a sensation in Britain. He was only able to give it because he knew that the Bolsheviks were unlikely to prosecute him for such a patriotic act – in any case they could not get their hands on him in Britain, and Britain was unlikely to surrender him to them even if they asked for it. The story was so bizarre that it needed no embellishment. It was widely reported in the press, and the record of the case is still in existence.

But was any of it in fact true? Police archives, recently uncovered by Brian Moynahan, a journalist and historian who came across the papers, tell a different story of Rasputin's murder, as does his most recent biography. He was lured to the palace, where he was met by prostitutes. Masked men emerged from the palace after two hours, not the four hours which Yusupov had claimed were necessary to subdue their victim. They were carrying a body, which they dumped in the river. The records show that the body died of gunshot wounds; a post-mortem examination found no traces of poison. Yusupov, who died in 1967, never retracted his story of the murder, though from time to time he changed the details. His version of events has until now never been challenged, but Moynahan says that the real story is much more mundane: 'The records show that the legend of invincibility was false, and was perpetuated by those who killed him.'

3:10

Stalin: 'Uncle Joe' or Mass Murderer?

The most ruthless and most effective mass killers in human history are those of the twentieth century; compared with them, Attila the Hun seems positively benign. The most destructive of the twentieth-century killers was Hitler, but Stalin runs a close second. Speculative estimates of the numbers killed by Stalin range from the 2 million admitted by Khrushchev to the 20 million suggested by the Soviet Union's bitterest critics. Is it possible to arrive at a more precise figure?

The cult of Stalin was not confined to the Soviet Union. Foreigners of left-wing persuasion like Bernard Shaw and the Webbs visited Russia in the 1930s and admired all that they saw. Nearly all outsiders believed in the justice of the 'show trials', including the well-known British lawyer D.N. Pritt. Historians fell over themselves to eulogise the Stalinist regime or at least to play down its deficiencies, and the works of R.H. Tawney and B. Pares are still widely used by students. Even later, after Stalin's death, historians like Christopher Hill and even Isaac Deutscher in places glamourised him and minimised his faults. Among approved Soviet historians the cult of Stalin became sickeningly sycophantic, even if Stalin's Trotskyist opponents took a more realistic view. During the Second World War opinion in the West did a U-turn from the days of suspicion and hostility in 1939/40 to admiration and adulation once the Soviet Union had been invaded in 1941. He became 'Uncle Joe' to the West – a hero, almost a saint, the notion that he could do wrong was almost unthinkable; the notion that Stalin was wicked was wicked in itself. But if a man's wickedness can be measured by the number of deaths for which he was responsible, all these admirers of Stalin were in serious error.

Good communists are hard to find; cynics have suggested that the only good communists are dead ones. Orthodox communists no longer fit the specifications laid down by Marx, and are more the product of 100 years of Marxist development and experience. Lenin's version of communism saw the political process as one of continuing revolution, and until this had been completed communists were engaged in a constant battle against counter-revolution. Singleminded commitment and ruthlessness were the hallmarks of the true communist. Stalin was more concerned with power than principle. By 1924 and too late, Lenin recognised Stalin's concern with self-advancement. Lenin had been ruthless, but his repression pales into insignificance against Stalin's purges, which Stalin justified as part of the ongoing proletarian struggle. But it is difficult to see any communist orthodoxy in Stalin's handling of the famine, treatment of the so-called kulaks, alienation of the peasants and the degradation of the industrial workforce. Stalin might claim to be another Robespierre, in that his killings were necessary to purify the state, but it is difficult to escape the conclusion that Stalin's killings resulted from paranoia rather than idealism.

It is important to decide which categories are to be included as Stalin's victims. Almost a million Russians died in the attack on Finland in 1939/40, but they are usually omitted as they were casualties of war. Over 20 million died as a consequence of the German invasion, and although Stalin must bear much of the blame for the initial military disasters of the war, it would be churlish to make him solely responsible for these Russian war casualties. Even so, some of the war casualties were his direct responsibility: the uprooting of Tartars leading to privation and much mortality, and the executions of many Russians, including partisans, on suspicion of collaborating with the enemy. It is usual to include all those who died in the gulags, although it must be admitted that some of them would have died of natural causes anyway.

There were spasmodic political executions throughout the 1920s – old Social Revolutionaries, former Cadets, Tsarist survivors and the like – but it was not until Stalin turned against the *kulaks* (wealthy peasants – [see page 281]) that the numbers of his victims escalated. It is estimated that there were 5 million whom Stalin labelled as kulaks. Of these some died at the hands of troops or commissars while resisting collectivisation, but about 3.5 million were sent to the gulags, and of this number fewer than a million survived. The purges followed. Stalin personally signed almost ¼ million death sentences during the 1930s, and undoubtedly these sentences were faithfully carried out. But many were shot out of hand, and probably ten times the number of those executed were sent to the labour camps, in which there was an average 30 per cent survival rate.

Official figures for the population of the Soviet Union in 1939 exceed the figures privately supplied to Stalin by 6.3 million, and it has been argued that this shortfall is made up of those who died in the famine and the purges. Since Stalin deliberately concealed the famine of the early 1930s from the outside world, and thus denied foreign aid to his country, it is usual to include those who died from the famine among his victims. But it is simplistic to ascribe the 6.3 million shortfall to Stalin-related deaths or even to deaths at all. Statistics can abound with inbuilt inaccuracies, and some of the victims of the purges were not even Russian nationals; foreign communists spending their exile in Russia were regarded as untrustworthy by Stalin and their numbers were decimated. Even so 2.5 million kulak deaths and a similar number of famine deaths seem fairly incontrovertible. And Stalin did not stop killing in the 1930s. From the Baltic states 170,000 were sent to the labour camps in 1940–41, and this was followed by the very high figure of ½ million during the late 1940s (almost 10 per cent of the population). The victims were the civil servants, teachers and intelligentsia of the former Baltic Republics. A similar proportion of the nearly 4 million Poles living east of the Curzon Line was also consigned to the gulags. Barely a third of these Balts and Poles survived to be repatriated after 1956. Of course, Stalin began executing Poles as early as 1941 when 15,000 Polish officers were put to death at Katyn [see page 30].

Nor in war did he stop at foreign nationals. Stalin's paranoia extended to any Russian who survived the German concentration camps or the German prisoner of war camps. The very fact of their survival implied to Stalin that they must have been collaborators, and many of these ex-prisoners returned to Russia to face immediate execution or further incarceration. And if Stalin was suspicious of those who survived German imprisonment he was even more hostile to those Soviet nationals who, through fear or conviction, served in German military units or civilian organisations. There were about a million of these, and Stalin demanded the repatriation of those he could not immediately lay his hands on. The Americans were uncooperative, but those handed over by the British were not far short of 100,000. Few of these survived [see page 286].

In the postwar years purges continued, but not on the scale of the 1930s. The deaths were not confined to Soviet territory. Trotsky was one of the first (1940) but by no means the last Soviet citizen to be hunted down and killed by Stalin's agents. In the late 1940s the Soviet show trials of the prewar years were mirrored by show trials in most of the satellite states. For these Stalin was directly responsible. And had it not been for Stalin's final illness and death the Soviet medical élite might well have been savagely pruned in 1953.

In all this there is a danger of double-counting: in which category do you place a Lithuanian who died of famine in a labour camp? In which category do you place a party member, who was also a kulak, shot during the purges? Moreover, there are no accurate statistics. On balance we can arrive at a rough figure of 30 million deaths during the Stalin era resulting from famine, purges or war. If the war deaths are removed we are left with about 10 million for which Stalin must bear responsibility. Here an estimate midway between the two extremes of 2 million and 20 million seems justified, but it is all very hit and miss, and could well be out by several million. Hitler is the champion killer because he takes responsibility for the deaths in the Second World War. If his responsibility is confined to political executions and the Holocaust he might well have to give way to Stalin.

3:11

Rudolf Hess: Devious or Deranged?

On 10 May 1941 Hitler's 47-year-old deputy, Rudolf Hess, piloted himself to Britain in a Messerschmitt, and parachuted into Scotland twelve miles from his destination – the Lanarkshire home of his prewar acquaintance, the Duke of Hamilton. Hess claimed that he had come to Britain on a peace mission, but the verdict of Hitler at the time, the Nuremberg trial later, and a number of eminent psychiatrists, was that

Hess was deranged. But there are still those who argue that Hess's peace mission in 1941 was official, that he was not deranged, and that the man who died in Spandau prison was not Hess. It is possible to assess the probable veracity of these arguments, but enough mystery remains to prevent a categorical assertion of their truth or otherwise.

Certainly if the official British version of Hess's peace mission is true it was bound to fail. Hess could hardly expect Churchill to agree to terms more harsh than those rejected by Chamberlain in 1939, and as exacting as those turned down by Churchill in the dark days of the summer of 1940. And seeing his old enemies the Bolsheviks taken on by Hitler would have been inadequate compensation for a humiliating peace. Hitler took great pains to dissociate himself from Hess's escapade as soon as he got news of it. He did not wait to see whether Hess would succeed in his peace efforts, and unless Hitler was a consummate actor, his initial bewilderment rings true. So an official peace mission seems most unlikely. Suggestions that Hess was jealous of his colleagues, and hoped that success in bringing peace with Britain would reinstate him high in Hitler's favour, support the view that Hess was acting on his own initiative without Hitler's prior knowledge. Its sheer foolhardiness also serves to reinforce the derangement theory.

But some, including Stalin, were highly suspicious. The timing of Hess's flight was only three weeks before the original date for the planned invasion of Russia. Was Hess, with or without Hitler's connivance, hoping to cash in on Churchill's dislike of communism to end the war in the West, so that Germany would not have to fight on two fronts? It seems very unlikely, and Churchill strongly denied it when he met Stalin at Teheran. And yet, while Hess seemed often to behave irrationally at Nuremberg – behaviour that probably saved him from the death sentence – his final years at Spandau prison did not reveal any eccentricity other than that to be expected from a man who had spent so long in solitary confinement. Many of the guards and certainly his own family regarded him as normal. Did he recover his wits, or had he never lost them? While the usual explanation that Hess was mentally unstable seems by far the most likely, there still remains some small element of doubt.

There is also some doubt arising from the manner and nature of his death. Hess was sentenced to life imprisonment at Nuremberg in 1946, and spent the next forty years of his life in solitary confinement in Spandau prison in West Berlin. He died at the age of 93 on 17 August 1987, in what appears to have been an act of suicide – he had already made several unsuccessful suicide attempts. That he had taken his own life was disputed by his son, who argued that his father was too frail to have engineered his own death (by strangulation) without assistance, as decided by the autopsy. But the son, Wolf-Rüdiger Hess, did not dispute that the dead man was indeed his own father. The existence of a double, trained in Norway in the spring of 1941, adds to the mystery, and gives some credence to the allegations that the dead man in 1987 was not Hess at all. But most senior politicians and generals on both sides were given doubles. More significant were the reports that dental records and the absence of surgical scars indicate that substitution had taken place. On this basis it is presumed that the man who flew to Scotland was the double and not Hess. Yet the very public Nuremberg trial would surely have brought the deception to light. Someone in the courtroom, or who watched the newsreels would have recognised the deception and would surely have felt obliged to draw attention to it. That the family, who had been visiting Hess for many years, dismissed the rumour of substitution seems to deny it any credibility, unless they too were a part of some elaborate deception. Doubts, therefore, persist about the precise manner of his death, but little about his true identity.

To an extent the mysteries about Hess remain mysteries. It is unlikely now that an authoritative resolution of them will ever be possible unless fresh evidence comes to light.

3:12
Was 'Lord Haw-Haw' Guilty of Treason?

*In London on 3 January 1946 William Joyce (alias 'Lord Haw-Haw')
was hanged for treason. The Nuremberg trials of the leading Nazis
had opened two months earlier; compared with the accused, Joyce's
offences were trivial. It has been argued that, as Joyce was not a British
citizen, he could not have committed treason anyway, and that
therefore his execution was a vindictive act of vengeance on the part of
the British. Was it?*

William Joyce was born in New York in 1906 of an American
father and English mother. He came to Britain in 1921 and
later graduated from London University. His admiration of
Oswald Mosley and Mussolini led him to become a Fascist.
He applied for a British passport in 1938 falsely claiming to
be a British subject, and he renewed this passport in 1939,
shortly before leaving for Germany. His great enthusiasm for
Nazism and Hitler caused him to become a naturalised
German citizen in September 1940, a month after his British
passport had expired. When he began broadcasting for the
Germans his upper-class and nasal accent ('Jahrmany calling')
soon earned him the nickname Lord Haw-Haw from his
British listeners. The broadcasts seldom had much specific
content, and were usually of a general and propagandist
nature. They caused more amusement than alarm in Britain
where many had heard of him but few listened to him. It was
rumoured that German spies fed him with detailed knowledge
about the timekeeping of British village church clocks and
other trivia, but in fact these rumours were apocryphal. If his
aim was to spread alarm and despondency among the British
population, he did not succeed; the few that took him
seriously would have been alarmists anyway.

After the war he was arrested in Germany, and brought to
Britain to be tried for treason. Only British citizens can commit
treason against Britain, and a British citizen he undoubtedly
was not. His British passport had been obtained falsely, and

falsely renewed a month before he began broadcasting in September 1939. Moreover, there was doubt as to whether he had retained his British passport after his German naturalisation. Nor was it easy to prove, in days before accurate identification of recorded voices, that he had actually made the broadcasts attributed to him. It was argued against him that, having sought the protection of a British passport, he owed allegiance to the British Crown, and the court found the treason proved.

In the months after the war liberated Europe was busily trying and executing its wartime traitors – Quisling in Norway, Laval in France were two among many. Britain had very few. Dispatching Joyce on the flimsiest of pretexts and evidence was the best Britain could come up with. Even the prosecutors at Nuremberg might have been hesitant in his case.

3:13

'McCarthyism': Did the End Justify the Means?

After the Second World War the United States experienced a wave of dread at what was seen as the relentless advance of communism. By 1948, the Russians had largely taken over control of eastern Europe, including parts of Germany, and the communists were also making rapid progress in seizing power in China. In 1949 the Russians also exploded their first A-bomb, long before the West expected it, and in the 1950s the H-bomb, too. The advance of communism now seemed inexorable and almost unstoppable, assisted, it seemed, by irresponsible left-wingers in the USA who were prepared to compromise the security of their own country for the sake of their personal ideology. Joseph McCarthy, junior Senator for Wisconsin, took up the cudgels in the fight against the creeping onslaught of communism in the United States from 1950 to 1952. What motives lay behind his campaign? Were they justified? Could the same unreasoning witch-hunt begin again?

Springing from total obscurity in this nervous atmosphere, McCarthy was regarded by many in America as an unscrupulous right-wing Republican who saw the chance for personal advancement in the prevailing panic and took it. In February 1950 he alleged that he had the names of 57 'card-carrying communists' in the State Department and that a further 205 people employed by the department were 'known communist sympathisers'. This startling pronouncement came directly after the conviction of Alger Hiss for perjury, and was used by Republicans to explain the failure of the Truman Administration to halt the advance of communism in China. Secretary of State Dean Acheson did all but admit that the communist victory in China was 'America's fault', and that a little more vigilance on the part of the USA could have, and should have, prevented it. His concern triggered the issuing of National Security Commitee Paper No. 68 by Truman's State and Defence department in April 1950 declaring that America must undertake: 'an immediate and large-scale build-up of military and general strength . . . with the intention of righting the power-balance in the hope that through some means other than all-out war we could induce a change in the nature of the Soviet system'. His concern seemed to have been justified by the outbreak of the Korean War shortly afterwards, the beginning of a struggle in Asia that was to last for three years.

McCarthy orchestrated a campaign against a large number of leading US figures, political, academic and artistic, many of whom were driven from public life by his insinuations. Although he never produced evidence to substantiate his allegations, his smears, half-truths and leading questions helped him to discredit prominent Democrats such as Acheson and Marshall, and later to embarrass many others such as leading scientific figures engaged in nuclear research, and entertainers like Charles Chaplin, Frank Sinatra and Paul Robeson. In 1950 the McCarran Internal Security Act was passed over President Truman's veto to tighten up on communist 'front' organisations and to forbid the entry of 'subversives' – even those with US passports – into the United States. McCarthy's practice of accusing individuals of belonging to political groups proscribed by the House Un-American

Activities Committee (HUAC), without producing evidence for the accusations, and his shameless employment of the tactics of 'guilt by association' created an atmosphere of 'red menace' that helped to bring the Republicans back to power in the presidential elections of 1952.

In January 1953 McCarthy became chairman of the Senate Sub-committee on Investigations and for twelve months conducted a campaign against suspected 'leftists' connected with the government, tearing to shreds the reputations of many public figures. But when in October 1953 McCarthy began to attack the US army, seeking to discredit the US Secretary of the army, Robert Stevens, he incurred the hostility of President Eisenhower. Counter-accusations by the army that McCarthy had sought to use his influence in favour of one of his aides called up for military service led to televised hearings for his Sub-committee in which his tactics were finally exposed to an alarmed and incredulous public. His brutal style of argument, his shouting down of witnesses and his bursts of table-thumping rage exposed the demagogic hysteria behind McCarthyism. Public opinion turned against him, and a Senate motion of censure condemning his methods was carried by sixty-seven votes to twenty-two in December 1954. A few days later, McCarthy attacked President Eisenhower himself, thus finally discrediting his cause. His career was at an end. Much of his appeal lay in his deep contempt for intellectuals, whom he berated as 'twisted-thinking eggheads' who were 'born with silver spoons in their mouths'. He appealed widely to the vulgar prejudices of social envy and resentment. His death in 1957 passed unnoticed by millions who had applauded him only a few years earlier.

After this time, American radicals, no longer under threat, were able to joke freely about 'McCarthy*wasm*' instead of 'McCarthy*ism*', and felt free to heap condemnation upon his memory for his exaggerations, his theatrical postures and his philistine small-mindedness. Yet the ripples he created spread widely. They could be seen again in the early 1960s when there was a flutter of apprehension over the growth of a new right-wing movement headed by the John Birch Society. 'Birchers' could see communism winning everywhere in the United States 'in the press, the pulpit, the radio and television media, the labour unions, the schools, the courts and the legislative chambers of America'. They even suspected the Supreme Court of subversion. Later in the 1960s, it was in evidence when the United States became so concerned about the continuing threat of communism in Asia that it produced the 'domino theory' to justify its interference in Vietnam, and in the 1970s, when it welcomed the advent of General Pinochet in Chile in place of the left-wing Allende. It is true that McCarthyism may be a spent force, but some of the attitudes which produced it still linger on in American minds.

Could the same phenomenon recur in American affairs? There is little doubt it could. The political leadership of the USA and the bulk of the American nation remain intensely patriotic in their feelings. They are starry-eyed to the point of mawkishness in their love of their homeland, whether or not the ideal qualities for which they regularly lay their hands on their hearts are as evident in their lives as they imagine. It is their firm belief that foreign states are deplorably feeble and cynical in not sharing their shining patriotic vision. To them, a clear-sighted grasp of America's national interests, a single-mindedness in their country's defence and a willingness to sacrifice themselves for their country are absolute imperatives, producing the same gut impulse to 'save America' as it did fifty years ago against communism. In this sense the McCarthyite spirit lives on, whatever may be the 'unseen enemy' that seems to threaten their sanctified vision of themselves.

3:14

President Nixon and the Watergate Scandal: How Damning an Indictment?

On 24 July 1974, the US Supreme Court, in a unanimous decision, adopted articles of impeachment against the Republican President R.M. Nixon for his conduct in office. Before this process was far advanced, he became the first US president to resign from office on 8 August, retiring into private life in California, and securing a comprehensive pardon in advance from his nominated successor, Gerald Ford. He has subsequently been regarded as among the least admirable of US presidents. His detractors allege against him a variety of charges ranging from conduct that was merely distasteful, petty and devious to those involving an attempt to undermine the whole basis of American democracy. In a television interview with David Frost two years later Nixon complimented himself on his handling of a number of domestic issues and for his resounding diplomatic successes in Vietnam, Israel, Communist China and the Soviet Union, with the words: 'I have done some stupid things, particularly in the handling of what was the pip-squeak Watergate thing; but I did the big things rather well.' Controversy still rages over which of these two verdicts is the more accurate one, for history has yet to decide on Nixon's true status in American and international affairs.

The Watergate affair arose in the context of a fierce controversy in 1972 between sections of the American press and the Nixon Administration, in the course of which newspapers accused the President of employing gangster tactics to further his career, through an organisation known as the Campaign to Re-Elect the President (CRP for short, but immediately dubbed 'CREEP' by Nixon's critics). These tactics involved mugging squads, sabotage, kidnapping, the use of call girls for political blackmail, and various forms of electronic surveillance and wire-tapping. They resulted in a break-in at the Democratic headquarters in the Watergate Building in Washington on the night of 17 June 1972 by a group of special operatives entrusted with the plugging of 'leaks' and hence known in the White House as the 'plumbers' unit'. The presidential Press Secretary dismissed the affair as some sort of prank, and the President himself claimed to have known nothing about it. In November 1972, Nixon and his Vice-President, Spiro Agnew, were convincingly re-elected to office, and little more was thought about the incident until early in 1973 when, after the conviction of five of the accused for burglary and conspiracy, Judge John Sirica imposed savage sentences on the convicted men, suggesting that these sentences might be reduced if any of the convicted men broke their silence and told the judge the truth about their clandestine activities. One of them did so, and the truth came tumbling out.

The shocking nature of the revelations persuaded the US Senate to set up its own investigation, and hearings were held in which a succession of White House officials admitted complicity in these covert activities, though several of them, including top aides John Erlichman and Bob Haldeman, continued to deny White House involvement. Former presidential counsel John Dean, however, gave the whole game away in his testimony to the committee in which he recounted the details of the entire cover-up. The question was now whether the President had been fully aware of the activities of these secret groups from the beginning, as Dean said, or whether he had been ignorant of them and had found them out only afterwards and little by little, as his defenders now alleged.

At this point the investigating committee learned that Nixon had for some time for reasons of his own been in the habit of tape-recording conversations of business transacted in the Oval Office. They therefore asked the President to hand over the tapes for purposes of the inquiry. This Nixon refused to do. He argued that such was the volume of business that it was essential for him to keep electronic records, but that these were private and highly confidential. It was said to be a vital matter of national security that they were kept from the investigators. Through his attorneys, the President refused to comply with a subpoena to surrender the tapes, putting forward the theory that they were protected by a hitherto undefined constitutional claim of *presidential prerogative* or *presidential privilege*. According to this, the President was entitled to act in matters of policy according to what he thought fit in the circumstances, without interference from the courts. As a result the investigating committee concluded its inquiry without ever hearing the tapes. Pressure mounted, however, for them to be released, whereupon Nixon suggested handing over transcripts of their contents. This compromise satisfied no one, and finally Nixon released the tapes to Judge Sirica. They were found to be interspersed with blank intervals, and even many of the parts recorded were obscured and distorted, as if there had been an amateurish effort to doctor them. Enough, however, was intelligible to confirm the worst fears of Nixon's critics, that the President was a mean-minded, foul-mouthed trickster who would spare no one and stop at nothing to further his own career. His reputation thereafter collapsed like a pricked bubble.

Part of the explanation for Nixon's consuming ambition is to be found in his diplomatic successes in a number of cases, and the successful relationship he managed to establish with Henry Kissinger, his Secretary of State. Exploiting the differences at the time between the Chinese and Russian communists, he abandoned America's usual obstructive tactics and accepted Chinese membership of the United Nations in 1971, later making a personal visit to Beijing in February 1972 and setting on foot more cordial Sino-American relations. In May 1972 he visited Moscow and extended the success of the SALT talks by reaching agreement with Brezhnev on limiting strategic atomic weapons. As part of this same 'shuttle diplomacy' in 1973 he visited the Near East after the war of Yom Kippur and began the slow process of repairing Arab–Israeli relations. He also negotiated a ceasefire in Vietnam in January 1973, as the result of which US forces were withdrawn and the Vietnam War was brought to an end. All this reinforced Nixon's reputation abroad and his self-esteem at home. He even began a process to repeal the Twenty-Second Amendment, so as to permit himself a third term of office, and perhaps further terms, as President.

But his reputation at home was shaky, and he showed no very

great enthusiasm for, or success in, solving domestic problems. Though he had some success with domestic initiatives such as setting up the Council for Urban Affairs to deal with the run-down condition of many American cities, it was US finance which plagued him the most. The enormous amount of overseas spending, not least on defence projects, led to a big outflow of currency and weakened the dollar. The result was a new phenomenon in the 1970s, 'stagflation', in which economic recession and high unemployment combined with a steadily rising level of wages and prices. Nixon made strenuous efforts to remedy this and to restore the Republicans' reputation as the 'businessmen's party', but he failed to carry the public with him. From the beginning he did not understand popular hostility to him and showed bitter resentment of critics, calling university protesters on their campuses 'those bums who burn their books', denouncing those who burned their President in effigy when they burned their draft-cards calling them to service in Vietnam, and lumping together his many other opponents as 'pinkos' or 'radiclibs' (i.e. radicals/liberals). He resented, too, the 'ecofreaks' who advocated the conservation of America's resources. Altogether he felt himself the persecuted victim of an ungrateful and uncomprehending public opinion.

At the same time, he had a subconscious feeling of inferiority directed against the eastern seaboard states, and in particular against the easy superiority of the Ivy League élite of New England, whose glamorous representative, J.F. Kennedy, had beaten him in the presidential election of 1960. He thought, too, that there was a press conspiracy against him. From 1971, when the Pentagon papers were published in the *New York Times*, revealing the bungling and deception that was going on in Vietnam, Nixon was firmly convinced that the media were out to isolate and expose him. This is one of the reasons why he was so obsessed with security that he set up his 'plumbers' unit' in the first place. At least as far as domestic matters went, he felt himself the victim of unpatriotic opponents who drove him to take technically illegal steps in order to preserve himself and his regime from their hate and malice.

Nevertheless, the overall indictment against Nixon is weighty. Even before any accusations of illegality had been made, he was accused of harassing opponents, imposing manifestly incompetent nominees for the Supreme Court and diverting funds properly appropriated to the details of Lyndon Johnson's 'Great Society'. Abroad he was bombing Cambodia in an undeclared war. Subsequently his Vice-President, Spiro Agnew, was disgraced for tax evasion and unceremoniously dumped, while Nixon himself was involved in a number of shady dealings quite apart from the activities in which he abused the office he was supposed to serve. But his main crime was to try to subvert and to obstruct the operation of the party in opposition, the Democrats, and hence, in a rather squalid way, hazard the future of the US political system. For this reason he will be remembered as the 'Watergate President'.

4

HISTORICAL DEBATES

The Terror: Has the Importance of the Bloodbath been Exaggerated?

Between 1792 and 1794, from the September Massacres, when France stood in real danger of foreign conquest, to the execution of Robespierre in July 1794, there took place a dark episode in the history of the French Revolution known as the 'Terror', when thousands of those allegedly opposed to the revolutionary regime perished in a bloodbath that shocked the world. Has the importance of this bloodshed been exaggerated?

The September Massacres were brought about partly by a conservative revolt in La Vendée challenging the right to rule of the revolutionaries in Paris, backed by the mob, and the rapidly deteriorating situation on the eastern frontier where Austrian armies were advancing in Belgium and where at the beginning of September news arrived of the seizure of Verdun by the advancing Prussians. The Revolutionary Commune in Paris called upon the citizens to arm themselves, and there was a general search for arms, in the course of which only about 2,000 were discovered instead of the 80,000 that the extremists had predicted were in the hands of counter-revolutionaries. Danton made a stirring speech, the tocsin sounded and at four o'clock on a fine Sunday afternoon, the massacres began. The first incident was an assault on a convoy of prisoners being taken by cart to the Abbaye prison. There followed an attack on clergy imprisoned in the Carmelite monastery, and the violence spread in four days to the other prisons where it was feared there were nests of counter-revolutionaries, and to seminaries, where priests were likewise objects of suspicion. The massacres were not systematically planned or directed, but the Commune made no effort to check them – indeed, the rhetoric of revolutionary leaders seemed positively to encourage them. All in all, about 1,400 people were killed in cold blood. In the light of the total population of Paris, then a city of ½ million people, their numbers swollen recently by masses of people from the surrounding area, this may not be a very large figure; but it was enough to spread horror stories about the nature of the revolution, graphic because they were spiced up by the grisly nature of most of the killings.

In the autumn and winter of 1793, after the replacement of the Girondin moderates in the Convention by Jacobin radicals, and particularly during the time of Robespierre's dictatorship until July 1794, the 'Terror' developed as an official instrument of government. It was part of a deliberate process of purification and was intended to elevate the revolutionary ideal by purging it of corrupt or impure elements. Alongside the 'economic' terror, which was designed to eliminate currency manipulators and food monopolists, and the 'religious' terror, which had as its purpose the destruction of the Christian religion, there was the 'political' terror, organised by the Committee of Public Safety and the Revolutionary Tribunal, to hound down and destroy aristocrats and other counter-revolutionary elements which were thought to be still at large. Every sort of fanaticism was encouraged, and it was thought perfectly proper to denounce neighbours who fell under suspicion as lacking enthusiasm for the radical cause. Later, by the Law of Suspects, such public-spirited individuals were even entitled to share in the estates of such persons after their conviction and execution. The efficient operation of the beheading machine so conveniently provided by the ingenuity of Dr Guillotin (originally a device to eliminate inequality in executions through the use of the axe for the privileged classes as against the rope for the common folk) enabled anything up to thirty or forty persons to be done to death in an hour in the name of Liberty, Equality and Fraternity. Not all were guillotined: some, especially outside Paris, were executed with sabres, bayonets or rifles, or even chained together and shot at by cannon. People were accused of a wide variety of crimes, from taking part in counter-revolutionary activities to secreting priests, assisting émigrés, selling bread at extortionate prices or uttering the phrase: 'Merde à la République!' In this way, over a period of nearly a year, a good many people went to their deaths.

The provinces were not slow to emulate the exploits of the capital. In Lyons, Marseilles, and Bordeaux, to name the most notorious, Jacobin commissioners vied with one another to see who could best demonstrate his enthusiasm for the revolutionary cause, and thousands perished – indeed Lyons was given the new name *Ville Affranchie* (Liberated Town) to celebrate its new status as being aristocracy-free. At the same time, in troubled Vendée, there was terrible violence both on the revolutionary side and on the side of their opponents. Royalist conservative peasants and lesser noblemen, anxious to give republican forces a dose of their own medicine, slaughtered hundreds of their prisoners and hunted down, tortured and killed their revolutionary opponents. The republicans retaliated vigorously. The lesser feudal nobles, in which the countryside abounded, were put to death; even crucifixion was practised on Nonjuring clergy. In Nantes and in Angers there was an orgy of killing. The commissioner in Nantes supplemented the guillotine with what he called 'vertical deportations', sending hundreds of prisoners out into the Loire in flat-bottomed barges with perforated bottoms which duly sank and drowned their entire cargo. Some of the victims of these so-called *'noyades'* underwent what became known as 'republican marriages', young men and women stripped naked and tied together before their drowning – anything to humiliate the enemies of the republican cause.

Apart from war casualties, perhaps 40,000 perished during the Terror. Such numbers themselves are sufficiently daunting, but contemporary opinion was especially horrified because, during the killings, such a high proportion of the old ruling class, the aristocracy, was weeded out and eliminated. Even more shocking was the fact that these excesses had taken place in a supposedly peaceful country at the heart of civilised Europe and, worse still, had been carried out in the name of the lofty political ideals which the revolution was supposed to represent. The actual *numbers* of the victims of the Terror may therefore have been exaggerated, but the moral and political *impact* of the Terror has not.

4:2

Was George III Really a Tyrant?

Unfavourable historical judgments on George III of Britain and Ireland (1760–1820) continued unabated throughout the nineteenth century and much of the twentieth. Eighteenth-century university specialists of today have a better understanding, but British school textbooks were still labelling George a tyrant at least into the 1970s, and in American school books George is still the tyrant king of the American Declaration of Independence. Is this a fair judgment?

In Great Britain the King's contemporaries did not seriously accuse him personally of tyranny, although some of the Whig fringe factions were ready, when it suited them, to accuse him of exceeding his powers, and agitators like John Wilkes thought that *ministers* were behaving tyrannically. However, it was not until after the 1832 Reform Act, which admitted the upper middle classes of Britain to a share of political power, that George III's tyranny became a commonplace accusation among British historians. The triumph of the Whigs in 1832 was reflected in the writings of the new generation of Whig historians. These were no longer content to be story-tellers or chroniclers, but believed it to be their mission to analyse historical persons and events and to make judgments upon them. They were confident of the continuing economic and political progress of the mid-nineteenth century, and they regarded all past persons and events which obstructed the smooth path towards that progress as dark and reactionary. Thus they developed the legend of George III personally driving his ministers into conflict with America, and seeking, but fortunately failing, to restore royal despotism. This legend does not stand up to close scrutiny.

Royal despotism in Britain ended with the Roundhead victory in the Civil War. A brief attempt to revive it by James II ended disastrously in 1688. The Glorious Revolution of 1688–9 made it virtually impossible for royal despotism to be revived, and when the last Stuart monarch, Anne, died in 1714, her German relations, the Hanoverians, who succeeded her, had little choice but to accept ministers from the triumphant Whig Party. The Tory Party, tainted with Jacobite treason, declined in numbers and influence, as did royal power. When George III succeeded to the throne in 1760 he declared his intention of acting constitutionally. He did not attempt to revive lost royal prerogatives; thus he did not resume the right to veto parliamentary legislation, last exercised by Queen Anne, nor did he resume *regular* royal attendance at Cabinet meetings. Senior government ministers, collectively known as the Cabinet, were the real political power in England, and they needed to enjoy the confidence both of the parliament and the Crown if they were to remain in office for long.

Confronted with a variety of warring Whig factions, and with the Tories virtually moribund, George decided to rise above faction and party, and to maintain a degree of royal independence, even though the Constitution as it then stood required his active participation. Thus the short-lived ministries of 1762–70 fell mainly because George III failed to give them sufficient support, not because he was looking for a puppet minister. Lord North, who became Prime Minister in 1770, was a man of impeccable Whig, not Tory, background, and his early policies gained him increasing respect, and thus strength, both from parliament and the Crown – although not from the Americans. North's resignation in 1782 George considered as a desertion, and North's seemingly impregnable political alliance with George's political enemy Fox in 1783 provoked George into influencing the House of Lords to bring about their downfall and into looking for a strong man to succeed them. The Younger Pitt's success in weaning parliament away from Fox and North gave the King not a weak puppet, but a man of proven political skills (despite his extreme youth – he was just twenty-four), and thus a Prime Minister deserving of the King's confidence. In 1801 Pitt was to respect the King's opposition to granting political rights to Roman Catholics. Whig historians regarded George's actions in 1783 and 1801 as evidence of his efforts to revive despotism, rather than as the legitimate use of the remaining royal prerogatives of the time, and they, too, blamed George for the loss of the American colonies.

During the earlier part of his reign the American colonies were engaged in their successful struggle for independence. In their Declaration of Independence, 1776, the American colonies accused 'the present King of Great Britain' of tyranny, and this accusation was the basis of their claim for independence. American historians habitually used to give George a bad press, and if they do not nowadays go so far as to accuse him of 'tyranny' they often assume that he played a greater role in formulating Britain's American policy than was actually the case.

The American patriots and Sons of Liberty saw with alarm during the 1760s the efforts of the British parliament to raise revenue from the colonies, to restrict their trade, and to send British and German troops to maintain order. The powers exercised by the British parliament in respect of the colonies were perfectly legal and proper according to the usage of the time. Parliament's mistake was one of tactics, in not realising that the colonies were a long way off, accustomed to having their own way, and unwilling to come tamely to heel when London required it. When hostilities broke out at Lexington those Americans who despaired of redress through negotiation found it easier to believe that the repression was the policy of a tyrannical monarch rather than that of a representative parliament; and it was easier to fight a king than a people. Of course, the American policies of Lord North and his predecessors did not have the unanimous support of parliament, but the policy was certainly that of the majority. And George III supported those measures which would retain and strengthen the ties between Britain and the colonies; he did not want to lose an empire. But there is no evidence that he, and he alone, was responsible for these policies. Even so, once the American view of George was taken up by the Whig historians, the labelling of George III as a tyrannical despot seemed to be unchallengeable and with it the corollaries that the American patriots saved America from George, and that the King's madness saved representative government in England. But the American patriots seized American independence from a reluctant Britain, not from a tyrant king, and George's mythical madness turned out to be bouts of febrile delirium brought on by the metabolic disease porphyria. It was not until 1811 that George, old and blind, sank into irreversible senile dementia.

4:3

Napoleon's Invasion Plans, 1805: Was Britain Ever Seriously Threatened?

In 1805 an isolated Britain faced the threat of a French invasion. It is usual for historians to assume that the invasion threat posed a real danger to Britain, and that the invasion scheme was a realistic plan to bring about Britain's defeat. Both assumptions are at best highly contentious and at worst seriously in error.

By 1804 Napoleon was at the height of his powers. He had become Emperor of France, and much of Europe was either under French occupation or an ally of France. Only Britain, of the major powers, continued to resist him, and Britain on its own could do little. But there was always the danger that Britain could form another European alliance against him (a coalition), and that while such a danger existed France could not enjoy absolute security. So in the latter months of 1804 and at the beginning of 1805 Napoleon devised an ambitious scheme for the defeat and conquest of Britain. Did Napoleon really intend to put this scheme into effect, or was its sole purpose merely to discourage Austria and Russia from joining a new coalition?

Some clue to the answer lies in the impracticability of Napoleon's scheme. In its final form the plan was basically simple. The three French fleets at Brest, Rochefort and Toulon were to break out simultaneously without engaging the blockading British forces. They were to release the Spanish fleets under British blockade at Ferrol and Cadiz. They were then to elude the pursuing British navy and to rendezvous in the West Indies. From there they were to double back to the English Channel ahead of the British fleet, hold mastery of the Channel for at least twenty-four hours, thus allowing the barges and flat-bottomed boats at Boulogne to convey 150,000 men, their supplies and their horses across the Channel. Once the army was across the Channel weak British resistance would be swept aside and the war would be over.

There were a number of weaknesses in this plan. For the fleets to break out simultaneously would be very difficult; to do so without engaging the blockading forces well nigh impossible. The Spanish fleets at Cadiz and Ferrol were in no state of readiness for active hostilities, and the assumption that any combined French and Spanish fleet would be able to reach the West Indies and double back unchallenged would depend very much on good luck and favourable weather. The scheme assumed that the British, faced with a threat to the West Indian colonies, would leave the Channel insufficiently defended as the British fleet was certainly overstretched. Moreover, even in summer the Channel could be an unreliable stretch of water; and, even if the French fleet gained a few days headstart, it would also need continuing favourable weather conditions. This was especially so in view of the nature of the barges and flat-bottomed boats. These were unsuitable for Channel crossing and were more appropriate to use on the Rhine in the

ever   If the weather was to be
suff   g the horses around and
bre   bably be too calm to get the
arn   ossing would take at least
tw   convenient landing place for
an   Kent and Pevensey in East
Su   ng from Boulogne of at least
ei   would arrive at its destination
ri   with horses suitable only to
su   n. It would take several days
b   fit enough condition to tackle
t   then its supply routes could
v   ritish navy. It is inconceivable
that Napoleon   unaware of these difficulties.

In the event the Brest fleet never got out at all, the French did not enter the Channel unmolested, but were beaten back at Cape Finisterre in July, and the formation of the Third Coalition meant that Napoleon had abandoned his invasion plan some weeks before Trafalgar put an end to any possibility of its revival. Whether an effective army could have crossed the Channel was never put to the test.

At the time, however, the British took the invasion threat very seriously, and there were moments of panic in Whitehall. The army and transport had been assembled by the French at great expense at Boulogne so how could it be a bluff? But Boulogne was sufficiently close to Germany and the mouth of the Rhine for the army and transports to be put to alternative use, and Napoleon had spent little on barges and ships specifically suitable for the Channel. It is always possible that Napoleon was hedging his bets. He had enjoyed such good luck before that he may have felt that good fortune would always smile upon him, and that the invasion scheme had at least a small chance of success. And if it failed he could always blame his admirals, like Villeneuve, or the weather, or Pitt's machinations, or the Spaniards. And, but for Trafalgar, he could always have tried again.

Conditions of Use

This transfer entitles you to transfer to other Metro buses, Sound Transit's (ST) Regional Express buses and Sounder commuter rail, or Community Transit (CT) buses, subject to the following guidelines:

- It is valid on the day of issue only, including the first trip on any Metro or ST route at the beginning of the next service day (starting at 4:00 a.m.) when designated OWL.
- It is not valid on the Seattle Center Monorail.
- It is not valid on Pierce Transit.
- It is not valid after 10:30 p.m. unless designated OWL.
- To be valid for inter-county transfers to CT buses, you must pay the full inter-county fare on Metro and the transfer must be punched accordingly.
- You must reboard before the expiration time indicated on the front.
- It is valid on Metro at an amount equal to the

4:4

Napoleon I: The Last of the Enlightened Despots?

The medieval idea that the universe was God-centred persisted well into the seventeenth century. But by then the new scientific discoveries had stood astronomy on its head and revolutionised the physical sciences. All knowledge now seemed within reach of mankind, and the world was regarded as man-centred, not God-centred. Enlightened philosophers asserted that since the world was made for man, man's progress and happiness were paramount. Thus the eighteenth-century Enlightenment looked with favour on those customs, laws and institutions which allowed man to develop his full potential, but savaged those which held him back. They were humanitarian: they wanted freedom of conscience, speech and press, and they campaigned for equality before the law, a humane criminal code, and free competition. These ideas were selectively adopted by some of the late eighteenth-century rulers, most notably Joseph II of Austria, Catherine II of Russia, Frederick II of Prussia, and more spectacularly among some of the minor despots, such as Duke Leopold of Tuscany. Napoleon I of France is often claimed to be the last enlightened despot. But such a claim is a very doubtful one since Napoleon lacked many of the essential qualifications for the role.

There is no doubt that Napoleon I was a despot. The complex constitution introduced in 1799 and retained, with minor modifications, when Napoleon made himself Emperor in 1804, paid lip-service to popular participation, but in effect made his despotism more unfettered than the eighteenth-century rulers, most of whom were in part constrained by outdated feudal restrictions. Napoleon's artificial court and resurrected nobility were sycophantic; Joseph, Catherine and Frederick were hemmed in by powerful nobility and provincial estates.

It is almost incontrovertible, too, that if Napoleon was an enlightened despot, he was the last. The French Revolution had killed off any desire of autocrats to dispense enlightened reform. For nearly a quarter of a century the absolute rulers of Europe had fought against the liberalising ideas of the French Revolution as spread by victorious French armies. After 1815 they were determined never to go through such an experience again. The Holy Alliance and Quadruple Alliance were designed for the preservation of autocracy. If reform was to come, it would be extracted by force from below, rather than benevolently granted from above. It has been argued that Alexander of Russia could be called the last enlightened despot, but his reforms were born out of necessity, rather than goodwill, and were rather late to be in the tradition of the Enlightenment.

So was Napoleon enlightened? The eighteenth-century rulers were acquainted with the works of the philosophers, and consulted them on occasions, although they did not always take their advice. By Napoleon's time the great philosophers were dead, and Napoleon's knowledge of their works was mainly limited to Voltaire, whom everyone read for his biting wit, and Rousseau, whose ideas Napoleon admired. But Rousseau was a theorist; his great work *The Social Contract* contains many contradictions, and Napoleon was to outgrow his youthful enthusiasms. Much of Napoleon's work, too, was born out of necessity; it was the legacy of the Revolution which had placed revolutionary changes side by side and overlapping with the laws and institutions of the *ancien régime*. Complexity bred confusion; the Napoleonic centralisation of local government was aimed at efficiency rather than enlightenment, and it consolidated Napoleon's despotism. The *Codes Napoleon* were urgently needed if the French system of justice was not to grind to a halt, but they did retain trial by jury and a more humane criminal code. The reforms in education were desperately needed because the Revolution had wrecked the clerical provision of elementary education without replacing it with anything as effective. But at least it retained the enlightened theory that access to academic and higher education was open to all, regardless of class or wealth.

Napoleon was not an admirer of the Physiocrats – the economic theorists of the Enlightenment. They favoured Free Trade; Napoleon favoured Protection. His reform of the currency and the creation of the Bank of France were essential to create financial and currency stability and to wipe out the legacy of the *assignats*. He built roads and subsidised industry, which would have pleased the Physiocrats, but they would not have admired an economy geared to war and financed by foreign loot.

In one particular Napoleon was not in the mould of the enlightened despots. He was not a hereditary ruler. He had come up from below, spawned by the Revolution. The enlightened despots had a historical legitimacy; Napoleon's rule was *de facto*, not *de jure*. For him change was dictated by circumstances and exigency, not to be doled out from above according to contemporary fashion, but to be engaged in where appropriate or necessary. Yet the Enlightenment had greatly influenced the changes brought about by the French Revolution, and Napoleon had always paid lip-service to the Revolution. Its changes were continued and retained, at least in part, by Napoleon and his reforms. Only in that sense has he some limited claim to be regarded as the last of the enlightened despots, but his reforms were inspired more by expediency than by true enlightenment.

4:5

The Speenhamland System: Was it a System at All?

In 1795 the magistrates of Speen, near Newbury in Berkshire, met to consider the recent rises in the price of bread and the growth of agrarian poverty. They drew up a scale of poor relief based on the price of bread and the number in the family and recommended this scale to the magistrates of the various quarter sessions districts of Berkshire. Within a few years the Speenhamland System became synonymous with the English poor law provision, and remained so until replaced by the new Poor Law in 1834. But the Speenhamland System was not a system at all, and the books which present it as a 'system' are quite seriously misleading.

The sixteenth-century Elizabethan Poor Law had created a system whereby the genuinely unemployed were to be found work or be put into workhouses, while the idle were to be punished, and confined to harsh conditions in a house of correction. As the financing of the new system was to be local, out of the newly devised system of rates on property, the details of the application of the new law were left in the hands of the local Justices of the Peace who constituted the local authority. It is not surprising that local magistrates soon discovered what local authorities have constantly found since: that the cost of looking after the poor in institutions is much greater than giving them meagre financial assistance so that they can support themselves. Thus by the eighteenth century houses of correction had virtually disappeared, and most parishes were too small to maintain a workhouse. The eighteenth-century poor who could not be made to work, or could not be found work, were almost invariably supported by money provided by local magistrates out of the rates. In order to prevent one district from being swamped by poor from other areas, strict settlement laws prevented the movement of the poor from parish to parish. Although the rich grumbled about the rates, until the latter part of the century the system seemed to work well enough.

But by then two major problems had arisen: first the breakdown of the parish system in areas of rapidly growing population, and second, the impact of wartime inflation. There was a world of difference between one overseer of the poor looking after a handful of destitute in one village, and looking after much larger numbers in a heavily populated urban sprawl. Moreover, fluctuations in employment, temporary layoffs, and wartime trade dislocation could increase unemployment to the point when those dependent on an overseer ran into several hundreds. As the industrial revolution got under way all attempts to maintain the settlement laws were doomed to failure. Poverty-stricken migrants, on their way to seek a new and more prosperous life in the factories and workshops of the new towns, swamped the villages. The war with France which began in 1793 brought matters to a head. It pushed up the price of bread, while wage increases lagged well behind prices. More and more agricultural workers were forced to apply to the parish overseers for help.

It was this situation which prompted the meeting at Speen in 1795. Normally the sum paid to the poor in each parish or group of parishes covered by the quarter sessions was a fixed sum which could be changed only by a full meeting of the magistrates. These were too irregular to cope with wildly fluctuating prices, and the Berkshire magistrates met in the comfort of the Pelican Inn to find a solution. In order to reduce the necessity of frequent meetings the magistrates drew up a scale of payments based on the price of bread and number in the family; it was anticipated that it would only be necessary to confirm or adjust the scales at an annual meeting.

The magistrates' intention was to provide a minimum living standard for the unemployed. But almost immediately the scales were used to supplement the wages of those rural workers with inadequate incomes. It thus became a means of subsidising wages: the employers could underpay their rural workers and the difference would be made up by the overseers out of the rates. The action of the Berkshire magistrates was so successful that it was not long before magistrates in other parts of the country began formulating their own scales and applying them. The scales were often changed, and varied considerably from district to district. Parliament had nothing to do with the Speenhamland scales and their imitators. They were drawn up locally for local use. Indeed, although scales were soon operating throughout the south and much of the Midlands, most of northern England was not covered by them. Rapid industrial growth and continuous labour migration made the scales unworkable in most of the northern areas where they were tried. Here the Poor Law was not used to subsidise the wages of those in regular work, but to provide financial relief for those without work of any kind. It was a financial cushion for those on piecework, such as handloom-weavers, whose earnings had become too meagre and intermittent for subsistence. So most northern poor received poor relief according to need, and not according to some arbitrary local scale.

Systems are usually uniform. There was nothing uniform about Speenhamland. It was not a national system of poor relief. It was not a national system for the subsidisation of rural wages, although it tended within a multiplicity of scales to be something of the kind in the south. The scales were not uniform or permanent. They varied from district to district within each county as well as between counties, and they were changed at frequent intervals. The one factor common to all of them was basing the amount of relief on the number in the family and the price of bread.

After the Napoleonic Wars national expenditure on poor relief rocketed, reaching an annual peak of almost £8 million in 1818. This was the consequence of postwar unemployment and high bread prices. Speenhamland got the blame, and it was convenient for its detractors to elevate it into a 'system' in order to prepare the way for its destruction. The 1834 Poor Law Amendment Act swept away outdoor relief for all except the sick and the aged, and the Speenhamland System came to an abrupt end.

4:6

The 1832 Reform Act: Did it Herald the Dawn of Democracy in Britain?

It is sometimes said that the reform of parliament brought about by the Whig governments of the 1830s marked the beginning of democracy in Britain and the start of the Liberal tradition of government which lasted for the rest of the century. It is, however, quite erroneous to call either the Reform Act or the reforms which followed it in the 1830s democratic.

For one thing, the Great Reform Act, though undoubtedly of immense importance, was not so vital as many at the time seemed to think. It made sweeping changes, but not as sweeping as was at first imagined. Indeed, in many ways, far from creating a democracy, the Act may be said to have staved it off. Though the Tories were weakened by the abolition of pocket and rotten boroughs, a good many small boroughs survived, and here patronage was as powerful as it was before. In elections, voting continued to be open, and corruption and bribery went on as badly as ever. Furthermore, Toryism was actually strengthened by the creation of sixty-five extra county seats, resulting from the out-of-date assumption that the rural interest should still dominate politics. Again, much of the old political routine stayed unchanged: the life of parliament remained at a maximum of seven years, and the powers of the House of Lords, the traditional stronghold of the aristocratic interest, were unaltered. No effort was made to modernise the procedure of the House of Commons, which continued to programme short sessions chiefly devoted to private business. Though the cry for democracy had been clearly made, parliament had given the vote only to the middle classes, and the total electorate had risen only to about 650,000 voters in a total population of over 16 million.

Furthermore, at the election of 1832, the first under the reformed system, the new House of Commons looked much like the old one. Over 150 MPs were related to members of the House of Lords. It was still composed of professional people: over 200 were lawyers, or serving officers of the army or navy, or were connected with the Established Church. Only 50 merchants or manufacturers were elected. Thus the composition of the new Chamber could scarcely be said to be democratic. Many radicals, aware that they had been cheated, began to clamour for further change, turning to direct political action instead of parliamentary pressure. Chartism was the natural outcome of this thinking.

The great reforms of the 1830s are likewise often regarded as the result of the new liberal politics, but this view also tends to be an exaggerated one. Many of the attitudes of the new House may not have been so aristocratic as before, but they were still markedly upper class in tone and intention. Nor was the legislation they produced in any sense democratic. Municipal reform, for example, brought a long overdue reshaping of the old corporations, largely passing control of them to the new business classes; Church reform, though it nibbled at ecclesiastical authority and finance, Church rates, tithes and the civil registration of births, deaths and marriages, was tentative and limited, and left many of the grievances of the nonconformists unremedied. Social reforms such as the education grant made in 1833 and the Factory Act of 1833, proved extremely timid and restricted, though at least they made a beginning with these problems. One, the Poor Law Amendment Act of 1834, was influenced by the thinking of Jeremy Bentham and was harshly utilitarian and unsympathetic towards the poorest in society, imposing on them the hateful 'workhouse test' before giving them any relief – though it undoubtedly satisfied the middle-class desire to keep the rates low and to ensure value for the money they spent. But this was cold comfort to the needy.

Royal influence over parliament, furthermore, still continued in a limited way in the 1830s under William IV, and this influence was hardly ever in favour of reform. The King actually drove the Whigs from office in November 1834 when they failed to provide the ministers that he desired, but Peel and the Conservatives did not last long, and an election in January 1835 brought an end to the old convention that MPs should support the ministers of the King's choosing. Thereafter he stopped trying to produce the coalition he had been seeking. At the end of the 1830s Victoria succeeded to the throne, and the influence over her of Lord Melbourne, the Prime Minister, was such that the Whigs were able to recover power when they had nearly lost it in 1839; Peel only became a real Prime Minister at the third attempt, in 1841. By the early 1840s the withdrawal of the Queen from a partisan role in politics was due to the influence of her new husband, Prince Albert; it was not that she ceased to take an interest in politics, but rather that, under Albert's influence, she began to recognise that there were limitations on her power, and tried to work within them.

Undoubtedly things were moving in the 1830s, and the Great Reform Act had averted the danger of complete stagnation in British politics; but to say that it brought about the beginnings of democratic reform is something of an exaggeration.

4:7

Bismarck: Planner or Opportunist?

Count Otto von Bismarck became Minister-President of Prussia in 1862. Within nine years he was Chancellor of a united Germany. He was soon credited with being the architect of German unity, a legend that he himself strengthened in his memoirs because of the need to enhance his reputation following his summary dismissal from high office in 1890. Certainly Bismarck must take the credit for unifying Germany, but whether he can take the credit for being the architect of it, which implies advanced planning, is another matter.

Germany was not high on Bismarck's list of priorities. It has been said that he had four concentric circles of obligation: first to the Hohenzollerns, second to Prussia, thirdly and only thirdly to Germany, and finally, occasionally, to Europe. So it is not surprising that when Bismarck took office in 1862 his immediate aim was to save the Prussian monarchy from liberalism and to expand Prussian military power. Once these had been achieved Bismarck could turn to his main aims in foreign affairs. Already, through the Zollverein, Prussia had economic domination over north Germany; he now wanted political domination. But that was impossible while Austria still headed the German Confederation and while small north German states looked to Austria to protect them against Prussia. So a challenge to Austria seemed desirable when opportunity arose.

But Bismarck could not create events, he could only attempt to control them; he could not really have anticipated Denmark's annexation of the Duchies of Schleswig-Holstein in 1863. But he saw how to turn it to Prussia's advantage. Holstein was a member of the German Confederation; Denmark's annexation of it was a challenge to the Confederation, and Prussia could pose as the Confederation's defender. Austria's participation in the war against Denmark in 1864 could not be avoided if Austria was not to lose its paramount position in the Confederation.

The war was brief and successful. It ended with both Duchies under Prussian and Austrian occupation, but Bismarck could see a way to exclude Austria from benefiting from the peace. The Convention of Gastein in 1865 placed Schleswig under Prussian protection and Holstein under that of Austria. Holstein was the larger province but it was hemmed in on its landward frontiers by Prussian territory. Austria was embarrassed by the cost of maintaining a presence in north Germany that it did not really desire, yet, challenged by Prussia, Austria decided to fight. The Austrians were overwhelmed at Sadowa in July 1866.

The consequences of Sadowa more than fulfilled Bismarck's aims when he took office. Not only was Austria driven from north Germany and a Prussian-dominated north German Confederation formed, but Prussia annexed those states north of the Main river which had fought on Austria's side. Most of north Germany was now Prussian territory and the rest of it consisted of princely satellites.

Did Bismarck now need or plan a war with France to make German unification complete? Millions of Germans were subjects of Austria-Hungary; to incorporate them into a German state dominated by Prussia would mean the disintegration of the Austrian Empire and great instability in central Europe. Bismarck shrank from this. Nor was he very enthusiastic about expansion into southern Germany. There the Catholic states like Bavaria were terrified of Protestant Prussia and looked to France for protection, now that Austria had been defeated. Bismarck's main hope was that the south German states would become so suspicious of France's intentions that they would cease their hostility to Prussia.

Bismarck used his diplomatic skill to encourage the French to demand compensation for Prussia's expansion. Napoleon III's confidential demand for Belgium could be used to sour

France's relations with Britain; his demands for territory in south Germany could be used to weaken south German mistrust of Prussia. Bismarck did not plan a war with France, but like any prudent statesman he had to be prepared for one.

The occasion was unexpected. Queen Isabella of Spain was overthrown by revolution in 1868. After unsuccessfully hawking the throne around Europe the Spaniards decided to offer it to a distant cousin of King William of Prussia. The French were horrified at the possibility of a powerful Hohenzollern alliance between Spain and Prussia. They demanded that the Hohenzollern candidature be withdrawn. Bismarck was well aware that to comply would mean a diplomatic triumph for France, and he tried to persuade William to refuse the French request. But William advised his cousin to withdraw. French newspapers represented the Prussian withdrawal as a French triumph, and Bismarck was so upset at this diplomatic reverse that he contemplated resignation.

The Ems Telegram, in which William gave a dispassionate account of his meeting with the French ambassador, was edited by Bismarck for publication. The editing made it appear as if the French ambassador had been snubbed, and that Prussia had turned a diplomatic humiliation into a diplomatic success. Subsequent events were not under Bismarck's control. He could hardly have expected that the Ems Telegram would arouse such war clamour in France, nor that Napoleon III would listen to it even when urged by his minister and by his wife, the Empress Eugénie. In fact if Napoleon had been a little more strong-willed he could have prevented the war with Prussia which he was so reluctant to undertake, as the war was by no means inevitable.

Prussia's speedy victory brought its reward in Alsace-Lorraine. An unexpected bonus was that of the south German states. These were so alarmed by the territorial ambitions of Napoleon III, now made public, that they saw Prussia as their only protector, and while the war was still in progress they joined the other German states under Prussian domination and turned the north German Confederation into the German

Empire. All along Bismarck had used events for the benefit of Prussia, and thus was a brilliant opportunist. And although in his youth he had, like so many Germans, talked vaguely about German unity, he could not, in 1862, have envisaged the German Empire of 1871. (See also 6:5.)

4:8

The Monroe Doctrine: The Basis of American Imperialism?

First propounded in his annual message to Congress by President James Monroe in December 1823, the Monroe Doctrine was reckoned to be of primary importance in the nineteenth and twentieth centuries. In this declaration he laid down that the American continents were not to be considered as 'future subjects for colonisation by any European powers', and that any attempt to interfere with the liberty of the newly independent Spanish colonies would be regarded as 'the manifestation of an unfriendly disposition towards the United States'. This policy was widely thought to be a warning to European powers in general – and to Britain in particular – not to meddle in American affairs. But, whatever its later significance, the Monroe Doctrine originated in a quite different context.

The Doctrine, though named after Monroe as President, was actually drafted by his secretary of State, John Quincy Adams. It was prompted by the threat of the European 'Holy Alliance' of Austria, Prussia and Russia, in which the royalist government in Spain concurred, to suppress the revolt of the Latin American states, which had been flickering in Spain's former colonies for the previous ten years. Originally, the idea was suggested by Britain's recently appointed Foreign Secretary, George Canning, and outlined the possibility of joint action by British and US warships to screen America from any possible European intrusion. The idea, however, was unacceptable to the US government because of continuing anti-British sentiment after the Anglo-American War of 1812–14.

Nevertheless, though Monroe took credit for it, the Doctrine proposed exactly what Canning had in mind when he said 'I called the New World into existence to redress the balance of the Old.'

Under it, the US government set out the policy (i) that the American continents were not territory for future European colonisation; (ii) that the American system of government was essentially different from European systems; (iii) that any attempt to extend their influence in American territory would be regarded as dangerous to its peace and security, and (iv) in return for European acceptance of this policy the USA would respect existing European colonies in the Americas, and would not participate in European wars.

This Doctrine is said to have provided the essential basis for US foreign policy for over a century. However, it was very flexibly applied: indeed it became the basis of what can only be regarded as American imperialism. President Polk in 1845 made warlike noises against both Britain and Mexico over US boundaries, declaring that 'the people of this continent alone have the right to decide their own destiny', and the policy was taken still further by President Theodore Roosevelt in 1904 when he asserted that the United States was 'an international police power' for the whole American continent. Outside the American continent, too, the USA was beginning to extend its feelers: in 1899 US Secretary of State John Hay announced a new policy, that of the 'Open Door' in China, demanding equal opportunities for all nations to trade in China, and in the following year insisted that all countries agree to respect Chinese territorial integrity. In 1912, too, Senator Lodge carried through Congress a resolution extending the Monroe Doctrine beyond the American continent by opposing external interference in Japan.

Between the two World Wars, the United States was beginning to intervene in European affairs, even in spite of the so-called policy of 'isolationism', and was tending to overlook its own promises not to do such things outside the American continent. Substantial interference in, among other areas of 'influence', Southeast Asia and Indonesia were to follow. After the Second World War, with the USA now one of the world's two superpowers, these promises were forgotten completely. In this situation, the United States invoked the Doctrine only when it was in their interest, or when there seemed to be an obvious need for it, as at the time of the Cuban missile crisis. In 1982, also, there were American demands that the federal government should invoke it, when Britain and Argentina came to blows over the issue of the sovereignty of the Falkland Islands – but these demands were resisted by President Reagan, who valued the friendship of Mrs Thatcher and Britain too highly for that. Overall, however, the policy came increasingly to look like: 'You keep your hands off America, but we will interfere in your affairs as much as we think fit.' This attitude was entirely understandable and was quite appropriate to the US position of world dominance in the late twentieth century.

4:9

'Manifest Destiny': A Cloak for American Expansion?

Around the midpoint of the nineteenth century there began a great expansionist movement of American settlers towards the west; a trickle that developed into a flood, reaching the Pacific coast in California. It claimed to be based on the justification that there existed a 'manifest destiny' on the part of the American people to occupy and to develop the vast emptiness of these lands. Was this excuse anything more than a cloak adopted to cover their imperialist instincts?

Foreigners certainly thought it was a mere excuse. British observers in particular dismissed it as an unwelcome mixture of bombast and ignorance. The contempt the Americans felt for the indigenous 'Indians' of the wide North American plains was well known, and the destruction of the native peoples was not universally approved. But the notion that the possessions of European powers on the American continent lacked legitimacy and could be set at nought simply because a jumped-up ex-colonial regime said so was as unattractive in Madrid, Paris or St Petersburg as it was in London. The world powers, if they acknowledged it at all, treated US chauvinism with the fastidious disdain they thought it deserved. Even the Americans themselves had their doubts about it. The more responsible thought that the notion was provocative and unnecessary, recognising in it the flavour of cheap, popular journalism. Indeed, the first mention of the idea of 'manifest destiny' did come from a journalist named John O'Sullivan in August 1845, when he wrote: 'It is the fulfilment of our manifest destiny to overspread the continent allotted to us by Providence for the free development of our yearly multiplying millions.'

This 'manifest destiny' came to carry conviction with many of the ill-educated mass who read the papers. These people were fed the idea that American expansionism was morally justified, and so they believed it was. Thus they could destroy the Indians in the belief that they were savages and sub-human, and they could quarrel with Britain, Spain and France in the knowledge that they had unimpeachable moral justification for their actions. To challenge this was to deny the Americans their patriotism, and even to challenge their manhood.

As early as 1838, Jackson had bribed and pushed the Cherokee out of Georgia and into Alabama, then west into the wilderness beyond the Mississippi. This great river highway was regarded by many as 'the valley of democracy', and by 1850 was well peopled and tilled, the indigenous tribesmen being unceremoniously shunted further west. The land east of the river had been divided into states, and a raft of them had entered the Union – Louisiana in 1812, Missouri in 1821, Arkansas in 1836 and Iowa in 1846. These new states and their settlers became a powerful new force in US politics. The 'log cabin' of this new westerner became the symbol of the new democracy and of its expansionism. O'Sullivan's refrain was taken up in Congress by representative Robert Winthrop of Massachusetts in a speech in January 1846. The belief reflected exactly the thinking of James Knox Polk of Tennessee, a man from the same mould as Andrew Jackson, who became

President in 1844, when he defeated the eastern Whig candidate Henry Clay. He immediately took up the cudgels on behalf of the expanding nation.

Friction along the Canadian border in the wake of the Canadian rebellions had led to the Webster–Ashburton Treaty in 1842 resolving disputes along the boundaries between New Brunswick and Maine, but in 1846 a graver danger presented itself further west, where Britain came into conflict with the United States over the boundary of Oregon. American interest in the far north-west had been increased by the successful opening of the Oregon Trail in 1842, which had brought settlers, traders and missionaries to the area. Polk now took up their cry of 'Fifty-four-forty or fight!', so laying claim to this latitude as the boundary between the United States and Canada. He asserted. 'Our title to the country of Oregon is clear and unquestionable.' But in fact he did not welcome a fight. Trouble was already brewing with Mexico, and Polk did not want to quarrel with Britain, too. In the end he negotiated with Lord Aberdeen, the British Foreign Secretary, an agreement whereby Britain abandoned a swathe of territory near the mouth of the Columbia river, but accepted the 49th Parallel as the mainland boundary, so long as Fort Victoria and the whole of Vancouver Island remained in Canadian hands.

So far, 'manifest destiny' had been restrained by Britain, as it was shortly afterwards when by the Clayton–Bulwer Treaty in 1850 US interest in Nicaragua was renounced in return for a British promise not to extend its settlement in Honduras along the Mosquito Coast, where previously it had been claiming a protectorate of the native tribes living there. Mexico had no navy and was easier prey. Trouble focused on Texas, renounced by the United States in the Florida treaty of 1819, but now rapidly filling with American settlers who had been allowed to live there. In 1834 Texas declared itself independent, and Mexican troops under Santa Anna invaded the country and massacred a number of Americans in San Antonio on the Alamo river. They were thrown out in 1836 by

Texan forces under Sam Houston, and in 1837 President Jackson recognised the independence of the 'Lone Star State'. Polk's war broke out in 1846, but did not last long. There were three chief theatres of war: California, where an expedition under John C. Frémont encouraged the inhabitants to rebel against Mexican control; New Mexico, where Col Stephen Kearny at the head of a small US army marched from Fort Leavenworth to Santa Fé to mop up Mexican resistance there, and then continued to California; and finally in Mexico itself. Here the main efforts were by General Zachary ('Rough and Ready') Taylor, who fought his way over the Rio Grande into the heart of this hostile country, before his opponents surrendered at Buena Vista; and General Winfield Scott, who landed from the sea at Vera Cruz in 1847 and in the full heat of summer marched up the 7,500 feet to Mexico City, which fell in September.

Peace was made at Guadeloupe Hidalgo in 1848, and gave the United States California and New Mexico (which included Arizona), and recognised the American annexation of Texas. In return the Americans paid Mexico $15 million, and assumed responsibility for further claims of US subjects against Mexico amounting to $3 million. As an addendum to this treaty, in 1853 the USA carried out the Gadsden Purchase, when 40,000 square miles south of the Gila river was added to New Mexico in return for a payment of a further $10 million. When, in 1867, the United States purchased the territory of Alaska from Russia, these additions completed the mainland territory of the United States.

No sooner was California acquired than gold was discovered there in 1849 and further impetus was given to the idea of 'manifest destiny'. A host of fortune-hunters poured into the territory, some by sea around Cape Horn and others by overland trail, to the gulches where nuggets could be washed out in pans. The mountains filled with roaring camps; San Francisco sprang up overnight into a metropolis filled with greed, vice and luxury, and the whole country in a few months was converted from a sleepy community of Spanish-American ranchers into a hustling community of Anglo-Saxons. In 1850 California became a new state, and in the next twenty-five years a further seven new states, nearly all of them in the west, were added to the Union.

Economic forces impelled this drive towards the west. The hard-working farmers who settled the prairie lands were quick to develop what soon became one of the world's greatest cornlands; in the drier areas, cattle-ranching grew, ushering in the age of the cowboy. In this development they were assisted by the development of the railroad. By 1850 there were only 6,000 miles of railroad, but by 1860 this had grown to 30,000, stretching westwards and replacing the old pioneer trails. Chicago, a small settlement in 1850, grew into a city of many thousands of inhabitants by 1860 and, with its place at the centre of the nation's meat-packing industry, was already a great railroad centre. The once-proud Indian nations were overwhelmed, their pitiful remnants confined to scattered reservations.

All this was the work of little more than a generation. From a timid little nation of 12 million in 1830, to a rapidly growing 45 million in 1875, America was developing into one of the world's great power-houses, its people, many of them newly arrived immigrants, carving out for themselves new ways of living, and new ways of thinking, not as submissive subjects of European regimes, but as pioneers who had grasped new lands and new aspirations. The expansion of the United States was not an accident, nor a conspiracy; and certainly not the outcome of some philosophic abstraction which gave the United States the divine right to fill the North American continent: it was the natural response to forces that were more demographic than democratic. But Americans believed in it, and that made it true.

4:10

Queen Victoria or Mrs Brown?

The personal relationship between John Brown, the manservant, and Queen Victoria created suspicions, assiduously hushed-up both during and after her lifetime, which have left something of a shadow on the royal reputation among commentators even at present. Was there anything in it?

John Brown was a Scotsman and came into contact with the royal family at Balmoral, their house in the Scottish Highlands. He had earlier served her beloved husband, Prince Albert, as a ghillie, i.e. his attendant and guide on hunting and fishing trips, and before he died in 1861 Albert recommended him to the Queen as a thoroughly trustworthy servant. A recommendation of this sort, especially from one whose advice Victoria so much revered, was enough to get Brown a position in the royal household, where he remained until he died in March 1883. There was a degree of intimacy between them, as could be seen from the numerous small items she gave him during his lifetime, cufflinks, brooches etc., none of them of any great value, but reflecting Victoria's conservative good taste in personal jewellery.

Victoria was far from popular in the years after the Prince Consort's death, at least partly on account of the way she withdrew herself from public life, living in mourning and seclusion in one royal residence after another. Her critics attributed undue influence to John Brown and even suggested an amorous relationship with the Queen, whom they unkindly dubbed 'Mrs Brown'.

In fact Brown turned out to be all that the Queen wanted him to be. She was a lonely woman, surrounded by a sycophantic court, and Brown's solid and reliable forthrightness came like a breath of fresh air. She saw in him, perhaps, an expression of the loyalty of her people, and a humble substitute for the helping character of Albert, on whom she so much relied. He always was at hand to seize a pair of runaway horses, or – as he did in 1872 –

a would-be assassin with a pistol. He drove away importunate newspaper reporters with a flea in their ear, and was always ready to offer blunt common-sense advice instead of courtly flattery if the Queen asked for it – and sometimes when she did not. He served her not only at Balmoral, but in her other residences, too, and frequently exchanged sharp words not only with the Queen's private secretary, but even with Prince Edward, the later Edward VII, of whom Brown held no very high opinion. Victoria liked him because he was honest and direct, and not afraid of showing his feelings. He wept readily at misfortune, and the Queen noted more than once in her diary 'good Brown was quite overwhelmed'. He also liked a regular tipple of whisky, though he was seldom drunk. He had, in short, a number of simple human qualities, joined with shortcomings, and this was probably the main reason that Victoria was attached to him.

Edward VII's destruction of all papers, monuments etc. relating to Brown immediately on his mother's death in 1901 reflected Edward and Brown's antipathy towards each other, but at the time and subsequently this was seen as a justification for the unsubstantiated rumours which fuelled the 'Mrs Brown' legend. On his death John Brown's diary, in which the details of his service and his thoughts were recorded, mysteriously disappeared, suggesting that someone at court thought that his unexpurgated comments might be explosive enough to warrant suppression.

New light was cast on Brown's supposedly 'missing' diary at the very end of the twentieth century by the discovery in the attic of one of his grandchildren of a number of the mouldering pages whose loss in 1883 had given rise to so much surprise. Even then they were not released for study or for publication – on the rather curious grounds that publication might give some disquiet to the then Queen Mother, Elizabeth, formerly Bowes-Lyon, widow of George VI. Herself a minor scion of the Scottish aristocracy, it is difficult to see what feelings other then hilarity the disclosure could have provoked. Whether this limp excuse provides evidence of Victoria's improper intimacy with John Brown, or whether it was part of an even subtler plot to conceal the fact that the diaries were entirely innocent, is quite impossible to say. What is certain is that the death of the Queen Mother on 30 March 2002, at the ripe old age of 101, removed the last scintilla of justification for suppressing them any longer.

Until then, Victoria must continue to enjoy the benefit of the doubt. It is still only gossip to suppose that there was anything indelicate in their relationship.

4:11

The Lusitania: Was it a Legitimate Target?

The sinking of the Lusitania *was one of the many 'evil deeds' attributed to the Germans in the First World War. It caused outrage in the USA, aroused much anti-German feeling and damaged the German cause. The British claimed that the* Lusitania *was an unarmed passenger ship which was not carrying contraband of war, and that its sinking without warning by a U-boat was an unpardonable atrocity. The Germans claimed that the ship was carrying contraband, and that it had been specifically targeted because of the contraband it was carrying. The British claim was a downright lie; the German claim was misleading.*

The First World War had erupted over most of Europe by early August 1914. Although most, though by no means all, of its citizens sympathised with Britain and France, the USA was determined to maintain a benevolent neutrality. But this was difficult to do while the British navy was attempting to blockade Germany, and while German submarines were sinking merchant vessels on route for Britain. At first German submarines observed the Cruiser rules by which they surfaced and gave merchant ships' crews time to take to the lifeboats before sinking their ships. But when the British Admiralty authorised merchant ships to carry guns and disguised naval vessels as merchant ships the Germans began to suffer U-boat losses. Cautious U-boat captains adopted the policy of 'when in doubt sink on sight', and they made no exceptions for passenger ships. This policy was given official German backing in 1915. It seemed inevitable that American citizens on British ships were at risk.

All the same, the *Lusitania* thought itself safe. It was the finest ship in the Cunard line. With four great funnels towering 75 ft over the boat deck, the liner was 780 ft long, had a displacement of 32,500 tons, and could reach a maximum speed of 26 knots, easily surpassing any other ship afloat. Its first-class accommodation was the height of luxury, with a gilt-and-white domed dining room, a drawing room panelled in mahogany, smoking room and libraries, and a 24-bed hospital. Its master, Captain William Turner, was immensely proud of his ship. When the Germans published in New York a notice to intending passengers warning them that they were in a war zone and were travelling at their own risk, he laughed it off. 'The best joke I've heard in many days,' he said, 'this talk of torpedoing the *Lusitania*!'

On 1 May 1915 the passengers, most of them British, went aboard. They were sailing from New York to Liverpool, and were expected in Europe in little more than seven days. But on 7 May, off the Old Head of Kinsale near the southern coast of Ireland, they had an unexpected encounter with the German submarine U-20. Its master, Kapitänleutnant Walther Schwieger, had been at sea since late April, and only the previous day had sunk two ships, allowing the crew to abandon one, but sinking the other without warning. He had only two torpedoes left. Sighting the *Lusitania* on the horizon, he approached cautiously and fired his first torpedo from periscope depth at a range of 700 metres. He saw the explosion and its results. Satisfied that the ship was rapidly foundering, he decided against firing his second torpedo, downed periscope and headed for home, leaving the *Lusitania* to its fate.

The ship sank in 18 minutes. 1,201 persons were drowned – 785 passengers and 413 crew. There were three further stowaways whose identity was never established, since several of the bodies washed ashore remained unidentified. The sinking was immediately condemned in Britain and the USA as an appalling act of murder. The Germans were said to have issued a limited edition medal in support of their claim that the liner was carrying war contraband – though in fact the so-called medal was struck privately by Munich metal-worker Karl Goetz, showing, on one side, passengers buying their tickets from a skeleton symbolising death, and, on the other, a prominent notice saying 'No Contraband' on a sinking ship loaded with aircraft and guns. It was intended as a criticism of German Imperial war policy and was immediately banned. Britain, however, replied by commissioning a replica from Gordon Selfridge (the owner of the London store) and issuing 250,000 copies of it mimicking the German one, implying that the Germans were gloating ghoulishly over so many deaths.

The Commissions of Enquiry into the sinking were both held before the war ended, the British one in June 1915, and the American in the summer of 1918. Both concluded that the *Lusitania* was not carrying war contraband; both were wrong. Several copies of the cargo manifest show that the *Lusitania* was carrying ammunition. There were 4,200 cases of rifle bullets (1,000 bullets per case), 1,250 cases of shrapnel shells (unfilled) and 18 cases of percussion fuses; all these were rather misleadingly labelled 'Non-Explosive in Bulk', and hence were allowed under the rules of war. These manifests, however, were incomplete, and the contents of two of the cargo holds have never been revealed. It seems likely, but not certain, that these contained quantities of gun-cotton – highly-explosive material produced by impregnating cotton fibre with nitric and sulphuric acid – possibly hidden in a consignment of furs. The German authorities in New York certainly suspected that the ship was carrying cargo that was forbidden by American law and should never have been carried on a passenger liner, but it is unlikely that they had any specific proof. The press warnings from the German consulate in New York against travelling on the liner did not, however, mention contraband. The German argument about contraband came after the sinking; the German commander of U-20 did not even know until the last minute what ship he was torpedoing, let alone what the ship was carrying. He had sunk the ship on sight, and the German defence that the ship was a legitimate war target on account of its cargo was shaky to say the least.

The action of the British Admiralty subsequently in trying to destroy the reputation of Captain Turner makes sense only if it meant it was trying to undermine the Captain's credibility in case of any revealing disclosures he might make later. Any other revealing disclosures were circumvented by the fortuitously incomplete state of the manifests. The Germans had some cause to feel aggrieved. The British had lied, and the German suspicions were correct. Yet Allied propaganda over the *Lusitania*, and the unfounded fear that it might bring the Americans into the war against them, caused the Germans to abandon their 'sink on sight' policy a few months later.

4:12

Was the Battle of Jutland a Great Victory for the British Navy?

The clash of the British and German navies at Jutland in 1916 gave rise to a great British myth. The British claim to have achieved a great victory came at a dark time in the war when any victory would have been a great morale booster, and a naval victory would reassure the British of the impregnability of their islands. In fact what was claimed as a victory was a near-disaster. Yet Jutland is still regarded by many as one of the most decisive battles of the war, although it did not actually decide anything, and to describe it as a victory is at best dubious and at worst erroneous.

On 31 May 1916 there occurred the only major naval battle of the First World War. Because of its proximity to the Danish coast it is known as the battle of Jutland, and there the main British and German fleets engaged in a battle that could easily have won or lost the war. In it the British lost three battlecruisers, three cruisers and eight destroyers, while the Germans lost one battleship, one battlecruiser, four light cruisers and five destroyers. The battle showed that the German naval armour, guns and gunnery were superior. And the British suffered more casualties: the 6,000 British sailors killed were more than double the 2,500 Germans lost.

So naturally the Germans claimed the battle as a German victory. They had done a great deal more damage than the British and their fleet was still largely intact. But the British pointed to the fact that the Germans had retreated back to port, that Germany had not broken the British blockade, gained command of the sea nor cut British communications with France. Therefore, Jutland had been a great British victory. But how could it be? A victory would have permitted a close instead of a remote blockade of the German ports and the removal of all threat to British naval supremacy. In fact, the presence of the German High Seas fleet in its home harbours posed just as much of a threat after Jutland as before.

Both sides had been afraid of losing, so both sides had contributed to the indecisive nature of the battle; the British claim that the threat of fog prevented close pursuit of the German fleet was little more than a flimsy excuse. German rejoicing that Britain could no longer take command of the seas for granted was mirrored in Britain by the disillusionment in naval circles that Britain could no longer win decisive naval victories like those of Nelson or Jervis. But Jutland was trumpeted in the British press as just such a victory. Meanwhile, the Germans took the view that, as their U-boats were about to master the seas, it would be rash to risk their surface ships when submarine warfare would soon bring Britain to its knees. If the U-boats had succeeded, then German tactics at and after Jutland would have been justified. As it was, the U-boat menace was eventually conquered, and the German High Sea fleet remained in port and mutinied when ordered to sea in the final stages of the war. The battle did very little; it did not change the situation at sea, nor did it enhance the naval reputations or the naval morale of either side. It was inconclusive; only in the sense that the British fleet still commanded the seas and the German fleet did not could Britain be said to have had the edge.

4:13

Did Lenin put Marxism into Practice?

It is the commonly held view that the whole work of Lenin consisted in carrying out in practice the ideas outlined by Karl Marx for a communist revolution mainly in his Communist Manifesto *of 1848, a work leading to his being charged with high treason in Germany, and in his epoch-making work* Das Kapital *in 1867. This view was assiduously fostered at a later date by Soviet leaders such as Stalin, but its persistence is based on a misunderstanding of the work and the importance of both men.*

To begin with, Marx's ideas were so general and theoretical that he gave Lenin very little to put into practice. Many of his books were highly critical books of popular history, commenting on contemporary happenings from a radical viewpoint. The *Communist Manifesto* is exciting enough, though stronger on rhetoric than on guidance, while all seven parts of *Das Kapital* are written in the same impenetrable professor-speak of the economics lecturer, which is essentially what they are. From time to time there are a few glimpses of sociological analysis, but generally to imply that the book would turn out to be the basis of world revolution seems about as improbable as the suggestion that John Kenneth Galbraith would turn out to be the second Messiah. Marx sets out no blueprint for revolution, and gives no hint of what a communist society would be like, and how, if at all, it would be governed. This meant in practice that Lenin, in planning for such a revolution, began with a blank sheet of paper and had to make up his revolution as he went along.

Lenin, on the other hand, was complementary to Marx in that he was more a man of action than a theoretician, and applied his considerable intellect to devising the institutions that would bring a socialist society, if not a fully communist one, into existence. His pre-revolutionary writings, therefore, are shorter and more practical. In 1902 he set out the principles guiding his early revolutionary activity in a pamphlet called *What Is To Be Done?*, in which he called for a tightly disciplined party of professional revolutionaries, an educated élite able 'to divert the labour movement from the unconscious tendency of trade unionism to march under the wings of the bourgeoisie'. This body would grasp what had to be done, and would provide the necessary leadership to achieve it. A body that was 'little but good' would stand a better chance of success than one that was diluted by mass parliamentary support. His 1905 pamphlet, *Two Tactics of Social Democracy in the Democratic Revolution*, was likewise a warning that the Russian bourgeoisie was generally too weak, vacillating and incompetent to be entrusted with the conduct of the revolution, and that the proletarian party should therefore support the 'democratic dictatorship of the proletariat' whose task should be to replace bourgeois society with a socialist one. The two pamphlets that showed some wish to discuss theoretical issues were *Materialism and Empirio-Criticism* in 1908, and *Imperialism* in 1916, the second of which aimed to explain how capitalist forces in the latter days of monopoly capitalism would for a time involve the workers in the exploitation process of colonial peoples as a means of deferring the evil day of revolution, but that in the end this tactic would be bound to fail, and revolution would come, none the less. This pamphlet had the purpose of explaining to the proletariat that the gradualist element of working-class leaders was being bribed by the 'superprofits' which the capitalists had decided to divert to them to purchase a longer lease of life for their system, but that the workers should pay no attention to this, and continue to struggle for the revolution. These two texts remained as authoritative statements of 'Marxist-Leninist' teaching for the rest of the century.

In a very real sense, therefore, Marx may be said to have been responsible for the *strategy* of the communist revolution, and Lenin for the *tactics* of the revolutionary coup. But as time went on, Lenin moved ever further from those ideals that he claimed as his inspiration, until finally his system was communist only in name.

Lenin's severest test came after the Bolshevik seizure of power at the end of 1917. His earlier optimism that the triumph of socialism could be achieved in a few short months, and that any mistakes made would not in the long run prove very important because 'the turning-point is at hand, and we are on the eve of a worldwide revolution', speedily evaporated in the light of harsh experience. He suddenly found himself saddled with the responsibility of governing the whole country, and of taking decisions for it that would sketch-in the outlines of the future communist state. With the help of a small unelected council and with the endorsement of a larger national congress of soviets, he cobbled together the semi-amateur administration which was to run the country, and took the first steps towards confiscating privately owned land, towards operating the railways, and managing and running Russian industry. Soon he had to deal with the problems of peace-making with the Germans, with famine and with civil war, trimming away the frills of Russian liberties in order to adapt the existing capitalist system to the stark realities of 'war communism'. He appointed 'bourgeois specialists' to help manage the factories, and tightened worker discipline in a determined effort to restore the economy. So extreme were the demands he made of the people that soon the Bolsheviks were as unpopular as the Tsarists had been, and in March 1921 the sailors of the Kronstadt garrison rose in revolt alongside the mass of the Petrograd workers, demanding 'Soviets without Communists', true industrial democracy instead of Bolshevik dictatorship. This warning signal made Lenin pull back from the brink, replacing war communism with the more moderate 'New Economic Policy', permitting more private property and the reintroduction of profit incentives. His critics objected that he seemed to think that the only way to make communism work was by abandoning it, and only his immense strength of character saw the new policy put into effect. All the same,

Lenin wore himself out in these chaotic years, dying in 1924 at the early age of 54.

Marx was thus the theorist and the philosopher, who dreamed the dream of unravelling the capitalist system and replacing it with a communist utopia; Lenin's was the much more gruelling job of building up from nothing a supposedly socialist system in the wake of a devastating war and an equally destructive revolution. Of the two, the second had much more practical impact on Russia and on the world, but the first produced a mental revolution that in the long run was perhaps more important.

4:14

Pearl Harbor, 1941:
Was the Japanese Attack a Total Surprise?

The Japanese attack on Pearl Harbor in Hawaii on 7 December 1941, which started the war in the Pacific, touched off a controversy in modern US history that has never been settled, and about which argument still rages. Why was the US Pacific fleet left in such a vulnerable position before the attack? Why were the secret steps taken by the Japanese not more fully known to the US authorities? Could the disaster have been averted? Why were more effective steps to prevent it not taken by the US authorities? And, perhaps the most interesting of all, how far did Roosevelt, in his anxiety to appear the innocent party, deliberately engineer the whole disaster? Perhaps, after half a century has elapsed, it may be possible to offer answers to some of these questions.

By the late autumn of 1941, relations between the United States and Japan had reached crisis point. Occupying large areas of the coastlands of China, the Japanese had plans for establishing supremacy over the whole Pacific hemisphere. Events in Europe had led to the signing of the Tripartite Axis Pact with Nazi Germany and Fascist Italy in September 1940, and the prospects for acquiring British, French and Dutch colonies in Southeast Asia seemed encouraging. In October 1941 the moderate government in Tokyo led by Prince Konoye had been replaced by the much more militant General Tojo. The Japanese government began to take a tougher line in lengthy negotiations with the United States that had begun in May. In July, they had already occupied French Indochina, and the USA had retaliated by freezing Japanese assets, and was contemplating placing an embargo on essential supplies of oil and other vital raw materials. All these factors drove the Japanese leadership in early November to take a fateful decision: they would continue their diplomatic efforts for three more weeks, but if agreement had not been reached by the end of the month they would go to war. The date was set for 8 December (7 December, Washington time).

Through the work of a brilliant cryptanalyst, Col Lawrence Friedman, who had cracked the chief Japanese diplomatic code (Code 'Purple'), President Roosevelt knew that the Japanese had set a deadline for a diplomatic solution at the end of November. US decoding machines named 'Magic' enabled the Americans to read encoded Japanese messages; unfortunately, no 'Magic' message ever contained precise information about when or where the attack was to be made. Roosevelt's main purpose in continuing the negotiations was not to appease the Japanese, which he had already decided not to do, but to stall the Japanese delegation while completing his war preparations, and to create a suitable political climate at home for acceptance of the inevitable war, when it came.

By the beginning of December, Roosevelt was waiting for the Japanese blow, wherever it was to be. One of his advisers, Harry Hopkins, asked the President why, if he knew war was inevitable, he did not attack first. Roosevelt replied that it was essential for him to appear to the world as the victim of Japanese aggression; in that way he would carry his people with him united into war. But US intelligence did not know precisely where the blow was to be struck. Their ignorance was compounded by the complete radio silence maintained by the Japanese flotilla stealthily approaching southwards from the

Kurile Islands 3,000 miles away, which they had left in mid-November in considerable strength. Roosevelt had a hunch that the attack would come somewhere in Southeast Asia, possibly in the Philippines or Guam; no one dreamed that the target would be Pearl Harbor. The US High Command ordered all merchant shipping into port, and all bases, including Wake and Midway, which were thought to be in much greater danger, were instructed to take 'all practical precautions' against imminent attack. The *Lexington* and the *Enterprise* were dispatched from Pearl Harbor carrying aircraft reinforcements for Wake and Midway, and though other vessels of the Pacific fleet were also at sea, the great bulk of the US naval strength lay at anchor there when the attack took place.

On 6 December 'Magic' began decoding a lengthy transmission from Tokyo to the Japanese delegation in Washington. It was in fourteen parts, and only the last one gave any indication of Japan's intentions. It announced that there was no chance of a diplomatic settlement 'because of American attitudes', and it instructed the delegation to break off negotiations on 7 December at precisely 1300 hours (about sunrise in Honolulu). Translation of the document was not completed until 0915; another 35 minutes passed before it reached the Secretary of State. Then, when it was decided to hand it over to the Chief of the US General Staff, he could not be found – he was out riding. The result was that the message was delayed until 1200, and by the time it arrived in Pearl Harbor it was too late. The attack had already begun.

US losses were severe. The Japanese sank or crippled 18 warships, destroyed 204 planes on the ground, extensively damaged 5 airfields, and killed nearly 2,500 US servicemen, over 1,000 of whom were entombed in the USS *Arizona* when it exploded and sank. What is a little surprising is that the Japanese did not follow up their strike by an outright seizure of the whole of Oahu Island, which lay at their mercy after the attack. This would have been comparatively easy for them to do.

Roosevelt's unwillingness to go to war, and his refusal to allow himself to be portrayed as the aggressor in the quarrel with Japan are readily understood, but the costly fumbling of his government's officials, and the lack of imagination of military intelligence – especially in view of the sterling work done in deciphering the Japanese codes – cost the USA very dear in the final attack. US Intelligence had a great deal more inside knowledge of what was going on in the events leading up to the assault than they could have expected, but their procedures were sometimes slow and bureaucratic. In any case their knowledge was incomplete. The clever way in which the Japanese High Command concealed the details of the impending strike, and the complete radio silence observed by the approaching Japanese fleet (in addition to their skilful avoidance of sea-lanes normally used by merchant shipping) all contributed towards hiding the truth from the Americans. Military and Naval Command were also to blame. In the last analysis, large warships are always vulnerable to air attack, and this does not seem to have been taken into sufficient account. Furthermore, gathering large numbers of such vessels together in a place as small as Pearl Harbor was bound to be an accident waiting to happen.

Even so, accusations of neglect or even treachery were not long in appearing. The highest American officials, from the President down, were alleged to be involved in a deliberate plot to drag the reluctant, isolationist United States into war, by enticing the Japanese into launching a pre-emptive strike sufficient to enrage the American people, but insufficient to damage American prospects for ultimate victory. One critic set out such a view in a book published in 1973 under the suggestive title *The Skeleton in Uncle Sam's Closet*, in which he made the bold claim that 'Roosevelt traded the military and civilian security of the Hawaiian Islands for his own political security.' Numerous similar allegations were made at later dates. One (*The Cruise of the Lanukai: Incitement to War*) implied that the President was trying covertly to provoke the Japanese into attacking him; another (*Infamy: Pearl Harbor and Its Aftermath*) alleged that Naval Intelligence had known all about the impending assault but had been persuaded to hush it up.

Closer examination of these charges proved nothing, and in 1981 Professor G.W. Prange in a book called *At Dawn We Slept* demolished the so-called 'devil theory' of Roosevelt's motivation. He doubted whether there was a conspiracy of officials to lure the Japanese into war, and particularly doubted whether, even if there were, the United States government would have been so foolhardy as to bait the trap with the bulk of the US Pacific fleet riding defenceless at anchor awaiting massacre on a Sunday morning. There was evidence of human weakness, mistakes, incompetence and opportunism, but not of deliberate conspiracy.

All the same it is true that the manner of the Japanese attack certainly helped in fostering the image Roosevelt wanted to give of himself as the injured party, and as a result helped considerably in allowing him to carry the nation with him united into the war. But to suggest that he cold-bloodedly allowed Pearl Harbor to happen when he could have prevented it, in order to put himself into the right for the final reckoning, is another thing entirely, and an accusation almost certainly without foundation.

4:15

The Yalta Conference, 1945: A Victory for East or West?

Controversy still continues over the importance of the Yalta Conference between the wartime 'Big Three', Roosevelt, Stalin and Churchill, towards the end of the Second World War. Was the conference a victory for the Western powers, or a victory for the Soviet Union and the communist bloc? Both these opinions have been advanced. Some observers, like the US Secretary of State at the time, have said that the United States and the other Western Allies secured all from the conference that they could have expected; while others have agreed with another more critical spokesman who said that the conference marked 'the high point of Soviet diplomatic success and correspondingly the low point of American appeasement'.

There is no doubt that the rapidly ageing President Roosevelt had for some time regarded Marshal Stalin with a political trust that bordered on indulgence. He had a sympathy for the Soviet Union's predicament and an understanding of Stalin's ambitions that were not shared by the allies of the United States, and not even by many American contemporaries. On the other hand, he regarded Churchill with more circumspection, seeming to fear a revival of British world imperialism. Perhaps he did not fully understand the extent to which Britain's world position had been undermined by its strenuous wartime efforts. As a result, even Roosevelt's advisers were surprised at the degree to which the President followed his independent line, largely impervious to their recommendations for caution.

As the result of the decisions made at the conference, Stalin, though remaining typically gruff and ungrateful for what he was given, made impressive gains. Roosevelt deliberately blocked Churchill's efforts to co-ordinate Anglo-American policy in advance, not wishing, as he said, 'to feed Soviet suspicions that the British and the Americans would be acting in concert'. The most important matter to be discussed by the conference related to Poland, where the USSR was already substantially in control. When the matter came up, Roosevelt appeared happy to agree to the Soviet suggestion that there should be elections in which 'all democratic and anti-Nazi parties shall have the right to take part'. Churchill pressed strenuously for international supervision of the polls, but all that Roosevelt would do in this direction was to ask for the signature of a Declaration on Liberated Europe, composed largely of reassuring promises, which Stalin was very willing to sign, especially when the President informed him that all American forces would be out of Europe within two years. At Yalta, too, in January, Stalin was promised substantial territorial rewards if he entered the war against Japan in August. This he duly did, though only a matter of days before the final Japanese surrender. The Far East did not figure largely in the Yalta discussions, mainly because Russia was not yet in the Pacific war, and hence consideration of Jiang Jieshi's (Chiang Kai-shek) problems was only sketchy. Hence the claim was later made that 'American diplomats surrendered the territorial integrity and the political independence of China, surrendered the principles of the Atlantic Charter, and wrote the blueprint for the communist conquest of China in secret agreement at Yalta.'

It is true that Stalin demanded, and secured, promises of outer Mongolia, the Kurile Islands, southern Sakhalin, the lease of Port Arthur, and the right jointly to operate with the Chinese the Chinese Eastern railway and the South Manchuria railway, which is probably the reason why the critics suggested that nationalist China had been betrayed; but on the other hand realists believed that the Western Allies conceded nothing that the Russians could not have taken for themselves. Averill Harriman said that nothing was done at Yalta that contributed to the overthrow of Jiang. The Russians did not betray the nationalists; they simply failed to carry out their promises to them, and left Jiang to sink under the dead weight of his own unmanageable incompetence.

Indeed, Roosevelt's defenders by no means thought that he had witlessly sold out to the Soviets. One US commentator, giving evidence to the Senate Committee, roundly refused to concede that even the Polish terms were unsatisfactory: 'I don't consider that the agreement at Yalta involved a surrender. The fact that the Russians violated it I don't think means that the agreement was bad. . . . I can't see that you could have done much more that would have been of benefit to Poland or the Polish people.' Secretary of State Stettinius went even further and claimed: 'The record of the conference shows that the Soviet Union made greater concessions at Yalta to the United States and to Britain than were made to the Soviets. The agreements reached . . . were, on the whole, a diplomatic triumph for the United States and for Britain.'

There are perhaps few who now would go quite as far as that in defending Roosevelt and his conduct of affairs, but it seems likely that Stalin was not quite as calculating or as treacherous as Western anti-communists would have us believe. He did, after all, agree to, and subsequently honour, what Churchill called a 'naughty document' in late 1944, which was in effect an attempt to exclude Russia from the Mediterranean at the price of giving him Romania and Bulgaria as satellites, provided he gave no help to the communists in either Italy or Greece. His motives, too, were purely defensive. What he held he was determined to keep. Even his chronic obsession with secrecy was largely dictated by his fear that the West might somehow find out how desperately weak the war had left his country. It is true that he treated non-communist opponents in the Balkans and in Poland with draconian severity; but that was his usual way of dealing with opponents. It was just that Western observers had not seen it operating before quite so publicly.

All the same, only a few days before his death, Roosevelt came to the bitter conclusion that he had been too generous with Stalin. In March he was persuaded by a series of furious messages sent him by Churchill that he had been over-optimistic in his expectations for the future. He is said to have banged his wheelchair with his fist and admitted 'We can't do business with Stalin. He has broken every one of the promises he made at Yalta.' Truman, his successor, would readily have accepted this view. Unfortunately, however, this interpretation of events is equally wide of the mark.

5

HISTORICAL REVISIONS

Samuel Plimsoll: Did He Bring About Marine Safety?

History textbooks often assert, hence history students usually believe, that the nineteenth-century pioneer Samuel Plimsoll, after devoting his whole life to the cause, succeeded by his Merchant Shipping Act of 1876 in improving the condition of seagoing vessels at that time and so saving the lives of thousands of crewmen who otherwise would have been lost at sea. This makes a good story, but is unfortunately almost entirely untrue.

It was not that there was no problem to be addressed. Conditions aboard ship were hazardous, and crewmen went entirely unprotected by the Factory Acts. A Merchant Shipping Act passed in 1854 extended earlier legislation on food, medicine, accommodation and wages for crewmen, but was spartan in its provisions, and paid no attention at all to questions of marine safety. It was not unheard of for shipowners to employ vessels sometimes so unfit for sea that they fell apart and sank during a voyage, causing the deaths of those serving in them. They might have rotten beams, disintegrated carpentry joints, or 'devil' bolts, which were sham bolts used for the sake of economy which in fact did not perform their function. Such ships were known as 'coffin ships'. Other owners picked up rotten ships cheaply, overloaded them with cargo, over-insured them, and then collected insurance on both ship and cargo after the inevitable disaster. A shipowner could load a vessel until its gunwales were within a foot or two of the water and then send it on a voyage from which it would never return; he might send ships designed for service on canals across the Atlantic, or use vessels loaded beyond the capacity of their engines, or deck-loaded until dangerously top-heavy – indeed one owner said the more bales of cotton on deck, the better the chances of the crew being saved when the ship foundered. He could conserve money by under-manning, or by employing as his crew only the dregs of the waterfront. Indeed, some owners had been heard to argue that if ships went down, they did so not because the ships were overloaded with cargo, but because their crews were overloaded with drink.

Samuel Plimsoll carried on a determined and often single-handed war against such abuses. Born in Bristol in 1824, he devoted his life to improving the state of merchant shipping by every means. It was his idea that ships should be required to carry a load line, as Venetian sailors had done nearly a thousand years earlier. This line at first simply allowed so many feet of 'freeboard' to so many feet of hold, whatever the width of the ship, but later more exactly was determined by what was known as *reserve buoyancy*, the proportion which the capacity of the solid part of the ship above the water bore to the capacity of the part immersed. Plimsoll entered parliament to secure the enactment of such a safety measure for shipping, and on more than one occasion created disturbances when members would not listen to him. He was firmly convinced that the shipowners were a gang of ruffians and murderers who sent hundreds to their deaths without a second thought. He believed anything he was told about them with absolute credulity, and usually was faced with a multiplicity of writs served on him for his libellous criticisms. Disraeli found him a pain in the neck and said some harsh things about him – writing to Lady Bradford in 1875, for example, he said of Plimsoll that he was 'the Moody and Sankey of politics, half-rogue and half-enthusiast'. In July 1875, having excluded Plimsoll from the House for a week for a particularly violent attack on members who defended criminal shipowners, and having accepted an abject apology from him for his behaviour, parliament took note of the strong public support he enjoyed and enacted a temporary Act which was later enlarged and made permanent in the Merchant Shipping Act of 1876.

This Act made a number of improvements to shipping law, but in its most important particular was plainly defective. It contained provision for a loadline, but allowed this to be fixed wherever the owner thought fit. One whimsical Cardiff skipper showed what he thought of the new load line when he had it painted on the funnel of his steamship.

The idea, therefore, that Plimsoll at a stroke solved the problem of the safety of merchant shipping does not bear a moment's examination. The fact that Plimsoll continued to work just as hard for these improvements as he had before shows that he was aware of the limitations of the new law. In 1880, for example, he travelled up to Birmingham on an impulse to badger the new Secretary of the Board of Trade, Joseph Chamberlain, over it, presenting himself at his door at seven o'clock in the morning, and insisting on interviewing him while he was still in his dressing-gown. Chamberlain gave some help but, noting that the 60 men killed each year at sea did not come up to the casualties in the mines, where the annual death toll was 315, he was not overwhelmingly enthusiastic. So Plimsoll continued his obstreperous behaviour, though always without a great deal of effect. Just before he died in 1898 he lamented the 'very little' he had been able to do for seamen.

It was not until the first decade of the twentieth century that parliament came round to agreeing with Plimsoll about the right way to calculate reserve buoyancy for placing a ship's load line. Even then it was not sacrosanct. Lloyd George, as President of the Board of Trade, raised the line in 1906, and was called a murderer by H.M. Hyndman for his pains. The placing of the line seemed to be the least of the sailors' worries in the First World War, though it was then moved up again slightly. Deck-loading continued until the Merchant Shipping Act of 1949, when it was restricted chiefly as a means of allowing the efficient operation of the radar equipment with which merchant ships in future were to be fitted.

5:2

Did Abraham Lincoln Seek the Freeing of the American Slaves?

President Lincoln is universally regarded as one of the greatest of United States Presidents, and is often credited with having fought the American Civil War in order to free the slaves. Is there any truth in this assertion?

Abraham Lincoln claimed to have been born of humble stock in a log cabin in the rather backward Southern slave state of Kentucky in 1809. This version of his background was designed for public consumption later in his career. Nor were his parents the God-fearing folk he made them out to be. His mother was 'poor white trash', his father a small farmer 'meaner than a rattlesnake'. When he was seven, the family moved across the Ohio into Indiana and then into Illinois, where his father resumed his farming. The young Lincoln, a tall, gangling and rather untidy youth, hated farm life, and soon left the farm. He became a storekeeper's assistant, which gave him enough money to build a flatboat, in which he floated down the river to New Orleans. There, by dint of sheer hard work he trained himself as a lawyer. He also went into local politics and entered the Illinois state legislature at the age of twenty-five, joining as a member the so-called 'Whig' Party of the well-to-do. He also began to earn enough money to make himself respectable by becoming a railroad lawyer. He did not come into national politics until 1846, when he was elected Congressman for Illinois. He took a major part in the movement which led to the formation of the Republican Party.

The pressing issue of the day related to slavery. Lincoln, though by no means a supporter of emancipation, had strong views on the subject. After the Missouri Compromise of 1820 and the 1850 Compromise, it seemed to him that the North was ducking this issue, and encouraging the Southerners to extend the grip of slavery into the US Federal Territories.

Until 1857, Abraham Lincoln had scarcely been distinguishable from hundreds of other lawyer-politicians in the North. It was his views on slavery that helped to bring him to the fore. These views are not always easy to ascertain, since they tended to be modified according to the audience he was addressing. To radical audiences he would rail against the whole institution of slavery, while to right-wing supporters he would affirm the racial superiority of the Whites. In modern terms, Lincoln would certainly have been regarded as a racist: he did not believe that slaves were the equals of Whites; he did not think they were fit to be either jurors or voters, and he would have opposed any suggestion (if any had been made) that they be integrated into society. Nevertheless, like many Northerners, he normally regarded slavery as an evil. In a speech at Peoria, Illinois, in 1854, he asserted that legislation should be framed on the principle adopted by the founding fathers that slavery was ultimately to be restricted or abolished. He maintained, too, that the idea of 'popular sovereignty' was unacceptable – hence his vote in Congress against the Kansas–Nebraska Act – since slavery in the territories was not only the concern of the inhabitants of those territories, but of the whole of the United States. The new Republican Party, which Lincoln joined and soon led, took the view that the Southern states should be allowed to keep their slaves – only a constitutional amendment could deprive them of that right, and this they would never accept; but that slavery should not be extended further, and should certainly not be adopted in the western territories.

In 1858, Lincoln engaged with Stephen A. Douglas, senior Senator for Illinois, in a series of debates on the future of slavery in the United States. The contrast between the two, in their persons as well as in their ideas, was great: Douglas supported the view of 'popular sovereignty', that the settlers in the territories should have the right to decide whether to have slavery or not; Lincoln maintained the Republican view that slavery must be outlawed in these territories in order to prevent its further spread. But he certainly did not campaign upon the issue of slavery and had no intention of abolishing it. Nevertheless, the South was deeply suspicious. They threatened to secede from the Union if any 'Black Republican', i.e. one committed to prevent the further extension of slavery, like Lincoln, should be elected. Nevertheless Southern Democrats were divided as to what to do about the threat: most were willing to settle for Douglas's views on popular sovereignty, but the extremists broke away and took their stand on the Dred Scott judgment – that all the territories should be open to slavery – nominating John Breckinridge of Kentucky as their splinter candidate. The effect of this in 1860 was to give the presidency to Lincoln by a large majority of electoral votes.

But it was the threat of secession from the Union rather than any plan to emancipate the slaves that chiefly concerned Lincoln. In 1858 he had said: 'A house divided against itself cannot stand. I believe that this government cannot endure permanently half slave and half free. I do not expect the Union to be dissolved; I do not expect the house to fall; but I do expect it will cease to be divided.'

The speech shows that while Lincoln envisaged an eventual end to slavery he was not proposing it yet. This did not prevent the Blacks from regarding him as a saviour, and looking to him with hope for the future. In fact the Southern states had all seceded by March 1861, even before Lincoln was inaugurated, and America was plunged into war, or, as Lincoln called it, 'rebellion'. Just as he had made no concessions in the early months of his presidency, so now, surrounded by demands for a compromise settlement, he revealed those traits of fortitude and tenacity that justified the Blacks' high opinion of his qualities. Though faced with a series of military disasters which would have deterred a lesser man, he persisted in his view that, whether there was slavery or not, what could not be permitted was that any state should leave the Union. He was execrated in the South, where he was regarded as the embodiment of all they hated most; even in the North he was despised as a political lightweight and an upstart with deplorable western habits. One critic dubbed him 'a plain President for a plain people'. This was perhaps intended as an insult, but Lincoln was very proud of it.

In the war which followed, the North had the resources for victory, but they lacked the spirit and the dash of the Southerners, and they conspicuously failed to carry with them the sympathy of the outside world. It was only after a gruelling four years of civil war that they were victorious. In the meantime, Lincoln's determination had never faltered; nor had his tolerance and his compassion. He resolutely refused to preach hatred; indeed, after Appomattox, when the crowds and their military band paraded in Washington for victory, Lincoln said when he was asked what music he wanted: 'Pray, bid the band play Dixie.'

Though he never claimed to be an orator, his speeches are still one of his lasting claims to fame. His Gettysburg Address in November 1863, following his Emancipation Proclamation the previous January, is perhaps the most famous speech ever made by a democratic leader, and at little more than 200 words one of the shortest. It also embodies his greatest legacy to his people, Black and White.

But he fought the war to save the Union, not to free the slaves. As Lincoln said in a letter to Horace Greeley, the editor of the *New York Tribune*:

My paramount object in this struggle is to save the Union, and is not either to save or destroy slavery. If I could save the Union without freeing any slave, I would do it; and if I could save it by freeing all the slaves I would do it; and if I could save it by freeing some and leaving others alone, I would also do that.

Lincoln perhaps, therefore, enjoyed a reputation as a champion of freedom that he did not entirely deserve. Nevertheless his assassination in April 1865, five days after Lee's surrender, in Ford's Theatre, Washington, was an act that appalled the North, but was disastrous for the South. Here there was soon unleashed a programme of wanton retaliation that Lincoln during his lifetime had always been at pains to avoid. His keynote had always been tolerance, compassion, restraint; but bitterness and revenge were easier, and more appealing to bigoted supporters. Lincoln, had he lived, might not have done much better; but, as things were after his death, it took over a hundred years to integrate the freed slaves into American society.

5:3

Was There Really a Scramble for Africa?

In the heyday of European empires at the end of the nineteenth century, history books were full of the story of the planting of colonies in Africa and the ensuing struggle for dominance among the major countries of Europe. The story was depicted as one of gallant and heroic pioneering in the unknown lands of what was then referred to as the 'dark continent', followed by a mad European 'scramble' to seize as much African territory as possible in the shortest possible time. This interpretation of the colonisation of Africa has later come to be challenged by many historians who now see it in vastly different terms, and regard the notion of the 'scramble for Africa' as a highly erroneous one.

Before 1870 most of the interior of Africa was unknown to Europeans. A few coastal settlements were under the control of European powers, the largest of them belonging to the British in Cape Colony and the French in Algeria. By the end of the century the whole of Africa, with the important exceptions of Ethiopia, Libya and Morocco, had been carved into European possessions. Ethiopia would have gone the same way had it not inflicted a humiliating defeat upon the invading Italians at Adowa in 1896, and Spain and France were already active in Morocco. Such a transformation within thirty years has given rise to the notion that the European powers were desperately competing with each other to acquire African colonies, and that this arose out of their commitment to imperialism. But this explanation does not stand up to close scrutiny.

Britain is usually regarded as the prime example of a nineteenth-century colonising power, and the British statesman Disraeli is credited with making the British people and the major political parties proud of their empire. Britain's great American empire, however, had been lost in 1783. Since then the British regarded their remaining colonies as expensive millstones, 'the white man's burden' of later years, which it was Britain's duty to govern and protect until they, too, followed America's example and broke free.

India was Britain's greatest overseas responsibility in the mid-nineteenth century, and it had showed its restlessness against British rule during the Mutiny of 1857. But despite the American experience and Indian unrest Britain was in no haste to divest itself of its colonies. Indeed its American policy was aimed at preventing the USA from acquiring Canada or any of Britain's Caribbean colonies. At the same time Britain had become established in New Zealand and was setting up new colonies in Australia. Disraeli's concern was that the Liberals might allow the colonies to go their separate ways rather than tying them in effective unity with the mother country. On 24 June 1872 Disraeli made a memorable speech at Crystal Palace, London. In it he urged the maintenance of the empire. He was particularly concerned that Britain should not abandon its role in India, but should strengthen the ties with India and with the other territories which Britain possessed. Contrary to later glosses on his speech, Disraeli was not advocating the *expansion* of empire.

If there was a mad rush for African colonies in the late nineteenth century, it is remarkable how reluctant the major powers were to take part. Some historians assert that the 'scramble' began with Leopold of the Belgians' International Association to exploit the Congo basin, but it was a private venture, and the Belgian government was most reluctant to become involved until forced to do so much later by world opinion. Most ventures began through private traders; they then tried to avoid the expenses of administration by persuading their national governments to take on the responsibility while they got on with the trading and exploitation, and missionaries got on with the converting. Britain gave up its interests in the Congo without too much of a struggle, and resisted pressure to turn Nigeria into a Crown colony until 1900. Britain's main concern was India and the trade routes to it. When the Turks were no longer strong enough to protect the overland route, and that was superseded by the Suez Canal, Britain acquired the major shareholding in the Canal in 1875, and trusted the Khedive of Egypt to protect it. But he could not. Britain joined in the international cooperation to prop up the Khedive, but then found itself on its own fighting to protect the Khedive against the revolt of Arabi Pasha in 1882. Far from trying to establish a foothold in Egypt, successive governments did their best during the next twenty years to rid themselves of the Egyptian burden. At several international meetings Britain showed willingness to give up Egypt, if the security of the Canal could be guaranteed in some other way. And Britain resisted for thirteen years popular pressure to avenge Gordon largely for reasons of expense and when Kitchener's expedition was finally sent in 1898 its main purpose was to remove the threat to Egypt posed by the Mahdi's successors.

Elsewhere in Africa Britain was in the main a reluctant coloniser. Fearful of a combined German and Boer threat to the Cape route to India, the British government declared a protectorate over Bechuanaland in 1885. But Britain did not obstruct the German acquisition of South West Africa in 1884, although it showed its concern for the Cape route by taking Walvis Bay. In East Africa the British even facilitated the German expansion, but took Zanzibar in 1890 to continue the policy of policing the slave trade. By the 1890 agreement with Germany Britain became the power of influence in Uganda, but Salisbury and Gladstone refused at first to annex it, and the country did not become fully British until 1895. Cape Colony was Britain's main outpost astride the southern route to India, and Britain was concerned to protect it. Since the Boers rejected British sovereignty, Britain was concerned to prevent the Boer Republics from becoming too powerful, or finding allies in neighbouring territories. Since the once-great Portuguese Empire was dying but not yet dead, Britain felt obliged to support its oldest ally, and would not allow either the Boers or any foreign power to take from Portugal the strategic Delagoa Bay. And to the north of the Boer Republics the establishment of the British South African Company in 1889 completed the virtual encirclement of the Boers, and dealt with the threat posed to them by the troublesome Matabele.

Kaiser William II was later to complain that Germany had arrived too late in the scramble for Africa, and had had to be content with what was left. This was not how Bismarck had seen it. Without a great fleet there was no call for Germany to have colonies. Thus Bismarck's acquisitions of territories, such as the Cameroons and South West Africa were intended as Germany's bargaining counters in European diplomacy, and the Berlin Conference of 1884 was as much about European relationships as about the allocation of lands in Africa. So the German colonies were not an end in themselves, they were pawns in the international chess game; later they were used to justify Germany's naval programme. In the 1880s Bismarck might well have disposed of a colony to buy a European advantage; in the 1890s that option was no longer possible as colonies had become possessions of prestige. Even so, there was no undue haste to carve up what was left.

As early as 1882 Bismarck encouraged the French to take Tunisia in order to drive the thwarted Italians to join the Dual Alliance. With their appetite for colonies thus roused, the Italians became active in Eritrea and Somaliland in the 1890s. But their interests, too, were European; after 1882 they did not wish to compete with other major powers in Africa, and were only looking for easy pickings. They readily limited their ambitions in an agreement with Britain in 1891, and only took on Ethiopia in 1896 because they expected little effective resistance.

France was far more interested in recovering Alsace-Lorraine than acquiring an African empire. Tunisia was an extension of France's interests in Algeria. France timorously left Britain to become established in Egypt, but later regretted it. Britain did not contest French influence in the Sahara, and by an agreement in 1890 gave France undisputed control of Madagascar. Col Marchand's Nile expedition was not intended as a serious challenge to the British position in the Sudan; it became an unsought confrontation and thus a matter of national prestige, but France had no intention of driving Great Britain into the arms of Germany, so backed down.

Imperialism was an expensive business. Only Kimberley, the Rand, and later the Congo offered a good return on European investment. No country acquired colonies in Africa for reasons that were nakedly imperialist; those who carved up Africa did so for a variety of reasons, and they did so amicably. Even Fashoda was less of a powder-keg than it appeared. Neither was there a 'scramble'. Most acquisitions were made reluctantly or at least with some presumption that they might be temporary. No one scrambled, no one raced for African colonies. After 1900 Europe's African colonies became identified with national pride and prestige, but that was when relationships had warmed into alliances, and differences had hardened into hatreds.

5:4

Was There a 'Massacre' at Tonypandy, 1910?

In South Wales, in the area of the former Welsh coal-mining industry, the story is still told of how the Liberal government of H.H. Asquith used government troops to shoot down Welsh miners who were striking for their rights. Winston Churchill, who was Home Secretary at the time, was said to have been responsible for this outrage. As a result, the Welsh people have never forgiven the English ruling classes for this act of barbarism. But did it really happen?

Churchill, who, in spite of his aristocratic connections with the Marlborough family, cultivated throughout his career a radical, truculent style in his speeches, had only recently in the House of Commons been denouncing the House of Lords in the debates over the Parliament Bill. Anyone might believe from his words that he was capable of harsh actions. If he were a radical, this should have pleased the Welsh miners, who shared his hostility to the 'boss class'. But as far as the Welsh were concerned his actions at Tonypandy seemed not only brutal, but a gross and unnecessary betrayal of the radical and working-class cause.

There can be no doubt that things were seriously amiss. Conditions in the coal-mining industry were at this time appalling throughout the country, but perhaps they were worst in South Wales. Hours were long, conditions dirty and dangerous, living conditions for the miners and their families dreadful, and wages extremely poor. In spite of a raft of legislation passed to protect them, many men supported wives and numerous children on a wage of less than £2 a week. That the miners' feelings ran high is only to be understood.

But did the government put the army on the streets to repress hungry and unarmed miners? The truth about the Tonypandy affair was much less spectacular. And those who were there knew perfectly well what actually happened.

The situation was certainly threatening. The rougher elements in the crowd of protesting miners in the Rhondda valley were getting out of hand, and local police forces were quite intimidated by their ferocity. Gangs of men armed with sticks and staves roamed the streets after dark; shops were broken into and property stolen or destroyed. Eventually the Chief Constable of Glamorgan requested that the Home Office send troops to maintain law and order. If a Chief Constable makes such a request, there are few Home Secretaries who will deny him. Churchill, however, in spite of all his aggressive declarations, was so horrified at the prospect of troops facing a crowd of rioters and firing on them that he countermanded the order for troops to be put onto the streets, and sent instead a body of plain, phlegmatic Metropolitan Police armed with nothing worse than their rolled-up mackintoshes. There were troops, it is true, held in barracks in reserve, but only unarmed policemen ever faced the striking mob. Thus the only real bloodshed in the affair resulted from a few bloody noses in the ensuing scuffles.

It was therefore only parliamentary posturing that caused the denunciations which followed in the House of Commons as the result of Churchill's supposedly 'unprecedented intervention'. His denials were all of no avail, and the idea that Churchill was a ruthless enemy of the working man lingered on for many years. This impression was actually reinforced by the extravagant words he employed at the time of the British General Strike in 1926.

5:5

The Angels of Mons: Divine Intervention?

The legend of the Angels of Mons continued for long to provide solace and satisfaction to the credulous and the patriotic alike. It is however utterly without foundation

In the early days of the First World War the 3rd and 4th Divisions of the British Expeditionary Force, under the command of General Smith-Dorrien, found themselves faced in Belgium by an enormous German army of about 400,000 men under von Kluck. It outnumbered the British by about four to one, so that they found themselves hard-pressed in their retreat from Mons, 27–28 August 1914. They were overawed by what they could see of the Germans' meticulous preparations, and the Germans in turn were deeply impressed by the skill and valour of the British, whose rifle fire was so rapid and accurate – 'fifteen rounds rapid fire' per minute – that they thought they were facing machine-guns. Sir John French, in overall command, found himself in a precarious position: hardly any troops at all on his left, the French on his right falling back so quickly that they were already miles behind him, and each one of his detachments, especially the one under General Smith-Dorrien, taking heavy and continuous punishment from hugely superior opponents. That they survived at all was attributed by many to divine intervention.

It seems on the face of it strange that the British foot-soldier, who would disbelieve almost anything (and especially what his officers told him), should have been so gullible as to give credit to the 'Angels of Mons' story. These were supposed to have appeared in the sky above the desperately struggling army clad in white and fighting with flaming swords against the German First Army. Yet many of the soldiers did believe it, and the Angels of Mons became one of the most lasting of legends from the First World War. How can this be explained?

Part of the answer is to be found in the conditions on the battlefield, the like of which in 1914 no one had ever seen before: devastating artillery fire that blew men into unrecognisable fragments, enormous and continuous casualties from hand-to-hand fighting with rifles and small arms, the support services completely overwhelmed by the ferocity of the battle and the intensity of the conflict continuing by day and night without let-up. Columns of dust and smoke eddied over the battlefield. It would be surprising if someone among this overwrought and exhausted mass of men had not thought he could see things in the haze that clouded his vision. So perhaps the phenomenon was no more than collective hysteria?

There is, however, a more prosaic explanation. On 29 September 1914, Arthur Machen published in the *Evening News* a popular fictional story, 'The Bowmen', in which he told how the spirits of the English bowmen dead at Agincourt came to the rescue of their hard-pressed fellow countrymen in 1914 by shooting their ghostly arrows at the advancing Germans and killing them without leaving any wounds. Machen described these bowmen, appearing between the two armies, calling them 'a long line of shapes, with a shining about them'. This word 'shining' was the magic one. Within days Machen's fictitious bowmen had become genuine angels, and fiction had been transmuted into fact. Their garb had become pure white, their bows flaming swords. What had been written as fiction came to be believed as fact. Machen, the author, was embarrassed by all this, but he was assured, especially by churchmen, that he had had a supernatural perception of what had actually happened at Mons – the angels were real, and they had appeared in the sky near Mons. It was unpatriotic to doubt it.

There were soldiers, too, who told of the 'elation' of moving up into the front line, of the 'estranging remoteness of battle', and of a sense of 'invincibility', almost as if they had been 'born again'. To common, uncultivated and ignorant soldiers, who had never given a moment's real thought to God or to religion, such an experience was entirely novel and deeply impressive. This might be called by professional psychologists the phenomenon of 'displaced Christianity'.

5:6

The Zimmermann Telegram:
Did it Bring America into the War?

A common error that is still widespread is that the sinking of the Lusitania *brought the United States into the First World War, although there is a gap of almost two years between the two events. A more sophisticated error is that it was the dispatch of the Zimmermann Telegram from Berlin to Mexico that caused the entry of the United States into the war. This is, however, if not an outright error, no more than a small part of the truth.*

On 19 January 1917, the German Foreign Office, headed by Alfred Zimmermann, sent a coded telegram to the German ambassador in Mexico City, proposing an alliance between Germany and Mexico if the United States went to war with Germany. Was this a serious proposal, and how far did it precipitate the entry of the USA into the war?

There is little doubt that by the beginning of 1917 Germany regarded the entry of the United States into the war as inevitable. Since Germany had decided to renew unrestricted submarine warfare, sinking of American ships and the deaths of American sailors could not be avoided. It seems likely that the decision, announced on 31 January had been taken several days earlier after considerable discussion. Thus the telegram of 19 January was sent with the knowledge that unrestricted submarine warfare was about to be renewed. The telegram proposed an alliance between Germany and Mexico, and Mexico would, in the event of victory, have restored to it the lands of New Mexico, Arizona, Texas and other territories lost in 1846. Mexico was to persuade Japan to make peace with Germany and declare war on the United States; just how the Mexicans were to do this was not made clear.

The sending of the telegram showed a remarkable ignorance of Mexican politics by the Germans. President Carranza owed his position to American support: General Pershing and an American force had driven his rival Pancho Villa into hiding in 1916. Fearing the loss of nationalist support Carranza had rather late and rather reluctantly used the Mexican army against Pershing's incursion into Mexican territory. But while Villa was certainly anti-American, Carranza could not afford to be. Perhaps the Germans thought that their offer would rally the Mexicans behind Villa, but his armies and support had already crumbled away. Furthermore, the sending of the telegram, although in code, was in itself a security problem. There was no certainty that the code had not been breached, or, more likely, that a decoded version of the telegram might not fall into the wrong hands. If the Americans got to hear of it the position of American isolationists would be undermined and America precipitated into the war. But the Germans would not have sent the telegram if they had not regarded American entry into the war as imminent.

In the event the British Admiralty decoded the telegram and communicated its findings to the American ambassador. To preserve the confidentiality of their source the Americans found it easy to bribe a clerk in the German legation in Mexico City to oblige with a copy of the deciphered text. In the meantime the USA broke off relations with Germany and Austria-Hungary on 2 February, ostensibly because of the German submarine announcement of 31 January. The Americans delayed publication of the telegram until 1 March. Why the delay? The White House had been in possession of the text of the telegram for a full month. It was not to protect the original British source. President Wilson was still hoping that the Germans would back down and call off unrestricted submarine warfare; after all, he had just been re-elected with the slogan 'He kept us out of the war'. Always a man of peace, Wilson moved towards war slowly and reluctantly. By the beginning of March, however, he saw no way of avoiding it; the publication of the telegram would strengthen the nation's support for war. Yet Wilson delayed his war message to Congress for another month, until 2 April. During that month the telegram had had time to foment anti-German feeling throughout much of the USA.

Even so, the telegram was not the major cause of war; nor did it even provide the occasion for it. Submarine warfare – the sinking of American ships, the loss of life by American citizens, the interruption to American trade – was far more crucial. Eastern bankers, moreover, were heavily committed to the Allied cause and had provided extensive credits which would be difficult for the bankers to recover if the Allies were defeated. The crucial votes for war were: in the House 373 for, with 50 against, and in the Senate 82 for, with a mere 6 against; these were convincing votes which did not need the stupidity of the German Foreign Office to consolidate them. The telegram was not a major cause of war – war was virtually inevitable anyway – but it certainly made it easier for the American people to reconcile themselves to it.

5:7

Was the German Army Defeated in 1918?

In the autumn of 1918 German armies were everywhere in retreat. Battlefields which had been the scene of horrific and costly fighting in earlier years fell into Allied hands, and the Hindenburg Line, on which the Germans pinned their defensive hopes had been, in places, penetrated and outflanked. The armistice of 11 November 1918 came in time to prevent a massive Allied invasion of Germany. But had the German army been defeated?

It later became one of the cardinal dogmas underpinning the Nazi movement in the 1930s that the German army had never been defeated. Even to think such a thing, German nationalists believed, was tantamount to high treason. Rather, the army had been betrayed by an odious combination of liberals, democrats and pacifists, and not least by Jews. This was the legend of the 'stab in the back' – that the German army in the autumn of 1918 was unbeaten, had shortened its defence lines and was ready to fight another day, had it not been for the politicians.

The German spring offensives of 1918 had won initial success, but like all previous offensives on the Western Front, had petered out without achieving breakthrough. To the German High Command the failure was little short of a disaster. It was necessary in the first place because of the US entry into the war in 1917 and the arrival, during the next year, of up to 4 million fresh American troops. It was vital for Ludendorff to win victory before that. Instead he won short-term success, and suffered the heavy casualties invariably sustained by the attacking side. Worse still, the German offensive had forced the Allies to have a united command under Marshal Foch, and the Allies, despite their recent defeats, were still able to mount a succession of counter-attacks, especially from August onwards. The Allied forces stumbled, whether by accident or design, on the new technique of attacking the Germans at their weakest points and then shifting the assault to other parts of the line when the initial strikes caused a stiffening of German resistance. By the end of September the Germans had lost not only the gains of recent months, but virtually all the gains made at great cost in 1916 and 1917.

Ludendorff, weakened by a slight stroke, and alarmed at the collapse of Bulgaria, decided at the end of September that Germany had now no chance of winning the war. The flower of his army had been decimated in the spring offensive, and the shortfall in numbers was being made up with boys of fifteen and middle-aged men. There had been some demoralisation when the German advance brought in captured Allied equipment and provisions far superior to those of the German army. The German troops had been promised victory: many could see for themselves that this was not achievable, and the Allied counter-offensive was fighting against a German army that had largely lost hope, but was still tenaciously contesting every inch of ground.

While the fighting continued unabated, Germany's request for an armistice in early October led to a series of exchanges between Germany and the Allies concerning Germany's acceptance of President Wilson's Fourteen Points, and the evacuation by Germany of all its conquests. Ludendorff's intention seems to have been to avoid a war on German soil, and to saddle the politicians with the responsibility for making peace. Thus he hoped an undefeated German army would live to fight another day. When he realised that the Allies intended the armistice to render Germany incapable of renewing the war, Ludendorff tried to halt the armistice negotiations. But once he had opened Pandora's box there was no way for him to close it again. The politicians in Berlin pressed on. In the meantime the Turks abandoned the war, Austria-Hungary disintegrated, and Germany lay open to invasion from the south. The mutiny at Kiel ended any possibility of a naval challenge at this late stage in the war, and fear of revolution made the civilian armistice negotiators willing to accept almost any terms no matter how harsh. A tense situation was partly relieved by the Kaiser's abdication; the armistice was signed on 11 November and Germany had not disintegrated.

Nor had the German army disintegrated. Devastated terrain, machine-gun nests, and determined German resistance held up the Allied advance. In some places the Allies were thirty miles beyond the Hindenburg Line, but Allied casualties were very heavy – the Americans suffered 100,000 in their Argonne offensive. At the armistice, apart from one small corner of Alsace, the German front line was everywhere on foreign soil. Haig thought that the Germans were capable of a formidable defence of Germany itself. Neither Foch nor Pershing considered that the Germans were finished. Certainly, although the Germans were in retreat along almost the entire length of the front line, they had nowhere suffered a major military defeat. Indeed, their retreat was shortening the line that had bulged out into north-east France, making the German positions easier to defend.

So it was not disaster in the field that led to the armistice. It was in part the result of Ludendorff's effort to protect the German army before nemesis in the shape of the Americans overwhelmed it in 1919. It was in part necessitated by the collapse of Germany's allies which made Germany's position untenable. And it was in part the work of the civilian politicians of the Old Reich who snatched at peace in an effort to preserve something at least of the old order. For the German forces defeat and disaster were imminent and inevitable, even though, by November 1918 their loss of territory was more through orderly retreat than disorderly rout. That the German armies still stood largely intact on the Western Front in November 1918 was to enable Ludendorff and others later to claim that Germany had not been defeated, but had been betrayed by the politicians. Thus the legend of the 'stab in the back' was born, and Hitler knew how to make good use of legends.

5:8

What Was the Importance of the British General Strike, 1926?

The General Strike in Britain in May 1926 is generally thought to have brought the country to the brink of the class war and the proletarian revolution. There is, however, no justification for such a view. The idea of a 'revolution' existed only in the minds of left-wing-inspired agitators, and no matter how long they thought it had been brewing, it was never likely to happen.

Conditions in the coal-mining industry had certainly been deplorable for over a century. Efforts had been made to improve them, but conditions remained difficult, dangerous and dirty, hours long and arduous, and wages extremely low. After 1918, the miners had found it hard to adjust to changed postwar conditions. Miners resented the importation of cheap coal from Germany as reparations, and resisted the efforts of the owners to restore their profits by further cutting costs. It was an industry where ill-feeling between owners and employees was a deeply rooted tradition. Ever since socialism had been seriously discussed, the miners had been in the forefront of those demanding the end of the capitalist system. They wanted nationalisation partly because they believed that only when the industry was unified, instead of being under separate colliery companies, could it be efficiently run, and partly too because they thought that under nationalisation their wages would be guaranteed at a reasonable rate and their conditions improved. In 1925 the owners gave notice of drastic wage cuts to make coal exports more competitive, and the miners appealed to the Trades Union Congress for support. The TUC threatened to activate an alliance already in existence between the dockers, the railwaymen and the coal workers and to call a General Strike, with which all trade unionists should be invited to comply. This was 'Red Friday' (31 July 1925).

To avert a crisis, the Conservative Prime Minister, Stanley Baldwin, promised a Royal Commission to examine all the problems of the coal industry. He even offered, during the nine months needed for the inquiry, to subsidise the coal industry at the taxpayers' expense: hours and wages were to remain unchanged during the inquiry, and any shortfall would be met by a government subsidy, which finally amounted to about £24 million. The Samuel Commission, headed by the Liberal Sir Herbert Samuel, produced a detailed report suggesting many changes in the organisation of the industry, but insisting that the miners would have to accept some reduction of wages, unless they were prepared to return to pre-war hours of working. Both sides rejected the report, the owners because it went too far, the miners because it did not go far enough. The Welsh communist, A.J. Cook, who was the miners' leader, summed up their objections in the slogan: 'Not a penny off the pay, not a minute on the day!' Punctually on 1 May (May Day) the miners stopped work, and three days later the other unions followed suit and the General Strike began.

The situation looked extremely threatening. There had already been a general strike in Glasgow and the more radical Clydesiders were anxious to spread their own particular brand of militancy. The British Communist Party was willing to support the call, turning respectful glances towards the Bolshevik example, and in this country within hours over seventy towns were being run by Strike Committees bearing a strong family resemblance to the Russian Soviets. The government invoked the Emergency Powers Act to seize land and buildings, food and other necessaries, to commandeer vehicles, and to take over railways, shipping, coal stocks and petrol supplies, and also supplies of water, gas and electricity. They assumed sweeping powers: they reserved the right to mobilise the police, the fire services and the armed forces; they controlled public meetings and threatened to exercise wide powers of entry and search in cases of suspected sedition. All this was justified by their claim that the strike created a 'constitutional issue'. Baldwin exhorted: 'Stand behind the Government. The laws are in your keeping. You have made parliament their guardian. The General Strike is a challenge to parliament and is the road to anarchy and ruin.'

In the absence of proper newspapers because of the printers' strike, the country was starved of news and rumours easily spread. Many turned to the new 'wireless', and those fortunate enough to own sets put them out on their window sills so that the BBC could be more widely heard. For the benefit of the remainder, the government launched the *British Gazette*, produced by non-union labour (or 'scabs') under the militant editorship of Winston Churchill. He referred to the strikers as 'the enemy' and called the strike 'a conflict which, if it is fought out to a conclusion, can only end in the overthrow of parliamentary government, or in its decisive victory.' The left-wing periodical *New Statesman* at the time headlined one of its articles 'Should We Hang Mr Churchill or Not?' though it gave scant regard to the alternative. For their part, the TUC produced the *British Worker*, countering government propaganda with propaganda of its own. They denied vigorously that they were attacking the constitution, though their message was hampered by their own decision to bring the printers out, and was often contradicted by the more militant spokesmen who were its mouthpiece in strike areas. One of them, an Independent Labour Party man, crowed exultantly in the north-east: 'Why man, there's never been anything like it! If the leaders here don't let us down we'll ha'e the Capitalists crawlin' on their bellies in a week. Oh, boy, it's the revolution at last!'

This enthusiasm, however, turned out to be misplaced. The British nation generally were a quiet, patient people, not easily stirred to extremism or violence. Though large numbers of special policemen were enrolled for the emergency, there was not much for them to do. As for transport, the new motor traffic on the roads ensured a reasonable distribution of supplies, while students, most of whom had never done a day's work before in their lives, indulged their childhood fantasies with more enthusiasm than skill by driving trains. It was said that the British revolution was as calm and orderly as a Victorian Sunday morning, though without the church. Rumour also had it that the special constables who had been enrolled to keep the strikers in order passed the time by playing football against them. After a mere nine days, the General Council of the TUC got cold feet and called off the strike, and everyone except the miners thankfully went back to work. The miners stayed on strike until well into the autumn, but eventually were forced to return on the employers' terms.

Baldwin maintained his image as a 'man of peace' by urging moderation in the settlement, but he was disappointed at the vindictive note struck by the Trade Disputes Act that followed in 1927. Not only did general and sympathetic strikes become illegal in future (a provision in practice very difficult to enforce), but there were a number of irritating limitations placed on the trade unions, which, for example, had to accept 'contracting-in' for their members to pay the political levy, instead of *not* to pay it as before.

All the same, though a dramatic episode, the General Strike turned out to have very little real importance. It did not change the policies of Baldwin's government, nor did it change the course of the economic trends of the time. The fall in wages and prices, the rise of unemployment, the extent of social welfare provision went on as before; the strike was merely an interruption. It was the end, not the beginning, of a period of unrest and possible revolution. Generally no one spoke of the 'class war' or the 'proletarian revolution' any more. During the 1930s the working classes tightened their belts and put up with the suffering inflicted by the slump; in 1945, after the Second World War, they captured power in the election of 1945, and embarked hopefully on achieving the revolution by democratic means.

5:9

Who Burned the Reichstag?

The burning of the German Reichstag early in 1933 created a controversy that took years to resolve. Clouds of left- or right-wing rhetoric have long obscured the issue. Even today the responsibility for the outrage is still sometimes debated.

On the evening of 27 February 1933, the German Reichstag

building went up in flames. Hitler, who had been appointed German Chancellor only a month earlier but who lacked a parliamentary majority and was badly in need of an anti-Red scare, decided to make what profit he could from the opportunity. He had already denounced the communists for subversion, but lacked convincing evidence for his charge. This act of arson provided him with an excellent chance to smear his opponents.

The Nazis said the outrage was the work of the communists, and afterwards staged a trial of the alleged incendiaries before the High Court in Leipzig. However, the trial, in spite of the best efforts of the chief prosecutor, Goering, was a failure, chiefly because of the brilliant advocacy of the accused. At the same time the obvious eagerness of the Nazis to secure a conviction led naturally to the belief that they were themselves responsible for the outrage. A number of leading historians, including Alan Bullock, repeat this erroneous idea in their work. What really happened?

About nine o'clock on that evening a university student who had been studying in the library heard on his way home the noise of breaking glass, and thought he saw a shadowy figure climbing into the Reichstag building through a first-floor window. He fetched a policeman, but they could not find anyone. The policeman did, however, discover flames, and at 9.15 called the fire brigade. At first they could not gain access. When they did, they wasted time on small fires in the corridor. It was 9.40 before the full strength of the fire brigade was mustered, and sixty appliances were sent to the building. By that time, the building was well alight, and soon was irretrievably lost. A minor Nazi figure, knowing that Goering, President of the Reichstag, together with Hitler and Goebbels, were at a party nearby, telephoned them with the news, which at first they simply did not believe. Hitler, however, sensing a chance to turn the situation to his advantage, worked himself up into a rage, and demanded that communists must be rounded up and shot, since this was clearly a communist plot.

Meantime, a half-naked young Dutchman by the name of Marinus van der Lubbe had been arrested in the building and was taken to the nearest police station. He was then questioned until the early hours, and gave a full account of his behaviour. His motives were unclear, based, it appeared, on some vague resentment, but it seemed at least that he thought the burning of the building would act as a 'beacon for revolt'. He impressed his interrogators with his clarity and intelligence. He described where he had bought the petrol and the firelighters, and told his listeners how he had stripped off his clothes before soaking them in petrol, scattering them about and setting light to them. The police checked the details he gave and established that they were all true. Fire officials confirmed that the arson was technically possible, with the design of the building and its central dome creating a chimney effect; and this, together with the regular oiling of its panelling for cleaning purposes, made it an ideal site for such a crime. They accepted that van der Lubbe had conceived and committed the act alone, and that the Communist Party were not involved.

This explanation was quite unacceptable to Hitler and his associates. At the ensuing trial they ignored the evidence of the investigators and their evaluation of van der Lubbe's personality, and insisted on making him out to be the half-witted dupe of the Communist Party put up to the job by his unscrupulous masters. They accused him of being an active communist, though in fact he had only vaguely socialistic left-wing views and was unknown to the communists. They stressed the improbability of one man starting such a massive conflagration unaided, and called numerous technical experts to prove that he could not have done it without assistance. But many of them were not fire officers or policemen, but professors of chemistry and criminology, some of whom had never even visited the Reichstag. Furthermore, only one of the accused – Torgler, leader of the communist group in parliament – had been anywhere near the Reichstag that evening, and he had left at 8 p.m. The others, the leading Bulgarian communist, Dimitrov, and two other Bulgarians, had been nowhere near, and in any case had no connection with, and had never even heard of, van der Lubbe.

This was awkward for the High Court judges. Before convicting, they usually would have preferred to have had some evidence of the guilt of the accused. Van der Lubbe made no bones over his guilt. He spoke clearly, coherently and accurately. He tried for six hours to convince the court that no one had instigated his behaviour, and rejected the evidence of the experts saying: 'I was there, and they were not. I know it can be done because I did it.' Most impressive was the court performance of Georgi Dimitrov, the leading communist on trial. He was lucid, convincing, and ran rings round the chief prosecutor, Goering, whom he reduced to gibbering incoherence.

In the end the High Court found van der Lubbe guilty and, even though arson was not a capital crime until Hitler made it so retrospectively, sentenced him to death. He was duly executed by beheading with an axe. The four communists were acquitted, but the court added the rider that van der Lubbe must have had assistance from 'persons unknown'.

Dimitrov put his finger on the weakness of the Nazis' case in court when he accused Goering to his face: 'Van der Lubbe had help. He did not get it from me. Therefore he must have got it from you.' The communists – who staged a counter-trial in London at which they proved to their own satisfaction that it was the Nazis who were responsible for the outrage – made much play with a 'secret' passage said to carry phone and electric cables and central heating pipes to Goering's house nearby (where the original informant who telephoned Goering at his party lodged) and alleged that the Brownshirts had used this to penetrate the building. There they laid the fires themselves, and at the last minute pushed van der Lubbe through the window to be picked up by the police and take the rap. This story was equally unlikely, and in any case ignored the fact that at 8.45 the building had been visited by a postman delivering the deputies' mail who neither saw, smelt nor heard anything suspicious. The evidence of this humble postman, who was not even called at the trial, shows that the Reichstag building was empty when van der Lubbe broke in at nine o'clock.

The most likely conclusion, therefore, appears to be that neither the communists nor the Nazis were responsible for burning down the Reichstag. Van der Lubbe did it all by himself.

5:10

The Battle of Britain: What Was the Role of the 'Few'?

Few myths have had so powerful or inspiring an influence over people today as that of the small gallant band of fighter pilots who fought in their Spitfires in the August and September of 1940 with phenomenal success against the overwhelming might of the German Luftwaffe.

The German army was at that time engaged in preparing for a full-scale invasion of Britain after recent events leading to the fall of France. In the four weeks following the start of the German aerial offensive on 15 August, Fighter Command lost nearly 500 aircraft, and the head of the *Luftwaffe*, Reichsmarschall Goering, was beginning to count the battle as won. Hordes of German fighters, 800 on 30 August alone, had strafed Fighter Command's operation centres in southern England, inflicting heavy damage on their British opponents. From their debriefings the German High Command had come to think that the Spitfire and Hurricane squadrons had been badly mauled, and that having lost so many fighters, the RAF had only about 300 left. So, by early September Goering felt it safe to change his tactics. On 2 September, partly in retaliation for RAF raids on Germany, he ordered the start of mass daylight bombing on London, and the blitz proper began. But although the whole of southern England took a terrible pounding from the *Luftwaffe*, victory in the air was denied to the Germans, and the legend of the 'gallant few' of the RAF who had saved their country was born.

The 'Few' were nearly all public-school boys, the product of England's residential academies for young gentlemen, still speaking in their clipped upper-class tones, but now fighting adorned with splendid handlebar moustaches, white silk scarves and flying goggles as they battled for the survival of their homeland.

The myth originated in the brilliantly successful wartime oratory of the British Prime Minister, Winston Churchill, in the broadcast tribute he paid to the pilots putting their lives on the line every day. While the outcome was still in grave doubt he echoed the sentiments of Shakespeare's *Henry V*, referring to 'this few, this happy few', and solemnly announced to an anxious public that 'Never in the field of human conflict was so much owed by so many to so few' (20 August 1940).

So they were a legend before the battle was half won. The truth, however, was more mundane. Swelling the numbers of the 'Few' were a great many ordinary grammar-school boys, though they were 'sergeant-pilots' rather than 'pilot-officers', and a large number of foreign pilots who came from countries recently occupied by Nazi Germany, such as Poland, France and Czechoslovakia, and from Canada and the Commonwealth, who were now helping in the fight against the common enemy. Although these may have lacked a little of the suave polish characteristic of the renowned 'Few', their contribution was invaluable.

Furthermore, they were not as markedly inferior in numbers to their enemies as their tactics suggested. Although the RAF usually attacked the incoming squadrons in small numbers, especially when they were engaged in hacking chunks out of the massed bombers of the *Luftwaffe*, they were striking approaching aircraft out of the sun, and flying in small groups for tactical reasons, rather than because they were greatly outnumbered. Indeed, even after their recent heavy losses in France, when about 450 British fighters had been lost, there were still in July about 700 operational planes ready to face the *Luftwaffe*'s 2,600 (a number which included the German bomber fleets). It was in fact the Germans who ran out of replacement aircraft and spare parts first, simply because their organisation was less efficient. Moreover, British and Allied pilots, shot down over friendly territory, could swiftly be provided with another aircraft (if they survived combat), while

Germans (if they lived) were taken prisoner. British losses, too, tended to be proportionately smaller, with the RAF downing two planes for every one they lost themselves. In October, for example, in the concluding stages of the Battle of Britain, the RAF lost 186 aircraft, but the *Luftwaffe* lost 379.

The legend was given even greater authenticity by the 'triumph' of 15 September 1940. The crisis of the Battle of Britain was reached on that day, when the *Luftwaffe* made its last and most costly effort to win control of Britain's skies. It failed. British radio and newspapers exultantly claimed that 185 German planes had been shot down as against a negligible loss by the RAF. German sources after the war revealed that the true German loss was between 56 and 60. British losses were 26. What accounts for this discrepancy?

During the heat of battle there was much confusion. RAF pilots who scored a hit on a German plane had not the leisure to see whether a German plane hit was a German plane lost. Some, with smoke pouring from them, limped back across the Channel and could be repaired to fight another day. These would be recorded by the RAF as successful kills. Even where a German plane blew up in the sky it was not always possible to say which British pilot had made the kill, especially if the German plane was under attack from several British fighters. So several RAF pilots might have claimed the same direct hit. Fighter Command was well aware that some of the claims to have destroyed enemy aircraft were conflicting and inaccurate, but it had no means of making any more than a wild guess at the true figures. It did not inflate the figures the pilots provided, they did not need inflating, but it passed them on to the government who exploited them to the full. The figures convinced the British public that there had been a tremendous aerial victory on 15 September, and the British public desperately needed some good news.

Even so the figures exaggerated the real losses by more than 300 per cent. If the RAF mistakenly thought that they were reasonably accurate, it also overestimated the total size of the *Luftwaffe*. The Germans, too, lacked accurate information on how the Battle of Britain was going. Goering's underestimate of the real size of the RAF proved costly to the *Luftwaffe*; the British overestimate on 15 September proved a great morale booster to the British public, and the date passed into legend as a miracle almost to rival Dunkirk.

But it was not a miracle. There were more secular reasons for the RAF's success. British Intelligence, having cracked Goering's code, knew what his orders were almost as soon as his own air staff. The engineering and specifications of British planes, too, were generally superior to the German, and radar was being rapidly developed to help by locating German aircraft even before they crossed the British coast. Furthermore, unlike Goering, himself an air ace of the First World War – where he fought as one of Baron Richtofen's 'circus' – British air leaders like Sir Hugh 'Stuffy' Dowding and later Air-Marshal 'Bomber' Harris were fully aware of the changed conditions brought about by modern technology, and were not so much 'knights of the air', jousting man-to-man in fair combat, as efficient organisers, planners and businessmen managing a formidable defence machine in every detail. One of them, and perhaps the least known, was Sir Keith Park, an abrasive, workaholic New Zealander, who made an enormous contribution to the Battle of Britain by his brilliant organising of the defence of the whole of south-east Britain (including London) from his 11 Group Fighter Command HQ in Uxbridge.

But it must not be denied that the young men of the RAF were worthy of their legend. The encouragement and help the elite 'Few' gave to their willing partners, their wry self-deprecating humour and their perpetual nonchalance was in marked contrast to the proud self-importance of the *Luftwaffe* aircrews. The achievements of all of them in a great time of crisis justified the admiration with which they were regarded. At the same time the legend of the 'Few' remains a legend. As the French writer Georges Bernanos said in his *Letter to the English* (Rio de Janeiro 1942; French edition 1946), it was 'a fairy tale, a tale that no serious adult could possibly understand – a children's tale'.

5:11

Barbarossa: Did Hitler Forget About the Russian Winter?

Hitler's armies invaded Russia in June 1941. By December his armies had come to a halt, paralysed by the onset of winter. Historians often take the line that the Germans had ignored the Russian winter in making their preparations, and that their lack of meteorological knowledge amounted to gross negligence. But this view is, in fact, a major error.

The Germans were well aware that Russia suffered from cold winters. Hitler, who had an amateur knowledge of history, knew of the fate of Charles XII and of the disaster that befell Napoleon. Nor was the German High Command completely foolish. Its meteorologists were conscious of Russia's extreme variations of temperature. They knew, too, that in an average Russian winter only January and February were likely to bring frost extreme enough to halt hostilities, and the generals planned to have brought the campaign to a successful conclusion by December. Of course, they were delayed by the Balkan campaign; on the other hand the meteorologists discounted the notion of a particularly severe winter ahead. The winters of 1939/40 (the winter of the Finnish War) and 1940/41 had both been uncommonly severe with intense cold well below the Russian winter averages; the meteorologists assured the High Command that three winters in a row of such severity had not been recorded since serious weather observations had begun in the seventeenth century, and that the chances of a third exceptional winter in 1941/42 were virtually negligible.

So Hitler expected that the main operations would be over before the worst of the winter. It was not to be. Winter came early and with great severity. Snow fell and settled in October as it often does, but on 13 November a temperature of –23°C was recorded (7°C lower than the mean minimum for January). On 5 December the temperature fell to –38°C, unusual even by

Russian standards. This set the weather scene for the rest of the winter. It halted the German advance, froze the oil and petrol in tanks and transport, caused widespread frostbite among the thinly clad German troops and enabled the somewhat better equipped Russians to counter-attack. Of course, there were other reasons why the German offensive had ground to a halt, but had the early Russian winter been an average one the Germans might have been able to carry on their offensive well into December, and the whole course of the war might have been changed.

Average temperatures in Moscow (°C)

	Maximum	Minimum
November	1.5	−3.3
December	−4.5	−9.5
January	−9.3	−16.2
February	−5.7	−13.6

6

HISTORICAL RE-EVALUATIONS

The Fall of the Bastille, 1789: How Significant Was It?

The Bastille was the royal fortress overshadowing the working-class district of Saint-Antoine in eastern Paris in the years down to the French Revolution. Was the existence of the Bastille the threat to the people of Paris that they thought it was, and did the fall of the fortress merit the enormous importance that was attached to it?

The Bastille had an exterior court generally open to the public, but it was nevertheless a formidable strongpoint, and could easily be garrisoned against the Parisian citizenry. Built at the end of the fourteenth century as a defence against the English, it had been transformed into a state prison in the reign of Charles VI, and was still spoken of as a sinister place of imprisonment. It had eight round stone towers, each with walls 5 feet thick; its battlements and platforms were supplied with batteries of artillery – nearly thirty heavy 8-pounder cannon and rather more than a dozen smaller pieces; there was a large powder magazine and arsenal, and it was believed (mistakenly, as it happened) to be the depot of a large supply of small arms and ammunition. It was thought in 1789 to house large numbers of prisoners of state. There were known to be deep, dank subterranean dungeons, their walls slimy with filth, and other cells up under the roof where the prisoners froze in winter and stifled in summer.

In fact, there were only seven prisoners detained there in July 1789, and the garrison of 82 military pensioners had only recently been reinforced by a draft of 32 extra men from a Swiss regiment. Initially, the defecting soldiers and the mob of citizens who attacked the Bastille on 14 July merely intended to arm themselves with muskets from its magazine and to neutralise the threat from its heavy guns, but the Governor, de Launay, refused their demands, and a lengthy stalemate resulted. They eventually forced open the outside gates, but then declined to enter, thinking that this was a trick by de Launay to get them to come in so that his artillery pieces could mow them down. Before the end of the day, patience had worn thin on both sides. De Launay contemplated firing his whole stock of about 300 barrels of powder, which would have demolished the whole fortress and the greater part of the entire district, but by evening decided to surrender instead with promises of safe conduct. Most of the garrison, nevertheless, were butchered; the Governor himself was hauled out, abused and finally kicked, bayoneted and shot, his head sawn off with a convenient pocket-knife and paraded on a pike.

The attack had shown that the Bastille was no more than a token of royal supremacy over Paris, and that its reality was much less frightening than its threat. The whole fortress, however, was literally torn stone from stone until it simply ceased to exist; even its plans were destroyed, so that its only representations either then or at present are purely fictional reconstructions. Even so, 14 July still remains one of France's great national holidays.

6:2

Did the Women March in the 'March of the Women', 1789?

The 'March of the Women' was instrumental in bringing back to the capital city, Paris, from their palace at Versailles, the King, the Queen and their son and daughter, or, as they were good-humouredly called, the 'baker, the baker's wife and the baker's little family'. The March has entered into legend as one of the turning points of the Revolution, but was it really, as its name suggests, a march of the women?

It was bread shortages in Paris that provided the underlying explanation of the affair. The harvest of 1789 was a good one, but the threshing and the slow transportation by wagon of the grain to the cities took time, and foodstuffs were desperately short. Farmers, too, had been hanging on to their stocks, hoping for price rises, and corn-dealers and bakers in Paris had been making the most of the shortage through higher bread prices. As bread queues lengthened, tempers shortened. Many Parisians believed that the King was simply out of touch with the situation, and that, if he knew about their plight, he would speedily take steps to put things right. The Paris Commune demanded urgent action by the National Assembly, also at Versailles. Numbers of popular newspapers such as Marat's *Ami du Peuple*, took up the cry to transfer the court and the Assembly to Paris.

The crowning episode sparking the affair was the summoning by the King of the Flanders regiment to Versailles to provide security against the threat of violence from the Parisians. When it arrived, it was given a banquet of official welcome in the Opera House, where the King and Queen mingled among the guests. Counter-revolution was cheered, black cockades worn, and tricolour ones and other revolutionary symbols were trampled underfoot. Rumours of these outrages were magnified in Paris, which simmered with dissatisfaction.

About 5,000 market women (or *poissards*, as they were known) gathered together in Paris and decided to march on Versailles. As they tramped along the Paris *quais*, they chanted their intention of bringing back to Paris '*le bon papa*'. They were in a good enough humour, but underlying the affectionate abuse there was an undeniable note of menace. Some of the 'women', true to the carnival atmosphere of the occasion, sported beards and moustaches and were in fact men in female attire, but most of the protesters joined the procession properly dressed as men, and brought with them their weapons so as to give strength to the occasion. These men were joined by some of the Bastille Volunteers and detachments of the National

Guard, nominally under the command of Lafayette, though they were commanding him, rather than he them. They also took with them pikes, muskets and even cannon. Something like 20,000 demonstrators were in the march, trudging about twelve miles to Versailles in the pouring rain. It was evening when they invaded the palace and the Assembly.

Louis, who had been out hunting at Meudon, rushed back to the palace to deal with the situation. He countermanded the military preparations that were under way, and after many hesitations, decided to agree to the demonstrators' demands. He promised measures to provision the capital, placed himself under the protection of the French Guards, and sanctioned the August decrees and the Declaration of Rights. He even agreed to speak to representatives of the mob, and met a small delegation of them headed by a well-spoken young market girl called Pierrette Chabry. She was quite overcome by the occasion, and fainted at his feet; the King – perhaps disliking public speaking quite as much as she did – revived her with his own bottle of smelling salts.

There were ugly scenes the next day, when two members of the King's bodyguard were murdered, and the Queen herself escaped with her life only by fleeing from her bedroom and taking refuge with Louis in his. The crowd took up the cry of 'The King to Paris!' and finally the royal family agreed to go back with the demonstrators to the capital, where they were afterwards installed in the Tuileries Palace. The move had the effect of thereafter depriving Louis of his freedom of action and placing the monarchy under the control of Paris, while at the same time putting Paris in charge of the Revolution.

There can be no dispute, therefore, over the historical importance of the 'March of the Women', though it is more doubtful exactly how much it owed to any women who took part in it. Legend, on the other hand, gives them the credit for it, and this is now part of its history.

6:3

Who Were the Revolutionary Mob?

During the Terror of 1793, the Parisian 'mob' played a major role. They are often reckoned to have been violent and unpredictable, a mixture of the capital's ruffians and layabouts together with the rougher elements of the adjacent countryside who had recently drifted into the city to find food and work. They are characterised by the ferociously bloodthirsty tricoteuses ('knitting women') who sat knitting at the foot of the guillotine to howl their derision at the 'aristos' as they were executed. The mob are sometimes referred to by their name of canaille *('dogstuff'), and have generally been the object of a good deal of vilification. But is this view of the character of the revolutionary mob a historically accurate one?*

There is not much doubt that they were freakish in appearance. Many of the men sported extravagant moustaches, with bushy sideburns and long unkempt locks; they wore revolutionary rosettes and other favours, carried a variety of weapons and generally behaved in a wild and threatening fashion.

But they were not scum. Many of them were solidly working class, with a good sprinkling of those who were better than they pretended to be – small employers, journalists, minor civil servants, clerks, shopkeepers, and even a few wine merchants and wholesalers. Some still wore the tight breeches of the middle and upper classes, but more of them wore the loose trousers of the labouring class – hence the name sans-culotte. There was an inverted snobbery about being a sans-culotte; many quite substantial individuals mingled with them and affected their dress and behaviour. The genuine sans-culotte lived in apartments on the fourth or fifth floor of lodging houses, where, on account of all the stairs that had to be climbed, rents were lower than on the lower floors. Many took an active part in the affairs of the local Jacobin Club in their *Section* of the city.

There were among them wildly radical leaders known as *enragés* ('mad dogs') with extremist views like those of Jacques

René Hébert, who eventually succeeded in his aim of abolishing the French Church. Some wanted price controls in the Law of the Maximum and one, Francis Noël ('Gracchus') Baboeuf anticipated later socialist theories. So outrageous were the views of the *enragés* that they antagonised mainstream Jacobins such as Robespierre, whose thinking did not go much further than petty bourgeois individualism; and early in 1793 many of them were purged. A number of them were women activists, but they all shared in the eclipse of extremism at this time. But the articulate members of the mob were not members of the lower social orders at all; in order to have ideas and be able to express them in public it was necessary to have a smattering of education, and not to be really of the 'mob'. As the historian George Rudé put it: 'It appears to have been a feature of the more organised political movements . . . that the driving elements were the small shopkeepers and workshop masters, who brought their journeymen and apprentices along with them.'

Hence the traditional view of a chiefly lower-class mob is something of a myth.

6:4

Who Really Won the Battle of Waterloo?

The fame of the Duke of Wellington was greatly enhanced by his victory at Waterloo. But to many Europeans, and especially Prussian and German historians, Waterloo was won not by Wellington but by Blücher, the Prussian commander. Although recognition of Wellington as the victor is largely confined to British historians, the Continental view does not stand up to close scrutiny, and to claim Blücher as the victor is undoubtedly an error.

On 18 June 1815, on a site one and a half miles south of the village of Waterloo, Napoleon fought and lost his last battle. The victory enhanced the already considerable reputation of the victorious Duke of Wellington. He, with inferior forces, two-thirds of whom were foreigners, withstood bombardments and hand-to-hand fighting of a ferocity that not even his Peninsular veterans had seen equalled. There were moments when Wellington had admitted that it had been 'a damned close thing'. But by late afternoon Blücher's Prussian troops began pouring onto the battlefield, and Wellington took the offensive, abandoning his defensive positions and pursuing the demoralised French army off the field until his exhausted troops were called to halt, and the pursuit was taken up by the eager Prussians. Continental historians have not, in general, supported the British view that Waterloo was Wellington's victory. They have taken the line that Blücher and his Prussians saved Wellington from destruction, and thus the victory was Blücher's not Wellington's.

In the first place the Prussians argued that, had it not been for Blücher's promise to link up with Wellington after the Prussian defeat at Ligny, Wellington would not have dared to fight at Waterloo at all. Napoleon had planned to destroy his enemies separately and both leaders were determined not to allow that to happen. But Wellington had given himself two options: he would fight to defend Brussels, twelve miles to the north, and if that failed, and if the Prussians were delayed or defeated, he would withdraw his forces in good order to the west to rejoin his ships. He did not fight at Waterloo by accident. In many ways the ridge of Mont St Jean which he chose to defend was similar to the ridges he had defended in the Peninsula where the disparity between French and Allied forces was even greater than at Waterloo. And he had chosen this ridge several days before, suggesting that whatever happened to the Prussians he had chosen a place to make a stand.

The French assault was delayed by the muddy state of the ground from recent thunderstorms. At first the French concentrated on Wellington's right flank around the farm of Hougoumont. But this was a diversion. At one o'clock the main French attack occurred against Wellington's centre. By now Napoleon was aware that the defeated Prussian army had not been fleeing east but had eluded Grouchy's army of 33,000 men and was now within sight of the battlefield. Napoleon had only about three or four hours to demolish Wellington before he would have to face the Prussians. This made him cautious about using all his reserves and in particular risking the Imperial Guard. Even so at three o'clock Napoleon tried again, and again the French were beaten off. This time Wellington might have turned to the offensive had not 2,000 of his best cavalry been mown down in overenthusiastic pursuit of the fleeing enemy. So far no Prussians had arrived on the battlefield but they could be seen advancing from the east, and Napoleon had to detach vital reserves under General Lobau to intercept them. At five o'clock Napoleon risked some, but not all, of the battalions of the Imperial Guard. For a moment it looked as if the British centre had been broken, but it held. It was Colburne's flanking cavalry attack, not the Prussians, which turned the tide. Prussian troops began moving into battle, at first a trickle, but by seven o'clock they had become a torrent. Wellington could now risk ordering a general advance, and exhausted British troops followed the fleeing French until the Prussians took over and turned the retreat into a rout.

So, of Blücher's army, all but a few advance contingents of Prussian troops had taken no part in the battle until the French were already in retreat. It was Wellington's army that had repulsed the French attacks, not Blücher's. It was Wellington who again showed how to hold on to a defensive position with inferior forces. The Prussian contribution was indirect rather than direct. The first sight of the Prussians away to the east in early afternoon must have boosted Allied morale. The non-arrival of Grouchy on the French right flank reduced Napoleon's attacking capability, and the pursuing Prussians prevented the French from regrouping. Without Blücher's promise Wellington might have found the opposing forces too great to risk battle, although it would have needed the arrival of Grouchy's troops to make that a likely decision. Blücher's warm congratulations to Wellington on the evening of the battle offer a more realistic view of the battle than those of Continental historians.

6:5

Did the Ems Telegram Cause the Franco-Prussian War in 1870?

In 1870, France and Prussia, the two most powerful military nations in Europe, met in the Franco-Prussian War, an episode characterised by one historian as a 'head-on collision'. France, its national pride nettled and its security threatened by the rapid growth of Prussian power and ambition, clashed with Prussia, whose leaders were anxious to save face and recover from a recent diplomatic rebuff received at the hands of the French government. Many people believe the immediate cause of the war was a telegram from the German emperor. Is this true?

The circumstances were as follows. Much against the wishes of his Minister-President, Otto von Bismarck, William I, King of Prussia, in the light of remonstrances made to him by Britain, Austria and France, advised his young relative Prince Leopold of Hohenzollern-Sigmaringen, a distant member of the royal house, to withdraw his candidature to the Spanish throne, which was at this time vacant. The candidature had seemed to the powers to threaten, however remotely, the balance of power, and in particular France, which might find itself threatened by a potentially hostile power on two fronts. Gratefully received in Europe generally, this withdrawal was trumpeted in the French press as a diplomatic triumph and an unmistakable snub for Prussia.

Bismarck was furious, especially since the King seemed unwilling to accept his advice on the matter, and threatened resignation. He was dining with two very senior military colleagues, von Moltke and von Roon, gloomily wondering how to recover lost face, when a telegram was delivered from King William, at that time taking the waters in Ems, a spa town on the Rhine. He had been badgered by the French Ambassador, Count Benedetti, for assurances that the Prussians would not permit the candidature to be renewed, and was now telegraphing back to his own government his refusal to provide these assurances.

With luck, Bismarck believed, the telegram could be made to serve his purposes. His aim was not to provoke a war with France (an error still widely believed) but to salvage a little of Prussia's pride, and to turn France's diplomatic victory into a diplomatic defeat. So he read the telegram aloud to his guests, and then, on the pretext that it was too long to be sent to the press unabridged, blue-pencilled substantial portions of the text. In the abbreviated version King William now appeared to say:

Count Benedetti spoke to me on the promenade in order to demand from me finally, in a very importunate manner, that I should authorise him to telegraph at once that I had bound myself for all future time never again to give my consent if the Hohenzollerns should renew their candidature. *I refused at last somewhat sternly, as it is neither right nor possible to undertake engagements of this kind for ever and ever. Naturally I told him that, as I had as yet received no news, and since he was earlier informed about Paris and Madrid than myself, he could clearly see that my Government once more had no hand in the matter. His Majesty has since received a letter from the Prince.* His Majesty *having told Count Benedetti that he was awaiting news from the Prince,* has decided *with regard to the above demand, upon the representation of Count Eulenburg and myself,* not to receive Count Benedetti again, *but only to* (and) let him be informed through an aide-de-camp that his Majesty *had now received from the Prince confirmation of the news which Benedetti had already received from Paris, and* had nothing further to say to the Ambassador. *His Majesty leaves it to your Excellency whether Benedetti's demand and its rejection should not be at once communicated both to our ambassadors and to the Press.*

Of course, the removal from the telegram of the words italicised above made the whole message appear much more brusque, and suggested that William I had given the imperial ambassador a flea in his ear. Its publication produced an immediate furore both in Paris and Berlin, and impelled the two governments within days in the direction of war.

The sending of the Ems Telegram cannot be said to have caused the Franco-Prussian War, but it certainly raised the diplomatic temperature in both countries. But Bismarck at this juncture wanted a diplomatic revenge rather than a military war. In any case France was not obliged to rise to Bismarck's provocation. Napoleon III, an ageing and a sick man, had the right instinct in wishing to turn aside from a final break with Prussia. But the Empress Eugénie was on the warpath, and the head of the French imperial government, the Duc de Gramont, threatened resignation if Napoleon III did not take up so clear a challenge. So war came; but it is quite mistaken to suppose that the Ems Telegram caused it.

6:6

Florence Nightingale: Was She the 'Lady with the Lamp'?

The image of Florence Nightingale as the angelic nurse caring for the maimed and the suffering in the military hospitals of the Crimean War gave rise to the legend of the 'Lady with the Lamp', a legend which appealed strongly to the British imagination in the mid-nineteenth century. Her very presence brought moral uplift to soldiers whose lives were sunk in filth and depravity, so that they kissed her shadow as she passed between their beds, thinking her a blessed saint. But in reality, the truth was far different.

For one thing, the 'Lady with the Lamp' was not the best-loved nurse of that particular war. That honour went to the Jamaican-born West Indian nurse Mary Seacole, who, on account of her selfless devotion to duty, was thought by British soldiers to be the true 'Mother of the Army'. Because so little was documented about her, she is now almost completely forgotten, though she was skilled and compassionate; indeed, the director of the Florence Nightingale museum at St Thomas's Hospital in London says of her that 'she deserves to stand alongside such contemporaries as Henri Dunant, the founder of the Red Cross'. Miss Nightingale on the other hand – contrary to her popular image – was a nursing reformer and the scourge of administrative lethargy and ineptitude rather than merely one of the bandage and bedpan brigade.

Indeed, for most of the time Florence Nightingale was not in the Crimea at all. While Nurse Seacole set up her own medical supply stores and treatment unit at Spring Hill, just five miles from the front at Sebastopol, and transported her own materials to the war zone, the hospital in which Miss Nightingale based herself was at Scutari, a suburb of Constantinople on the Asiatic side of the Bosphorus, to which many of the sick and wounded were shipped 200 miles across the Black Sea in a journey which should have taken four days, but which in bad weather might last two or three weeks.

Florence Nightingale saw herself not as the 'Lady with the Lamp' but as the avenging enemy of sloth and complacency in official quarters. Wounded officers were dismayed to see her sweep past them busily and without a word, absorbed in her problems. She was a worker of inexhaustible enthusiasm, and the sharp-tongued critic of opponents who were for the most part bumbling and slipshod. She had to contend with the abysmal standards and the low expectations of members of the nursing profession at that time, nearly all of them coarse, stolid and brutal in the style of Charles Dickens's Mrs Gamp. Far from welcoming Seacole on her arrival, Florence Nightingale, already established at Scutari with a team of thirty-eight nurses, snubbed her consistently and placed many obstacles in her path. Her hostility was perhaps more on social than on medical grounds. Seacole herself believed that Nightingale rejected her because she was black; besides, she thought she was looking either for ladies, who would be in charge, or for skivvies, who would do the hard work. Nurse Seacole fitted poorly into either category: she was no 'lady' (in Nightingale's narrow sense), but with a long and successful career behind her in nursing she was far too overqualified to be a skivvy. Rejection of Mary Seacole was one of the few things that Florence Nightingale and the military establishment could agree upon.

Otherwise, the military authorities and Florence Nightingale were constantly at loggerheads. In Scutari she was distracted by having to face the indescribable filth and squalor prevalent in her hospital and an almost complete lack of the most elementary necessities of nursing. She was not only aghast at the sufferings of the sick and wounded in her charge, dreadful though these were, but appalled at the breathtaking incompetence and indifference that pervaded both the War Office and the Army Medical Board which was supposed to be managing field hospitals during the war.

While never losing her composure, and without ever even so much as raising her voice, Florence Nightingale single-handedly revolutionised the organisation of military hospitals. She mercilessly harried her superiors in Britain and in the Crimea in her ceaseless efforts to get things done, bombarding them with an endless barrage of letters which she refused to let them ignore, and forcing them into the realisation that at least she, a mere woman, grasped the importance of the work to which they paid no attention. She pestered them until they came to dread the sound of her name. Although she was relatively frail, she worked harder than anybody, driving herself beyond human endurance in her self-imposed service.

She did herself find time briefly to undertake inspections of the field hospitals in the Crimea itself, though she largely ignored Nurse Seacole, who was already there. Conditions in the Crimea were even more dreadful than she expected. Serving army officers faced her with a blank wall of apathy and incomprehension. There was a total lack of cooperation from those supposed to be in authority, who took no notice of her and left her to her own devices, not even providing food or accommodation for her small party. She wore herself out over some weeks until she was stricken by fever and, semi-delirious, had to give up the work. Even then she refused to go back to England, and simply resumed her thankless toil at Scutari.

At the end of the war she was rewarded by public repute, by officialdom, the medical profession and even by Queen Victoria, who met her at Balmoral and presented to her the brooch specially designed for her by Prince Albert. But she found that a great deal of administrative reform still remained to be done. She ruined her own health in doing it, continuing with the same energy as before until she became an invalid. Her dominant aims throughout her life were for medical reform, for the improved treatment of patients and for the enhanced status and the better training of the nursing profession. She was awarded the Order of Merit in 1907, and died at the age of 90 in 1910.

6:7

Prince Albert: Statesman or Foreign Meddler?

Opinions about Albert, husband of Queen Victoria and Prince Consort of Britain, have varied enormously. His contemporaries gave him little respect, and after his death opinions even among historians have been highly controversial. Some have belittled him, regarding him as halfway between a busybody and a buffoon; others have accorded better recognition to his positive features. It is now possible to say that the rehabilitation of Prince Albert is almost complete.

Prince Albert, second son of the Duke of Saxe-Coburg-Gotha, was born in Germany in 1819 and, though a delicate child, grew up into a healthy young man, with good looks and bearing. In February 1840 he married the young Queen Victoria of Britain. Of average intelligence, the young prince was very Germanic in his bearing and rather priggish. His tutor, Baron Stockmar, supervised a somewhat superficial education – a smattering of Roman law, economics, history, philosophy, modern languages, music and science – and commented rather dourly on the prince's habit of 'not dwelling too long on a subject'. There is no doubt that the marriage had long been arranged – the young Queen is said to have had a free choice between Prince Albert and his elder brother – and this reflected the social ambition of the Saxe-Coburg family.

Albert made an unfortunate impression in Britain. He was awkward and tactless, and unwilling to change his rather rigid styles of thought. To perceptive English observers he appeared to be something of a careerist. The Queen had been advised not to share with him the powers or the responsibilities of monarchy, or to accord him any precedence in the House of Lords. Indeed, the Prime Minister, Melbourne, whose judgment the young Queen much admired and respected, had at first preferred a marriage match with the House of Orange, and regarded Albert unkindly, concurring, albeit reluctantly, in the House of Commons to a reduction of the Prince's allowance from £50,000 per annum to £30,000, a decision which the Prince primly denounced as 'a truly unseemly vote'.

Victoria, however, soon came to respect the Prince's judgment, which in many ways was a sound one. She found not only that his advice was good, but that he lightened the burden of her work. At the same time he had only the haziest grasp of the workings of the British constitution, and sometimes sought to interfere in matters not properly his concern. Palmerston, whose authoritarian and unpredictable foreign policies offended the Prince's sense of propriety, was often rather nettled by his influence over the Queen. The two soon came to read Foreign Office dispatches together line by line, and the Prince's views became ever more obvious in the Queen's attitudes. For example, Palmerston sympathised with the Italians in their struggle against Austria in 1848, but Albert and Victoria were both traditionally pro-Austrian, and objected to the tone of his dispatches to Vienna. In May of that year she refused to initial a dispatch, saying: 'The Queen returns this draft to Lord Palmerston which she thinks had better not be sent. It would be, in the Queen's opinion, unnecessarily irritating, and increasing the distrust with which they view our sentiments on the question without doing any good.' Palmerston, who thought he saw the influence of Albert in her refusal, replied to the Queen rather stiffly: 'Viscount Palmerston presents his humble duty to your Majesty and will, according to your Majesty's wishes, withhold the proposed dispatch.' But his irritation steadily increased, and he fell into the habit of sending dispatches to Victoria late, or when he knew she was going riding – even, in some cases, removing or ignoring her comments after the dispatches were returned. This conduct elicited from her a sharp rebuke in the Queen's Memorandum of 1850, in which she requested that 'her minister should state what he proposes to do' and directing that a measure sanctioned by the Queen 'should not be arbitrarily altered or modified by her minister'. Palmerston cheerfully concurred, but was soon doing the same thing again.

Friction between Palmerston and Albert, who had come to dislike him heartily, came to a head over the crisis resulting from the *Trent* affair in 1861, when the federal warship *San Jacinto* stopped a British steamer on the high seas and arrested two passengers bound from Havana to Southampton as accredited representatives of the US Confederate government. Palmerston, who was then Prime Minister, dispatched the Guards to Canada and was on the point of sending a curt and swingeing rebuke to Washington which might easily have led to war between the USA and Britain. Prompted by Albert, already suffering from the typhoid which was to kill him, Victoria toned down his dispatch, leaving the US government a tactful loophole to avoid the apology or the reparations on which Palmerston was inclined to insist:

> The Queen returns these important drafts, which upon the whole she approves, but she cannot help feeling that the main draft is somewhat meagre. She should have liked to have seen the expression of a hope that the American captain did not act under instructions, or, if he did, that he misapprehended them – the United States government must be fully aware that the British government could not allow its flag to be insulted, and the security of her communications to be placed in jeopardy. . . .

The federal government gratefully scrambled through the loophole she provided, leaving poor Captain Wilkes to carry the can for his 'excessive zeal'.

In retrospect, however, the views of the Prince seem modest and reasonable, and more in accord with Britain's interests than the excited and often synthetic indignation of Lord Palmerston. Victoria wished her husband to be known as the 'King Consort'. This idea, however, caused bitter resistance, and it was not until 1857 that, as a compromise, she conferred on him the title 'Prince Consort' by royal letters patent. Opposition to Albert sprang fundamentally from his misreading of his own and his Queen's constitutional rights in government, and also from the fact that he was a foreigner. As a German princeling of sometimes rather quaint views he aroused the latent insularity, if not the xenophobia, of the ruling classes in England in the nineteenth century. Victoria became ever more deeply attached to him and personally and politically dependent on him; and this is shown by the devastating loss and isolation she suffered at his death.

Albert may have been regarded by some of his contemporaries as something of a meddler in diplomatic and political matters, but there were other sides to his character. He showed himself genuinely interested in agriculture, industry and commerce, and was a notable patron of music and the arts. The Great Exhibition of 1851 was largely his creation. Always extremely conscientious, he wore himself out in his achievements, and this work helped to undermine his strength and render him vulnerable to the disease that finally killed him. His own generation, except perhaps for his wife, regarded him as unqualified and pushy, but history has come to assess him more generously.

6:8

Did the Civil War Bring US Slavery to an End?

It is sometimes said that the US Civil War brought about the end of slavery in the United States, and that this outcome was something that would not otherwise have happened. On the other hand, some American scholars have maintained that slavery, as an economic system, was already doomed, and would not have survived even without the Civil War to bring about its abolition. This is a controversy that has raged for more than a century, and which still goes on. Is it possible to bring it to a conclusion now?

There is no doubt about the importance of slavery to the states of the pre-war South. Leaving aside the cultivation of sugar and tobacco, the massive boom in cotton production in the first half of the nineteenth century was striking evidence of its importance at that time. Cotton output went up from about 100,000 bales per year to over 4.5 million bales between 1820 and 1860, while raw cotton exports topped the export list, chiefly to British mills in Lancashire. In 1860 the population of the Southern states was about 9 million, of whom about 4 million were slaves. At the same time, slavery was not evenly spread; it tended to be concentrated in the cotton-growing districts, where there had been little advance in mechanised methods of agriculture. Only 50,000 Whites owned slaves; of these, about 8,000 owned more than 50 slaves. It was this cotton area that was the heart of the US slave dominion; but perhaps by 1860 the economic situation was changing.

For one thing, the importance of the South was declining, and the expanding west proved a much more powerful magnet for immigration and resources. At the same time, cotton proved an exhausting crop to produce, and wore out the soil quite quickly. Cotton prices, furthermore, did not rise much on the markets: prices had risen by about 5 per cent per year before 1860, but by this year the rise had diminished to less than 1 per cent. The price of slaves rose much faster. The effect of this was to force the plantation owners to look more closely at mechanisation as a means of easing their labour problems. Such statistics reveal that slavery was doomed to die anyway.

Economic historians have examined closely the conditions prevalent in the antebellum South in recent studies. Conrad and Meyer, writing in 1956, took the view that slavery was at least as profitable an investment as any other; the rise in the prices of female slaves shows that owners expected slavery to continue along with an increase in the value of their slave estate. Fogel and Engerman, in 1974, reinforced this opinion: they tried to show that slave economies were efficient and economic, and that overall conditions for slaves at work were improving as owners recognised their value. Efforts have been made to extrapolate statistics to show how slavery could have been the basis of a flourishing Southern economy even after the Civil War.

But there is always a good deal of guesswork in such predictions. The continuing growth of the US economy, its diversification into new products, the improved transport network – even the appearance of new types of fabrics – produced new trends in the statistics that could never have been accurately predicted. Perhaps the current rise in slave prices would not have been maintained after 1860, especially when cotton prices were failing to advance.

The basic question remains: is slave labour ever likely to be more efficient than free labour? Slavery tends to retard mechanisation and to act as a brake on technological innovation, as well as providing little incentive for effort to the workforce. There are many reasons for thinking that slavery had a poor outlook in America after the Civil War: the state of the market in cotton and its overall price-levels were not likely to improve much; the North and the west were beginning to grow much more rapidly, with massive immigration and considerable technological improvement, while the South seemed to be stuck in a time warp. Its economy in 1860 was seriously unbalanced; it was based on a poor and unenterprising workforce whose aggregate demand would never amount to a mass market, and the country's wealth was gravely maldistributed between a small number of rich property owners and the bulk of the impoverished many. The truth seems to be that slavery in the South had little future and was about to enter into terminal decline, whether the Civil War had taken place or not.

6:9

Who Should Take the Blame for the Fall of Khartoum, Gladstone or Gordon?

The death of General Gordon in the Sudan in 1885 was blamed at the time, and by many historians since, on the obstinacy, tardiness and deliberate policy of the then Prime Minister, W.E. Gladstone. But, in fact, Gordon's fate was determined, not by Gladstone, but by Gordon himself, and by his would-be rescuer, Lord Wolseley. Gladstone's contribution was his delay in sending a force to rescue Gordon, but Gordon should not have got himself into a situation requiring a relief force in the first place, and Gladstone's delay was not the vital factor in the relief force's failure to reach Khartoum in time.

In 1883 a nationalist tribal leader and Muslim fanatic styling himself the 'Mahdi' overran most of the Sudan, apart from the areas still under the control of Egyptian garrisons. At the end of the year General Hicks and his army were destroyed by the Mahdi's forces. After some hesitation the British government decided to send General Gordon to report on the situation. Rather than withdraw he decided to stay and fight it out. The Mahdi invested Khartoum; it fell on 26 January 1885, Gordon was killed, and the relief force sent by the British government arrived two days later.

This tragic episode raises a number of questions. The outrageous suggestion that Gordon was addicted to the bottle has no evidence to support it but a good deal of evidence to the contrary. What is much more arguable consists of four main issues: Why did the government send Gordon to the Sudan, and was Gladstone the prime mover in sending him? Why did Gordon ignore his instructions and make a stand in Khartoum? Why did Gladstone hold out so long against sending a relief force, and was he therefore responsible for the fact that it arrived too late?

General Charles Gordon honed his military skills during the 1860s against the Taiping rebels in China. His work there enhanced his reputation and gave him his appointment as General by the grateful Chinese authorities. His country, however, tended to employ him on more menial tasks, and it was not until 1873 that he first went to the Sudan as Governor of the equatorial provinces and then as Governor-General of the whole of the Sudan. When the revolt of the Mahdi led to the destruction of Hicks Pasha and his army and threatened the remaining Egyptian garrisons in the Sudan, the government was faced with a decision. It should not have been a difficult one. Gladstone's government rejected Disraeli's imperialism and intended only to retain a British presence in Egypt until the Khedive had introduced effective government there. If Egypt was to be given up there was obviously no point in hanging on to the Sudan. But not all of Gladstone's government agreed with the notion of withdrawal. The imperialist wing of the Liberal Party led by Lord Hartington wanted to explore the possibility of preserving British influence in Egypt, and this would involve trying to maintain a presence in the Sudan. It really depended on how strong the Mahdi was, and what show of force would be necessary to keep him at bay.

As Gordon's service in the Sudan made him an expert in the area, the government had already in early December 1883 consulted Sir Evelyn Baring, Britain's Consul-General in Egypt, about sending Gordon on a fact-finding mission to the Sudan. Baring had clashed with Gordon before, and twice made clear his opposition to Gordon's appointment. But a newspaper campaign, which may well have been orchestrated by Liberal imperialists, gathered momentum in the following month, and Gladstone was persuaded to ask Baring's opinion again. A small group of ministers, meeting as a committee, agreed to ask Gordon to go to the Sudan and to report on the situation there. Most of these ministers were on the imperialist wing of the Liberal Party, and if sending Gordon was a mistake, they, rather than Gladstone, must bear the responsibility for it. But their choice of Gordon does not mean that they were secretly trying to manoeuvre their colleagues and Gladstone into maintaining the Sudan garrisons. Gordon was chosen because, although he publicly stated that he would like to hold on to the Sudan if possible, his military experience and his local knowledge seemed ideal for the task in hand. Moreover, his reputation for ruthless efficiency did not necessarily mean that he would be unable to organise a defensive withdrawal, and a withdrawal was his specific instruction from the committee and to which he agreed. Obedience to this instruction was what Gladstone and the government had a right to expect.

But no sooner had Gordon arrived in Egypt than the Khedive appointed Gordon as Governor-General of the Sudan. Thus his mission from the British government was to report and evacuate, while what the Khedive, from whom Gordon now took direct orders, wanted him to do was not clear. Accepting the Khedive's commission could well mean an unacceptable conflict of interest; Baring's reservations about Gordon seem to have been justified. Gordon did not see any conflict of interest. He was the man on the spot; lack of effective communications would mean that Gordon would need on occasions to take the initiative and make important decisions. His assessment was that the Mahdi's popularity was a very temporary thing, that a British presence in the Sudan was necessary to protect the isolated Egyptian garrisons, and that British and Indian troops could soon dispose of the Mahdi and his forces. But the British government, still expecting Gordon to carry out his instructions, withdrew what British troops were left in the Sudan. Khartoum was soon closely besieged, and Gordon's only hope was a powerful British relief force. The British Prime Minister, Gladstone, was not happy about the invidious position in which Gordon's disobedience of orders had placed the British government. Gladstone was no pragmatist. He could not adapt to changing circumstances, and once he had made up his mind he believed that those who opposed him had the basest, or at best the most mistaken, motives. Gladstone resisted public pressure for some time, even when the Queen played an active role in it. Eventually, with the greatest of reluctance, and believing from the nature of Gordon's dispatches that the situation was less serious than was actually the case, Gladstone agreed to send a relief force. Lord Hartington's threat to resign from the Cabinet helped him make up his mind. In August Lord Wolseley was appointed to command the expedition and it arrived in Egypt in early September, four and a half months before Khartoum was to fall. From Cairo to Khartoum is about 800 miles.

Wolseley had about 10,000 of the best British and Indian troops, and he planned to embark them on a flotilla of ships, using the Nile river to avoid a long and arduous desert march. It was not until the middle of November that Wolseley realised that the river approach had to be abandoned as the river had become too shallow for the cataracts to be negotiated. The Nile is usually at its lowest in the autumn. As the expedition had not been sufficiently equipped for the whole force to make a long march across the desert, another long delay occurred. It took nearly six weeks to find enough camels. Lord Wolseley set off at the very end of December and arrived at Khartoum too late. Gordon's death forced only a very temporary change of government policy, because the government ordered Wolseley to evacuate the Sudan as originally planned.

The delay in sending Wolseley was due to the fact that Gladstone, of all prime ministers, would not allow government policies to be changed by wilful subordinates. On Gladstone, therefore, descended the blame for the disaster. But Gladstone's delay did not in itself determine Gordon's fate. Had Wolseley prepared an overland advance in the first place he would have arrived at Khartoum several weeks before and not two days after Gordon's death. And while Gladstone and Wolseley must share some of the responsibility, the main blame must attach to the man who disobeyed orders, who disbelieved reliable reports, and refused to take the opportunity to escape while an escape route was still open. The excoriating attacks on Gladstone after Gordon's death were, therefore, unjustified.

6:10

Parnell and the O'Shea Divorce Case: A Case of Victorian Prudery?

The British reputation for 'fair play' has a long and mainly praiseworthy history, but it is in fact a myth. This myth has been exploded on numerous occasions, but one of the most dramatic occurred in 1890 when the Irish leader Charles Stuart Parnell was brought down by a combination of moral rectitude and political vindictiveness. Parnell's ruin effectively scotched any chance that Ireland might have had to move peacefully further along the road to semi-independence and Home Rule. The affair effectively exploded the myth of British fair play and common sense, since its disastrous outcome was out of all proportion to the gravity of the moral offences which led to it. For many years historians judged that Parnell had only himself to blame for what occurred; only a century later can we begin to ignore the shock and outrage that the affair produced at the time, and see the tragedy for what it really was.

In 1889 Charles Stuart Parnell was at the height of his political career. Since 1878 he had been leader of the Irish Party in the British House of Commons, and his political honesty and personal integrity had recently been vindicated when incriminating letters, alleged to have been written by him, but in fact composed by a man called Richard Pigott, were proved to have been forgeries. Up to this time Parnell's private life had not been a matter of public comment. It was known to a number of Parnell's friends and political colleagues that, from 1880, he had been living with Kitty O'Shea, the wife of Captain W.H. O'Shea, an Irish Member of Parliament. O'Shea was an ex-officer of the Hussars and a man of extravagant and dissolute habits. He left politics in 1886, and might have sued for divorce soon after, but failed to do this. Part of the cause of his inaction may have been that he did not wish to embarrass Parnell personally, or the Irish cause generally, during Parnell's political crisis years of 1887–9; more likely, it was due to hopes of sharing in Kitty's expected inheritance from an aunt. When this inheritance failed to materialise, or for whatever reason, O'Shea delayed his divorce petition until November 1890. He cited his wife for adultery and Parnell as co-respondent, and thus wittingly or unwittingly ruined all the main characters in the drama, including himself. Why should this divorce petition have brought Parnell's career so abruptly to an end?

At first it seemed that the affair had done no great political damage. At the end of November Parnell was unanimously re-elected leader of the Irish parliamentary party, and Gladstone had said that the leadership was a matter for the Irish to decide. But all soon changed. The English Liberal Party depended for much of its support on the votes of nonconformist Scotland. To nonconformists adultery and divorce were sins, and therefore anathema; to Roman Catholics divorce was anathema because marriage was a sacrament; to Anglicans divorce was a scandal and a disgrace. It may well be that the Victorians had double standards: they indulged in their private lives and they abstained in their public lives, but they vigorously drove from public life any who offended their moral standards. Perhaps it was fortunate for Gladstone that his well-intentioned forays to save the souls of London's prostitutes were not more widely known.

Three days before the Irish Party re-elected its leader Harcourt told Gladstone that, if Parnell won, all cooperation between the Irish Party and the Liberals would be at an end. The day before the election Gladstone informed Parnell by letter that his re-election would have 'disastrous consequences'. Parnell either did not receive or certainly did not read the letter. When informed of it on the evening after the election he refused to resign, merely commenting that he had expected Gladstone to attack him. Whereupon Gladstone published the letter. Parnell was now alone. As a Protestant he could not expect support from the Roman Catholic Church. Indeed, as early as 1882 the Pope had forbidden faithful Roman Catholics to contribute to a fund for Parnell's personal support; it could hardly rally to him now, when his sin was not only being a Protestant but a scandalous one at that. Not surprisingly the Irish bishops publicly condemned him.

The Times set itself up as the guardian of moral standards and extracted its revenge for its humiliation by Parnell over the Pigott forgery. His colleagues abandoned him in early December and elected Justin McCarthy in his place. The general public supported the almost universal chorus of disapproval, perhaps subconsciously feeling that being sanctimonious conferred upon it a saintliness it strove after but did not always live up to. Gladstone was renowned for being self-righteous, and in Victorian society he had many, and often less worthy, imitators. Parnell battled on for nine months. Twenty-six of his Party continued faithful to him. But it was a losing battle that ended with Parnell's premature death in October 1891.

Parnell was not alone in being hounded from public life through scandal. There were a number of others: Sir Charles Dilke was also ruined by a messy divorce scandal in 1885, even though, unlike Parnell, he was not even a guilty party, and fair play gave way to a vindictive and rigid morality. The British have, in the twentieth as well as the nineteenth century, expected high moral standards from their politicians. Victorian prudery gave this expectation an extra dimension.

6:11

Edwardian England: A Golden Age?

The age of King Edward VII in England is often regarded as the country's 'Golden Age' of influence and prosperity. But is this judgment entirely a fair or accurate one? Part of the explanation for the 'Golden Age' idea must lie in the sentimental reverence that was accorded to the decade after the First World War and the dismal 1920s. After so spectacular a start, what followed in the twentieth century turned out to be a bitter disappointment for the British people.

The Edwardian decade marked the zenith of the British Empire and was hymned by the stirring patriotic verse of Rudyard Kipling and the equally grandiose music of Sir Edward Elgar.

The British presence in India, always a matter of great pride and moment in the Viceroyalty of Lord Curzon, soon culminated in the Great Durbar of 1911, when the new sovereign, George V, together with his Queen, visited the subcontinent in great pomp and was installed as Emperor of India. Britain at the same time abandoned in its foreign policy the traditional isolationist stance in respect of diplomatic alliances and became a major European player in the Triple Entente it formed with France and Russia. Already the possessor of a navy that had ruled the seas for upwards of a century, Britain embarked on a vast programme of naval rearmament, reinforcing its world reputation for riches and influence with one for irresistible armed might.

At home, the Edwardian Age was synonymous with ease and luxury. Great families lived in fine houses in the country's cities, and owned palatial mansions and vast estates in the countryside, attended by fifty or more domestic servants and many more estate workers. Their food, supplied from their own gardens and prepared by the hands of their own kitchen staff, was varied and always plentiful. Their smallest whim was catered for. One leisured gentleman even insisted that his newspaper should be lightly ironed of a morning so that it did not reach his breakfast table creased. Together, this ruling class created some of the most impressive domestic architecture and the noblest public buildings in Europe in an age noted for the splendour of its arts and the glitter of its entertainment.

But the age was fundamentally based on an inequality that stemmed in the main from the maldistribution of its income. Ranking below the classes living in luxury there were the modest bourgeois, and supporting groups of clerks and artisans, in ever meaner ranks down to the very dregs of Edwardian society. There were many for whom the careless sixpenny tip from a 'gent' was more than they could expect to earn in an hour or even, in the case of domestics, in a day. These included men who worked on the docks and recently had struck for the famous 'Dockers' tanner', and women in their appalling tenements who earned no more than a penny a dozen for scraping clean the skins of dead rabbits or a penny a hundred for gluing together by hand paper bags for use in the retail trade. Their children were often dirty, ignorant and in rags and were usually hungry. In the absence of organised public welfare many in this underclass were dependent on the sporadic and grudging provision of private charities such as the Salvation Army or Dr Barnardo's Homes, at the mercy of sharp-eyed professional carers always desperately short of funds. And, within a few short years, the glaring cracks in the foundations of Britain's military and technological 'superiority' were to be made all too apparent.

So, for the great majority who always lived on the brink of penury and had nothing to look forward to in their old age except the workhouse, the Edwardian Age was not the Golden Age. Only in one sense was it an age of gold: it occurred before the advent of a paper currency and the intricate machinery of credit, with the golden sovereign in circulation and at the foundation of Britain's global dominance. Those who dealt in postwar paper might therefore look back on Edwardian times as the real Golden Age.

6:12

Lloyd George, the Father of the Welfare State?

Lloyd George was Britain's Chancellor of the Exchequer from 1906 to 1915 and he is usually credited with laying the foundations of Britain's welfare state during those formative years. This interpretation is over-generous and erroneous. Lloyd George did not have in mind the creation of a welfare state, nor were his reforms so sweeping as is often supposed.

The attitude of the Liberals to destitution had traditionally been to encourage self-help and thrift, since state intervention merely subsidised idleness and dependency. This was not entirely Lloyd George's view. He had a genuine concern for the less fortunate. The researches of Booth and Rowntree (among others) had touched the social conscience of the late Victorians and Lloyd George was determined to address the worst social evils of his day. He believed that where self-help and thrift were insufficient the state should become involved to plug the gaps. That it was necessary for him to wean his own colleagues away from *laisser-faire* attitudes is demonstrated by the fact that every social measure that he proposed encountered obstruction and opposition from Cobdenite traditionalists on his own side. He had, therefore, to proceed cautiously. Anyway, a welfare state savoured of socialism, a philosophy with which Lloyd George was not in sympathy. He visited Germany in 1908 partly to see how to tackle social evils effectively, but also to see how German welfare reform had spiked the socialist guns. He wanted to help the poor but he did not want to turn Britain into a socialist state. In the event Lloyd George's reforms, coupled with the financially crippling effect of the Osborne judgment, which undermined trade union financing of Britain's new Labour Party and stunted its early growth. In any case, this new party could hardly be called a true socialist party. So with the aim of stealing a march on socialism Lloyd George's reforms were effective. Were they also effective in his other aim of providing a safety net for the poor?

There is no general answer to this. Each reform had a qualified measure of success, but some were much more productive than others. The School Meals Act of 1906 permitted local authorities to provide free school meals to needy children. After a slow start the number benefiting from the free meals reached 150,000 by 1914; the number of needy children was probably well in excess of 1 million, and the Act was only permissive. The compulsory medical inspection of schoolchildren in 1907 led to many local authority reports about the prevalence of under-nourishment and rickets, but no remedies were provided except possibly for the endemic headlice. The Mines Act of 1908 was a landmark in that it was the first to limit the working hours of adult males in any industry, but the Shops Act, while legislating for mealtimes and half-holidays, failed to address the question of shop hours.

Labour exchanges (1909) brought employers seeking workers and workers seeking employment more easily into contact, and saved the unemployed the long and fruitless tour of workplaces in search of work. Its aim of increasing mobility of labour had some success occupationally but very little geographically.

Lloyd George's greatest triumph was the Old Age Pensions Act of 1908. This had wide, but not universal, cross-party support, and had been initiated by Asquith. The 5s non-contributory pension (7s 6d for married couples) did not commence until seventy years of age – Lloyd George ruled out giving it at sixty-five on the grounds of expense. Qualification for the pension was hedged with numerous exclusions, some of which were lifted before 1914. It was also means-tested so stringently that the combined pension and other income of those qualifying inevitably fell below the poverty line. The purpose was not to keep the aged out of the workhouse; the aged, unlike the able-bodied, were entitled to outdoor relief, and in fact the number of workhouse inmates fell by only 1 per cent to 3 per cent per annum in the years 1909–14. But the number of over-seventies on outdoor relief fell from 170,000 in 1908 to fewer than 10,000 in 1914. It looks as if the old age pension merely replaced local poor relief with national state aid, but where the pension supplemented the income of the aged it often reduced the financial burden on the immediate relatives. It would be churlish to be too critical; with increasing longevity the numbers benefiting rose rapidly and expenditure on pensions greatly exceeded Lloyd George's original estimates. And expectations had always been realistic; only in the late twentieth century was it ever mooted, and that briefly, that old age pensions should on their own provide an adequate standard of living.

The other great social achievement of Lloyd George was the Insurance Act of 1911. The provisions for health looked far-reaching. Some 15 million workers were compulsorily included in a contributory health scheme which provided free medical care and sick pay. But many of the 15 million were covered already by their voluntary membership of health schemes run by Friendly Societies and trade unions. This scheme, therefore, topped up existing provision and used unions and Friendly Societies to run it. Yet it did not cover wives (except for maternity) and children. They continued to depend on Friendly Societies for their health care, and those who could not afford even the Friendly Societies' very modest subscriptions could always obtain treatment in the outpatients' department of the local free hospital. The lot of general practitioners working with the poor certainly improved. The low pay and insecurity of those working under contract for the Societies and unions ended with the introduction of medical panels to which general practitioners were to belong and by which they were to be properly remunerated. After the Act the number of outpatients' treatments fell and the number of hospital admissions increased – some indication that panel doctors were doing their job properly.

The insurance provisions of the Act were more limited. Contributory insurance against unemployment was to be provided in the major industries – engineering, building, shipbuilding, vehicle manufacture, iron founding, saw-milling – where unemployment was cyclical rather than structural. Thus it was intended as a cushion against temporary layoffs and not as a palliative for the long-term unemployed. Since unemployment pay was to be only 10s a week and sick pay 7s a week workers would, when unemployed or sick, be expected to supplement their state payments from their own resources if they wished to avoid the workhouse. There must have been some beneficial impact since, at a time (1911–14) of rising unemployment, workhouse numbers continued to fall. And the Act did make provision for other trades to be added; 2.3 million were covered in 1911 and the number had quadrupled by 1914.

The greatest disappointment of Lloyd George's work was the failure to reform the Poor Law itself. Both the majority and minority Poor Law Reports of 1909 recommended major changes, but nothing was done. John Burns, President of the Local Government Board, is usually saddled with the blame for the inertia, but too radical a departure from *laisser-faire* might have been too much for many Liberals to stomach. Lloyd George and his colleagues were patching up rather than sweeping away, and the Poor Law was too big an issue to tackle during the crisis years of 1909–11. After that other problems, both political and social, were more pressing. When the First World War ended in 1918 Lloyd George was absolutely dependent upon the Conservative majority in the House of Commons, so further major welfare reform was not really an option. Even so his Conservative-dominated government extended unemployment insurance to cover most industries: this had the unexpected and dramatic effect of undermining the Poor Law that the government had failed to reform in 1909. The Addison Housing Act of 1919 gave state subsidies for the building of houses by local authorities, and imposed on the local authorities the duty of providing such houses when the need was established; this was to supplement, not to replace, private building. And in the strike-ridden years 1919–21 Lloyd George was suspected of having more sympathy with the strikers than the Conservative MPs who kept him in power. Yet there was less need in the postwar years for Lloyd George to worry about his supporters' susceptibilities over *laisser-faire* when he had a Conservative majority rather than a Liberal one. Even so, the pre-war and postwar reforms did not amount to the setting up of a welfare state, and they were not intended as the precursor of one. But they marked the final abandonment of *laisser-faire* in social questions. They attempted, with some success, to find palliatives for the worst social evils of the day, and they prepared the way for the substantial reforms of the interwar years and the 1940s. Sir William Beveridge's experience in working with Lloyd George was to prove invaluable to him when he drew up the far-reaching Beveridge Report in 1942.

6:13

Was the Gestapo the Instrument of Ruthless Tyranny?

The Gestapo and the SS were among the grimmest of the instruments set up by the Nazi regime in Germany to liquidate their real and imagined opponents. These organisations were frequently regarded as instruments of a totalitarian tyranny, whereas in truth their operation was often arbitrary, random and even trivial. This suggests that it is appropriate to attempt a re-evaluation of the effectiveness of the Gestapo and the SS as instruments of coercion.

At the head of the machinery of repression was the Gestapo (the *Geheime Staats Polizei* or Secret State Police) created by Goering. Its executive organs included Himmler's SS (*Schutz Staffeln*, or Security Guards), the black-uniformed élite, creamed off from the SA and a far more effective instrument of terror than Roehm's turbulent body of brown-shirted storm troopers. They had the task of enforcing submission and obedience not only from politicians, government officials and the judiciary, but from the body of the nation as a whole. Judges especially had to conform to the new Nazi maxims of law, such as 'The judge's task is not to do justice, but to annihilate the enemies of National Socialism.' The Gestapo, created by Goering, passed into the control of Heinrich Himmler, the SS Chief, and under him became a branch of the Security Police, led by the second-in-command of the SS, Reinhard Heydrich. It became their duty to administer the concentration camps, which absorbed at first thousands, and later millions, of victims.

Of course, not all of these 'enemies of the state' were in fact true opponents, but since no process of law was required before a person could be imprisoned other than a signature from a Gestapo official, there were a good many irregularities in the way the camps operated. Among the many socialists, communists, trade union leaders and Jews who were imprisoned, there were also many professional people such as doctors or dentists, newspaper workers, pacifists, Jehovah's Witnesses, priests, lawyers and figures from the arts or the theatre.

The system was calculated to strike terror into the hearts of the populace. Hitler, with all his supposed devotion to the German people, in fact held them in total contempt and encouraged their exploitation: 'You can do anything you want with them. They will submit to you . . . they are insignificant little people, submissive as dogs, and they sweat with embarrassment when you talk to them.'

Nevertheless, not too much stress must be laid on the hideousness of this system of policing. Terror was used, and was always frightening when it occurred. But the system operated randomly and quite arbitrarily, and was characterised quite as much by its inconsistency as by its harshness. Gestapo officials, puffed up by their own importance, were capable of making the stupidest mistakes and of overlooking the real problem in favour of some trivial peccadillo.

Not many records of the camps survive, since those involved in running them took care to burn much incriminating material at the end of the war, when the country was liberated. Some written records have accidentally survived, however, from the office buildings where the SS had their notorious headquarters. It seems unlikely that these findings have been doctored to prune out the worst cases, although this must remain a possibility. Generally, though, these records show the true level on which the Gestapo appears to have operated. It seems to have acted on local gossip or on malicious reports from busybodies: perhaps a person, living alone, was unfriendly, or did not show proper respect for the swastika; perhaps they dressed only in black, or kept a dog that never stopped barking. In this way unpopular people, those who did not conform, or were perhaps a bit odd in their behaviour, were weeded out and removed – the same method as was commonly used to identify witches in medieval times. As a method of maintaining internal security it was highly unreliable in operation, and produced inconsistent results. There is also oral evidence from victims who managed to elude the clutches of the Gestapo that officers could behave unpredictably, as in the case of one music-loving officer who was sent to arrest and detain a Jewish woman, but who turned a blind eye to her escape because she happened to be related to an orchestral conductor whom he much admired. In cases such as this, it would appear that the lack of a proper administrative framework for the conduct of officers, together with some vagueness in their briefing, contributed towards an overall haphazardness in their operation. One of the least acceptable features of such a terror was its casual application as well as its pitiless consequences.

6:14

Did Hitler Follow in Bismarck's Footsteps?

It is sometimes alleged that Bismarck and Hitler occupied a similar position in German history during their lifetimes, and did much the same kind of work in the course of their political careers. Both men had a good and a bad side to their characters. Both did a great deal of good for Germany in their domestic policies, conferring material benefits and a sense of pride in their country's achievements. Both rejected democracy. Both knew how to deal ruthlessly with their opponents, and to produce discipline and a sense of service in the hearts of the people. Both conferred national unity on the Germans, set their feet on the road to militarisation and war expansion, and both finally landed them with a war against their European neighbours, bringing to their country disastrous defeat and humiliation. Is this comparison a fair one?

It is true that there are some superficial similarities between the two, but no one could really offer any serious evidence for the assertion either that Hitler was the Bismarck of the twentieth century, or that Bismarck was the Hitler of the nineteenth. For the differences between the two men are much greater than the similarities.

To begin with, Bismarck was a gentleman and Hitler was a guttersnipe. This is not merely a snobbish social comment; it explains a great deal about the two. Bismarck, though something less than the *Junker* aristocrat he liked to claim to be, had a comfortable, secure background and was an educated man. He moved easily in the upper echelons of European society, had a good working knowledge of diplomatic French and a useful smattering of other languages, and had an inherited respect for a system of law and order on which his knowledge of German society was grounded. He had clear personal convictions of his own in politics, morality and religion, but respected the convictions of others. His patriotism was orthodox, even conventional; in his day he was regarded as the arch-conservative of Europe.

Hitler, on the other hand, lacked nearly all of these qualities. He was the lower-class product of petit-bourgeois ignorance and prejudice; only incompletely educated, though his head had been stuffed with erratic and quite irrational whims which he never ceased to peddle on the subject of history, art, philosophy, politics and science. He was the unattractive product of the social and political dissolution that followed upon the destruction of the old authoritarian framework of the Hohenzollern Empire after 1918. Deeply insecure himself, he was pitilessly cruel to real and imagined opponents. Throughout his life he devoted himself to the pursuit of an ideal of racial exclusivity and domination that proved itself as absurd as it was dangerous. He had no discernible principles and, like a gangster, devoted himself solely to his own personal aggrandisement. At the same time, he was unreliable, lazy and inconsistent, delegating anything that bored him to his sycophantic underlings, and spending much of his time watching old films and trashy sentimental operettas. His tastes were populist and coarse. Significantly, he adored the brassier passages of Wagner (whose anti-Semitism he shared) and modern architecture in the excessively brutal style. Bismarck would not have acknowledged his existence; if he had, he would have locked him up as a lunatic agitator.

It is only to be expected, therefore, that their policies were different. If Bismarck was the arch-conservative of Europe,

Hitler was the arch-revolutionary. He did valuable work largely to benefit the German working class, but other aspects of his work were more threatening. Hitler set himself the task of bypassing or demolishing the framework of law and administration inherited from the old empire, substituting for it compliance with an ideological *diktat* that was as imprecise as it was arbitrary. His policy of *Gleichschaltung* (the *assimilation* of the social and legal framework of the state into the Nazi Party) was dangerous and meaningless, and was aimed solely at conferring legal force on his personal will. Even his most devoted followers gave up trying to grasp what Hitler was trying to do, and substituted a heightened spiritual devotion for intellectual understanding. Others, more perceptive and realistic, mouthed the appropriate slogans and set about the much more congenial task of building up their own personal power-base in Germany, or, more simply, feathering their own nests with the plunder they stripped out of the system. The social, economic, commercial and financial policies of the Third Reich were at heart incoherent and inconsistent: predicated on war, they created that catastrophic conflict that limited the life of the Reich that was to last 'for a thousand years' to a fleeting episode of little more than ten.

Their external policies were also in complete contrast with each other. Bismarck was interested in a stable Europe and was anxious to make friends and allies in order to protect his infant Germany. On the one hand Bismarck strove to prevent a major European war – indeed, the First World War resulted from the abandonment of his policies after his dismissal by the young Kaiser in 1890, and was brought about despite him rather than because of him. But Hitler thought more of conquest than of coexistence, and his policies led inevitably to war. He was interested in exploiting and finally dominating his neighbours, and believed the only way to create real stability was to establish an unchallengeable military hegemony over Europe based on his theories of racial purity and supremacy.

The divergent attitudes of the two men to Austria illustrate this difference. Bismarck valued the solid and powerful rock of the Habsburg Empire to the south as a guarantee of peace and stability. He wished to preserve it not only because it was a force for discipline and conservatism, but because he wanted to live peaceably alongside the Catholic Church, which he recognised as a powerful force better outside a mainly Lutheran Germany than included within it. Hitler simply did not grasp this. He had no use for ideologies other than his own, and so unwisely brought about the *Anschluss* to join Germany and Austria together purely on racial grounds. In doing so, he ignored both history and the stabilising influence of Austria in central Europe, and so contributed indirectly to the political fragmentation of the area. This removal of Austria also incidentally eased Soviet Russia's path to communist dominance in the area for a half century after 1945 and, after that, helped to produce the disintegration of Yugoslavia in the 1990s, so accelerating further progress on the road leading to what was once appropriately termed 'Balkanisation'.

6:15

Indian Independence: Did Britain Bungle It?

In 1947 India and Pakistan became independent, but their independence was not achieved peacefully. It was not that Britain, the colonial power, resisted granting independence. It was the outbreak of sectarianism which set Hindu against Muslim and Sikh, caused massive population migration and at least half a million deaths. For the chaos and the slaughter Britain has been blamed both at the time and since, but this blame is largely undeserved, and those who see independence as hasty and badly planned are in fact in error.

The British claimed to have given India peace, unity, equal religious rights, modern communications and some economic growth. These benefits, however, were not acceptable substitutes for independence, and during the 1930s the British government introduced reforms which gave to the Indian provinces a large measure of self-government. Proposals for a federal India foundered on the opposition of the Indian princes, but apart from a few lone voices like Churchill, Britain favoured moving India cautiously towards some form of Dominion status. The war intervened. After the war the new Labour government, impatient at the failure of Hindu and Muslim leaders to agree, granted a partitioned India independence ten months earlier than originally planned. The religious hatred and massacre that ensued provide a superficial case for saddling the Labour government with mishandling independence, but a closer examination leads to a different conclusion.

United India was a British creation. India had only been united previously and temporarily by force. The Great Mogul had latterly been little more than a figurehead. Thus if Britain wanted to grant independence to a united India, much careful preparation and goodwill would be needed. Britain began badly by imprisoning the leaders of the Indian National Congress Party during the war. These leaders were unnecessarily made pro-Japanese by this British foolhardiness. After all, there was little to be gained by substituting Japanese rule for British rule; it was unlikely that the Japanese would keep in place the local self-government the British had already granted. The Cripps Mission of 1942 promised Dominion status after the war. The Indian leaders wanted immediate independence: Gandhi is supposed to have called the British offer 'a post-dated cheque on a bank that was obviously failing'. The British government was unwilling to grant immediate independence with Japan poised to invade. The Congress leaders organised a 'Quit India' campaign. Britain replied by once again imprisoning the Congress leaders.

After the war the British believed that a united India could be created with safeguards for the Muslim minority. The Muslim leader Jinnah disagreed. He wanted partition and an independent Pakistan. He did not trust the Hindus, and although he joined the interim government set up in September 1946, he refused to take part in the discussions for a new constitution. There were now virtually no British troops in

India, and none to spare to be sent there; the Indian army was now almost entirely Indian, even its senior officers. The civil service had been Indianised during the 1930s. So while the Indian leaders, restrained only by Gandhi, whipped up nationalist and religious fervour, there was no British authority to maintain order. Violence and disorder were on the increase. Unable to maintain effective control in India the British government wanted a solution acceptable to both main religious groupings as quickly as possible before the subcontinent relapsed into anarchy. To the British government it seemed that only partition, as demanded by Jinnah, would limit sectarian bloodshed, and that the longer it was delayed the greater the violence and disorder that would accompany it. In order to push the arguing factions into agreement the British government, without prematurely committing itself to partition, announced in February 1947 that Britain would transfer power to the Indian leaders not later than June 1948. Lord Mountbatten was appointed the new Viceroy with the task of bringing this about.

Mountbatten soon realised that partition was inevitable. He persuaded Nehru, the Congress leader, that Indian unity could not be preserved without the most appalling civil war accompanied by enormous bloodshed. He recognised that partition, too, would lead to bloodshed, and decided that the quicker partition and independence could be achieved the less this bloodshed would be. It was impossible to produce a partition frontier that would place all Hindus on one side of the line and all Muslims on the other. But if rough justice to both sides was the best that could be done, the quicker the better. A new date for independence was fixed: 15 August 1947. Mountbatten completed his work in great haste, and it was his British officials who decided on the partition boundaries; there is no indication that Indians could have drawn the frontier any better. Ethnic and religious minorities would remain on the wrong side of the frontier virtually wherever it was drawn. Some problems, such as Kashmir, were not resolved, and have continued to defy solution.

The deaths of the half million or more Muslims, Hindus and Sikhs in 1947 cannot easily be blamed on Britain. Britain's main failure was that its strength had been sapped by five years of world war, and that as a result it had not the will or the capacity to maintain its erstwhile pre-eminence. No one had anticipated bloodshed on the scale that hit the Indian subcontinent in August and September 1947. It might have been reduced if Britain had had the military capability and will to delay independence for some years and impose an acceptable unitary solution. But Britain no longer had the power or resources to enforce that option. It might have been reduced if Britain had stuck to the original June 1948 date and not shown such undue haste. But this is doubtful; the fear was that the longer independence was delayed the more likely Jinnah or Nehru would raise some new obstacle or renounce decisions already agreed. After all, it had taken a very long time to get Jinnah to agree to anything. The best opinion at the time was that every day of delay would lead to more deaths. There might have been less bloodshed if national and local politicians had not cultivated racial and religious hatreds in pursuit of their political aims. In some ways it could be argued that Britain's policy had been a success; it had forced a pragmatic solution to a seemingly intractable problem, but at tremendous cost.

7

POLITICAL RE-EVALUATIONS

The New Deal: Did it End the Great Depression?

In the early 1930s the USA, along with most of the rest of the developed world, was struck down by the Great Depression. By 1933 the number of American unemployed was approaching 13 million, farmers were facing bankruptcy and banks were often unable to meet their obligations. President Hoover had made some effort to tackle the problem, notably by giving federal help to the banks and by encouraging public works both state and federal. But the presidential election of November 1932 had swept him aside and replaced him with Franklin D. Roosevelt, whose public utterances proclaimed the need for a 'new deal' to confront the Depression head-on. In the early years of his presidency the New Deal took shape from a welter of legislative activity by President and Congress. But it is an error to believe, as many continue to do, that the New Deal was the sovereign remedy that achieved all it set out to do.

Roosevelt did not have a coherent economic programme. His attack on the Depression was a series of separate measures each intended to tackle one aspect of it. If the measure did not work then he would try something else. He was no socialist: his aim was to save capitalism, not to destroy it. Indeed, some of his policies were borrowed from his Republican opponents. Nor was he a Keynesian. His understanding of economics was limited, and he and his treasury officials baulked at the idea of deficit financing and federal spending. He was prepared to borrow in the short term, but eventually the budget must be balanced if inflation was to be avoided; and the German inflation of the 1920s haunted all those across the world who had the responsibility of tackling the world economic crisis. The USA was the world's biggest creditor and the world's biggest consumer, yet the shrinking of exports exacerbated by the Smoot-Hawley tariff of 1930 was a major factor in the American slump. An American revival could only be partial unless the rest of the world recovered too.

According to orthodox economic theory the turnaround would have come anyway. The fall in labour costs and the fall in prices would eventually increase consumption, demand for labour would rise, and the economic cycle of boom following slump as slump follows boom would continue as it always did, although this time the slump was so severe as to make the upturn a long time in coming. Roosevelt's aim was to speed up the cycle and advance the recovery.

A good deal of economic activity is based on confidence: confidence in the currency, confidence in the banking system, confidence in the market. Roosevelt had considerable success here. America's small local banks were particularly vulnerable, as the collapse of one major borrower or the defaulting of a number of local farmers could bring a bank to its knees. A number had already foundered before Roosevelt took office, and local banking failures could undermine the major banks who had supplied the local ones with credit. The Emergency Banking Act gave federal guarantees to sound banks only, thus forcing the weaker ones out of business. The Glass-Steagal Banking Act further strengthened confidence in the banks by forcing them to separate their commercial and investment activity and to curb banks' involvement in speculation. Thus the surviving banks gained credibility, while falling prices damped down fear of inflation and restored faith in the currency. Investment confidence revived with government measures to limit fraudulent, speculative and marginal dealings on the Stock Exchange.

Most of the banking legislation was enacted during the '100 days', and, together with low interest rates, did much to prepare the ground. Of course, renewed confidence alone was not enough. Roosevelt attempted to make exports cheaper by taking the USA off the Gold Standard, but exports languished until world recovery began. He had more success with agriculture. Banks were encouraged not to foreclose on mortgages, and the Agricultural Adjustment Act provided for the destruction of crop surpluses, the reduction of the acreage under cultivation, and the encouragement of cooperative practices. A Federal Farm Loan Act provided help to existing mortgagees and credit to new ones. Although the Agricultural Adjustment Act was declared unconstitutional by the Supreme Court, new legislation in 1937 and 1938 revived most of its provisions, and by 1939 agriculture was making a modest improvement. Credit and cooperation led to increasing mechanisation and in many areas farms were making a profit again. Even in the 'dustbowl' the flight to the towns slowed down considerably as farmers rediscovered enough hope and confidence to cling on. And the Tennessee Valley Authority was a great success, bringing employment to seven states, providing cheap hydroelectric power and increasing the fertility of thousands of square miles of farming land.

Roosevelt's efforts to tackle unemployment in other ways were less successful. The Civilian Conservation Corps provided temporary work for young men. Most of the work was in forestry and infrastructure, but it was much criticised for giving federal pay for very little work. The Federal Emergency Relief Administration gave similar assistance to adults. The Public and Civil Works Administration (in 1935 replaced by the Works Progress Administration) gave greater emphasis in providing construction work for federal and state projects, but it gave only a very limited boost to the construction industry, beset as it was with administrative caution and management incompetence. The National Recovery Administration tried to help industry and encourage cooperation between management and unions, but it neglected small firms in favour of big organisations and was to an extent undermined by excessive bureaucracy. Nevertheless, where these 'Alphabet Agencies' paid workers and bought raw materials, tools and vehicles, they created consumption demand, and helped to lift the economy off the floor.

Similarly, although the welfare provisions, such as the Social Security Act of 1935, were intended to deal with the social rather than the economic effects of the Depression, they had no more than a marginal effect in lifting demand; unemployment insurance and old age insurance did not have an immediate major impact, and they would not do so for some years, but they did help to raise public and consumer confidence, as did the fireside chats on the radio and the Blue Eagle badges.

Roosevelt's New Deal thus reached out in all directions. And it soon made enemies. In 1935 the Supreme Court had paralysed the New Deal by declaring much of the legislation unconstitutional. Most of what was salvaged in the late 1930s was watered down. But unemployment had fallen quite dramatically by 1937, by over 5 million. It did not last. Unemployment rose by over 2 million in 1938, and was still stubbornly above the 1937 level in 1940. So, of course, Roosevelt did not end the Depression; the Depression lingered on throughout the 1930s. Recovery was only partial and spasmodic. And some of what recovery there was depended on improved world trade, although this in itself was dependent on the revival of the American economy. War in Europe ended the Depression. From 1939 New Deal policies took a back seat while the USA concentrated on rearmament. Unemployment took a nose-dive; exports of food, war supplies and armaments escalated. By 1940 the Gross National Product (GNP) was 26 per cent higher than it had been at the onset of the Depression in 1930. Roosevelt's achievement, therefore, was not to bring the Depression to an end, but to restore the financial and economic confidence of the nation, and to show that the Depression could at least be contained, even if it could not be defeated.

Churchill: Was He a Great War Leader?

Winston Churchill became Prime Minister of Great Britain in May 1940, and he led the country from the dark days of 1940 and 1941 until final victory in 1945. To Churchill went the credit for Britain's part in the Allied success, and universal gratitude to him meant that he was compared with the Elder Pitt, who led Britain to victory in the Seven Years' War. But Churchill's war leadership has been attacked; it is alleged that he had no idea of strategy, and that he made many mistakes. So his wartime leadership has become a controversial area over which the dust has not yet settled.

When Churchill came to power Norway had fallen, the Low Countries were under German attack, and the blow that was to knock out France was imminent. These disasters were blamed on Churchill's predecessors when Churchill had been a voice in the wilderness urging his fellow countrymen to take the danger of Hitler seriously. So when Churchill faced the Battle of Britain, as the German air force tried to soften up Britain preparatory to invasion, he was regarded as one of the few leaders Britain could trust. The Labour Party, who had always hated Churchill, accepted that he was the best Prime Minister available, and served him loyally throughout the war. None tried to stab him in the back, so enabling him to escape the fate of Asquith in the First World War.

One way in which he consolidated support was in his sense of urgency and his insistence on getting things done. He certainly worked hard, and took only a minimum of sleep, and he expected others to do the same. He kept a very close eye on the war effort as well as the war, which meant that he often interfered in the minutiae of lesser government departments. At least he kept them all on their toes, but perhaps some of the time thus used could have been spent in developing war strategy with his advisers.

But was he an expert on strategy? In the early days of the war his aims were survival and victory, with little idea how these were to be achieved. During the most crucial months of the war (June 1940–June 1941) when Britain stood alone, or had only Greece as an ally, Britain's meagre forces were divided between home defence, a campaign in North Africa, offensives in Eritrea and Abyssinia, the defence of Greece and the defence of Crete. It was fortunate that Britain emerged from these relatively unscathed.

When the USA entered the war in December 1941 Churchill persuaded Roosevelt that Germany must be dealt with before Japan – a decision of the greatest importance for the later stages of the war, and one which the Americans at first had been most reluctant to accept. But here Churchill had Stalin on his side. Churchill met Roosevelt and Stalin a number of times, but apart from this decision he was unable to exert much influence on either of them. His appeals to Roosevelt before the American entry into the war did not result in military intervention, only the draining of Britain's foreign reserves to pay for American armaments. Later Roosevelt was afraid that Britain wanted to use the war to advance British imperialist aims, and he failed to see that Britain's imperialist days were over, and that the Soviet Union had from its beginnings been an imperialist power. So at the three-power meetings Churchill was usually unable to get his way. He tried in vain to win their support for a major Allied attack in the Balkans (shades of Gallipoli) and Churchill was lukewarm about the Second Front almost up to D-Day.

Nor was Churchill always at his best in dealing with his subordinates. Members of his Cabinet and certainly of his government were often left unaware of Churchill's most recent decisions concerning their departments. Yet they remained loyal. To his service chiefs he insistently demanded action, even when action was not possible, or might lead to disaster. Thus when pressed by Churchill to attack the enemy, General Wavell, in Egypt, said that he needed three months to prepare and a massive influx of tanks and supplies. These were denied him. Wavell was sacked; his successor Montgomery was given the reinforcements denied to Wavell, and he was allowed five months to prepare; the fact that Montgomery was successful obscured Churchill's high-handed treatment of Wavell. While he prodded the commanders in the field, and swapped them around if they failed to take the offensive, he could be over-indulgent to those personally linked to him. Perhaps his trust of both Beaverbrook and Brendan Bracken was a little excessive, and he supported Air Chief Marshal Harris almost single-handedly against his service critics. On the other hand he had difficulties with de Gaulle, but so did virtually everybody else!

Occasionally his ideas bordered on downright stupidity, as, for example, when George VI had to scotch Churchill's plans to be present at the D-Day landings; the triumph of common sense over exuberance. And his proposal for union between Britain and the collapsing France in 1940 was more pathetic than prophetic. But it is comparatively easy to produce, by selection, a negative catalogue out of Churchill's five years of war leadership. His greatest achievement was the sense of determination with which he began his ministry. He was a man who could get things done. He told the country so, in parliament and on the radio. When there were disasters he did not (normally) conceal them from the public. When he talked of 'blood, sweat, toil and tears' men and women rose to the challenge. When decisions had to be made Churchill made them, whether right or wrong. There was no other who could have fired Britain's determination to resist as he did in 1940 – those in his Cabinet who, when France fell, wanted to consider a compromise peace might have had a better chance under another leader. He was by no means perfect, or a superman, but without him Britain could well have succumbed to Hitler, leaving the USA with an almost insurmountable task on its hands.

7:3

What Was the Origin of the 'Iron Curtain'?

On 4 March 1946 Winston Churchill gave a speech at Fulton, Missouri, in which he referred to the 'Iron Curtain' that had descended across the Continent of Europe. By this he meant the ideological, and in practice physical, barrier which rigidly separated communist Europe from non-communist western Europe. Many would argue that with this speech the Cold War began in earnest. It is, however, an error to suppose that the term 'Iron Curtain' was originated by Churchill.

It is probable that its first use was in a newspaper article by Goebbels in February 1945. It was certainly used in a similar sense in a radio broadcast by Count Schwerin-Krosigk, Nazi Germany's last Foreign Minister, at the end of April 1945, when the Nazis' final forlorn hope was to detach the Western Allies from the Russians. Churchill himself used it in a message to President Truman as early as June 1945. Churchill was never one to waste a good phrase, no matter what its origin, and his reference to the 'Iron Curtain' at Fulton gave it an international currency that passed into general usage.

7:4

How Much did Chinese Communism Owe to Stalin?

Students of history often imagine that it was through the supportive efforts of Stalin and the Russian communists that Mao Zedong (Mao Tse Tung) was able to establish the People's Republic of China in 1949, by defeating the nationalist forces of Jiang Jieshi (Chiang Kai Shek). In fact, Stalin's policies, for all that he was a communist, were extremely conventional, cautious, and even conservative. It was only after 1950 that he reconciled himself to the existence of Mao's regime in China. In short, it is an error to suppose that the People's Republic of China was established through the encouragement and support of the Soviet Union.

Political Re-evaluations

In the 1920s and 1930s, Stalin saw himself as the champion of popular communism against the forces of world imperialism, and therefore took the side of the nationalists in China, against capitalist and colonialist intervention in China's affairs by the Western powers. As early as 1922 the Chinese popular leader Sun Yatsen had been persuaded to accept Russian help, and Mikhail Borodin was sent to advise Sun on transforming his organisation into an effective government, and creating a nationalist army to police the infant Republic. When Sun died in 1925, Jiang, himself trained as a soldier in Japan and later in Moscow in 1923, took up the reins. Jiang, however, was no lover of communism. In 1927, when the nationalists took Shanghai, he carried out a massacre of thousands of communist supporters of the Kuomintang, working hand-in-glove with the propertied and banking interests of Shanghai, whose ranks he joined when he married Soong Meiling, sister of Mrs Sun, and a Christian. The communist left wing of the Kuomintang fled and were scattered, and Jiang spent the next ten years trying to hunt them down and eliminate them, regarding them as a more dangerous enemy than the Japanese who invaded the country after 1937.

Stalin was slow to learn from all this. Partly because he saw the nationalists as resisting the Western powers and Japan, Russia's traditional enemies in the East, and partly because no one among his advisers had the courage to give him contrary advice, Stalin persisted in his pro-nationalist attitudes long after they had ceased to be useful. When he was threatened by Nazi Germany in Europe, he consented to sign a non-aggression pact with Japan in April 1941, and later, during the Great Patriotic War, was fully occupied with ensuring the survival of the Soviet Union against the Nazi invasion. The effect of all this was that he played no part in Chinese affairs at all during the war, and only came into the war against Japan in its closing stages, when he advanced into Korea and Manchuria, and actually returned Manchuria to the nationalists. In the later stages of the Chinese civil war, Mao had little more than bare recognition from Stalin, and certainly very little help, while Jiang had massive support from the

United States, and hoped to use this to defeat his communist foes, who by this time enjoyed the support of the bulk of the Chinese peasantry. It was only when Stalin came to realise that Mao was not the loser he had believed him to be that a trickle of support began to come through. Meantime, Jiang had launched offensives to capture the country's main cities, but in doing so had spread his forces very thinly. Peking (Beijing) fell to the communists in 1949, followed by Nanking (Nanjing), Chungking (Chonqing) and Canton (Gwangzhou), and finally in December 1949 Jiang fled with his whole regime to Formosa (Taiwan), from which the Japanese had been recently expelled.

Thus the success of the Chinese communists owed very little to the Soviet Union. From 1927 to 1947 they had received little help from Stalin, who until then seems to have imagined that Jiang was going to win. Only in 1950 did Stalin and Mao sign a thirty-year Treaty of Friendship and Alliance between the two great communist powers, under which the Russians began to provide much financial and technical assistance for the People's Republic, and a good deal of industrial expertise for modernisation.

It may therefore perhaps be thought that Stalin missed a great opportunity for cementing the bonds of the twin forces of Russian and Chinese communism. This, too, however would also be wrong. The Chinese communists were much less docile than the Soviet satellites in Europe. They expected a dominant role in Asian affairs; they tried to encourage the smaller European powers, such as Albania, to pursue policies of independence; they frequently adopted a very independent line in their dealings with the Third World, and finally they felt themselves entitled to share in the USSR's nuclear secrets. This was not always welcome to Stalin, and certainly not to his successor, Khrushchev. He came to regard his friendship with Mao as a very mixed blessing.

7:5

How Deserved was the Reputation of President Reagan?

During his two periods of presidential office, Ronald Reagan enjoyed an enviably high public reputation in the United States, and was one of the few presidents who left office more popular than when he was inaugurated. There is still, however, a good deal of controversy about the extent of his achievements, and even on the question of his abilities as President.

To foreigners it seemed that Reagan was painfully ignorant, badly briefed and, though intuitively keen, intellectually rather lazy. He did not like to be bogged down in detail and was often guilty of amazing superficiality. Throughout his life, both as a successful movie star and later in the Gubernatorial Lodge of California, he took a lot for granted and avoided asking too many questions. He had a mind that had never submitted itself to rigorous challenge, but on the contrary was happy with surface judgments. As a result, his advisers prepared him as carefully as they could and hoped that the decisions he faced would coincide with the areas they had prepared. He was capable of spectacular errors. William Safire, the *New York Times* columnist, gave an unusually harsh judgment on him when he said: 'The president has been skimping on his preparation. He thinks he can wing it. Some member of the inner circle should tell him that in a democracy a leader's range of comprehension is put to the test, and that he has been flunking the test.' In news conferences Reagan was capable of fluffing the answers to his questions quite remarkably. This was partly because his hearing was not good, but chiefly because he often could not get to grips with 'White House speak'. He had so much difficulty that eventually his aides installed a small loudspeaker just out of sight of the cameras from which questions were translated into terms he could understand. This was a cause of some amusement on the part of foreign newspapermen, who maintained that someone was telling him the answers. His weaknesses were compounded by a failing memory for names and faces that some believed were early signs of the onset of the Alzheimer's disease that was soon to plague his old age. His failings were further aggravated by the not uncommon American trait of insularity, a neglect of things strange and foreign that was simultaneously irritating for foreigners and understandable and rather lovable to fellow Americans.

Reagan had, however, a secure and uncluttered concept of the presidency modelled on his early rather sentimental recollection of the presidency of Franklin Roosevelt. From this sprang both his delegative style of decision-making and his natural gift for public appearances. He saw himself as the 'Great Communicator' – a talent reinforced by his professional training as a movie actor – able to rally the country by the power of his voice and to harness public opinion as a catalyst for change. Like his father, he was a compelling salesman who knew that a salesman must believe in his product before he can persuade others to buy it. Believability was the key. Even when he was wrong or misinformed he was so convincing and assured that others believed him. He did not exhibit defensiveness, or duplicity or aggression, but spoke in homely pieties that people could relate to. At the time of the 1980 primaries an aide climbed into a taxicab and asked the driver what he thought of Reagan. 'He's the only politician I can understand' was the reply. His skill as a communicator drew on other assets. Though he knew little about world geography, or economics, or rocket science, he had a clear picture of what he wanted and a clearly drawn political agenda and, like Margaret Thatcher in Britain (with whom he had a complete rapport), simple moral values clearly grasped and consistently applied. He was a President with few doubts – perhaps, as his critics said, too few.

As well as being the 'Great Communicator', Reagan was also the 'Great Delegator'. When he arrived in Washington, he brought with him the desire to have the same type of cabinet government he had used as Governor of California. He had promised to use the cabinet as the working arm of the government, and he took this promise as seriously as he took promises to reduce the burden of taxes and to end the welfare mentality. Though the cabinet was too big to work efficiently (one of his aides observed that the cabinet was 'about as useful as the vermiform appendix') he continued to delegate work to it much more extensively than his predecessors, giving them broad authority and considerable freedom of action. While they were slaving away in a hot office he preferred to take a nap in the afternoons. This was not due to any natural indolence, but simply because he was not a detail man. He was appalled by how Carter had become involved in unnecessary detail, and saw himself as executive decision-maker, or 'chairman of the board'. A distinctive feature of his presidency was how his advisers were encouraged to comment on matters outside their expertise. As a believer in general principles himself, he indulged his suspicion that energy was much too important to be left to the Department of Energy and foreign affairs much too important to be left to the State Department. To Alexander Haig this was strange; to a man like Henry Kissinger it would have been absolutely intolerable. Whatever its implications, the system suited Reagan. He preferred back-and-forth discussions with his colleagues rather than wearisome and often prolix briefing papers. Some members of the government, increasingly compartmentalised into more or less autonomous sections in their duties, did not like this system. Some of them, on the contrary, wanted no more than a perfunctory nod from the President, and might well have been happy to have had no President at all. But this was not how Reagan saw his responsibility to the nation that had voted for him. He had no wish to become a cardboard cut-out.

So, throughout his two periods of office, Reagan spoke directly to the people and nourished the simple ties he had with them. But though people loved him and valued him, he always remained a leader of limited vision with limited achievements both at home and abroad. Indeed, to intellectuals and to professional critics he was a poor President, as one would expect of an actor playing a presidential role. In terms of what he actually did as President his record remains a very thin one; yet paradoxically the reputation of the presidency under Reagan had never stood so high.

7:6

Did Harold Wilson Lie Over the
Devaluation of the Pound, 1967?

There has been a tendency for successive British Prime Ministers and Chancellors of the Exchequer to pass off devaluations of the currency as mere matters of technical adjustment without significant consequences, and there is evidence that people generally have accepted such excuses.

Thus it was, in 1967, when, contrary to pledges given and repeated until the very moment he acted, James Callaghan as Chancellor devalued the pound. On that occasion the Prime Minister, Harold Wilson, stated to the nation his opinion: 'From now the Pound is worth 14 per cent or so less in terms of other currencies. It does not mean, of course, that the Pound here in Britain, in your pocket or in your purse, or in your bank, has been devalued.'

This was simply untrue. A devaluation of 14 per cent, from an exchange value for the pound of $2.80 to $2.40, meant that exports were cheaper, i.e. industry was working for a smaller reward in the price of exports, while imports were dearer, meaning that the charge to the UK consumer of imported goods was correspondingly greater. Callaghan recognised the truth of this by resigning from office as the result of breaking his promises; Wilson maintained the fiction until his death.

7:7

Margaret Thatcher:
The White Hope of British Conservatism?

Margaret Thatcher, first woman Prime Minister of Britain and leader of the Conservative Party in the later years of the century, excited strong feelings during her long term of office, and has subsequently become one of the most controversial political figures of her generation. To her supporters she represents a uniquely important figure who helped materially to shape the country in the later twentieth century and to give it the character it possesses today; to her opponents she remains a loud, dreadful woman; obsessive, blinkered and tyrannical in office and misguided and meddlesome out of it. Maybe the time has come to attempt a historical reassessment of her importance.

Margaret Thatcher, (née Roberts), was a grocer's daughter born in Grantham in 1925. Educated at Grantham High School and Somerville College, Oxford as a chemist, she became a barrister and was elected Conservative MP for Finchley in 1959, holding minor office in 1961–4. Then, in 1970, she was appointed Minister of Education by Edward Heath. After the fall of his government she was, perhaps surprisingly, elected leader of the Conservative Party in 1975, and became Prime Minister after winning the general election of May 1979. Her period in office witnessed sharper and bitterer disagreements within the party than at any time since Joseph Chamberlain's tariff reform dispute, and a lot of the rancour is still in evidence.

In the first place, Thatcher's style was deliberately confrontational. She rejected the notion of consensus pursued by Neville Chamberlain, Harold Macmillan, Edward Heath and other 'one-nation' Tories and tried to redefine the meaning of Conservatism in individual moral terms. She made it clear that to her Conservatism 'meant governing a society rather than managing an economy'. Secondly, she remained something of an outsider. Her social background was surprisingly similar to Heath's, yet she was never accepted as completely as he was.

Her plain, unsophisticated ways were ridiculed in private, and she remained the target of that snobbish élitism that is one of the less attractive features of Conservatism. One critic observed that 'she is still basically a Finchley lady'. Francis Pym revealed his essentially dismissive attitude towards her when he said: 'We've got a corporal at the top and not an officer.' These superior 'one-nation' Tories seemed to think that their polish would eventually rub off onto Thatcher and 'civilise' her, thinking that her directness betokened the insecurity of a woman who had not yet gained the easy self-confidence of being 'at the top'.

Her critics were dumbfounded when she continued to nag at what she believed to be the Tory 'basics'. As Nicholas Ridley, one of her admirers, put it in 1979: 'Her basic beliefs were clear enough: sound money, reform of the trade unions, targeting welfare to where it was needed, low taxation, rebuilding Britain's position in the world. . . . The 1979 election was to be the start of a long period of rigorous reform.' The battle within the party soon came to be described as one between the 'Wets' and the 'Dries'. It centred on monetarism, and featured in her budgets from the start. The Wets were 'one-nation' Tories, some of whom, like Heseltine, wanted to use the powers of the state to pursue a more effective economic policy; the Dries, on the other hand, like Biffen, and later Howe and Lawson, became monetarists by different routes and soon counted themselves among her supporters. Old Etonian Ian Gilmour, perhaps the most articulate of the Wets, had published a book, *Inside Right*, in 1977, in which he stressed the importance of creating what he called a 'sense of community'. But Thatcher was more individualistic and more radical than that. She even went so far at one point as to say 'There is no such thing as society.' When her monetarist policies brought soaring inflation in the early 1980s, and unemployment topped 3 million, the Wets thought that their hour had struck, but Thatcher stuck remorselessly to her guns and said, 'There is nothing else to try. *There is no alternative*.' This phrase, sometimes abbreviated in the press as 'TINA', and other similar phrases such as 'The lady's *not for turning*' were characteristic of her simplicity, frankness and conviction: 'Deep in their instincts people know that I am saying and doing right. And I know it is, because that was the way I was brought up. I regard myself as a very normal ordinary person, with all the right, instinctive antennae.' Sustained by this inner conviction, Thatcher went on to weed out those whose dryness she doubted, replacing them with her own creations, and simultaneously extending the limits of Prime Ministerial power. She carefully controlled Cabinet agendas, limiting discussion of controversial issues. She used her Press Office, and her loyal henchman, Sir Bernard Ingham, to watch over her ministers and to leak information on them in order to damage them if they had outlived their usefulness. Those who succumbed – St John Stevas, Gilmour, Prior, Pym – lost any influence they had once had; others, like Heath, glowered from the benches and kept aloof from any kind of public comment on her. By 1985 her supremacy was almost unchallenged.

Above all, she wanted to give the country leadership, and a leadership they could understand. She hated the muddle and drift of the 1960s and 1970s – the endless stop-go, the crippling strikes, the country's ailing industrial performance, continuing national decline – and wished to regenerate prosperity and success.

Throughout her period of office, Thatcher had two great advantages: grass-roots support and a parliamentary party close to her both in her views and in her social background. Grassroots support showed itself at Party Conferences, where she was in her element – unlike most Cabinet ministers, who loathed them. Thatcher saw conferences as an annual opportunity not to decide what to do, but to re-bond with right-thinking folk. To her mind these ordinary people represented precisely that sort of public opinion with which the Tory grandees were out of touch. The obsequious attention of television cameras, with the best 'sound-bites' reported on the evening TV news, all confirmed her easy and familiar ascendancy.

But Thatcherism was never an 'ideology'. To her the word *ideology* meant slavish adherence to some abstract blueprint created in advance. She rejected such a notion vigorously. Yet she gave many observers the impression of being ideological herself. This was because her policies conveyed a similar feeling of movement, direction and purpose. Thatcherites aimed to 'do the right thing', and shared fairly definite ideas as to what the 'right thing' was. She sometimes made references to what she called 'Victorian virtues', giving the impression that she was perhaps a nineteenth-century Gladstonian Liberal. But it would have been more accurate to say that she went back further than that, perhaps to Adam Smith. Her view of Britain was drawn in three concentric circles: starting with the individual, it moved to the family to foster the individual's development, and arrived only last at the state, where the individual and the family could flourish and develop. It was in this sense that she meant that there was no such thing as society – rejecting the corporatist view that society exists in its own right as a vast welfare agency and assimilates the role of the individual to its own pattern. It was not for nothing that she was brought up as a Methodist. Her view was profoundly religious, moral and individualistic.

Likewise, her impact on late twentieth-century society must not be underestimated. It is true that she did not always show an infallible judgment – as when she allowed herself to be ensnared in the poll-tax trap, or when she lectured foreign politicians on the virtues of fiscal autonomy and struggled to hold aloof from a common European currency. But after November 1990, when suddenly – and to her mind inexplicably – she fell from power and was replaced by the mild-mannered John Major, she left behind her a different kind of Britain.

The whole scenario had changed. Her obsession with national sovereignty – in a curious way, the counterpart to individual sovereignty – led her to resist further subordination to a supranational Europe, and to reject a common currency. At the same time, at home, the state had dumped whole areas of responsibility where previously it had been very busy on people's behalf. It scrapped, or sold off, vast networks of economic activity such as the gas and electricity industries, coal-mining, the water industry, the railways – called, significantly, by Tory statesmen such as the geriatric Harold Macmillan 'the family silver'. She was even suspected by her opponents of wishing to privatise the Post Office and the National Health Service. She had cut down the trade unions to size, stripping them of their cherished illusion that it was really they who ran the country. She had lowered the burden of taxation. However, her ultimate aim of making the individual pay for his enfranchisement by shouldering his share of the poll tax foundered on the reluctance of those who demanded their share of political power but were happy that others should foot the bill. She had so far redefined public attitudes towards the state that even when Blair led Labour's return to power in 1997 he dared not reverse the innovations she had introduced, but instead redefined Socialism just as she had redefined Conservatism. As the result of her Prime Ministership, the whole of British politics had been shunted decisively from corporatism to individualism.

7:8

Was the End of World Communism an Unqualified Benefit?

Few events have been so important and yet, simultaneously, so enigmatic as the collapse around 1990 of communism in large parts of Europe and Asia. China still remains as one of its longest-surviving citadels; Cuba clings on; but the former USSR and all of the satellite states of eastern Europe have now passed away, unhonoured and unsung. There still remains, however, considerable uncertainty and controversy over the historical significance of this development.

The sudden and unexpected shift in power that took place at the end of the 1980s set in train the disintegration of the whole Soviet bloc in eastern Europe, and was followed shortly afterwards in 1991 by the collapse of communist power in the Soviet Union itself. At the time the West regarded these developments with approval, partly because they involved the destruction of the Warsaw Pact, and hence simplified the problems of the West's diplomatic relations with its eastern neighbours, but also because the West felt genuine delight that the masses of people previously under Soviet political control could now enjoy a freer and happier way of life. Ten years on, the question of whether the collapse of communist power was as beneficial as was at first thought is still being debated, as is the question of whether the different political regimes that have succeeded to the old order can in fact be regarded as an improvement.

There may be something to be said for the opinion that it is not the wicked perversity of political systems that bring the infliction of suffering on so much of humanity, but rather the moral shortcomings of humankind itself, both of rulers and ruled.

The Soviet Union. What collapsed in Russia in 1991 was not only communism, but also Leninism. Communism was a corporate state system dating from the late nineteenth and early twentieth centuries that was vaguely rooted in Marxism and socialism; Leninism was a system whose essential features lay not in ideas or policy programmes, but rather in principles of organisation enabling the leadership to construct and maintain a mono-organisational state and a central ruling state party. In fact, however, both of these 'isms' notoriously failed to deliver.

Socialist methods were incapable of organising the economy effectively, and Russia's industrial progress groaned at the burdens imposed on it, stagnated and fell further and further behind the West. At the same time the party, originally intended as an agent of rejuvenation became, after Stalin's time, steadily more atrophied. It imposed centralised discipline and curbed independent thinking. It became an ever-more arrogant and besieged ruling class (somewhat like the Tsarist bureaucracy) that thought only of holding on to power. Gorbachev's intention was to remedy these weaknesses through his policies of *glasnost* (openness) and *perestroika* (restructuring). His success, however, was limited. He made little progress towards the rule of law in everyday life and neglected to develop legal procedures that could be trusted. He was also unable to dismantle the state-run economy. There was little sign of the new enterprise or the new market that were meant to replace it. And finally he failed to transform a monolithic unitary empire into a free federation of states, thus accelerating the disintegration he meant to check. He was one of the most gifted men of his generation, but his own limitations and the complexity of the situation drove him from power. His failure was partly due to the survival of the old monolithic state in a non-communist form, and partly to the survival of the *nomenklatura* with their ambitions for supreme military or political power. The continuation of the old form of state, with little broadening of its bourgeois base, and the widespread frustration brought about through the crumbling of the economy led speedily to feelings of nostalgic regret at the passing of the communist era.

The failure of the Gorbachev experiment can be put down to three things. Firstly, he overestimated the capabilities of the bourgeoisie, and the sense of public service of the political *apparat* and the military; and, underestimating the importance of nationalism, allowed – and even encouraged – separatism. Secondly, he showed far too much optimism in tackling the problems of democracy, law, the market, the economy and the empire simultaneously, instead of proceeding piecemeal and gradually. Thirdly, he continued to insist on shouldering the responsibility himself in the Stalinist fashion, instead of developing presidential institutions and delegating to them departmental responsibilities, for example in the case of the economy, that were really full time. If he had been a better team worker, and if the former ruling class had been as public-spirited as he was, the story might have had a different outcome.

The nationalist virus speedily infected the Soviet Union itself. On 25 December 1991 the major element in the Union, the Russian Soviet Federative Socialist Republic (or RSFSR), the largest state in the Union, was transformed into the Russian Federation, and the hammer-and-sickle flag replaced by the traditional tricolour of horizontal red, blue and white stripes. Boris Yeltsin, who had been narrowly elected as Chairman of the Soviet Union in March 1990 and now became President of this Federation, agreed to the formation of a new union, the Commonwealth of Independent States (or CIS), to which a number of Russian states, like Belarus and the Ukraine, adhered. By December eleven states had joined, leaving outside the CIS only Georgia and the three Baltic republics. The industrial and nuclear resources, the nuclear armament and the conventional land, sea and air forces of these states were now no longer under a single unified command, but divided up between them.

The result was that the Western nations found themselves faced with a many-headed monster instead of a single-headed one, in a situation that was less threatening but considerably more dangerous than it had been before under the monolithic control of the Communist Party of the Soviet Union (the CPSU). The dangers now sprang from the ambitions of the military élite, the anger and the frustration of the *apparatchiki*, the dissatisfaction of the labouring masses at their poverty and powerlessness, and the lawlessness and gangsterism that replaced the orderly and closely regulated Russian society. Without the necessary training and experience it was simply too much to hope that Russia could make the transition from centralised dictatorship to liberal democracy all in one jump. Faced with this new situation, the West had no idea how best to react, and their attitude swung uncertainly between the one extreme of benevolent neutrality, leaving the Russians to resolve their own difficulties, and the other of more positive intervention, usually in the form of solving Russia's problems by throwing Western money at them.

Eastern Europe. A very similar story took place in the formerly communist oligarchies of eastern Europe. The people here had already demonstrated simmering dissatisfaction with communism, and from time to time had broken out in open insurrection. In general their discontent was based on low living standards, poor wages, chronic shortages and industrial backwardness; but it tended also to focus on the ruling élite – that fortunate group who seemed to be the main beneficiaries of the whole system. Eastern European leaders reacted in the only way they understood, by clamping down on discontent and tightening their control. Gorbachev's attitude, when he visited such countries, appeared to be one of mild encouragement for the reforming process. He seemed to think there was no reason why *glasnost* and *perestroika* should not be given a place in their policies too. Eastern European leaders, with a real dread of political disintegration, thought – quite rightly – that he was pulling the rug from under them, while eastern European peoples, scenting a whiff of political freedom, clamoured all the harder. Cracks began to appear in the monolithic structures in eastern Europe in 1988 and 1989. In Poland, power was handed to moderate reformers in August 1989, and in 1990 the first free elections were held for over half a century. The Baltic States made a good transition (momentarily Gorbachev hesitated on the brink of repressing them) though their main problem was that of a substantial Russian minority – in the case of Latvia, almost a majority problem. In East Germany, too, there was relaxation: restrictions between East and West Germany were loosened, and at the end of 1989 the Berlin Wall came down. Democratic reforms also began in Hungary and Czechoslovakia. In Romania, one of the most repressive communist regimes was overthrown, and the dictator, Nicholae Ceausescu, was seized with his wife and both bloodily executed. Finally Albania, the harshest and most primitive of the Balkan dictatorships, also overthrew its communist leaders and made a bid for freedom.

Whether all this disintegration constituted an improvement on the earlier monolithic dictatorship still remains an unanswered question. One of the criticisms made of this area of Europe in earlier years related to this very disunion. Indeed the word 'Balkanisation' was invented to express it. As Yugoslavia crumbled into its squabbling national units during the 1990s, the suspicion began to dawn that whatever other evils the communist oligarchy there had previously concealed it had at least kept the peace between the different ethnic divisions, and had checked the violence of national and religious wars. The grim and relentless faction fighting that brought suffering and destruction to Croatia, Bosnia and to Kossovo showed that nationalism was just as brutal and even more destructive than anything that Marshal Tito had ever employed to subdue and unify his people. Western observers might think in their heart of hearts that it was better for these eastern European factions to be killing each other, rather than killing them, but given the choice between factional national strife and single-minded communist repression, the answer remained far from obvious.

8

INTERNATIONAL RE-EVALUATIONS

Munich: The Policies of Betrayal?

Late in September 1938, Hitler, Mussolini, Daladier and Chamberlain met at a crisis conference in Munich to discuss the future of the Sudetenland area of Czechoslovakia. In the accord that was eventually signed, it was finally agreed to surrender the disputed area to Germany within a matter of days, and shortly afterwards German troops, acting on behalf of the substantial minority of ethnic Germans living there, entered and occupied the whole region of the Sudetenland. This action was bitterly denounced by the Czech government as an act of betrayal by their treaty allies, a view that came later to be shared by many in these countries themselves. But even today controversy still surrounds the question over whether the policies followed at Munich constituted a betrayal of the Czechs.

The Czech attitude was clear. Their position in the Sudetenland rested on the authority of the Treaty of St Germain (1919) with the Austrian government at the end of the First World War, a treaty that assigned the area to them.

The region was highly industrialised, Pilsen being the home of the Skoda armaments works, and was well fortified, its defences so effective that even the German troops who took control of them in 1938 were impressed. The forty divisions of the Czech army were among the best trained and best equipped in Europe. Furthermore they could rely on the support promised by two major powers: France, whom they accused specifically of betrayal at Munich, and the Soviet Union, whose representatives, like their own, were excluded from the conference. The Czechs believed that a firm stand by the Western democracies would not only have stopped Hitler in his tracks and saved their country, but would also have given the German Chief of Staff, Ludwig Beck, the chance he had been waiting for to rally the German officer class and put an end to the Nazi regime altogether. At Munich, however, France, instead of fulfilling its treaty obligations to its ally, had taken part in a craven conspiracy to strip it of one of its richest and most important provinces and to reduce it to impotence in the face of the German threat.

Czechoslovakia was prevented by these actions from resisting Nazi Germany alone. On the face of things the decision to fight alone does not seem unreasonable. The Czechs had a front-line army of 800,000 men and reserves that would increase that to 3.5 million. This army was almost as large as that of Germany. In addition the Czechs possessed an air force of 1,600 planes; the Germans had 2,600. The Czechs could put 470 tanks into the field, and these could have given a good account of themselves against the 720 of Germany. The concrete defences along the mountains of the Bohemian frontier were formidable and judged by the German generals who inspected them later as almost impregnable. Field Marshal von Manstein said: 'There is no doubt whatever that had Czechoslovakia defended herself, we should have been held up by her fortifications, for we did not have the means to break through.'

But the Czech advantage was an illusion. The Bohemian flank had been turned by the *Anschluss*, and German troops could take Czechoslovakia in the rear by crossing the Austro-Czech frontier. Fortifications here were only primitive. Besides, a surprise German attack could well have destroyed the Czech air force on the ground, as later was to happen in Poland; and had it come to air battles, German planes would certainly have been technically superior.

So much for the Czechs themselves. The other powers involved in the Czechoslovakian problem did not think their actions involved betrayal so much as self-preservation. In their eyes, their own interests came first, and if the only way that peace could be maintained was the sacrifice of Czechoslovakia to Nazi Germany, such a price they were willing to pay.

Soviet Russia claimed to be affronted at the failure of the Western democracies to invite their representatives to Munich, leaving them with the idea that the Russians were willing to give their full support to the Czechs as they had promised in 1935. That impression was itself part of the problem: in fact neither Britain nor France was anxious to see Soviet influence extended any further in central Europe. Both preferred to solve the problem in their own way. But in truth the Soviet Union had little real desire for any entanglement over Czechoslovakia, and certainly no wish to pull the Western powers' chestnuts out of the fire for them. Stalin had already shown a marked coolness over involvement in Spain, where he was willing to allow Spanish communists to fight for the Republic, but wanted only to play a minor part himself – a part for which he insisted he should be handsomely paid. His priorities remained chiefly domestic, and he continued to smear foreign adventures with the epithet of 'Trotskyism'. He revealed his real attitude to foreign involvements when he said in 1931: 'We are fifty to a hundred years behind the advanced countries. We must make up this gap in ten years. Either we do this, or they crush us!'

This meant that he concentrated on the collectivisation of agriculture, the industrialisation of Russia, and on maintaining discipline and cohesion within the party, rooting out deviationists and purging the dissidents. These defensive attitudes prevented any active involvement in Czechoslovakia, the outcome of which, even if favourable, could only be of marginal importance to Russia. In truth, in spite of the obvious Slavonic connection, he rather despised the Czechs, whose democratic system he dismissed as bourgeois and reactionary. It is perhaps unfortunate (though entirely understandable) that Stalin was not invited to Munich. If he had been – and if he, or Molotov, had agreed to attend! – his bluff would have been

called and everyone would have seen his lukewarm enthusiasm
for the Czech cause.

France, denounced by the Czechs as being chiefly responsible
for the Munich betrayal, was apparently in a strong position in
Europe. It had the biggest army in Europe and was linked to
the Soviet Union by the Franco-Soviet pact of 1935, which also
contained pledges for the defence of Czechoslovakia. But
French strength was illusory. The Popular Front government,
which had introduced an ambitious programme of social
reform, had led the country to devaluation, unemployment,
strife and social conflict, and had been replaced in 1938 by a
right-wing government of National Unity, conscious of the
country's divisions and weakness. The much-vaunted French
army, furthermore, was ill-equipped, its fighting morale shaky.
Paralysed by divisions in French opinion and incapable of
providing a firm lead, Daladier's government feared the
growth of communism in France and was willing to leave the
initiative to Britain, fully aware that Britain had made no
promises to Czechoslovakia and was unlikely to provide the
support which France felt it needed to defend the country. At
Munich it became obvious that the French lacked the resolve
to honour their promises and that they were prepared to sell
out to the Germans in the interests of their own survival.

Britain, for its part, was ill-disposed to come to Czechoslovakia's
rescue. The British Prime Minister, Chamberlain, referred in a
broadcast to the crisis as a 'quarrel in a faraway country between
people of whom we know nothing', and seemed anxious to
preserve peace almost at any price. The Cabinet discussed the
problem, and in Chamberlain's words: '. . . was unanimous in the
view that we should not utter a threat to Hitler, and that if he went
into Czechoslovakia we should declare war on him. But it was of
the utmost importance that the decision should be kept secret.'

Since such a decision in order to be effective should be well
publicised, the secrecy he suggested seems incomprehensible,
except on the assumption that the British did not want to harden

France's resolve to hold out against Germany's demands, and further that they did not wish to topple Hitler by encouraging the military to remove him from power. Chamberlain seems to have thought that Hitler's removal would expose Germany to the danger of a communist takeover, saying that 'the disappearance of Hitler would lead to another ten million communist votes in Germany'. This may help to explain why Chamberlain, though he hated air travel, made three flights to Germany in September 1938, and why, though he disliked Hitler intensely, he strove to patch up an agreement with him that would avert war. It also explains his eagerness to strike a bargain with him the day following the Munich conference, when the two men signed the famous 'piece of paper' in which Britain and Germany pledged their joint commitment to future peace. It was this piece of paper that Chamberlain waved triumphantly on his return to Heston airport, and to which he was referring when he told the cheering crowds in Downing Street later that evening 'I believe it is peace for our time'. It is in truth very doubtful whether he accepted Hitler's assurances. He had already been thoroughly disabused of his earlier view that the Chancellor was a reasonable man who would be prepared to settle, and expected that he would soon produce another 'absolutely final demand' that would expose Europe to a new danger of war. But Chamberlain felt he had to make sure of the support of the Commonwealth and the approval of the United States when war eventually came, so that no one would make the mistake of thinking that it was the British who were the aggressors. He also imagined that Britain could take advantage of the breathing space provided by Munich to complete the country's war preparations. In fact, Britain's efforts remained sluggish, while Germany used the interval to close the armaments gap between the two countries: Britain would have had a better opportunity (even if Hitler had not been overthrown) of defeating the Germans in 1938 than it did in 1939. Indeed the British government was so obsessed by its gnawing fear of communism that all its judgments at the time of Munich appear to have been tainted by it.

So it would appear that the doctrine of 'collective security' at the end of the 1930s became the doctrine of 'devil take the hindmost'. No power had the clear intention of betraying Czechoslovakia, and yet the Czechs are to be understood in their opinion that in effect this is precisely what happened.

8:2

How Complete Was US Isolationism Between the Wars?

It is sometimes said that the United States between the wars followed policies of 'isolationism' in its external relations, seeking to minimise its dealings with the outside world. To what extent was this idea no more than a cherished myth in the American tradition, and to what extent was it a reality?

In fact there were many forces pulling the Americans into world affairs. The USA, one of the great manufacturing countries of the world, was constantly seeking new markets for its produce, and searching for supplies of raw materials necessary for its manufacturing industry. Its great corporations, like Ford, Woolworth and Standard Oil, opened outlets all over the world, and simply could not afford to turn their backs on them. Cultural links between the USA and the outside world also flourished very strongly: the literature, broadcasting, films and music of the United States became part of the fabric of world life. American customs, speech patterns and even cigarette tobacco became as familiar to most people as even their own native equivalents. In fact, in many countries of Europe and the world, Hollywood and jazz music dominated the entire cultural scene in the years between the wars.

However, isolationism was essentially a diplomatic rather than a social policy. The idea behind successive American governments was to keep the country out of trouble by keeping out of foreign entanglements. This was not always easy. Policy had the unfortunate habit of getting itself involved with matters of money and trade. As far as trade went, the desire for separateness could be seen in US immigration and tariff policies, aiming at cutting down on foreign contacts; but in the end America depended on foreign trade and would suffer if this were unduly hampered. America, too, also needed and wanted foreign immigrants; its policies were directed not to abolishing immigration, but to controlling it. War debts, too, arising from the First World War were a persistent source of US irritation, and the more Europe wriggled, the more insistent America became. The American attitude was expressed very simply if rather harshly by President Coolidge, when he said 'They hired the money, didn't they?' To them, it seemed right and proper that the borrowers should pay back what they owed.

Essentially, however, the USA had as its main diplomatic aim the wish to keep out of foreign alliances or out of binding commitments to the outside world. This could clearly be seen at the time of the Senate's refusal in 1919 to ratify the Treaty of Versailles, with its clause committing the USA to membership of the League of Nations. Instead, the United States made a separate peace treaty with Germany in 1921. The same could be said of the Neutrality Act of 1935, which tried to prevent the USA becoming involved in any European war, by banning American exports of arms to either side in any war and forbidding American ships from carrying goods for either side. This Act was revised in 1937 and was put into force in the Spanish Civil War.

But it would be a mistake to think that US diplomatic activity was significantly reduced through the existence of such a policy. The United States was deeply involved in what might be termed preventative diplomacy. After the Washington Conference of 1921–2, the US government, concerned at what they saw as the expansion of Japanese power, signed in 1922 both the Four-Power Treaty (with Japan, Britain and France) arranging mutual guarantees of each other's positions in the Pacific, and the Nine-Power Treaty of all the major Pacific powers upholding the independence of China, and the policy of what Senator Hay had called the 'open door' in China. These were linked with a third treaty, the Five-Power Treaty, between the major naval powers, agreeing to restrictions in naval armaments in the Pacific hemisphere. This treaty enjoyed only limited success, and efforts were made to improve it in naval conferences in Geneva in 1927 and in London in 1930, but little came of them.

The United States was also a prime mover in another of the idealistic schemes of the interwar years, the Pact for the Renunciation of War in 1928, commonly known as the Kellogg Pact after the US Secretary of State, Frank B. Kellogg. The US Senate, contrary to its usual inclinations, offered no objection to this agreement between over sixty world powers, but the scheme turned out to be quite useless in practice. Indeed, a number of them, including Italy and Germany, treated it as something of a joke.

In its relations with other American states, which it saw as being in its own sphere of influence, the United States government could scarcely claim to be isolated at all. US troops were involved in what they viewed as 'police action' in various Latin American and Caribbean states, when troops were sent to, and later withdrawn from, Santo Domingo (1924), Nicaragua (1925) and Haiti (1934); and there was an ongoing presence both in Cuba and in Panama. During his presidency, F.D. Roosevelt made the conscious effort to foster friendly relations with Latin American states as part of what he called his 'Good neighbor' policy, and conferences took place at Montevideo (1933), Buenos Aires (1936) and Lima (1938), to promote good relations in that part of the world, and at the same time to assure the security of US dollar investments there, which by this time were running at more than $4,000 million.

In the interwar years, the United States also became involved with other international institutions. It took the practical step of becoming a member of the Universal Postal Union (as did even Nazi Germany and Soviet Russia). The Senate cautiously agreed in 1926 to accept the Permanent Court of International Justice at the Hague, but they hedged their acceptance with such unacceptable conditions that their application was turned down. President Roosevelt carried this unofficial cooperation with the

League of Nations further in 1934 by joining the International Labour Organisation, although once again care was taken that there should be no derogation from US sovereignty.

So the United States was isolated between the wars in international diplomacy only as far as it suited the convenience of the federal government. The policy always had a good deal going for it in terms of American political opinion, as Roosevelt discovered when he encountered difficulties in pushing through the Cash-and-Carry programme and the Lend-Lease programme for Britain on the eve of the American entry into the Second World War. But in fact isolationism imposed very little restriction at any time on America's diplomatic freedom of action.

8:3

Hitler and Mussolini: Were They Friends and Allies?

It is customary among students of history to regard Hitler and Mussolini, the two principal members of the Axis Pact and wartime allies, as close collaborators and even personal friends. This view of their relationship, however, is quite mistaken.

The majority of those who have considered the subject in any detail seem to be agreed that the relationship between the two men was not an intimate one. Both had serious flaws in their characters, rendering them to a greater or lesser degree unappealing to their fellows. Mussolini was proud, imperious and vain, though some who knew him, such as Anthony Eden, found him quite an attractive figure. Hitler was boorish, bullying and rather uncouth, and though he was able to attract devoted followers who were loyal literally to death, he often filled those who came into contact with him with revulsion. Perhaps it would have been surprising if the two men had got on well with each other.

Of the two, Hitler seems to have felt quite warmly towards Mussolini. When he was still labouring in obscurity he looked up to the other as a brilliant success and a powerful and attractive leader. The two did not meet until June 1934, and their initial meeting was not a success. However, in September 1937 he invited Mussolini to successful military manoeuvres in Mecklenburg, and later gave him a tremendous reception in Berlin, where the two stood side by side on the Maifeld in front of a massed crowd of 800,000, an experience that made a lasting impression on the Fascist leader. In 1938, when Mussolini withdrew his opposition to the Nazi takeover of Austria, Hitler was extravagant – almost comical – in his expressions of gratitude. Thereafter Hitler's admiration for him continued quite unfeigned: like himself, Mussolini was a man of the people, with whom Hitler was able to feel at ease as he never felt with members of the traditional ruling classes, least of all Victor Emmanuel and the other crowned heads of Europe. It is true that he was disappointed in Italy's performance later in the war, and came to regard Mussolini as something of a military liability, losing no opportunity to lecture him at length on his shortcomings; but he remained loyal to him to the end, and even arranged his rescue from captivity in the mountains in September 1943 after his dismissal from power. Installed in the short-lived Republic of Salo in northern Italy, he visited Germany several times in 1944, where, numbed by embarrassment at his own inadequacy, he had to submit to further lengthy harangues on the failures of Fascism and the cowardice and treachery of the Italian army, which had brought their joint cause to the brink of defeat.

For his part, Mussolini was initially less than impressed with Hitler. At their first meeting in northern Italy in 1934, Mussolini noted Hitler's nervous and diffident manner, in particular his lank hair and watery eyes, and remarked to one of his aides that he did not like the look of him. Another observer said Hitler was wearing a yellow mackintosh and patent leather shoes, and was clutching a grey felt hat in front of him 'like a little plumber with one of the more embarrassing of his tools'. But Mussolini's first reactions of amused contempt gradually underwent a change. Later meetings impressed him increasingly with Germany's greater power. He still continued to refer slightingly to Hitler's rouged cheeks and unimpressive appearance ('I don't know why the Germans are taken in by him!'), but he was clearly struck by, and more than a little jealous of, Hitler's easy ascendancy in their relationship, and his vanity was affronted by having to play second fiddle to a man he secretly despised. But it was Hitler's lecturing and his priggish self-righteousness that repelled him the most. Ciano, present at one of their meetings in 1942 at Salzburg, reported:

> Hitler talks, talks, talks. Mussolini suffers – he, who is in the habit of talking himself, has instead to remain silent. On the second day, after lunch, Hitler talked uninterruptedly for an hour and forty minutes. He omitted absolutely no argument. . . . Only Cavallero, who is a phenomenon of servility, pretended he was listening. The Germans, poor people, have to endure it every day, and I am certain there isn't a word or a pause they don't know by heart. General Jodl, after an epic struggle, finally went to sleep on the divan.

The trouble was that, however bigoted and objectionable were his views, Hitler had behind him the organised resources of perhaps the most powerful state in Europe, with the clear capacity for putting his will into execution. Mussolini, on the other hand, became increasingly a shadow of his former self, until finally he was executed by partisans and strung up by the heels in a garage forecourt in Milan in 1945.

8:4

Were the Nuremberg War Trials (1945–6) a Travesty of Justice?

The actions carried out by the Nazis in the Second World War led the Allied powers as early as 1943 to promise to bring war criminals to justice. These trials were held in Nuremberg between November 1945 and August 1946. The Allies set up an international Military Tribunal to judge the accused, the bench comprising four judges, with a deputy for each in case of illness, representing the four main Allied powers: Britain, France, the USA and the USSR. Some 199 were accused at Nuremberg, but thousands of others were tried elsewhere: in Allied military courts, by their own countrymen after the Allied withdrawal, and in former occupied countries. Important questions about the legality of the trials were raised even at the time, and continue to be asked by those who think they were inspired more by vengeance than by justice.

At Nuremberg, the prisoners were tried on four counts: crimes against peace – preparing and carrying out acts of aggression; war crimes – the ill-treatment of prisoners of war and civilian populations; extremes of brutality against individuals or groups; and conspiracy – participation in plans to commit the other three offences. A number of the accused, including Hitler, Goebbels and Himmler, were already dead. Another, Robert Ley, former Head of the Nazi Labour front, hanged himself before the trial started; another, Hermann Goering, swallowed cyanide when it was over in order to avoid the gallows. Another, Gustav Krupp, was senile and did not understand the charges; his son Alfred was later tried and sentenced in his place. Of the twenty-four who were brought to trial, three were acquitted. Three, including Hitler's deputy, Rudolf Hess, received life imprisonment. Two got twenty years, one fifteen and Doenitz, who had made the final surrender to the Allies, got ten years' imprisonment. A number of the accused, including Adolf Eichmann (responsible for administering the 'Final Solution' for the Jews) and Franz Stangl (the former Commandant of the camps at Treblinka and Sobibor), were later found abroad, brought to trial and convicted. Twelve were hanged on 16 October 1946.

Week after week, the evidence had mounted up during the trial, evidence at the same time chilling and overwhelming. One of the accused, Hess, gave every sign of mental derangement; only Goering maintained his quick-witted awareness to the end. The others were broken men. One, Hans Frank, whose thirty-eight volume diary gave irrefutable evidence of his involvement in murder, starvation and extermination, despaired completely and summed up what many of them felt when he said: 'A thousand years will pass, and this guilt of Germany will not pass away!'

How justified was this trial and its outcome? Few disputed the moral justification for it. The crimes involved were so dreadful and so overwhelming that no one imagined there was no redress; everyone supposed that the legal basis for the trial lay in The Hague and Geneva Conventions. The general reaction, therefore, was to welcome the trial as going some way towards atoning for unprecedented atrocities.

Yet there remain disturbing features. How could aggression be illegal if there was no legislative agreement under which it could be punished? It was highly unusual for any state or individual ruler to be punished for breaking a treaty, though a number of such trials have been held since Nuremberg. To spare the Soviet Union's embarrassment, for the USSR had also been guilty of exactly the same offences against Poland and Finland, the charge was confined to aggression by the Axis powers alone. Thus the offence seemed to be specially designed to fit the crime and was applied only selectively. No Italians were ever charged. Italy had changed sides, and to indict an ally would have opened the door to a similar indictment against the USSR.

The accused were also condemned for crimes that were not crimes in international law at the time they were committed. If extreme crimes against humanity, or conspiracy to commit such crimes, were now offences against international law, the same charges could have been brought against Churchill for his complicity in the bombing of Dresden, if the Germans had been victorious instead of defeated.

Furthermore, the accused were not allowed to say: 'But I was only obeying my orders.' To expect an individual subordinate to be able to distinguish between a legal order and a criminal one was quite unrealistic. The Allies themselves, throughout the war, considered men bound by superior orders, and not legally liable for them. But now the Allies were saying that obedience to orders was not a defence, but only a mitigation. This would have certainly been bad news to the bombardier aboard *Enola Gay* who was ordered to drop the first atom bomb on Hiroshima.

But the most fundamental criticism was the simplest. For punishment to have at least the appearance of justice, the prosecutor must not also be the judge. The judges at Nuremberg represented the nations that were parties to the action, and therefore could not be said to be impartial. It would have been better that the judges should have been empanelled from among neutral nations such as Sweden or Switzerland, for this would have given a greater impression of impartiality. The partiality of the bench gave ammunition to those who maintained that the trials were merely acts of vengeance carried out by the victor against the vanquished. As Goering himself shrewdly observed at the trial: 'The victors will always be the judge, the vanquished the accused.' Such a criticism will always weaken the moral justification of the Nuremberg Tribunal, though it will not lessen the frightfulness of the crimes that brought the trials about.

8:5

The Korean War: Was Stalin to Blame?

In June 1950 a North Korean army of 130,000 men crossed the frontier and invaded South Korea. At the time it was widely believed that the Soviet Union was the main instigator of this invasion, and the charge has been repeated many times since. It still occurs in most historical accounts of the war. But almost from the beginning there have been those who have put forward reasons for doubting this interpretation. Even so, their revelations have never successfully overturned the established view, and this continues to be accepted as the true explanation for the war. The theory of Soviet aggression, however, is open to very serious doubts.

The first thing that casts doubt on Russian scheming as the main origin of the war is the inherent implausibility of the motives attributed to Stalin. Only a few weeks before the Korean invasion began, the Russian delegates had walked out of the Security Council of the United Nations in protest against the refusal of the Western powers to admit the representatives of communist China to membership in place of Jiang Jieshi's (Chiang Kai-shek) nominees. The US view was that the Chinese nationalist regime, currently exiled in Taiwan, was the legitimate government of China, and that the Chinese communists who had seized power in Beijing at the end of 1949 were no more than a purely temporary *de facto* leadership with no right to claim China's place in the UN. There was, of course, no reason why the Russians should not have returned to the Security Council table after the invasion took place, but the fact that they did not do so suggests that they were as much taken by surprise as anyone else. The official Soviet view was that the illegal exclusion of Mao's delegation from the Security Council invalidated all the council's actions, so that there was no need to veto them; while the US view – backed by the other Western powers – was that the mere absence of the Russians from the Security Council did not in itself constitute a veto and so did not prevent the UN taking decisions while they were not there. Both interpretations have some plausibility about them, but it seems overwhelmingly probable that if the Russians had engineered the invasion as their opponents advocated, they would have taken care to be present so that they could veto any UN proposals to deal with the war. As things turned out, the council's decision to take police action in Korea against the invasion went unchallenged, and the Soviet Union could not prevent UN intervention in the war.

Quite apart from this, there is a good deal of evidence to suggest that the war started because both Syngman Rhee in the South and Kim Il Sung in the North were unwilling for Korea to continue as a divided nation, and both had plans to reunite the country, by force if necessary, after the Allied withdrawal. There is no doubt, also, that both sides behaved equally provocatively in the weeks leading up to the war. President Syngman Rhee's defence minister told General MacArthur before the war that his troops were now ready to drive into North Korea, and the President himself had boasted as early as 1949 that his forces could take Pyongyang, the North's capital, in three days. Kim Il Sung behaved equally provocatively, spurning the hundred seats set aside for him after the recent elections in the South to be filled after reunification, and permitting, if not encouraging, numerous frontier 'incidents' between the two countries to stir up ill-feeling. The language of his tightly knit clique was disfigured with the usual communist rhetoric and was equally intemperate in tone. There seems little doubt that in its origin the war was a civil war, with each side trying to jockey the other into making the first move.

Foreign states, at least at first, were little more than bystanders. Russian observers saw through Kim's bombast and doubted his capacity for a full-scale war. General Kalinov noted the North Korean preparations, but commented on their failure to provide a modern air force. General Zakharov warned against the Soviet Union becoming automatically involved: 'It is necessary to be careful with these Koreans. . . . We are not going to act like the sorcerer's apprentice, creating a force that could make mischief in the Far East.'

Kim consulted with Moscow, but Stalin shared these doubts. Nevertheless Stalin decided to ask Mao Zedong for his views, and learned that Mao thought the war would be over quickly and the USA would not have time to intervene; in any case, said Mao, the war was an internal affair that the Koreans would settle for themselves. This did not increase Stalin's enthusiasm for it.

The United States was also beset by ideological prejudices, but of the contrary variety. The idea began to take root after 1949, sedulously fostered by Senator McCarthy in Washington, that only Western cowardice had brought about the fall of Jiang Jieshi, and that a little more American resolution would have enabled him to survive in his struggle with Mao. President Truman had a deep personal distrust of Russian communism, and was already more than half persuaded to stand firm against the USSR. US commentators began to suspect the existence of a worldwide communist conspiracy which sooner or later America was going to have to confront, a feeling reinforced by the appearance of a defence document known as NSC 68 (National Security Committee paper No. 68) which plainly stated that the USA should

> . . . strike out on a bold and massive programme of rebuilding the West's defensive potential to surpass that of the Soviet world, and of meeting each fresh challenge promptly and unequivocally. . . . This new concept of the security needs of the nation calls for an annual appropriation of the order of 50 billion dollars, or not much below the former wartime levels.

Hence a note of toughness crept into US attitudes towards the communist states. The diplomatic note fired off by the Truman administration at Moscow on 27 July 1950 gave evidence of this new belligerence. At the same time, the public announcement made in Washington to intervene in the dispute on behalf of South Korea – even before the UN had had the chance to discuss it – shows that the United States had already decided to enter the struggle and to 'go it alone' if necessary.

Stalin, on the other hand, was very conscious that the West had the massive technological advantage of nuclear armaments, and so seems to have been anxious to avoid confrontation with the West. What the USSR needed above all at this juncture was a spell of peace and quiet in which to lick its wounds. Stalin knew perfectly well that the Soviet Union had been exhausted by the struggle just ended with Nazi Germany, its forces dangerously depleted, and the Red Army now spread very thinly over eastern Europe. This was certainly not the time to pick a fight over a matter in which the Russian leadership was not primarily interested. The fact that Stalin still got the blame for the Korean War in spite of all these facts shows that the Western powers in general, and the United States in particular, profoundly overestimated the power, the wickedness and the satanic cunning of the Soviet leadership. In the light of its economic and military weaknesses, the USSR must have been delighted to be treated with such circumspection by the West.

8:6

Was the Hungarian Rising of 1956 a Total Disaster?

The Hungarian Rising of October 1956 is often regarded as an attempt by the country to break away from Soviet control, but an attempt that failed, plunging the country back into submission to the USSR for the next three decades. This may have been true for the first few years, but it is an error to suppose that the rising in the long run achieved nothing worthwhile.

Hungary had been at first under Soviet military occupation directly after the war, and then under a communist regime that enjoyed the full backing of the USSR. At the Twentieth Party Congress, however, in February 1956, the new Russian leader Khrushchev had arraigned Stalin on a number of charges, one of which, by stressing that there were 'different roads to socialism', suggested that Stalin's demand for monolithic control over the satellite countries was on the point of being relaxed. The Hungarians were encouraged in this expectation by events in the summer of 1956 in Poland, where there was clear dissatisfaction with Soviet influence, and where Polish pressure had led to the release and return to power of the popular leader Wladislaw Gomulka.

So Hungarian radicals in October brought pressure to bear on their new leader, Ernö Gerö, to call back to power the popular Imré Nagy as Prime Minister. However, at the same time, Gerö called on the Soviet troops stationed in Hungary to help him control the situation. But instead of controlling the situation his action inflamed it. During the last week in October fighting broke out in Budapest and other cities. Political prisoners were released and members of the secret police, or AVO, were attacked in the streets and killed. Nagy boldly abolished the one-party state, and there was talk of holding genuinely free elections. Most threatening of all to the Soviet Union, Nagy put forward the idea of 'non-alignment', i.e. withdrawal from the Warsaw Pact in favour of an independent foreign policy. Cries of 'Russians, go home' were heard in the capital. Student demonstrators captured the radio station and began broadcasting in the name of Radio Free Budapest, and in one of the city's parks youths hitched a cable round a great bronze statue of Stalin and with the aid of a heavy lorry toppled it, leaving a huge pair of bronze boots on the plinth while the rest of the metal body was hauled round the city at the back of a refuse cart. Nagy appointed his first non-communists to cabinet posts and negotiated a ceasefire. The Hungarian War Minister, Pal Maleter, entered into negotiations with Soviet officers for the planned withdrawal of the entire Soviet army from the country.

This occurred at the same time as an Anglo-French ultimatum was delivered to Israel and Egypt over the security of the Suez Canal, an ultimatum that was the pretext for an Anglo-French invasion of Egypt. These developments signalled the preoccupation of the Western powers with Near Eastern affairs and tipped the scale in favour of Russian intervention in Hungary, where American propaganda broadcasts were already urging the Hungarians to leave the Warsaw Pact. Many Hungarians expected American help. Perhaps Khrushchev felt threatened by this turn of events. Certainly he decided to act.

Within days masses of Soviet troops, reinforced by heavy tanks, returned to crush Budapest. Tanks roared at full throttle along the city streets, pumping gunfire into buildings right and left. Nagy appealed frantically for Western help, but without result. He and Maleter were whisked off to Russia by plane on a promise of further negotiation, but on their arrival were imprisoned, later to be secretly tried and executed in 1958. In Nagy's place the more conformist János Kádár became Prime Minister and was entrusted with returning Hungary to its former submissive condition as a Soviet satellite.

The Red Army restored order in Budapest at a frightful price – the death of 30,000 Hungarians, many of them mere bystanders, and almost 7,000 Russian troops. All the old terrors about Russian imperialism came flooding back. As one US observer commented: 'Liberation was a sham. It always had been a sham. All Hungary did was to expose it to the world. However deep Eisenhower's fear of communism, his fear of war was deeper. . . . The Hungarians, and other eastern European peoples, learned that there would be no liberation, and that their policy of playing off East against West was finished.' Meantime, the new Hungarian regime, Soviet-installed, came to heel obediently, and ruled the country with rigid orthodoxy, to the silent fury of the people. Khrushchev's brief flirtation with liberalisation, and Hungary's, was at an end.

On the face of it, then, it would appear that the Hungarian Rising achieved nothing that was worthwhile. Its results seemed to be a total disaster for Hungary. However, things were not quite as simple as that. For one thing, the Soviet Union afterwards modified its tone towards its eastern European partners, and did not repress them so thoroughly as before. For instance, when the Czechoslovaks rebelled in 1968, the Russians took care that the tanks of other Warsaw Pact countries as well as their own were in evidence on the streets of Prague. Furthermore, though there was a threatening stand-off between troops and Czech civilians, there was little if any actual bloodshed. The Czech leader, Dubĉek, was sent to work in a woodyard, rather than being shot in the Lubyanka. Nor were the affairs of these former 'satellite' states regulated quite so closely as before.

Hungary's case appeared to be different. Kádár appeared on the surface to be quite conformist and indeed completed the collectivisation of agricultural land in 1961. But he soon embarked on policies which introduced, stealthily, those policy modifications that the earlier leadership had been warned against. Thus Hungarian communism soon acquired its own national flavour. In the 1960s, political detainees were set at liberty and the vigilance of the secret police was slowly relaxed.

An atmosphere of greater freedom pervaded the country, and press censorship was less severe. In 1964 Kádár reached a religious compromise with the papacy and the Catholic Church (though Cardinal Mindszenty refused to accept it and took refuge in the US Embassy, and only left there when he went into exile in 1971). Also, in 1968, economic decentralisation was launched. Contacts with the West increased, foreign investment began, and there was more competition between business firms. In 1983, political elections began to be contested in a way entirely untypical of the communist system. In 1987, an income tax was introduced on the Western model, and shortly afterwards the Value Added Tax (or VAT). When Kádár retired from the political leadership in 1988, the new Prime Minister Károly Grosz went even further by recognising free trade unions and by legalising rival political parties. The following May, a new constitution was adopted, based on multi-party democracy and a new presidential executive. But by 1990 the dissolution of the eastern European bloc was well advanced. A right-of-centre group won the elections, and in 1991 devalued the currency, awarded compensation to landowners and businessmen expropriated by the communists, and signed a pact beginning the association of Hungary with the European Community. It is not an exaggeration to say that the whole of this modernising process can be seen to date back to the events of the Rising in 1956.

8:7

The Cultural Revolution: What Were Mao's Real Motives?

The Cultural Revolution in China is often presented by Western historians as an attempt made by Mao Zedong to identify and eliminate his political opponents, and so continue his personal dictatorship of the Chinese people. Not even Jung Chang, in her graphic account of this period given in Wild Swans: Three Daughters of China, *published in the West in 1993, sufficiently explains its brutal terrors. But it is a*

fundamental error to regard the Cultural Revolution as no more than a
destructive and autocratic caprice on the part of Chairman Mao. Much
more sober reasons underlay it.

Mao had certain deep misgivings about the course he saw being plotted by the People's Republic in the years after 1950. This can be seen at the time of the 'Hundred Flowers' campaign as early as 1956, when Mao had for a short time actively encouraged the growth of dissident opinions and even open criticism of the communist regime. The reasons for these misgivings arose out of the unfavourable comparisons Mao made with the objectives and the workings of Soviet communism in Russia. To Mao, Russian communism was too much dominated by modernisation, industrialisation and Westernisation, all of which he mistrusted in greater or lesser degree; it was too dominated by cliques and committees, and controlled by technicians and experts who paid too much attention to output and too little to building the socialist character of the citizen. Above all, he felt, it ran the risk of creating a new ruling class of administrators with their powers, perks and privileges, so that in the end the country was run by a self-absorbed and self-interested clique not much different from the Manchu mandarins who had failed the country before the revolution. It was his idea, therefore, that the revolution should be kept in motion, aware of its ideals and purposes, and not allowed to fossilise into smug self-satisfaction with what had been achieved so far. He also felt, after Stalin, that the Russian communists had ceased to oppose Western capitalism, but were now bent on imitating it. Their emphasis on more cordial relations with the West, their willingness to do deals with them in limiting the spread of armaments, their new concentration on consumer goods to buy off worker pressure – all this lay behind Mao's belief that the Soviet leadership was composed of the 'new tsars' who were almost indistinguishable from the old ones. In other words, his approach to politics was more strictly spartan, almost more puritan.

The gist of the Cultural Revolution, therefore, was Mao's

attack on formal institutions, and his effort to keep alive the original spirit that had united the early heroes of the revolution in the days of the Long March. All his attempts to jolt the personnel of the new Republic out of the ruts into which they had allowed themselves to sink – the effort to make electronic engineers do automobile maintenance, or doctors of philosophy scrub out the latrines – are to be seen in this light. All institutionalisation of functions he saw as inherently contrary to the spirit of revolution, and therefore he did his best to resist.

There were two consequences of his actions to which he perhaps gave insufficient thought. The first was his reliance on the Red Guard, many of them half-educated youths who terrorised towns and cities by mass parades, and blindly demonstrated their loyalty to what they thought were his wishes by waving their 'little red books' of the *Thoughts of Chairman Mao* and threatening and humiliating academics, officials and party bigwigs who represented, to their thinking, the old revolutionary order. Even the senior ranks of the ruling élite were reorganised, and men like Liu Shaochi expelled from it. The second, and more important, effect of this was that the country was brought to a standstill. Schools, universities and other places of learning were closed for a time in 1967 to permit a complete rethinking of the educational curriculum and its purposes; examinations were suspended, and the associated scientific research and practice was discontinued. So communist China, already seriously behind in its progress, slipped further down the competitive league, and the revolution ground to a halt. It was only in 1968 that China began to recover something of its former momentum.

Outsiders found it strange and frightening as millions of uniformed Chinese youngsters abandoned themselves to a frenzy of revolutionary enthusiasm in which there was a good deal of disrespect but very little constructive purpose. In the end, the Red Guard went further even than Mao hoped they would, disrupting the whole life of the country in their ideological enthusiasm. The final outcome, after the death of Mao in 1975, was the hardening of the political line between the moderates, who sought to adapt the revolution to the changed political situation in the later twentieth century, and the radicals, who were really extremely conservative in the way they continued to cling to the old revolutionary forces.

8:8

The Falklands Crisis, 1982: Should Britain Have Gone to War?

The Falklands crisis of 1982 illustrated perfectly the dangers into which its latter-day policies of colonialism led Britain in the late twentieth century. It is doubtful, however, whether the British government took the right course before and during this crisis, and it would be a mistake to imagine that there was no alternative to the policy that the Thatcher government followed at that time.

At first sight it would seem that Argentina had a good claim to the Falkland Islands. These lie about 400 miles off the eastern seaboard of Argentina, and, since they form part of the same landmass, might appear by the so-called 'proximity argument' to be properly part of the same territory. Unfortunately the 'proximity argument' is not generally accepted in the world at large. Such an argument would cause endless trouble if it were extended to places like the Channel Islands, Corsica or Rhodes – or even in the case of Britain itself, which lies not 400 miles but 22 miles off the coast of France.

Fortunately the Argentinians did not employ the proximity argument. Their claim was a historical one, and went back to the attempted partition of the world in the Treaty of Tordesillas by Pope Alexander VI in 1493, when he divided the globe into the eastern hemisphere, which he awarded to Portugal, and the western, which he gave to Spain. However, few nations afterwards accepted either the award or the treaty (some indeed did not even accept the Pope). In particular, Britain and France would not accept any claim to a territory unless the nation making it had established a permanent settlement there. This could not have been done in the case of the Falkland Islands, which were not even discovered until the mid-sixteenth century – and then by a Frenchman, not a Spaniard. It was not until the mid-eighteenth century that any settlement was established, when the French set up sheep farming there. The British drove out these settlers at the end of the Seven Years' War. The French then transferred their claim to the Spaniards, but the British navy established a trading post, which the Spaniards removed by force in 1770. War threatened, but eventually Britain and Spain signed a treaty in 1771 settling a number of outstanding differences, in a secret clause in which both sides agreed to quit the islands and leave them uninhabited.

When Spain's empire in South America began to disintegrate during the Napoleonic Wars its claim to the Falkland Islands was taken up by the state of Buenos Aires; and when Buenos Aires became part of Argentina in 1816 the Falklands claim was transferred there. Argentina placed a garrison on the islands four years later, but Britain took the view that a military garrison did not constitute a proper settlement, and that in any case the Argentinians were in breach of the 1771 treaty. The Argentinians objected that they were not party to the 1771 treaty, and so were not bound by it. All the same Britain expelled them. But then Britain rather spoiled the effect of this legalistic gesture in 1832 by setting up a settlement of their own – admittedly a civilian one – and proclaiming the Falklands a British colony. That was how the situation remained until the twentieth century.

The first modern problem over the ownership of the islands occurred after the Second World War, when Argentina referred the dispute to the United Nations in 1947. Britain proposed to refer the whole question of British possessions in the area to the International Court of Justice, but the reference was rejected by Argentina (and by Chile) on grounds of their 'indisputable rights' over the area. In 1955 Britain referred the dispute unilaterally, but the court declined a hearing on account of Argentina's refusal to submit to its jurisdiction. Several anti-British demonstrations subsequently in Buenos

Aires led to the decision of the Labour government of James Callaghan in 1977 to send ships to the south Atlantic, while trying at the same time to produce a settlement. When Mrs Thatcher took office she sent Nicholas Ridley to Argentina with proposals, which went further: he suggested a long-term freeze on the dispute, a lease-back arrangement whereby titular sovereignty would be vested in Argentina, and a joint Anglo-Argentinian administration. This, if pursued, would have provided an admirably sane and practical alternative to the policies later followed.

Unfortunately, there were a number of difficulties here. One was that the plan was heavily criticised in London by Conservative, Labour and Liberal MPs as lacking in backbone. Most of the critics wanted a firmer line with Argentina. Another difficulty arose out of the attitude of the Falkland Islands' Legislative Council, which naturally was unwilling to see the area handed over to Argentina, even though the Argentinians offered to make the Falklands their 'most pampered region'. But the third difficulty arose out of the uncompromising refusal of the Argentinian delegation to the settlement talks to contemplate further delays. They made an offer to each and every of the 1,800 inhabitants of the islands of compensation to the tune of £17,000 if they would agree to accept Argentinian sovereignty, but this was brushed aside. The Argentinians therefore said that 'unless a speedy negotiated settlement was reached, it would end the negotiations and seek other means to resolve the dispute'.

It seemed to be at about this point that the Thatcher government decided to tough out the dispute. She concluded that mounting Argentinian impatience was the direct result of the recent reduction, for reasons of economy, of British naval strength in the south Atlantic, and that the correct way to handle the situation was to send reinforcements. Mrs Thatcher discovered to her dismay that there was only a small detachment of seventy Royal Marines on East Falkland and one ice patrol vessel armed with two 20-mm guns to protect the whole colony. British weakness became evident in March 1982, when an Argentinian warship landed a party of sixty 'scrap dealers' on South Georgia, who were able to seize the island without difficulty. Voices in Britain began to be raised for a more vigorous response, including that of Denis Healey, the Labour foreign affairs spokesman, who called the government's actions 'foolish and spineless'.

At about the same time in the mind of Mrs Thatcher, the idea of a small, victorious foreign war to restore the fortunes of a government that was going to have to seek re-election in little more than a year took root. Her resolution hardened when, at the start of April, Argentinian troops landed at Port Stanley and took over the islands in little more than three hours, deporting the British Governor, Rex Hunt, to Uruguay and setting up an Argentinian administration. Thatcher was not slow to pick up the gauntlet. There followed for ten weeks an undeclared war in the south Atlantic between Argentinian and British forces.

In a remarkable demonstration of logistical improvisation Britain assembled a task force of some 30 warships and supporting vessels, a fleet of the most modern aircraft and 6,000 fighting troops, which were efficiently conveyed 8,000 miles to recover the islands by force of arms. South Georgia was repossessed on 25 April and Port Stanley in East Falkland on 13 June. The Argentinian army of over 12,000 men eventually surrendered to the British task force. Argentinian casualties amounted to about 400; British casualties to about 50. The Royal Navy lost two destroyers and two frigates to missile attack from the air, and an Exocet missile also sank the chartered Cunard container ship *Atlantic Conveyor* off San Carlos during the landings there. For their part, the Argentinians had lost nearly 400 more when the cruiser *General Belgrano* was torpedoed and sunk by a British submarine in May. The conflict served to reaffirm the vulnerability of warships to air attack. It also led almost automatically to the overthrow of President Galtieri shortly after the end of hostilities.

The United States, in trying to find a solution to the dispute before and during the war, was placed in a very difficult situation because it was friendly to both sides in the dispute.

President Reagan attempted unsuccessfully to mediate, sending Alexander Haig to London to represent the State Department and the National Security Council in efforts to avert or contain the conflict. Haig was contemptuous of the matters at issue. When he was shown maps he could not understand why the British were so upset. 'Gee, it's only a pimple on their ass!' he is supposed to have said. The matter, however, was particularly difficult for President Reagan, who was not only trying to uphold Security Council Resolution 502 against the use of force, but was simultaneously supplying both sides with materials of war. Mrs Thatcher, however, was resolute. She refused to budge from the position she had adopted: 'We made it clear to Mr Haig that the withdrawal of the invaders' troops must come first; that the sovereignty of the islands is not affected by the act of invasion; and that when it comes to future negotiations what matters most is what the Falkland Islanders themselves wish.'

This admission enshrines perhaps Britain's most fundamental mistake. It is true that the Thatcher government was returned with a increased majority in 1983, and that it had the satisfaction of gratifying all the latter-day 'Jingos' who wished to defend the traditional notion of the British Empire. But whether the hundreds of millions the war cost and the essentially unstable position in the south Atlantic that it helped to preserve were ultimately worthwhile is still very much an open question. At the time, having abandoned the earlier plan for a transfer of titular sovereignty to Buenos Aires, there seemed perhaps to be no alternative course of action, apart from backing down to 'dago threats'. The Junta in Buenos Aires were a 'gang of thugs' (as Haig told the Cabinet), and the United Nations had condemned them. Resolution 502 required the Argentinians to withdraw, but, if they did not, Britain had the right under article 51 of the Charter to repossess its territory by the use of reasonable force. This they duly did. Nevertheless it seemed to be a quixotic motive to engage in a war on behalf of less than 2,000 settlers (but more than 600,000 sheep) who claimed they wanted to continue under the Union Jack instead of under the Argentinian flag.

At the same time, however, it appears not much worse to require the Falkland Islanders to live under a rather remote Argentinian suzerainty than to hand back nearly 5 million Anglicised Hong Kong Chinese to Chinese communist control on the expiry of the ancient treaty in 1997, or to restore Gibraltar to Spain. What the latter-day Palmerstons who criticise British policy have perhaps forgotten is that Britain is no longer an imperial power, and the gestures of imperialism at the end of the twentieth century are more expensive and less appropriate than they once were.

8:9

The Cuba Crisis, 1963: Did Kennedy Save the Free World?

Historians are generally agreed on awarding to President Kennedy high honours for the courage and firmness shown in his handling of the Cuban Missiles Crisis in 1962, which, it is said, saved the world from nuclear destruction. Yet this view of his intervention in the affair requires considerable modification.

There can be no doubt about the seriousness of the situation in Cuba in October 1962. A U-2 reconnaissance flight over the island had recently revealed nuclear missile sites being installed under Russian supervision in Cuba, from whose weapons it was calculated most of the United States would be vulnerable. Kennedy's advisers informed him that they had to be removed. But how could he get the missiles out of Cuba without triggering a nuclear war? Some advisers wanted surprise attacks on the bases, that were likely to eliminate the threat but would kill Russian technicians and Cuban soldiers at the same time; some wanted an armed invasion of Cuba, which it was hoped would be more successful than the previous year's 'Bay of Pigs' fiasco. Robert Kennedy, however, said (whatever he meant) that he wanted 'no Pearl Harbors on his brother's record'. So the US Secretary of Defence eventually settled for a naval blockade of the island that would prevent the delivery of further shipments of nuclear weapons. In a TV broadcast on 22 October, President Kennedy imposed what he called a 'quarantine' on the island, and threatened full-scale nuclear retaliation if President Castro attempted to use the missiles against the USA: 'It shall be the policy of this nation to regard any nuclear missile launched from Cuba against any nation in the western hemisphere as an attack by the Soviet Union on the United States, requiring a full retaliatory response.'

Kennedy therefore confronted Khrushchev with the threat of war if he did not disown this risky initiative and remove the weapons. Khrushchev for his part resorted to bluster, first denying that in fact he was installing nuclear weapons in Cuba, and then attempting to assert that they were for defensive purposes only. It was calculated, meantime, that the sites would become operational in only a few days. The country was on red alert: the air force prepared to take out the sites before they could be used; the navy moved into position to stop the first of the approaching Soviet ships, and a fleet of B52 strategic bombers took to the skies with nuclear bombs on board in preparation for war.

But the crisis blew over, for neither side wanted war. The first Russian ships submitted to be stopped and searched; the flow of nuclear armaments to Cuba ceased. Khrushchev wrote to Kennedy offering to remove the missiles from Cuba if Kennedy would give his guarantee not to attack it. Kennedy accepted the offer, but before he could reply Khrushchev sent a second letter, demanding that the USA also remove its nuclear bases from Turkey. Kennedy refused to bargain. He agreed to the demand in the first letter, but ignored the demand in the second. On the evening of 27 October, Robert Kennedy met with the Soviet ambassador, Anatoly Dobrynin, and required 'a commitment by tomorrow that those bases should be removed'. He threatened that if the Russians did not agree, United States forces would remove them themselves. He also added that, though not part of the deal, if the Russians complied with US wishes, American missiles in Turkey would also be dismantled.

The crisis subsided as quickly as it had arisen. Khrushchev began to remove the missiles, claiming that he had achieved his objective of protecting Cuba from American attacks. Shortly afterwards, under UN supervision, US missiles were removed from their bases in Turkey. Later a 'hot-line' telephone and telex link were set up between the White House and the Kremlin to help to avert similar crises in future, or to prevent the accidental outbreak of war caused by faulty intelligence or malfunctioning equipment. Later still, in 1963, the first of a series of Nuclear Test Ban treaties was signed, to be followed in 1968 by a Nuclear Non-Proliferation treaty. These marked the beginning of a slight thaw in Cold War temperatures.

The Americans claimed this as a great victory for the 'free world' and complimented Kennedy on his firmness and determination. Western opinion generally agreed with the White House official, Dean Rusk, who said 'We were eyeball to eyeball, but I think the other fellow just blinked.' Less generous observers accused Kennedy of manufacturing the crisis to silence his Republican critics and advance his party's chances in the midterm elections in November 1962. He had been campaigning chiefly on domestic issues such as the New Frontier programme, but this crisis reinforced the impression he wished to give of himself as a wise, strong leader. He knew that the installation of forty-four missiles in Cuba did not significantly alter the nuclear balance of power when America had four times as many missiles as the USSR, but he knew that their proximity to the United States was bound to give rise to apprehension among the American people, and this uncertainty he was fully prepared to exploit. In this light, the Cuban crisis was seen by some observers as a disgraceful and rather perilous exercise in nuclear brinkmanship.

As for Khrushchev, the rebuff proved fatal to his political career, and within a year he fell from power. Some agreed with the American analysis, believing that he had been worsted in this encounter; indeed, under Brezhnev, who succeeded him in 1964, the USSR embarked on a crash programme to expand the armed forces and the Soviet navy, and to bring the Soviet

Union up to full parity with the USA in nuclear armaments. Khrushchev himself afterwards remembered the affair rather differently. Though he held no very high opinion of his opponent, whom he considered inexperienced and rather shallow, he thought President Kennedy was honest and meant well. Unfortunately he believed him to be the tool of America's vast military–industrial complex that was jockeying him towards war. He seems also to have believed Robert Kennedy when he allegedly said to Dobrynin that unless he complied with their wishes the President was in danger of being overthrown by the military. He thought that domestic political pressures were compelling the President to strike a stubborn patriotic pose in order to improve his party's chances and to secure support at the polls. Of course, it is only to be expected that Khrushchev would attempt to justify his actions in some such way as this, but his analysis of the position in 1962 presents the whole Cuban missiles problem from a different angle and in a new light.

8:10

How Sensible Was the 'Domino Theory'?

In the course of the 1960s the idea gained ground that the United States was obliged to do all in its power to check the growth of communism in East Asia in order to shield countries against powerful communist neighbours threatening to bring the whole hemisphere under their domination. This US strategy, however, proved to be a gross strategic and historical error. In any case the execution of the policy was almost totally ineffective.

After 1945, the USA struggled desperately to avert a civil war in China, and when the struggle began, went on to try to mediate between the warring parties. Successive US governments, feeling threatened by the success of communism in China and suspecting the growth of a worldwide communist plot to subvert democratic states, continued to give help and encouragement to the Nationalist leader Jiang Jieshi long after his flight to Taiwan, and for more than twenty years refused to recognise the communist regime in Beijing. Further communist outbreaks in neighbouring states suggested that the whole of East Asia was susceptible to the same complaint.

This was particularly true of Indochina. At first, successive US administrations were reluctant to become involved in any exploit that might smack of 'colonialism', but the persistent appeals of the crumbling French regime in Indochina helped to change its mind. With the development of the power of Ho Chi Minh in the northern part of the country, and his defeat of a large French army at Dien Bien Phu in 1954, these fears of Asian communism grew. By 1960 the 'domino theory' had gained influence over American thinking. This was the view that the collapse of one local regime to communist aggression must lead to the collapse of others in their turn, one after another, like a row of dominoes, and therefore that the sooner the United States took a stand for the defence of the area the more of it could be saved from communist domination.

As the result of this conviction, the USA in Kennedy's presidency became more and more involved in the defence of Vietnam against Ho Chi Minh's attacks, sending first 'advisers' and later combat troops to the country. President Johnson grimly declared in 1966 that the 'Americans would stay and fight beside the people of South Vietnam . . . until aggression has stopped.' By 1968 the United States had become entirely responsible for the war, with American money, supplies and armaments being pumped into the country, and over half a million troops sent to fight there. When he became President, Nixon declared his intention of withdrawing from the war, but it took several years more before he eventually disentangled himself from it under a ceasefire agreement reached in Paris in January 1973. The last US troops were to leave Vietnam within two months, prisoners of war were to be exchanged, and the United Nations were to be invited to provide a truce supervision force.

The South Vietnam that the USA had been at such pains to uphold fell into Northern hands like ripe fruit. By 1975 communism was triumphant throughout the length and breadth of all Vietnam. The armies of the newly victorious state went on before the end of the 1970s to flood over into the neighbouring, recently independent state of Laos. They also invaded Cambodia, or Kampuchea as it came to be called, where they defeated the Khmer Rouge, whose leader, Pol Pot, since his seizure of power from his predecessor, General Lon Nol, had governed his unfortunate people with appalling barbarism. So hideous were the methods employed by Pol Pot that he wiped out about half the population, and the Vietnamese invasion came almost as a relief. From Vietnam itself, where the communist oligarchy was busy weeding out their old opponents, there followed in 1979 a huge exodus of the so-called 'boat people', mostly middle-class and supporters of the toppled Saigon government, who fled the country in anything that would float in order not to be forced to live under a communist regime. All these events led observers to think that perhaps the initial blunder of the United States in entering Southeast Asia had now been compounded by the worse blunder of leaving it. Perhaps there was something in the 'domino theory', for now the whole area was threatened with communism.

However, events soon proved that American fears of communism were hysterical and exaggerated. In the 1980s, Vietnamese forces were withdrawn both from Laos and Kampuchea, and peace returned to Vietnam itself. Communist China, instead of making common cause with the new Vietnamese government, was so upset by the unruly behaviour of its former protégé that it quarrelled with it. There followed a short frontier war in 1979 from which it was the Chinese who retired first to lick their wounds. Relations between the states of the communist bloc, and especially those between Russia and China, did not present the USA with the monolithic foe that McCarthy and many other American observers had imagined. They, just as much as the rest of the world, were at sixes and sevens with each other. It began to dawn on the

United States that the 'domino theory' was no longer important, if it had ever been.

What they had imagined to be the immense ideological monolith of communism was really only the much less threatening and entirely conventional danger of nationalism. The leaders they had supposed to be part of the communist conspiracy were in reality seeking only to oust unwelcome foreigners from their country and to govern it in their own fashion. So there was no steady slide into communist dictatorship in Southeast Asia. The United States had overestimated the dangers the American people thought were confronting them. Where communist rulers still clung to power, as in North Korea and Vietnam, they speedily took on the protective colouring appropriate to their own circumstances, and, thinking only of themselves, followed policies that were as much nationalist as they were communist.

8:11

How Successful Was East–West Détente?

After their 'eyeball to eyeball' confrontation at the time of the Cuba crisis of 1962, and in an effort to avert a nuclear holocaust, the US and the USSR pursued diplomatic policies aiming at détente and disarmament. Generally, however, détente produced very limited effects. It is a mistake to suppose it achieved more.

The two powers agreed the Nuclear Test Ban Treaty in 1963, to cease nuclear testing in the atmosphere or under water, so as to lessen the danger of 'nuclear debris', or 'fall-out'. They also agreed to the Nuclear Non-proliferation Treaty of 1968, whose aim was to check the further spread of these weapons. Both treaties gained wide acceptance by other powers, though not by France or communist China. It suited the objectives of the signatories at that time to go along with the idea of détente. This was because the USA, at that time absorbed in Vietnam, was disinclined to embark on other commitments, while for its part the USSR under Brezhnev, in spite of its lip-service to hard-line policies, went on nevertheless seeking an accommodation with the United States, much to the annoyance of communist China. President Nixon made successive visits to Beijing and Moscow in the early 1970s, further improving relations with both of them. During the Moscow visit, two important new agreements were signed as the result of what was called at the time Strategic Arms Limitation Talks (conveniently referred to by the acronym SALT). The first related to anti-ballistic missile systems (ABMs), and sought to restrict the areas in which such weapons could be deployed; the other restricted the total numbers of intercontinental ballistic missiles (ICBMs) and submarine-launched ballistic missiles (SLBMs) held by the two powers. Brezhnev returned the compliment by visiting the USA in June 1973, where a second summit was held.

The improvement in the relations of the two powers, however, was not sustained. Enthusiasm waned in the 1970s. Some unease had been expressed in Moscow with the existing treaties, partly because they did not take into account the new American Multiple Independently targeted Re-entry Vehicle (or MIRV) which was capable of showering from the same missile a wide spread of targets with separately guided warheads. These misgivings grew with the Yom Kippur War of 1973, where both sides, though officially neutral, continued to supply their traditional allies with arms. Brezhnev, indeed, even threatened the Israelis with attack if they ignored the Security Council's call for a ceasefire.

Nevertheless the two countries did not altogether abandon their efforts to reach further agreements. Nixon, once more in the USSR in 1974, initialled a number of such agreements with Brezhnev: one banning underground tests for weapons in excess of 150 kilotons, another agreeing to deploy only one ABM system, and a third imposing further limitations on strategic arms. These were endorsed by President Ford at a meeting with Brezhnev in Vladivostok in late 1974. Nixon and Brezhnev also took the first tentative steps towards the much more ambitious, but ultimately abortive, plan to establish a Conference on Security and Co-operation in Europe (or CSCE). This plan produced the Helsinki Conference in 1975, whose Final Act included pious paper declarations on a variety of subjects such as frontiers, human rights, disarmament, economic and scientific cooperation and the like. None of these, unfortunately, produced any discernible results.

The underlying reason why these plans failed arose from the continuance of the distrust between the USA and the USSR. For one thing, Brezhnev was under considerable pressure from Soviet hardliners to take a firmer stand against the capitalist West; for another, the Soviet Union by a tremendous effort had achieved a near-equivalence with the United States in its nuclear weaponry. The USA, for its part, had now been liberated from the burden of war in Vietnam and was once again beginning to raise its head above the parapet. As a result US military spending, including that undertaken on behalf of America's allies, shot up from $45 billion in 1976 to $70 billion in 1979. In the light of this spending, the conclusion of SALT 2 in Vienna in June 1979 was little more than an empty gesture. US–Soviet relations became even worse as the result of the Russian invasion of Afghanistan in 1979. This invasion, together with suspected Soviet 'adventurism' in parts of Africa such as the Sudan, Somalia and Mozambique (together with support for Cuba in Angola and Zaire) made the incoming Reagan Administration in 1981 much less inclined to bargain with the Soviets. As a result, one of America's first acts was to reject the SALT 2 treaty when it came before the Senate for its ratification. Not even the death of Brezhnev in 1982 and the swift succession of elderly leaders that followed altered US attitudes much. The accession to power of Gorbachev in 1985 likewise left the Americans deeply suspicious of Soviet intentions.

But Gorbachev's astonishing proposals for disarmament at Reykjavik in 1986 stunned both Reagan and the US delegation, and for a time they did not seem able to take them in. It took two more years of close negotiation before the two powers were ready to sign the first major treaty, abolishing medium-range ballistic missiles. Soon Gorbachev ordered the Soviet withdrawal from Afghanistan, and this was followed by the even more radical offer to withdraw his troops and equipment from eastern Europe, and even to allow US inspectors to visit top secret Soviet army bases to witness the dismantling and destruction of surplus missiles there.

None of this, however, was due to a sudden outbreak of reasonableness on the part of the USSR. Gorbachev's flexibility was due less to inherent moderation and much more to the stark bankruptcy facing Russia as the result of the crippling burden of arms expenditure (see also page 257). It was also due to Gorbachev's determined effort to do what he could to resolve his country's problems. Détente had produced only limited results since 1963 chiefly because the leaders of neither side trusted each other, nor wished détente to be successful. Furthermore, the limited agreements merely to reduce nuclear stockpiles did not undermine the capacity of either side to wage effective nuclear war. So it would appear that both sides thought that détente and disarmament were good things in principle – provided the other fellow did it first.

Perhaps détente achieved some easing of international tension. In the later 1970s and in the '80s the danger of all-out nuclear war seemed to have receded in spite of continuing differences between the powers. This may have been because détente was slowly improving international confidence, lessening the danger that things would be pushed as far as they once had been at the time of the Cuba crisis. However, by 1991 the whole international scene had been irrevocably altered. Communism was collapsing, and with it the Soviet satellite 'empire' in eastern Europe. Even Soviet provinces such as Armenia, the Ukraine and the Baltic States were demanding freedom from centralised control. Taken together, it meant that an arms race between East and West was no longer as important as once it had been. So in the end détente succeeded only because there was no longer any need for it.

Did the Strategic Defence Initiative End the Cold War?

The Strategic Defence Initiative, or SDI, often popularly referred to as 'Star Wars' by reference to a popular science-fiction movie of the time, is sometimes credited with playing a significant part in the ending of the Cold War between America and the communist bloc in 1990. This notion, like the scientific theory that supported it, was a complete myth, and it is an error to think that it made the slightest difference to the ending of the Cold War. Or, if it did, it did so in a way quite different from that in which it is usually perceived.

The idea, in any case, was purely science fiction in itself. Its main purpose, expressed with such conviction by President Reagan, was to shelter the whole of the United States under an umbrella of protection by anti-missile missiles which would infallibly intercept incoming Soviet weapons and destroy them while they were still approaching in space. If perfected, the strategy would mean that the USA would be impregnable against Soviet attack, while the Soviets would be defenceless against an American attack. But though immensely reassuring, the whole idea, for a variety of technical reasons, was totally impossible to achieve.

Reagan, who had himself featured in a science-fiction film in the 1950s whose plot closely resembled this project, was keen on SDI, though there is no reason to suppose that he really believed a word of it. It also threatened to be hideously expensive, and that in the end turned out to be the main point in its favour. Reagan began his term at the White House in 1980 partly by accelerating more mundane projects such as MIRV (the Multiple Independently targeted Re-entry Vehicle), which was designed to shower a wide spread of targets with separately guided missiles from the same warhead; but more fancifully, he convened a conference of leading science-fiction writers in Washington and asked them to work on detailed proposals for SDI. Thereafter, he spoke of the fictitious technology as if it really existed, and even threatened the Russians with it.

They took the bait, and set about discovering similar strategies of their own. It was imperative for them to redouble their scientific research programme, for no amount of espionage would avail them to penetrate strategic secrets, which after all did not exist. When Gorbachev met Reagan at the Reykjavik summit in 1986 the threat of SDI was hanging over Soviet heads.

The main value of SDI turned out to be that the Russians could not afford it. The research involved, when added to the heavy cost of Soviet rearmament, created a crippling financial burden that threatened the stability of the whole Soviet economy. The Soviet military budget, further aggravated by recent military spending in Afghanistan, was now set to rise from $45 billion per year to over $90 billion. Gorbachev, sensing the danger to his country's already unsuccessful command economy, pressed keenly for cuts, first at Reykjavik, and then, more successfully, at Washington in 1987. His reform schemes, too, were aimed at broadening political consent and improving the efficiency of the whole economy. In fact, however, they led to the complete collapse of the USSR and the disintegration of the whole Soviet bloc.

There is therefore some truth in the view that SDI helped to bring about the collapse of world communism, though for economic rather than military or strategic reasons. It was an inspired bluff that paid handsome dividends.

8:13

Did Stalin Fake the Photographic Evidence?

Pictures often convey a stronger and more lasting image than words. This belief in the absolute veracity of photographs is utterly misplaced, for photographs can be falsified like any other form of evidence.

In the course of his career, not only did Stalin purge his enemies from political life in the Soviet Union, he also attempted to expunge them from history by doctoring the photographs in which they appeared. Of these, perhaps the most famous is the photograph of Lenin addressing his troops outside the Bolshoi Theatre in 1920, when he was photographed on a wooden rostrum in full oratorical flow, Trotsky standing by the side of the platform with Kamenev close behind. When Stalin removed Trotsky from power in the USSR at the end of the 1920s, he also had him touched-out of the photograph. The same treatment was meted out to Kamenev as the result of the 'show trials' of the 1930s.

Stalin also made political capital out of another simple photographic trick: he succeeded in enhancing his public reputation by publishing, spliced together, two altogether separate pictures. In one of these he was shown, apparently sitting amicably alongside a reclining Lenin in 1922 (after his recent stroke), so as to emphasise the close relations between the two men, when in fact they were completely at odds. Stalin used this supposed closeness to show how, after 1924, it was he, and not Trotsky, who was Lenin's true political heir.

9

LONG-STANDING PUZZLES

Major André: George Washington's One Mistake?

On 2 October 1781 Major John André, a British army officer, was hanged as a spy at Washington's headquarters on the Hudson river. All appeals to Washington for clemency were ignored, and Washington was accused by the British of barbaric vindictiveness and even by some of his own side of being lacking in humanity. This episode has cast a shadow over Washington's otherwise spotless career.

In September of 1781 Major André was instructed to negotiate with the American commander of West Point, Benedict Arnold, for the surrender to Britain of that vital fortress. Arnold, smarting from the indignity of his recent court martial, and devoted to his loyalist wife, decided to abandon the patriotic cause and betray his country to the British. Major André was taken by boat to a point between the British and American lines, received a safe conduct from Arnold, and a number of vital papers concerning West Point and the plan to surrender it. He concealed these in his boots. He had no intention of crossing the American lines, and indeed was wearing his British uniform under a light overcoat. But the boat was not available the next day to take him back to the British lines; the only way back was overland through the American lines, and he was advised that he would have a greater chance of success if he abandoned his British uniform altogether. So unforeseen circumstances had forced André into this change of plan. At first all went well: he crossed the last American line and was entering no-man's land with some relief when he was suddenly confronted by three local militiamen. Taken by surprise he failed to use Arnold's flag of truce, gave confused answers and aroused the militiamen's suspicions. They searched him and found the incriminating evidence.

Washington appointed a board of officers to look into André's case. In the meantime Arnold saved himself from inevitable arrest by hasty flight. The board spent several days considering the evidence, and then condemned André as a spy. It has been suggested, but evidence is lacking, that the board was not unanimous in its verdict. The British, meanwhile, had been putting considerable pressure on Washington for André's release, pointing out that the British had not exacted the supreme penalty upon any American who claimed loyalty to Britain while spying for the American side. It was all to no avail. Washington would not even consider André's request to be shot as a soldier rather than hanged as a spy and, possibly to avoid further representations, the execution took place within a few days of sentence. The episode tarnished Washington's reputation even with his own side.

But what was Washington to do? It was true that André had become a spy by accident rather than by design. But that in itself was no real excuse; he certainly had behaved like a spy, hiding by day, masquerading as a loyal American, and wearing civilian clothes. Washington's main concern was the discipline and morale of his troops. His own recorded comments on the André case showed that he was not motivated by a vindictive desire to punish André because he could not touch the real villain Benedict Arnold. He admired André's courage, and his behaviour and deportment as an officer. But the parlous position of his army was uppermost in Washington's mind. Pay was often hopelessly in arrears, discipline had collapsed in some units, and there was an ever-present danger of mutiny. Arnold's betrayal was an example of the disaffection in the American ranks, even, it was suspected, among others of his staff officers. Washington could not let it be thought that treason was to be easily disregarded, nor that British officers were free to explore strategic areas within the American lines with impunity. If André was to be punished for his part in the treason Washington had no alternatives: spies were not shot, they were hanged. A commuted sentence would be difficult in wartime, as facilities for long-term imprisonment were rare in the states and non-existent in the army. To restore him to the British lines was unthinkable. It seems that Washington felt he had no alternative but to proceed with the hanging, and not to raise false hopes by delaying it. He had done his duty as he saw it, and salved an uneasy conscience by the generous tribute he paid to André after his death.

9:2

England, Britain and the United Kingdom: Why the Confusion?

In many history books, 'English history' includes not only the history of England but also of Wales; it also usually includes parts, if not the whole, of Scottish and Irish history; then, there is Northern Ireland, sometimes known as Ulster. . . . And what is the status of 'Great Britain'? These national distinctions are often muddled and imprecise; foreigners are confused, and mistakes are frequently made even by people within the country itself. So, can their meaning be clarified? Just what is the 'United Kingdom'?

At the time of Britain's late nineteenth-century imperial grandeur, 'English history' also included the history of the colonies and even of India. It came to be used for all English-speaking areas (and a number *not* English-speaking) that were under British control. After 1783, however, this did not include the United States of America – though in this case the attitude long persisted among Englishmen of a certain class that it should have done, since undoubtedly Americans were no more than renegade colonists.

More precisely, the whole group of islands off the north-west coast of Europe (and forming part of that Continent) is called by the name of 'the British Isles', the largest, i.e. without Ireland, being referred to as 'Great Britain'. After the Act of Union in 1800 between Ireland and Britain, the British Isles were synonymous with the 'United Kingdom of Great Britain and Ireland'. This became the 'United Kingdom of Great Britain and Northern Ireland' after the partition of Ireland went into effect in 1921.

As for Great Britain itself, there are three components, England, Wales and Scotland:

England is the dominant one of the three, by far the most important from the point of view of resources and population, though the custom has grown up in the course of the present century for its people to call themselves the *British*, partly out of consideration for the considerable non-English minority of Great Britain, and partly for the convenience of foreigners, who cannot be expected to be familiar with the intimate detail of British affairs.

Wales was never a separate kingdom recognised as such by England despite the claims of princes such as Owen Glendower (1405); it was conquered piecemeal in the thirteenth century, and was administered as if it were part of England – though recently it has been granted an assembly of its own. Its inhabitants are known as the *Welsh*, a word sometimes used in colloquial English as a verb, unhappily meaning 'to cheat'.

Scotland was a separate historic kingdom which had a common sovereign with England after 1603, and became united with England by the Act of Union of 1707, but thereafter was treated as if it were part of England – though recently it, too, has been granted a parliament of its own. Its inhabitants are known as the *Scots*, a word whose adjectival form is *Scottish* (the word *Scotch* referring only to the whisky distilled there, for which the country is famous).

While considerable areas of both Welsh and Scottish history appear in English history books, both of these nations claim separate nationhood, and have their own national language, though English is widely spoken and even more widely understood there. The basic national division is between the Anglo-Saxon and the Celtic nations. *English* is the language of the majority and remains largely Anglo-Saxon based, with considerable additions from Latin and Norman French. As for the *Celtic* tongues, there are marked similarities between Scots Gaelic, Irish Gaelic, Welsh and even the forms of Gaelic spoken in Brittany, Asturias and formerly in Cornwall (where a small minority continue to demand separate treatment for the lands west of the Tamar under their ancient name of *Kernow*).

In the course of the twentieth century both *nationhood* and *language* became politically sensitive subjects in many parts of the world, and the same trend was evident in Britain, too. Towards the end of the century, as the immigrant population of Britain grew, the terms 'Britain' (from the Brythonic 'Prydain') and 'England' became curiously unfashionable names, a trend which was emphasised by the establishment of separate assemblies for Wales and for Scotland, and the attempted revival of an assembly for Northern Ireland. As of May 2002, English regional assemblies have also been proposed. Broadcasters started to talk about holidaymakers returning 'to *these islands*' from abroad, while even a Cabinet minister spoke of the need to be 'representative of all the interests in the United Kingdom, and that includes *all the nations* of the United Kingdom'. Such a development seemed to make the British Isles even more polyglot than it was before. It was almost as if the word 'Britain' should not be mentioned. The word 'England' was not mentioned either, except in connection with sport, when the use of it could hardly be avoided. The polite equivalent for 'England' seemed to have become the 'Regions', and that for 'Britain' 'the United Kingdom'. It seemed as if the concept of one-nation 'Britain' was outmoded, the country drifting apart internally, and likely in the long run to submerge more of its identity in Europe. Perhaps, at the beginning of the third millennium, this was no bad idea.

9:3

How Did Napoleon I Die?

St Helena is a rainy, windswept island deep in the South Atlantic, used by the British as a staging post. It was here that Napoleon I of France spent nearly six years in exile, and here that he died on 5 May 1821. But what was the cause of death?

It was not long before rumours began alleging that Napoleon did not die of natural causes. After all, he was only in his early fifties and both his French entourage and his British guardians would have much to gain by his death: they could go home. Arsenic or strychnine administered over a period of time were alleged to have killed him; the French accused the British of deliberately revenging themselves on Napoleon for the long period of warfare to which he had subjected both Britain and Europe. This seems highly unlikely. Sir Hudson Lowe, the governor of St Helena, kept strictly and unimaginatively to the letter of his instructions, and lacked the initiative to commit murder on his own account. His subordinates, both civilian and military, were on limited postings and expected to go home when their time was completed. Not so the Frenchmen who shared Napoleon's exile; they would be obliged out of loyalty to stay on St Helena and serve him until the end. But all Napoleon's entourage were so devoted to him that it is impossible to find a murder suspect among any of them. Accusations against General Montholon, who was one of the former Emperor's companions and quarrelled with him, lack supporting evidence; disagreements among the exiles and under such circumstances were only to be expected and are not, in themselves, indicative of a greater likelihood of murder. There is a recent suggestion that Montholon or one of his aides was in a secret plot with Charles, the heir to the French throne, to murder Napoleon. The evidence is thin and circumstantial; Montholon may well have wanted to return to France, but whether he would have countenanced treachery and murder to do so seems highly improbable.

The post-mortem was conducted by both British and French doctors who disagreed on the cause of death. The French doctors claimed that Napoleon's health had been undermined by so long a sojourn in so unhealthy a place, and pointed out his ulcerated stomach. The British doctors insisted that it was stomach cancer, for which the climate of St Helena and the conditions of his captivity could not be held responsible. The discovery, with the aid of modern methods of analysis, of traces of arsenic in a lock of Napoleon's hair has not advanced the argument much. Arsenic contamination can occur both before and after death, and certainly the walls in Napoleon's room had some arsenic in the wallpaper paste. It seems reasonably clear that Napoleon died of some kind of stomach complaint, whether cancer or severe ulceration. Those who assert otherwise still have to prove their case.

9:4

The Alamo: What Happened in the Final Hours?

Among the great heroes of American legend and folklore are Jim Bowie and Davey Crockett. The Bowie knife and the Crockett hat of beaver fur give them idiosyncratic individuality, but it is the manner of their deaths that casts them in the heroic mould. On 6 March 1836 the Mexican army under Santa Anna broke into the Alamo mission building in San Antonio, Texas and massacred the entire garrison. Bowie and Crockett fought desperately and to the last in the cause of Texan independence. Or did they?

The Texans had proclaimed their independence from Mexico early in 1836. This brought down upon them the full might of the army led by the Mexican President, General Santa Anna. At a conservative estimate he had 3,000 trained soldiers under his command and the Texans had had little time to coordinate their defences. Scattered Texan settlements were soon overwhelmed and the residents of San Antonio, despairing of outside help, took refuge in the large fortified mission house. For twelve days from 24 February, 200 civilian defenders held the Mexicans at bay. When eventually the defence crumbled there were no adult male survivors left, and Bowie and Crockett and the co-commander William Travis were assumed to have been among the slain. When last seen the three men were still fighting and exhorting others to continue to do so.

But the last hours at the Alamo were a time of chaos and confusion, and the evidence of the survivors is conflicting. No reliable witness actually saw any of the three leaders fall. While the Texans claimed later that the garrison had been massacred, the Mexicans stated that those killed had still been under arms. They did not claim to have taken any prisoners, or that any of the fighting men had tried to surrender. It has been recently argued that Crockett and six others were taken prisoner, and were massacred after the surrender despite Crockett's plea that he was a civilian unfortunate enough to be caught up in the battle. The evidence for this is the diary of Lt-Col Jose Enrique de la Peña who served with Santa Anna at the Alamo. The diary first came to light in 1955, late enough to arouse suspicion, but it is written on paper authentic to the period, and is believed by some scholars to be genuine. If true the popular and heroic version of Crockett's death needs some modification, and the Mexicans emerge as cold-blooded murderers rather than hot-blooded killers.

Another hypothesis is that Bowie, Crockett and others survived the battle and that they remained in captivity for some years. There is no reliable evidence to back this version. Sam Houston and other Texan leaders would have good reason for keeping quiet on both these variants: they did not want Texan heroism tarnished by the tameness of surrender. But with the captivity theory it must seem a little odd that Santa Anna, who was himself captured a few weeks later at San Jacinto, did not reveal this knowledge to his captors in order to effect an exchange. Nor does it seem likely that, if they were prisoners of the Mexicans, no hint or rumour of their captivity ever leaked out.

The Mexican version that they died fighting supports the heroic legend, and offers no credibility to the de la Peña version. Either of the alternatives would have made the Alamo much less of a Texan rallying cry ('Remember the Alamo'). In our present state of knowledge it seems that the Alamo ended in a massacre, but whether the massacre took place during or after the battle hinges upon the authenticity of de la Peña's diary.

9:5

The Scottish Tartan: Ancient Custom or Modern Fiction?

Those with certain Scottish names claiming membership of particular Scottish clans often claim – and would even reserve – the right of wearing a particular tartan to themselves, more or less as a heraldic badge. Numerous books have been written claiming a long historical lineage for the 'wearing of the tartan'. There seems to be no grounds for such a claim.

There is no particular reason for regarding the type of weaving pattern usually known as 'tartan' as being especially Scottish. It is one of the simplest forms of pattern to invent, and examples of it have been found in prehistoric Mongolia, in medieval Italy and in fabrics originating in China and Japan. The fact that they should occur in Scotland among the small-scale domestic industries of the country is scarcely surprising.

The myth that it was the Scottish national dress claims to have ancient roots. This myth has been in part perpetuated by the fact that after the Jacobite Rebellion of 1745 an act of the English parliament forbidding the wearing of 'Highland dress' was usually assumed to refer to the tartan, which, however, it did not specifically mention.

It is true that some time after Culloden a number of Highland regiments were given the right to agreed patterns of tartan, and the wearing of these regimental tartans was systematised by the end of the century. But reports of the earlier wearing of tartan seem to have been without foundation. Evidence from eighteenth-century family portraits suggests that Scottish gentry chose their clothes with an eye to quality, cut and fashion rather than because of some family or clan custom. Likewise, David Morier, Cumberland's official military artist, painted the Highlanders at the battle realistically, but not in clan tartan, rather in a variety of different garments – waistcoats, jackets, belted plaids, trews and hose of varying patterns, with no two of them being dressed alike. In the early nineteenth century two Polish brothers, friends of Sir Walter Scott and blessed with the extraordinary name of Sobieski-Stuart, claimed not only to be descended from Bonnie Prince Charlie but also to have in their possession an ancient tome which laid down the historical record of all clan tartans. This document, however, they never succeeded in producing. Sir Walter Scott himself, of course, had a romantic interest in Scotland and would dearly have liked to produce some evidence, but was never able to do so.

Some actual impetus for the more widespread use of the tartan seems to have come from a royal visit by George IV to Edinburgh in 1822, but it was not until the reign of Victoria and the beginning of the Balmoral connection that much interest was taken in it. The Queen visited Scotland for the first time in 1842, and from the very first pages of her later journal *Our Life in the Highlands* enthused on the subject of 'Highland dress', by which she meant the tartan. Whether she was aware that it was a confection prepared for her delight or whether she accepted it as totally genuine is not clear, but she certainly enjoyed its finery and pageantry. Then it became all the rage, and it is understandable that Scottish families should have made the effort to dignify the practice by creating for it and for themselves an ancestry that would provide a romantic historical appeal for this supposedly ancient custom.

9:6

The US Civil War: Was the North Bound to Win?

It is often said that the Northern states were so much stronger than the Southern Confederacy that any war between them was bound to result in victory for the North. Historical judgments are often made, however, on the principle that what happened was bound to happen. Such a verdict is by no means inescapable.

At the outset of the Civil War in 1861, the North seemed to have every advantage. With a population of nearly 20 million, reinforced by a steady stream of immigrants, it enjoyed a numerical preponderance over the South, which had a population of about 9 million, of whom almost half were black slaves whom the government dared not arm. The North was linked together by a railway system valuable for strategic as well as for industrial reasons. Whereas the South depended for manufactured goods on the factories of the North and on imports mainly from Britain, the North had superior industrial capacity and could produce plentiful munitions. Technological innovation was another characteristic of the North, as was the plentiful finance which flooded the floors of the stock and produce exchanges. The war caused the national debt of the North to escalate sharply to over $3 billion, but nevertheless the resources of the country were by no means exhausted; indeed, even allowing for the war, the per capita income of the North doubled between 1860 and 1870. The North also possessed most of the navy, and from the beginning controlled the sea and prevented the Southern states from continuing their trade with Europe. The armies of the North also enjoyed numerical superiority, enlisting over 100,000 men, three-quarters of whom were under twenty-one. Though ill-trained and often undisciplined, they eventually formed a formidable army and were able to overrun the South. Finally, the North possessed in Lincoln a leader far beyond anything their opponents could produce in courage, political wisdom and good judgment.

On the other hand, the Southern Confederacy constituted a formidable foe. On the military side, the Southerners were more used to the outdoor life, and formed a more disciplined force, most of whom believed in what they were fighting for. The Northern army, later augmented by the admission of conscripts, contained many inferior persons, weakened by industrial drudgery and sometimes indifferent to the outcome of the war. Again, the South produced at least as many able generals as the North, and the two outstanding ones, Robert E. Lee and 'Stonewall' Jackson, both of whom were Virginians. They enjoyed the advantages of interior lines of communication, and a social organisation more appropriate to the creation of an efficient fighting force. The South, furthermore, commanded the unquestioning loyalty of the body of its citizens, who were fighting for all they held dear – for liberty and self-government, even for hearth and home. At the same time they enjoyed the sympathy of a number of European governments. Lord Palmerston, for example, even toyed with the idea of coming to their assistance. The war was, curiously, a class affair: many of the upper classes, dominating the membership of governments, sympathised with the South, yet the working classes – even those of Lancashire, denied their raw materials, and therefore their employment, by the blockade of the South – sympathised and identified with the common people of the Northern states. But the North at first had to live with the mistakes of indifferent or poor supreme commanders until the appointment of Ulysses S. Grant. Northern victories were long coming, and when they came they were bloody, costly and purchased with enormous effort.

The war, however, required this effort. The South had withdrawn from the Union; the North had to force it back again. Not until then would it have won. Any settlement which acknowledged the independence of the South, or its right to extend slavery, would be the equivalent of Northern defeat. The Confederacy did not have to defeat the North; it merely had to avoid being defeated by it. The North could win only by defeating the South and conquering it. Nevertheless, though it was not fighting for its existence, the North was fighting for an idea – the idea of Union. The idea of Negro emancipation was very much an afterthought. The 'Battle-Hymn of the Republic', to which they marched, focused on Union and Freedom, but made no mention of slaves.

All in all, the outcome of the war was far from a foregone conclusion. The South American republics and the Italian states had achieved their independence against greater odds; even Hungary might well have done the same but for the intervention of the Russians. The South's victories, as at Bull Run, seemed to show that the Confederacy was in earnest, while the Union had no stomach for the fight. Who can say what might have been the effect on the resolution, the morale or the political stability of the North if a few more of the spectacular victories which graced the military fortunes of the South had been won in the neighbourhood of Washington in 1861? There were few public figures in Europe even in 1864 who doubted the permanency of the separation. But if the irreversible Union for which the North fought had not been preserved, the United States of America would have become the 'disunited states' of America, and the whole course of world history would have been changed.

9:7

Did the Colonies Reflect Greatness or Dishonour on Britain?

By the eighteenth century Britain had developed into an imperial power. Following in the footsteps of the Portuguese, the Spaniards, the Dutch and the French, the British developed their colonial empire mainly for commercial reasons and as a by-product of their great naval strength. They found lands that were supposedly empty, like Australia, New Zealand and the fertile eastern coast of North America, and, ignoring the rights of the native peoples thinly scattered there, 'planted' their colonies among them. The search for precious metals in distant parts of

*the world was reinforced by new needs for tropical crops and raw
industrial materials, and the wish to find markets for manufactures
was reinforced by the need to find new homes for a burgeoning
population and to provide an outlet for the proselytising activities of
chapel and church among the 'heathen'. By the end of the century, the
peoples of the British Isles were developing a taste for their new status
as a world power. But was the empire ever an economic benefit to the
'mother country'?*

The American War of Independence checked the growth of
British imperial sentiment. Ascribed on the one hand to the
ingratitude and the wilfulness of the colonists and on the other
to the harsh tyranny of George III and his governments, the war
illustrated to a nicety the difficulties of administering colonies
3,000 or more miles away from the home country: how could it
ever be possible to permit the democratic freedoms the colonists
demanded for their citizens, while avoiding entangling the home
government in distant and expensive commitments? The result
of the war was a national humiliation at the hands of the
colonists and their European allies and a peace treaty which
solved the political problem by giving the Americans the
independence they demanded. But it taught a sharp lesson to
politicians at home and took a good deal of the shine off their
imperialist pretensions. A colonial empire after 1783 was
regarded as an expensive and troublesome commitment.

The British, however, were slow to learn the lessons the
Americans had taught them. They went on accumulating
colonies during and after the Napoleonic wars in the West
Indies, South Africa and elsewhere, seeing these acquisitions as
important strategic outposts signalling the establishment of
British influence in Africa, India and the Far East; but
at the same time they failed to solve the fundamental problem
that had led to the US War of Independence. They found
themselves ensnared in expensive foreign entanglements on
behalf of people to whose fate they were largely indifferent. In
Canada they were involved in the conflict between the settlers
of French and British origin; in New Zealand they found

themselves caught up in the Maori Wars, and in South Africa they found themselves at loggerheads with the small but stubborn Boer population they had inherited when they took over control from the Dutch. At the same time there was a series of niggling problems with the newly established USA over the clarification of its boundaries, all of which the home government found tedious and costly.

Though Lord Palmerston (himself a relic of the eighteenth century rather than a genuine Victorian) for a time seemed proud to assume the imperial mantle in his dealings with 'Johnny Foreigner', the empire by the mid-nineteenth century was something of an irrelevance. Disraeli at first thought that 'the colonies were millstones round our necks', troublesome when they were still dependent, and ungrateful when they demanded independence; while Gladstone and the Liberal Party – though they represented commercial and industrial interests – earned for themselves by their indifference to colonies and to foreign problems generally the name of 'Little Englanders'. It was only in the 1870s that, at Disraeli's behest, Britain rediscovered the idea of world eminence and imperial greatness.

In the fifty years after 1870 Britain built up a vast overseas empire in all five continents and, aided by the flattering picture popularised by Mercator's geographical projection, painted nearly half the world red. In the later days of Victoria's reign and well into the twentieth century Britain saw itself as a world imperial power. When, after the First World War, the substance of this world greatness began to slip away, Britain contented itself with the civilised fiction of a 'Commonwealth of Nations' under the Statute of Westminster in 1931, when it began to preside over formerly colonial nations that were now in effect quite independent. Only in the later years of the century did the words 'colonial' and 'imperial' acquire a derogatory tone, and Britain begin to apologise for its once splendid past.

Some writers, like Colin Cross (*The Fall of the British Empire*, 1968) and Edward Grierson (*The Imperial Dream*, 1972) saw this decline as part of an inevitable process; others, like Corelli Barnett (*The Audit of War*, 1986) regretted the decline of

Britain's position in the world after 1945, believing that the country's continuing obsession with the fiction of imperial greatness when the country was no longer able to sustain the reality overextended its commitments, bankrupted it and forced it into a humiliating dependence on the USA, the last remaining superpower. It took many years for the imperial idea to pass, and for Britain to begin to restrict its horizons to a narrower compass.

This change could be seen in popular attitudes to the imperial idea. Rudyard Kipling became quaintly comic in his talk of the 'white man's burden' and of native peoples being 'half devil and half child', and books such as *King Solomon's Mines* and *Sanders of the River* came to be replaced by less self-satisfied accounts like *The Jewel in the Crown* and *Cry, the Beloved Country*. In schools and examining boards there was a vast reduction in the teaching of colonial history and in history syllabuses on the empire. By the end of the century the British, now residual possessors of Gibraltar, St Helena and the Falkland Islands, had almost forgotten they had ever had an empire.

Is it possible to arrive at a final balance sheet on the costs and the values of the empire? As far as the 'mother country' went the empire was the natural product of Britain's industrial and commercial strength and its naval power in the nineteenth century, and as such yielded more value than it levied cost. To the colonies themselves it had a greater significance. On the one hand it brought to a number of developing nations the benefits of railways, the telegraph, trade, mechanisation, dams, cheap electric power, schools, medicine and hospitals; on the other it exposed them to the risks and dangers of contemporary times which otherwise they would not have known, and dragged them into the glare of international world politics. Yet we must not overdraw this contrast. It would be just as true to say that we gave them cheap textiles and they gave us rice, or that we gave them syphilis and they gave us Aids.

Those who saw the beneficial hand of progress in the spread of colonies now perceive that same progress in their passing away. This perception depends on the length of the observer's vision. But the fact is that there are fashions in political values as there are in women's hats. Currently empires have had their day. But it is at least as much owed to the dwindling of the self-confidence of the modern post-colonial West as it is to any shortfall that has been discerned in the efficacy of colonialism that overseas empires are now treated with a scepticism bordering on complete rejection.

9:8

What Part Did the United States Play in the Ending of the First World War?

In Europe generally, and in Britain in particular, the opinion took root in 1917–18 that the United States had kept out of the First World War until it was as good as over, that they joined in chiefly in order to secure influence over the peace settlement that was made at the end of it, and that their contribution to the eventual victory in practical terms was small. Such a belief, then and afterwards, however, is quite erroneous.

It is quite true that the United States hesitated for a long time before joining the war. This was due mainly to the peculiarity of America's world position. The country was the 'melting-pot' of Europe's peoples, and could hardly take sides in any quarrel that was mainly a European one. By long tradition, the United States was neutral, and since the days of Monroe's famous Doctrine had kept out of other people's quarrels. Woodrow Wilson, whose government had been subject to a series of provocations from Germany, had nevertheless managed to keep out of the war. It was only the German threat to Mexico as revealed in the Zimmermann Telegram, and the German announcement of unrestricted submarine warfare in the spring of 1917 that jolted the USA into the war.

It is also true that at the outbreak of Wilson's war the United States was ill-prepared for combat. The US army was small and equipped with out-of-date weapons. Its most recent campaign, to catch the Mexican bandit Pancho Villa who had carried out daring raids into New Mexico during civil troubles in his own country, had lasted nine months and produced little in the way of a result. But American efforts to prepare for the First World War were rapid and extremely successful. Congress enacted a Selective Service Act that conscripted about 5 million men, and a further 24 million were registered for the draft. Of these, 2 million were sent overseas, and 1½ million fought in France. This did not compare, pro rata, with the scale of the war effort made by the main combatants, but it certainly made a considerable contribution to the Allied victory when they began to arrive in Europe in June 1917. By the end of that year there were over 200,000 of them.

The situation on the Western Front at this time was very finely balanced. Both sides had expended huge amounts of men and armaments in desperate efforts to break through the opposing lines, and were now on the verge of exhaustion. When General John J. Pershing led his American Expeditionary Force into battle he refused to allow them to be fed into the mincing machine, but built up his forces until March 1918, when he employed them to stem the last great German spring offensive. Undoubtedly the arrival of these new forces tipped the scales decisively in the Allies' favour, and helped, between June and November 1918, to bring the war to an end. In June, US forces drove the Germans out of Château Thierry; in July, they joined the battle along the Marne, helping to flatten out the German salient between Rheims and Soissons; in September, over a million of them drove into the Argonne Forest towards the formidable Hindenburg Line. Here their lack of experience, and Pershing's employment of the Allied strategy of attacking the enemy at their strongest rather than their weakest point, brought heavy casualties. American losses, considering the short time they were in the front line, were thus very heavy, with 50,000 men killed and over 200,000 wounded.

At sea, too, the US contribution to victory was considerable. By 1916, seaborne trade with the Allies, in spite of the submarine campaign, had grown from $750 million to over $3 billion, while in the same period German trade had shrunk from $350 million to less than $30 million. By 1917, however, U-boat attacks on Atlantic shipping were so successful that British stocks of grain were reduced to a six weeks' supply, and the country stood on the brink of starvation. Again, the intervention of the United States tipped the balance. Many new ships were built and pressed into service: on Independence Day in 1918 alone, for instance, no fewer than ninety-five vessels were launched. American merchantmen helped increasingly in the importation of vital supplies, while warships assisted in the implementation of Lloyd George's convoy plans, enabling large numbers of ships to be shepherded across the Atlantic by armed escorts. The United States also began to supply scientific equipment for the detection and destruction of the German U-boat packs.

Much of the wartime trading was financed by credit extended by US banks. They had already loaned Britain nearly $2.5 billion before the United States entered the war. There was indeed criticism from Wilson's Republican opponents that the war would 'benefit only the class of people who have already made millions of dollars, and who will make millions of dollars more if we get into the war'.

These loans were themselves one reason for the US entry into the war – to protect the financial investment. The United States went on, by the end of the war, to lend over $10 billion to its European Allies. Altogether the war cost the United States over $20 billion, about a third of which was raised in additional taxes, and about two-thirds by the flotation of vast 'Liberty Loans', issues of war bonds whose sale was organised by William McAdoo, Secretary to the Treasury, by public canvassing and even street-corner sales. Without these resources the task of the Allies in defeating the Central Powers would have been much more difficult.

In this light, the contribution of the United States to the outcome of the First World War was of critical importance. Without their help, the Allies might well have taken several years more to defeat their enemies, if, indeed, they were able to win the war at all.

9:9

Did Lloyd George Double-cross Sinn Fein?

In 1922 Lloyd George masterminded an Irish settlement based on partition. To his supporters, he had secured the best settlement that could be got under the circumstances, and had dealt with Nationalists and Unionists alike with scrupulous fairness. To his critics, and especially his Irish ones, Lloyd George had secured Sinn Fein's consent by dubious tactics, false promises and devious political manoeuvring. Did he deceive and trick Sinn Fein into accepting the settlement, or were his genuinely meant plans and promises ruined by Conservative intransigence? The controversy still rages.

Faced with the impossibility of maintaining British power in Ireland by force, but with the equal impossibility of forcing Northern Ireland (Ulster) to accept rule from Dublin, Lloyd George needed to be a political superman, for his large majority in parliament consisted mainly of Conservatives who would never abandon the Unionist cause in Ireland.

Lloyd George's original proposals of 1920 would have placed Ulster under the rule of Dublin and provoked a rebellion there. However, it was, in effect, vetoed by Lloyd George's Conservative colleagues. So in 1921 Lloyd George proposed several options, of which one was partition, with both Belfast and Dublin having their own parliaments. This was readily accepted by the Ulster Unionists who saw the threat of a united Ireland recede. So how could he reconcile this with Sinn Fein's determination to secure a united Ireland? Their representatives, weary of fighting the British, were given a virtual ultimatum by Lloyd George's threat to call off the negotiations. They seized on his hint that the Boundary Commission, which was to determine the boundary between Southern and Northern Ireland, would so draw the boundary (especially eating into Tyrone and Fermanagh) that Ulster would cease to be viable, and would in the end have to seek union with Dublin. Since this hint was corroborated by some of Lloyd George's senior

Conservative colleagues, the Sinn Fein representatives took Lloyd George's promise at face value and accepted the proposed arrangements, known as the Irish Treaty (ratified in the British parliament in December 1921 and in the Irish Dáil in January 1922). Lloyd George's overweening self-confidence, and his belief that his Conservative colleagues owed their positions to him, suggest that the hint was genuine and that he expected to be able to honour it; if not, after all it was only a hint.

Sinn Fein, therefore, expected that the Anglo-Irish Boundary Commission would be given a free hand. In the event the commission was set up by the minority Labour government in 1924 and, among others, Lloyd George himself said that only minor boundary rectifications would be allowed. Since these were so trivial in Tyrone and Fermanagh and were expected to be balanced by nationalist concessions elsewhere, the Irish withdrew from the commission, and the six counties of Ulster retained their boundaries virtually unaltered.

Was that Lloyd George's original intention? In which case he had deliberately deceived the Sinn Fein negotiators. Lloyd George had suggested in December 1921 that the majority of the inhabitants of Tyrone and Fermanagh counties would probably wish to be ruled by Dublin, surely an oblique support for a free Boundary Commission? The change of mind between 1921 and 1924 sprang in part from the fact that he was no longer in office, and any Conservative government would want to keep the six counties intact. Possibly Lloyd George did originally intend a free Boundary Commission, and it had been enough to bring Sinn Fein to the negotiating table in 1920. When Lloyd George discovered that the Unionists and his Conservative colleagues would never consent to the drawing of new boundaries for Tyrone and Fermanagh, he stated that that had never been his intent in the first place. Thus it was not malice aforethought that determined his policy, but typical Lloyd George pragmatism which (for him) turned out well. But Sinn Fein and Dublin had some right to feel betrayed.

Who Were the Kulaks?

In the 1930s, Stalin launched in the Soviet Union an attack on the kulaks *as the enemy of the communist revolution, rounded them up and deported them to death or imprisonment in the labour camps of Siberia. This, however, in truth, tells us very little about who the* kulaks *were, and perhaps is more significant as a subtle, but often unchallenged, piece of Stalinist propaganda in defence of his sweeping agricultural changes.*

The Soviet leader claimed the kulaks to be a class of rich peasants and an obstacle to his plans for the wholesale collectivisation of Russian lands. He denounced them for having petty bourgeois beliefs in profit-making and private enterprise, and accused them of sabotaging his five-year plans for Soviet agriculture, either by actually thwarting the achievement of his objectives, or else simply by failing to help enough. He succeeded in arousing the envy and mistrust of the poorer peasants for the kulaks' privileged position, and so enlisted their cooperation in 'eliminating them as a class'. It is estimated that about 2 million of the kulaks perished in the course of Stalin's campaign.

  Information about the kulaks seems limited, although references to them date back to the nineteenth century, where they are mentioned after the emancipation of the serfs in 1861. But unfortunately there was little empirical evidence about them from the point of view of income, taxation payments or family budgets. There was some information from excise statistics implying a higher consumption by the peasantry generally of many items like sugar, tea and cotton goods (though not of alcohol, much of which they produced themselves in illegal stills), but this does not advance our knowledge of the kulaks very much. They also aroused little controversy before the communist revolution. Anecdotal information suggested that they might form about 15 per cent of the peasant population. They often acquired more land, by breaking up new lands or by absorbing common land. They also rented more land, went in for more scientific methods, and grew newer crops such as flax. There were also signs of new enterprise, with local factories putting out work to cottage workers, for instance in textiles, especially in wintertime, when farm work was slack. There is little evidence that the kulaks were wealthy: their redemption payments for the land they were buying were often in arrears and, being peasants, they usually avoided whatever taxes they could.

There is likewise little evidence that their landlords oppressed them, or that in their turn they were the oppressors of the lesser peasantry. Indeed, there is not even any clear social division between the kulaks and peasants who were lower down the scale. The whole class position at the time seemed, on the contrary, to be very fluid: the same family might move up and down the scale. When the peasant was young and had small children he was often badly off, as he was when he grew older and could not work so much; but in his middle years, when his children were in their youth and still working for him at home, he might for some years become better off and even appear to his neighbours to have become a kulak. Then he would try to improve his farming methods, get more machinery or buy new stock. His family would dress better and eat better. He was generally on the lookout to improve himself, and this was not an attitude confined to the kulaks – all peasants thought alike on the matter.

So it would appear that the word 'kulak' was little more than a name given in communist propaganda to those who resisted the regime's agricultural reforms. In truth, however, the kulak who was the class enemy implacably opposed to the communist revolution may have been little more than a figment of the Soviet dictator's mind, some kind of ogre (as Trotsky was) created to frighten the peasants into submission, or to excuse Stalin's own shortcomings when the promised collective utopia did not materialise in the course of the changes. Envious neighbours might denounce him and be quite happy to see him carried off to detention by local party officials, but that did not make him a kulak or a counter-revolutionary. He probably was neither.

9:11

Guernica: Who Was to Blame?

The responsibility for the destruction of Guernica created a bitter controversy that raged for many years after the event, giving rise to angry accusations between the various parties until recently. Only now, sixty years after the dust has settled, is it possible to allocate blame for the bombing, and perhaps to draw the controversy to a close.

Guernica is a small town in the Basque province of Vizcaya in north-eastern Spain which found itself caught up in the violence of the Spanish Civil War in 1936. The language, culture and traditions of the Basque provinces were, and still are, vastly different from those of Castilian Spain, and there was little sympathy here for the centralising nationalist forces of General Franco. The Spanish Republican government in October 1936 delegated a freedom to the Basques similar to that already conceded to the Catalans in Barcelona and, under the oak tree in Guernica, traditionally the spot where the Kings of Spain swore to respect the special liberties of the Basque provinces, a separate government known as the *Euzkadi* was formed, whose legality the nationalists immediately challenged. With a population of only 7,000, and lying in a steep valley six miles from the sea and only twenty from Bilbao, the most important town in the area, Guernica at first sight seemed distant from the war, a haven for the many refugees who streamed northwards towards the French frontier from the conflicts raging to the west and south.

It was in Guernica, in April 1937, that massive devastation wrecked the town, destroying much of it and killing up to a thousand of its inhabitants. The explosions and the raging fires were witnessed by the town's mayor, the British consul and a number of foreign correspondents reporting from the area. They maintained the town had been bombed by German Heinkel 111s and Junkers 52s, and that this force of over thirty bombers had been supported by fighters, Messerschmidt 109s and older Heinkel 51s which had machine-gunned fleeing civilians as the bombers destroyed the town. Later Pablo Picasso produced a painting, perhaps his most famous, depicting the stark horror that the war had visited on the town.

Initially, the nationalists denied that Guernica had been bombed at all, saying that few bomb fragments had been found and that most of the damage had been done by incendiary devices planted by Basque extremists who had blown up their own town, to 'inspire indignation against the Nationalists'. Franco's top leadership, when they got to know, were horrified at the completeness of the destruction, and denied that it had anything to do with them. Franco in particular was said to be shocked and furious about the raid. It was only in 1970 that the nationalist government of Spain eventually admitted that Guernica had been bombed from the air, and that there was plenty of evidence of high explosive damage as well as of fire-bombing. Even then, they maintained that they had neither ordered nor condoned the destruction.

The blame was commonly laid at the door of the German *Luftwaffe*, whose planes had carried out the raid. Numerous admissions, public and private, by members of the bombing squadrons responsible (the so-called Condor Legion) are on record, the usual German explanation being that the town was a justifiable military target, with a small-arms factory nearby – though in fact this was unscathed – and an important bridge over the nearby Oca river, vital in case of a Republican evacuation of the area. This bridge also escaped destruction. If the idea was a Nazi one, however, there are some features of the raid that remain puzzling. Why did the Condor Legion use relatively old planes for the job, instead of the supremely accurate Stuka dive-bombers that were available? And why was the aim of the German bombers so lamentable that their main objectives were never hit? The excuse that the smoke and dust from the town was so thick that the pilots were prevented from taking accurate aim seems a rather feeble excuse for an organisation like the *Luftwaffe*, which took such pride in its professionalism. Moreover, the diaries of a few of the key officers in the *Luftwaffe* make it clear that the nationalists knew about the raid beforehand, however much they protested their innocence afterwards.

The real truth is probably that the raid was inspired by the nationalists, and carried out rather perfunctorily by the German *Luftwaffe*, few of whose officers were very keen on the idea. The notion that they were simply practising for their later blitzkrieg raids on major European cities during the Second World War seems fanciful and quite unlikely. Both the Spanish nationalists and the Germans, however, seem to have been ashamed of the episode, and subsequently tried to deny that they were in any way responsible.

9:12

The Hindenburg Disaster: Was it Sabotage?

The disaster which struck the German dirigible Hindenburg *in 1937 (coming so soon after the disaster which befell the airship R101 at Beauvais in France on its maiden voyage in 1930) and which effectively put an end to further commercial airship development was at the time and thereafter put down to the highly dangerous properties of hydrogen as a lifting agent. This verdict, however, was mistaken. Recent research has suggested a quite different cause.*

The *Hindenburg* was a 245-metre-long airship of conventional Zeppelin design built and launched by the Zeppelin Company at Friedrichshafen, Germany, in 1936. It had a maximum speed of 84 mph and a cruising speed of 78 mph, and could carry upwards of 100 passengers and a considerable amount of commercial freight. During 1936 the vessel inaugurated commercial air services across the North Atlantic by carrying over 1,000 passengers and substantial cargoes between Germany and the United States on ten scheduled trips, as well as a number of other voyages to other destinations in the New World. Hitler was very proud of the vessel, and wished it to be known as the *Adolf Hitler*, a request that its owners politely refused.

On 6 May 1937, while landing at Lakehurst, New Jersey, the hydrogen-filled *Hindenburg* burst into flames and was completely destroyed. Thirty-six of the ninety-seven persons aboard were killed, and a larger number injured. Since the weather at the time was stormy and the airship had been delayed in landing by the need to manoeuvre between two nearby thunderstorms, the fire was generally attributed to the discharge of atmospheric electricity in the vicinity of hydrogen gas in the process of being vented from the airship. The accident caused a sensation throughout the world, and prompted the setting up of a commission of inquiry by the US Department of Commerce which spent some time investigating it. The Zeppelin Company, whose prestige was also involved in the disaster, established an inquiry of its own, though the results of this were not published.

Theories explaining the disaster abounded. Suspicion fell for a time on a German citizen, a professional acrobat, who was suspected of climbing up between the lifting bags inside the shell with a view to taking photographs with a flash camera, but in the end this hypothesis was discarded. There was speculation, too, about the possibility of sabotage by anti-Nazi fanatics seeking to discredit the Third Reich. Though closely examined, no proof of this suggestion was ever produced. In the end, the investigators put the blame on the highly inflammable nature of hydrogen, concluding that it was too dangerous to be used in such quantities for purposes of transportation. The *Hindenburg* disaster in fact marked the end of hydrogen-filled rigid airships in commercial air transport. Though there was one already nearly finished in Germany, further research and development were abandoned and with the outbreak of war in 1939 no more was heard of airship transportation.

NASA rocket scientists, however, in the 1990s remained dissatisfied with this verdict. They were convinced that hydrogen, far from being dangerous, was one of the best and most environmentally friendly forms of fuel, whether used as a fuel or as a lifting agent. They believed that for all the time and energy spent on the *Hindenburg* investigation, the inquiry had never got down to the basic causes of the disaster, and had taken the easy course of blaming the accident on hydrogen. For one thing, the observations of the onlookers, all of whom made detailed depositions to the inquiry, and the behaviour of the fire and the colour of the flames – which were said by all to have been red and orange instead of the almost transparent blue of a hydrogen conflagration – were inconsistent with the supposed cause of the disaster. Masses of evidence was re-examined, and the private report of the Zeppelin Company was for the first time analysed and aligned with that of the Department of Commerce report. Research was also carried out into the findings of the enquiries, and experiments devised to test their conclusions.

In this way, new explanations began to emerge to account for the disaster. For one thing, captive hydrogen did not behave in the way that the enquiries had supposed. When vented normally it did not catch fire, even in the presence of considerable voltages of static electricity. But other aspects of the *Hindenburg*'s structure and operation were brought under suspicion. The fabric which covered the shell and the hydrogen bags had been doped to give it durability and to increase its reflectivity (so that the hydrogen inside would not become overheated or expand), and the separate panels of which this outer cover was constructed were firmly laced together with rope to make them easier to handle. The problems caused by static electricity had been well known by the Zeppelin Company, who believed, with good reason, that any accumulated voltage would be discharged by the lowering of the landing rope on arrival. Unfortunately the dope used consisted of powdered aluminium and other constituents such as iron oxide, which were exactly the materials used as solid fuels in the Apollo missions, and therefore highly inflammable. Furthermore, the covering panels being separate, but laced together, would discharge separately and would be to a degree insulated from each other by the small gap of about an inch between them, since the rope lacing them together, even if wet from rainwater, would not have as high a conductivity as was required to drain the charge. The smallest of static sparks to bridge this gap would be all that was needed to ignite the rocket fuel with which the airship was painted.

The modern researchers discovered, therefore, that the presence of masses of hydrogen in the airship's bags was quite immaterial in causing the accident, though after the fire started it helped to intensify the flames. It is their view that further attention should be devoted to the possibilities inherent in the airship as an efficient and economic mode of air transportation.

9:13

Was Hitler's Rise to Power Inevitable?

Students of history often make the mistake of thinking that in the latter days of the crumbling Weimar Republic the emergence of Hitler and his Nazi followers to power was inevitable, the consequence of the chronic political disorder afflicting Germany as the result of the crippling damage inflicted on the country by the Great Depression of 1929–33. They simply fail to see that the problems of the era could have had any outcome other than the one that eventually transpired. This opinion, however, when examined, turns out to be quite erroneous.

The Nazi Party in 1929 was far from being the most important political party in the Weimar Republic. In the recent elections of May 1928, its representation in the Reichstag stood at no more than 12 seats out of 491. In the meantime there were a number of street scuffles between their supporters and those of the

Communist Party, though only in a few cities did these constitute any threat to public order. It was only when there was a big swing to Nazism in July 1932 that Nazi representation went up: it was then at 230 seats, but still only about one-third of the total number of 608. It actually fell back at the elections of November 1932. It was only by means of their intrigues and political posturing that the Nazis managed to secure power in the following year: it was by no means inevitable.

It is true that the roots of democracy in Germany were rather shallow, and the democratic Republic unpopular because it had saddled itself with the bitterly resented Treaty of Versailles, the burden of reparations payments and the humiliation of losing German territory, especially to 'inferior' neighbours such as Poland. The economic crises of 1923 and 1929 had also played their part in destroying the Republic's credibility. But democracy was not necessarily condemned to fail. It had done well in the middle years of the 1920s and, when the economic blizzard had died down, might easily recover in the 1930s. Scaremongering by opponents played as much a part in discrediting the Weimar Republic in Germany, as scepticism about Ramsay MacDonald's government in Britain did for Labour. The bulk of Germany's increasingly influential middle classes expected the Republic to recover from this crisis, and was disappointed and humiliated when it failed to do so.

A good deal of the blame must be laid at the doors of the right-wing parties for their mishandling of the situation. They feared an inflationary surge that might re-create the 'galloping inflation' of 1923, and sought to keep their hands clean by breaking with the ruling SPD in 1929 when it stepped up social insurance benefits to respond to the needs of the unemployed at the time of the slump. Brüning faced the same problem in May 1932, and tried a policy equally unpopular with the right when he proposed settling the unemployed workers on Junker estates (a suggestion which they condemned as 'a Bolshevik agrarian policy'). His government fell and was replaced by von Papen in June 1932. He was a born intriguer, and sought a right-wing solution in the form of a 'Government of National

Reconstruction', chiefly as a way of building an authoritarian system, which would avoid the irksome democratic restraints of the Republic. Though this manoeuvre failed it had the unforeseen consequence of strengthening Hitler's appeal. In December von Papen was forced to resign and was replaced by von Schleicher as Chancellor. Hitler, however, responded with a deal with Papen: Hitler was to be Chancellor and Papen Vice-Chancellor. Hitler came to power in January 1933 when President Hindenburg accepted the arrangement. But neither Papen nor anyone else took this turn of events seriously.

After his appointment in January, Hitler called an election for March 1933, so providing himself with another, this time quite spurious, claim to legality. This election – to choose the national Reichstag for the third time within a year – was ostensibly free, though throughout it was marred by violence and intimidation. Even so, the Nazis did not secure a majority; they held only 288 seats out of 647 and polled less than 45 per cent of the votes cast. Hitler had been legally appointed to the Chancellorship by Hindenburg but, for all his insistence on 'legality' as the basis of his government, he fell short of being elected directly to power by the German people.

Nevertheless it was not uncommon in 1933 to hear even intelligent people in Germany say: 'Let Hitler have a taste of power. Six months of it will show up his inability to run a state – the responsibilities of office will ruin the Nazis, and then we shall be rid of them forever.' This constituted a very serious underestimation of the threat from Hitler. In 1947, A.W. Dulles, in a book called *Germany's Underground*, pointed out this fatal weakness in the outlook of the German intelligentsia:

The intellectuals failed to realise that democracy must never be taken for granted. They did not see the need to come to its defence. To the staid and aloof professors in the German universities Hitler's movement, exemplified in the incoherent book *Mein Kampf*, was so ridiculous that they did not take it seriously. Before they knew it, many were removed, imprisoned or forced into silence or exile.

Dulles goes on:

> By the time the German people realised what 'national
> rebirth' and 'moral reawakening' meant, one of the most
> ruthless police states the world has seen was firmly
> established. . . . Modern technology – the radio, tele-
> photography, the concealed dictaphone – and the most
> efficient methods of detection and torture were devoted to
> suppressing freedom and ferreting out any who dared to
> oppose the Nazi dictatorship.

So it was a bad mistake to underestimate the ruthlessness or
the low animal cunning of Hitler. The main theme of his
speeches was that he alone could save Germany from disaster;
he wanted, he said, a four-year 'probationary period' to prove
himself, after which he would go back to the electorate to ask
for a 'renewal' of his mandate. He was always careful to portray
himself as a democrat and a populist. But once in office he
began to pay off old scores and to intrigue for the consolidation
of his power. For example, before the election in March, the
Reichstag building mysteriously burned down, and Hitler was
so prompt in turning the episode to his advantage by accusing
the communists of having perpetrated it that he incurred the
suspicion that the Nazis must have arranged it themselves. He
not only arranged the state trial of the communists for the
offence, but persuaded the decrepit President to rush through a
raft of emergency decrees (which he was fully entitled to do
under Article 48 of the Weimar Constitution) by which he
suspended the guarantees of personal liberties written into the
constitution, banned the Communist Party on the eve of the
election, and proclaimed the 'co-ordination' (*Gleichschaltung*) of
the whole of Germany's government with Nazi principles,
supposedly in the interests of 'protecting the people'. In March
he went on to bring in the so-called 'Enabling Bill' under which
he successfully superseded the operation of parliamentary
government in Germany by permitting national laws to be
enacted by the cabinet as well as in parliament. This step,

together with the packing of the Reichstag with his own supporters, his employment of his Brownshirts as hall guards to line the walls of the Chamber and deal with critics, and his use of the Chamber as a theatrical stage to popularise his speeches, effectively reduced the Reichstag to absurdity and eventual disuse, though he never formally abolished it. Thus the Weimar Republic withered away rather than was officially ended.

None of this, however, was inevitable. Hitler deliberately engineered these developments as means of consolidating his own power. A more genuinely democratic leader, more sincerely concerned with the welfare of the nation, would have acted entirely differently. This was an early occasion by which an unscrupulous leader used the apathy of the masses, or pandered to their ignorance and prejudice, in order to outwit and intimidate the intelligent and the articulate, and to rivet on all German wrists fetters which only national disaster could remove. Hitler knew the secret of the demagogue, offering some explanation, no matter how specious, for national grievances, and then promising some amelioration of them. His success in securing a devoted popular following should teach intelligent people in future that it does not take much probity or culture to run a state.

9:14

How Much Did the German People Know About the Concentration Camps?

When the full extent of the Holocaust became public towards the end of the Second World War it was argued in defence of the German people that its worst horrors were known only to a limited number of senior Nazis, and that the German people knew nothing of what had been going on. This version of events, however, was a myth studiously fostered by many Germans in their anxiety to plead ignorance for the excesses perpetrated by the Nazis, and the myth continues to be peddled as truth even to this day.

When the Allies took German civilians to see for themselves soon after the camps were liberated, most expressed surprise and shock; some broke down at what they saw. But only a few Germans lived near enough to the death camps to make personal visits. Instead, the camps were filmed and shown on cinema screens throughout Germany. The typical reaction of a people brainwashed by Nazism for twelve years was that the concentration camp films were fake Allied propaganda.

But the German people had been aware of concentration camps from the outset. The first ones were established in Germany in 1933 and no attempt was made to keep their existence secret. They employed German civilians, German firms provided goods and services, and some of them were close to main German urban centres. The Night of the Long Knives (1934) had accustomed the German people to Nazi political killings, and it would have been widely known that death by brutality or execution was common in these camps. Camp regulations, which were not classified documents, provided the death penalty for the most trivial offences.

It was somewhat different with extermination camps, which were established to carry out the 'Final Solution'. These were all situated outside Germany's pre-war borders: Auschwitz and Treblinka were the most notorious, and the Nazis naturally did not wish to publicise their sinister purpose. Even so, knowledge of what was going on in them reached many more people than a few senior Nazis. Most of the SS must have known, and they went on leave and some must have talked to their families about what they had seen. German firms like IG Farben who made the Zyklon B for the gas chambers must have known what it was for, and so would many, if not all, of their employees. German banks could not have been ignorant of the origins of their plentiful supply of dental gold. Many smaller German firms were involved with the camps and would have been aware of the situation there; medical specialists must have had some idea of their colleagues' active participation in concentration camp 'research'. And if most Germans lacked relatives or friends with direct knowledge of the camps, they must have wondered about the railway trucks, laden with human cargo, that incessantly rumbled their way eastward. Did they really believe they were destined for łabour camps?

Undoubtedly some Germans, especially those living in the countryside and at a distance from the main east–west railway lines, could have been unaware of the existence of the extermination camps. Some Germans, a not insignificant minority, would have direct knowledge of the camps and what was taking place in them. The majority would have heard rumours of varying authenticity. They could dismiss them if they lacked substance; if they rang true it was better to keep quiet about the rumours rather than fall foul of the Gestapo, and anyway the moral sense of the German people had been blunted by years of Nazi propaganda. The German people as a whole knew about the early concentration camps, but most of them lacked authoritative information about the extermination camps, and lacked the moral will or political means to do anything about them had they known.

9:15

How Much Did the Allied Leaders
Know About the Holocaust?

After the Second World War, war leaders on the Allied side protested complete ignorance of the mass killings of Jews that had been going on in Nazi Germany and in other parts of occupied Europe during the previous ten years. These protestations in most cases were false. It is true that at the time they had not mentioned their knowledge and took no steps to make use of it while the war was on, but this silence sprang more from cunning than from ignorance.

Though they made little propaganda or strategic use of any knowledge that they had, it seems fairly certain that many politicians, at least in Britain, had more than an inkling of what Nazi Germany was doing in eastern Europe and western Russia.

Professor Breitman, of the American University in Washington, in a book published in 1998, *Official Secrets: What the Nazis Planned, and What the British and Americans Knew*, declared that the British were aware of the Nazi policy of the mass killings of Jews as early as the late summer of 1941, though the information was not passed on to the Americans until 1982 as part of a US investigation of suspected war criminals. He speculates about the reasons why there was reluctance on the part of the British to make use of their information.

One reason seems to have been that there was some disagreement among British leaders whether the information was true and, if it was, whether it was a good idea to make use of it. The British Foreign Secretary, Anthony Eden, was one of those who advised against it, apparently on the grounds that any use of the information would play into the hands of Goebbels's propaganda, that the Allies were 'fighting the Jews' War'. Another reason was that the British were unwilling to let the Germans know that they had been successful in breaking German codes, when it came to their notice, as early as July 1941, from coded police messages, that there were massacres of Jews on the Eastern Front. But the main reason, it is suggested, for holding back the information was the substantial mistrust existing between London and Washington on Jewish issues. For one thing, to British right-wingers, President Roosevelt was suspected of being 'soft' on the Jews; for another, the Jewish 'lobby' in Washington was reckoned to have exercised an extremely powerful influence over US policy-making. When Roosevelt learned independently in December 1942 of the Nazi atrocities he reacted in a joint statement issued by him and Churchill denouncing Nazi actions very strongly; but at no time did Churchill admit to Roosevelt that he knew about them already.

Spokesmen for British Jewry, on the other hand, anxious to butter up the British authorities by salvaging Churchill's reputation as a man of probity and honour, have denied that he was implicated in the deception. They say that Churchill, always an intelligence enthusiast, had been in receipt of decoded messages up to September 1941, but then stopped reading them, one reason being that reported killings by this time were so frequent that he looked upon them as 'merely routine'. Such an admission, however, scarcely seems consistent with the previous assertion that the British authorities could not be sure whether the information they had picked up was true. The spokesmen, furthermore, produce the even more incredible opinion, denying that there was any organised anti-Semitism existing among senior members of the British government at the time, and putting down the calamity to 'a massive and unworthy misjudgment' of the importance of the reports received.

It is true that there were a number of quite spectacular blunders made by the Allies at the time, and this was one of them. But even if they had acted on the information available, their action might not perhaps have saved Jewish lives. It is hard to see what, in fact, they could have done before 1944, by which time the camps were being wound up. This, however, does not excuse the British failure to share their wartime intelligence with the Americans.

9:16

Enforced Repatriation, 1945: What Really Happened?

The enforced repatriation of over 70,000 Cossacks and Yugoslavs in May and June 1945, at the request of Stalin and Tito, Britain's communist allies in the East, is said to have been one of the most shameful episodes in modern history. Rifle butts and pick-axe handles were used by British troops to herd thousands of people onto cattle trucks for transportation to concentration camps in the East, where many of them were imprisoned, tortured and even executed. What was the truth about this grim affair?

At the Yalta Conference in February 1945 Churchill and Roosevelt had promised Stalin that those he claimed as 'Soviet citizens', whether or not they had fought for Hitler, would be sent back to Russia. Tito, too, anxious to get his hands on Croat extremists who had wrought vengeance on Serbs during the war in ways that made even the SS go pale, was demanding similar treatment for Yugoslav nationals. British garrisons in Austria, keen to show themselves loyal allies, set about this task with gusto, rounding up not only suspected Nazi sympathisers, but many who were innocent of such charges, and thousands of them women and children.

In 1988 the historian Count Tolstoy, grand-nephew of the Russian author of *War and Peace*, together with an associate, Nigel Watts, accused Lord Aldington, Chief of Staff at the time of V Corps of the 8th Army, of being a war criminal for exceeding his duty in committing thousands of innocent people to the tender mercies of intolerant Stalinist regimes. Tolstoy lost his case and was condemned to pay £1.5 million in damages to Aldington. However, Tolstoy pleaded poverty and paid very little of the sum awarded in damages and none of the £350,000 legal costs. Instead he counter-claimed for libel. Twelve years afterwards, in 2000, while Tolstoy contrived to live in some style, Aldington, who had been living in straitened circumstances and at the age of 86 was almost blind, finally died of cancer. This seemed to put an end to the controversy.

Research, however, shows that the matter was far from being an open-and-shut affair: the evidence is massive and confusing, consisting of thousands of files and microfilms pointing confusingly in different directions. More seriously, it has been suggested that there was an official cover-up not only of the events of 1945 but also in the circumstances leading to the trial. It is said that an 'old boy network' of old Wykehamists and others, including ministers in the Thatcher government, helped Lord Aldington to prepare his case. Files relevant to the case were withdrawn from the Public Record Office, where they had been lodged, and then buried away in the Ministry of Defence and the Foreign Office, and said to be 'lost' or 'unavailable' when Tolstoy needed them. Lord Younger, Defence Secretary from 1986 to 1989 was approached by Lord

Aldington, also a former pupil of Winchester College, and asked to remove the files from the PRO to the Ministry of Defence so that he could examine them there. A similar request was made to the Foreign Office, and again files were moved. The result was that the documents were not available to Tolstoy when he wanted them.

The possibility that such a conspiracy existed tends to show that there must have been at least some truth in the original complaints. Perhaps it is hardly surprising that the matter has not yet been resolved. However, the main thrust of the accusation must relate to what happened in 1945. Looking at the situation as it was then, it has to be said that those involved in the enforced repatriation were taking the line of least resistance by simply carrying out their orders. They were weary after six years of war, and just wanted a quiet life. They felt some sympathy for the Soviets and did not want any further trouble from them. They lost little sleep over the future fates of those they were sending back. It was only after the end of the communist regime that the wisdom of their decision has come to be seriously doubted.

10

ON-GOING CONTROVERSIES

Was Washington a Great General?

If, in 1783, the Americans had been asked to whom they most owed their success in the War of Independence, they would have been virtually unanimous in naming George Washington. Without him could anyone else have welded the frontiersmen and sharpshooters into an effective military force? Without him could anyone else have suffered so many defeats and yet win the final victory? Contemporary American observers glossed over Washington's failures and extracted as much propaganda as they could out of his victories, turning Washington into a military genius. Contemporary British observers attributed American successes not so much to Washington's military skills, but to the gross incompetence of the British military commanders, especially General Howe. The truth lies somewhere in between.

Washington did not have a military background. He worked at first as a surveyor on the western frontier, which gave him plenty of opportunity to observe Indian fighting tactics at close quarters. His knowledge of the terrain led to a military appointment by the colony of Virginia, and his part in the ill-fated Braddock expedition to take Fort Duquesne in 1755. Here Washington showed great personal bravery and considerable skill in extricating the remnant of Braddock's forces from the disaster. The colony rewarded Washington by appointing him commander of the forces of Virginia, and he took part in the capture of Fort Duquesne in 1758, thus avenging the defeat of three years earlier. After this Washington returned to his estates, gave up his military career and entered local politics.

As the quarrel between Britain and the colonies escalated, Washington became a delegate to the First Continental Congress in 1774. Hostilites broke out at Lexington in April 1775, and the Second Continental Congress decided to appoint a Commander-in-Chief of the colonial armies of Congress in order to coordinate the fighting. Washington was not the only candidate available. In fact some of Washington's later troubles were caused by disappointed aspirants like General Lee. But Washington's combination of military and political experience won the day and he was appointed in June 1775.

There was no doubt about the bravery and commitment of most of the men Washington had under his command. But, in order to render them capable of taking on Britain's professional armies, he had to turn them into soldiers. Skilled horsemen, expert shots, willing fighters they may have been, but they were not soldiers, nor did they constitute an army. During the next two years this was Washington's main task. He won the respect of his men; he even got them to acknowledge and respect their own officers. An army was created. It was not great in numbers, nor did it have the professional skills for Washington to risk it in open battle except on rare occasions. But his army became a thorn in the side of the British. It would have been an even greater threat to them if Washington had created a cavalry section out of the excellent horsemen he possessed. Cavalry was invaluable in the battle tactics of the eighteenth century, but military tactics were not Washington's strong point.

His capture of the Dorchester Heights in 1776 led to the fall of Boston, but it was a rather rash venture of which the British failed to take advantage. He allowed his army to become dangerously exposed in its dispositions for the unsuccessful defence of New York, and at White Plains his weak centre and isolated right courted disaster. But perhaps some risk was worth taking if he had accurately assessed Howe's incompetence. He was much lauded for his crossing of the icy Delaware river at Trenton in December 1776, but the crossing was slow; the Americans did not reach the main camp of the German mercenaries until daylight, and a better defence would have placed the Americans in extreme peril. In open contest the Americans were usually no match for the British, as was shown by Howe's defeat of Washington at Brandywine in September 1777. That he was better on strategy was evident in Washington's encampment at Valley Forge in the winter of 1777–8. It enabled Washington to harden his troops to the rigours of a New England winter; it enabled him to continue to weld his disparate army into a cohesive unit; and above all it enabled him to render General Howe impotent in his winter quarters at Philadelphia, some twenty miles away.

But the old tactical weakness showed up again at Monmouth Court House in New Jersey in June 1778. Washington had the chance to defeat Clinton if he had attacked the British centre instead of the British rear. He again neglected to make use of his horsemen who, for want of a trained cavalry, would have played havoc with the retreating British infantry. This was the last open engagement of the war. Clinton's British army remained on the defensive in New York while Washington encamped nearby on the Hudson to keep watch on the British. Washington's difficulties mounted. He was short of supplies and even shorter of money. His political skills in negotiation with the parsimonious authorities of the various colonies were called into play as Washington strove to keep his army in being.

Washington's great moment came in 1781. Uncertain whether to attack Clinton's reduced army in New York (Clinton had dispatched Cornwallis to Virginia) or to attack Cornwallis instead, his mind was made up when he heard that the French had now gained command of the sea and that Cornwallis could be trapped in his Yorktown stronghold. Deluding Clinton with a feint towards New York, Washington moved his army 400 miles to the South in less than a month, and combined with Lafayette's French army and De Grasse's French fleet to bring about Cornwallis's surrender with 7,000 men. This was a masterpiece of strategy. It brought the war effectively to an end.

Washington was thus a greater military strategist than

military tactician. Perhaps, with greater numbers, better supplies, and more political support, he might have achieved more in battle. He might have achieved more, too, had he made better use of his Virginian horse. But he had made a greater contribution to victory. His later work, as President, was mainly devoted to strengthening in peacetime the ties that had bound the United States in war – another task just as daunting.

10:2

Louis XVI of France: Tyrant or Incompetent?

Louis XVI was accused before his death by many of his political opponents and critics of being remote, extravagant and tyrannical. Is there any truth in this view, or is it merely a myth? The story was sometimes told of his ordering of the execution of two hapless peasants close to the hunting field in order that he could have their throats cut, and bathe his weary feet in their fresh blood. The fact that this absurd fantasy gained credence illustrates the fear and horror that his name sometimes evoked. But was he in reality a tyrant?

Louis succeeded to the throne of France on the death of his grandfather Louis XV in 1774, his father Louis the Dauphin having predeceased him almost ten years earlier. He was a stolid and unimaginative young man, and his grandfather rather despaired of him, while he, for his part, was much more interested in outdoor pursuits, together with a little tinkering with clocks, than he was with affairs of state. In his personal journal he had been known to write 'Today I did not do anything' if he had not been on the hunting field, no matter how weighty were the affairs of state that had been referred to him for approval. Whatever else it might have been called, such conduct hardly constituted tyranny. He was a tyrant only in the sense that he controlled great powers by virtue of his position as absolute ruler of one of the greatest of the European states.

Indeed, the French constitution, informal and unwritten

though it may have been, conferred enormous powers upon him. He was free to make or to change laws, and the limitations theoretically imposed on him by the various parliaments were flimsy and easy to circumvent. He could impose or modify taxes, make war or peace, and appoint or dismiss his own ministers as he thought fit. He could even imprison his own subjects by special warrant indefinitely and without trial if he wished. He could not be forced into doing anything against his will – though perhaps he could be persuaded by the hosts of courtiers who surrounded him at his court in Versailles. The presence of large numbers of professional troops stationed around his capital and in the country, together with the massive presence of the royal fortress in Paris itself (it struck fear into Parisians and was known to them simply as 'the Building', i.e. the Bastille) meant that his power and authority were unchallengeable.

The trouble was not that he overused his authority, but rather that he did not use it at all. He had too fine a regard for the grandeur of his position and the strength of the traditions surrounding the monarchy to wish to exercise his powers. Certain of his critics wished him to be more dynamic and vigorous rather than less, and criticised him for his apathy and indolence rather than for his tyranny; they saw him as 'King Log', wallowing ineffectually in his pond, rather than as 'King Stork', watching over his people and picking off his opponents with his beak. Thus France drifted leaderless at a time when political and financial problems were mounting.

Various Controllers-General of Finance, such as Turgot and Necker, wanted Louis to redesign the whole structure of French finance, and in particular to check the growth of sinecures, or immunities and of aristocratic privilege so as to make the yield of taxes approximate more closely to the country's taxable capacity. But Louis drew back from such radicalism. He did this partly because he recognised that many tax exemptions had been legally bought, and that it was sharp practice to sell immunities and then to cancel them, or to invent new taxes on which there were no immunities. Nor had he the determination to sweep away the dead wood of outmoded institutions, or the imagination to approve some new way of financial accounting to speed up the process of collection or the auditing of accounts. It was sometimes said of him that his views of the policies necessary for France were the views of the adviser who had spoken to him last. He lacked the ruthlessness of a Napoleon to understand that in order to make an omelette one has first to break a few eggs.

When he faced his nobles who blocked his reforms in their assembly in 1787, or when he faced his country's first elected Estates General since 1614, he had not the wit nor the personality to take the lead, though France would have worshipped him if he had. All he could do was to stamp his foot and become even more petulant than usual. His indecision in crucial matters proved to be fatal, his regard for his subjects so tender that he could not bring himself to hurt anybody. Meantime, the forces of progress and reaction in France were shaping up to one another, preparatory to the final showdown. Even when he attempted to flee to the Austrian frontier at Varennes in order to secure foreign aid to put down what by this time had become a revolution, the plan was recklessly botched by the Queen and he was brought back to Paris a political prisoner. Whatever may be said about his political wisdom, however, there can be no doubting his personal courage. On the occasion of the march on Versailles in October 1789, or of the attack by the mob on the Tuileries in August 1792, Louis was steadfast in the face of personal danger, and tenderly solicitous of his wife's safety. On the latter occasion he found himself surrounded by an immense crowd of angry demonstrators armed with pitchforks and pikes, but showed no sign of flinching. He spoke calmly to them, and even humoured them by donning the red 'cap of liberty'; but he still refused to agree to their demands. He was equally calm and dignified at his trial, a few months later, when he was tried for crimes against his people (a novel interpretation of the concept of treason), and went to the guillotine in January 1793 with no stain of cowardice on his character.

Louis XVI was not an odious tyrant; he was merely an honest incompetent promoted beyond his capacity.

10:3

Robespierre: Statesman or Terrorist?

Maximilien Robespierre is probably the most famous of the French revolutionaries. He is inextricably linked with the bloody ruthlessness of the Committee of Public Safety, thus making him symbolic of the Terror. But is this a fair picture?

Robespierre has been something of an enigma both to his contemporaries and to historians. On the one hand he has a reputation as an idealist – the man of noble principles – Carlyle's 'sea-green incorruptible'. On the other he is remembered for his ruthlessness as the principal architect of the Terror. That he dressed in the meticulous style of the aristocracy he was helping to decimate does not make him any less a terrorist. Nor does the fact that he was unsure of himself, nervous and withdrawn in company and timid in his personal relationships. And his incorruptibility and idealism were shared, to some extent at least, by many of his colleagues, and were not in themselves incompatible with ruthlessness.

He can be regarded as a political puritan a leader who reached, often vainly, for lofty ideals; who grew impatient with those who did not share his ideals; who rejected half-measures or compromise; and who believed that individuals were capable of realising a vast potential if only they could master their own frailties. His belief that opposition was perverse led him to self-righteousness and a rigidity in his views, which was eventually to destroy him.

He began his career as a lawyer and entered politics as deputy for Artois in 1789. Mirabeau thought him a dangerous maniac, whose abstract speeches on the rights of man were expressed with such passion and personal ambition that they were bound to lead the nation to disaster. The flight to Varennes made Robespierre a republican, in order that the goals of the revolution should not be betrayed by counter-revolution. At first he opposed both war and violence. Later he came to support war, even though it had been instigated by his opponents. He saw the revolution as a necessary and inevitable stage in the liberation of man. Elected to the Convention in 1792 he was soon championing the policies of the Jacobins against the moderates who waged war ineptly, and who opposed centralisation. When war brought extreme foreign danger, Robespierre became convinced that the Revolution could be saved only by purging the nation of those who threatened it, and his refusal to condemn the September Massacres committed him to a theory of popular justice that was little short of lynch-law. When the trial of the King took place, he pressed for the death penalty in spite of his views on capital punishment ('Because the country must live, Louis must die'). Yet he had refused to become a judge before the Revolution as he was squeamish about the death penalty, and not surprisingly he secluded himself in his shuttered house on the day of Louis XVI's execution.

Thus he campaigned for blood-letting and purification; yet many of his interventions in the work of the Revolutionary Tribunal later were on the side of clemency. He did not see purification in terms of people being put to death; he saw it as a means of cutting out the diseased portion of society. His stress on virtue, purity and religion made him unpopular among his colleagues, who feared his inquisitorial eye, but he was a valuable member of governing committees and a popular public idol. At the same time, his stress on purification struck hope and fear simultaneously into the hearts of the people ('Without Terror, Virtue is impossible; without Virtue, Terror is pointless').

So social justice was to be achieved at a cost. While danger threatened, during the crisis months of 1793 and 1794, purification by guillotine would continue. Danton's proposals for a Committee of Clemency seemed to Robespierre as dangerous as sans-culottism and Hébert's demands for atheism. It is sometimes said that such men threatened Robespierre's own position of control; that social ideals gave him his justification in seeking for power, but that love of office made him cling to it; that even the deism to which he adhered seemed almost as much an opportunity to parade himself in his sky-blue suit as affirmation of the spiritual needs of the nation. But the truth is that Robespierre's character lacked both the cynicism and the brutality of most dictators. There is no reason to doubt that he aimed at political liberty according to his own definition, and saw the revolutionary dictatorship as purely temporary in a time of crisis.

But there are doubts as to whether he was really a dictator, let alone a tyrant. He exercised no dominant authority in the Committee of Public Safety; he was not a permanent member until July 1793, and Barère, Carnot and Prieur de la Marne signed far more decrees than he did. Nor does he bear sole responsibility for the intensified Terror of 1794. While he agreed that the enemies of the people deserved death, he was never as severe either as the members of the Committees of General Security or as the more fanatical of his colleagues, such as St Just (the 'Angel of Death'). Some of his policy decisions may have been of questionable wisdom. Paying volatile sans-culottes to attend Section meetings, and walking the political tightrope by striking simultaneously at the left (Hébert) and right (Danton) were perhaps risky and dangerous decisions. And when in July 1794 he tried to browbeat the Convention by making non-specific threats against unnamed members he was repeating previously successful tactics in a different, more hostile situation. Thus his statesmanship is to be found more in the quality of his beliefs than in the efficacy of his actions.

The fact remains that historians have overrated Robespierre's importance on account of the exaggerated attention paid to him by his Thermidorean opponents: Robespierre came to personify the Terror without being fully responsible for it, and in the end the Terror with which he is identified claimed him as a victim.

10:4

General Custer: Foolhardy or Just Unlucky?

General Custer was one of the soldiers sent in 1876 against the Sioux and a force of assorted Cheyenne and Arapaho Indians, an army of about 12,000 warriors altogether, in the valley of the Little Bighorn river in Montana. Some say that Custer was a hero who fought to the last against overwhelming odds; others say he was simply unlucky. Yet others believe he disobeyed orders and acted foolishly, seeking only glory for himself. Perhaps it is unlikely that we shall ever know the truth behind the Custer legend.

The position of the Indian tribesmen in the Middle West was already desperately weak. When the US Civil War ended, General Sherman had threatened to drive them from their hunting-grounds, and in the next twenty years about 200 pitched battles were fought against them. The technological supremacy of the Whites, the drive for western railroad building, the search for gold after the discoveries in California in 1849, and the steady extinction of the buffalo herds which provided the tribesmen's staff of life all contributed to the plight of the Indians, who were being hunted down and murdered, or confined in 'reservations' to do the work of women on the farm.

Born in 1839, George Armstrong Custer was, while training, a brilliant if rather unpredictable student in the military academy at West Point, and a dashing and ambitious officer during the US Civil War. He became the commander of the 7th US Cavalry in 1866. He was already known to indian leaders as the man sent to the Black Hills on the Dakota border in 1874 to subdue the Sioux there and to further the settlers' search for gold. Generally thought to be strong-willed and reckless, Custer regarded the indians contemptuously, and sought to further his military career by achieving a spectacular victory over them.

In 1876 an expedition of crack White troops was sent into the Bighorn Mountains against Crazy Horse and Sitting Bull who, with their group of warriors, had refused to go to their reservations as ordered. General Terry, in overall command, planned to march Colonel Gibbon and the main body of his troops south up the Bighorn river, while Custer and the 7th Cavalry would march round the Wolf Mountains and then north down the Bighorn to meet him at the point where the rebel Indians were camped. Custer, however, had ideas of his own. He divided his force of cavalry into three: one to search the mountain ridges along the route, the second to continue the advance down the right bank of the river, and the third, a force of 215 men under his own command, to outflank the Indians with a move down the left bank. Both of his subordinates, however, were faced with superior numbers and compelled to retreat, and Custer found himself cut off and surrounded. He fought bravely, but in the end his small force was wiped out to the very last man. At what point in the struggle Custer died is not known. He may even have shot himself, for people sometimes 'saved the last bullet for themselves' rather than be taken by the indians. This may be true, since his body was not mutilated nor his scalp removed, and indians were known not to meddle with the corpse of a suicide. Nevertheless, oral tribal histories relate that two native women, angry at the way Custer had ignored unwritten agreements so often entered into in the past, sought him out among the dead and, without marking the body, pushed slender metal needles into his ears and into his brain, 'in order to improve his hearing' of the treaty conditions they expected him to honour.

It certainly appears that an element of foolhardiness came into Custer's defeat, since he would have been safe if he had followed his orders exactly instead of trying to make a name for himself. What his motives – other than vanity – were, however, has never been established.

10:5

Were the First World War Generals Criminally Incompetent?

Bitter criticism both from historians and non-historians has for long been heaped on the heads of the First World War generals of both sides for their conduct of the war during the years 1914–18. There can be no doubt that these accusations were over-harsh, and at least in some cases undeserved.

During the four years of war over 3½ million men were killed on the Western Front. These colossal casualties, the result of repeated failed offensives, caused disillusionment in Britain, mutinies in France, and desperation in Germany. By 1916 the British and French generals were beginning to be blamed for the huge death toll, but as they could only retain their positions by military success they continued to embark on new and costly offensives. So it is not surprising that many historians have concluded that the Western Front generals were incompetent, incapable of learning from their mistakes, and criminally overconfident as they sheltered in their headquarters, many miles from the front line. The words of one general who is supposed to have said 'We shall have heavy casualties, but at least we shall kill more of them than they of us' was often quoted as a stereotype of the top leadership of all armies. Most attempts to defend the generals are to be found in the works of their biographers, which are usually too partisan. Yet it is possible to find excuses for the generals, even though these fall well short of justification.

Military training before 1914 had assumed a war of movement. As in previous wars the cavalry was to achieve a breakthrough and the infantry was to follow up and mop up remaining resistance. Although both barbed wire and machine-guns had been used in the most recent wars, their value in a static war was not yet realised. So when the fluidity of the Western Front during the first three months of the war ended, and both sides dug in, a new and untried military situation arose. It became necessary to pierce the enemy line of trenches, and to do so meant to attack. It took a long time for generals to appreciate that in all major battles, except Verdun, attackers suffered higher casualties than defenders.

Of course, the Allied generals were under political pressure. Early expectations of a rapid end to the war resulted in disappointment. The war could only be ended through successful military offensives; so generals engaged in strikes on heavily defended positions in order to avoid being dismissed. This was illustrated early on by what happened to Sir John French, the commander of the British Expeditionary Force. He had not distinguished himself in the early war of movement, but when it became a war of attrition he found himself under pressure both from the French commander General Joffre and from Field Marshal Lord Kitchener, the British Minister of War. Goaded by both into a frontal assault on the enemy trenches at Loos, he attributed his failure to an inadequate supply of shells. This angered the British government, led to French's dismissal, and acted as a salutary warning to other generals who might wish to step out of line. German generals, too, knew that they were at the mercy of political pressure, in this case from the despotic Kaiser.

Thus they felt obliged to attack, but it is a mistake to assume that the generals were indifferent to casualties. After all, an army decimated by casualties would be in no position to continue the war. So, except for Verdun, the Germans avoided major offensives until 1918, and simply built defensive lines superior to those of the Allies and waited to be attacked. This is what the Allied generals would have preferred to do. But on the costly French defence of Verdun seemed to hinge the whole fate of France, and the French begged for a British offensive to distract the Germans.

This needed weeks of careful preparation, so that by the time of the opening of the battle of the Somme, that at Verdun was almost over. General Sir Douglas Haig, the new commander of the British forces, convinced himself that the enemy front line could be obliterated by artillery bombardment: he expected the army to march into abandoned positions, so that casualties would be very light. He was wrong. The artillery threw the enemy barbed wire into the air and it fell to the ground more entangled than it had been before. Minor and localised successes, and the need to help the French whose armies were on the verge of mutiny, persuaded Haig to continue the Somme battle long after the casualty lists should have urged him to call it off. The Germans, too, had persisted with the attack on Verdun, despite the casualties, because they believed that the fall of Verdun would lead to the fall of France; the French thought likewise, and over 600,000 men died in the slaughter there.

For a while the French fell back on defence and the British lay low. From April 1917 both were content to await the arrival of the Americans. But Haig's success in blowing the Germans off Messines ridge in June 1917 restored his confidence, and he was sure that the German line could be breached. The British army now had tanks and these would achieve the breakthrough. He did not want the glory of victory to pass to the Americans and he was alarmed by suggestions that the war would prosper better if efforts were concentrated on the Italian front. Most of his own senior staff and most of the Cabinet had doubts and wished to avoid further heavy casualties. Perhaps Haig really thought that he could end the war in 1917, but the ensuing battle of Passchendaele got bogged down in the mud of Flanders. It would have been excellent tank country, flat and open, had not the unseasonal summer rains which continued well into the autumn rendered it an impenetrable quagmire. Once again the attackers suffered more heavily than the defenders.

In 1918 the Germans, fearing the impending arrival of countless American troops, decided to strike while the rival armies were still evenly matched, and while they were able to divert troops from the Russian front. Ludendorff decided to avoid the attacking mistakes of his enemies: he moved troops by night to confuse Allied intelligence; above all he advanced without a preliminary bombardment, the cause of so many

Allied failures. But one lesson he had not learned: he, like his opponents, persisted in attacking the enemy's strong points rather than its weak ones, and so his costly offensives ran out of steam. Even the American General Pershing was guilty of this at first, and there were heavy American casualties. It was Marshal Foch who devised, or as some say, hit upon by accident, the shifting attack which moved from the more strongly defended areas of the line to the weaker areas as occasion demanded. By the time of the armistice in November 1918 trench warfare had been abandoned except in a few locations, and the war had become a war of movement which the generals on both sides had wanted all along.

It took a long time for the generals on the Western Front to learn from their mistakes. There was no alternative but for them to attack if the war was to be won, because an interminable defensive war would be intolerable both for themselves and for the nations they led, not to mention their political leadership. But the generals were not cynically indifferent to casualties, and did not order offensives regardless of the cost. No general included heavy casualties in his plans. Nivelle and Haig both thought that their offensives would succeed at little cost and they were appalled at the losses. Rarely did the most senior officers visit the front line to assess conditions for themselves. They were perhaps therefore guilty of callousness, and of allowing themselves to become ensnared in their own red tape – for modern war had speedily become a very bureaucratic business. But it should not be suggested that they did not care. Even if they had visited the front line frequently it is difficult to see how the generals could have ended the trench stalemate. Their critics are better at recording what they should not have done rather than what they should have done.

10:6

Lenin: Demagogue or Statesman?

Vladimir Ilyich Lenin was revered in his lifetime as the father of the Bolshevik revolution. After his death in 1924 his embalmed body lay in state in the Kremlin, the object of pilgrimage of every true Russian communist. His enemies regarded him as no more than a demagogue who swayed the masses with his oratory and who subverted communism from its ideals. His admirers claim that his pragmatism showed true statesmanship, and that, had he lived, the Soviet state would have demonstrated how communism should really work. While the controversy rages Lenin is still awaiting an objective assessment.

There is no doubt that he could play the demagogue. In the heady days of 1917 Lenin could as easily sway a committee as inspire a mob. To a sophisticated audience he was an intellectual; to a crowd of factory workers he was a workmate. And in 1917 the Bolsheviks needed demagogues. But more than that, in Lenin's view they needed someone to urge them against the dangers of collaborating with the politicians of the February Revolution; they needed someone to urge them that the time was right for the Bolshevik takeover; they needed someone to convince them of the necessity for government by a small party élite. Many vital and hasty decisions had to be taken in the first days of the October Revolution. The Bolshevik leaders would not have turned, as most of them so readily did, to Lenin if he was a demagogue and nothing more. But he was much more. Above all he had clarity of thought and single-mindedness of purpose which his colleagues readily recognised.

So there was more to Lenin than mere demagoguery. But can he be called a statesman? In one sense not. He was not an *international* statesman. After 1917 he never left Russia. He did not meet foreign statesmen and, in so far as the Soviet Union had a foreign policy other than isolation, he entrusted its conduct to others. But statesmanship does not need to be of the international kind. Ordinary politicians are party hacks who follow the party line and are prepared to subordinate their personal opinions to the party dogma. Statesmen are those who rise above party and address themselves to the needs of the state, even if it means unpopularity or deviation from party principles.

Lenin had considerable room for manoeuvre. Karl Marx had established the general principles of communism and Lenin did not deviate from these. But Marx had not set out in detail how communist theory would work in practice; he had been good on dialectical analysis but vague on constructive recommendations, and this gave Lenin the scope to create as well as to interpret policy. He made bold decisions. On the Constituent Assembly and the war with Germany he was decisive if controversial. And Lenin proved to be right when he persuaded his colleagues that Brest-Litovsk would be short-lived, even though it was not the expected world revolution which overturned it.

During the civil war Lenin showed skill in his choice of military commanders, and he was not averse to using ex-Tsarist officers like Brusilov. And he showed a great deal of tact in handling men like Trotsky and Stalin, whose personal animosities could have endangered the war strategy. The postwar famine was a tragedy of enormous proportions. Unlike Stalin later, Lenin did not try to deny the existence of famine and was not too proud to ask for international aid. The famine highlighted the failure of communist economics, and Lenin found it necessary to abandon strict communist orthodoxy when he replaced War Communism with the New Economic Policy (NEP). The Kronstadt Mutiny (1921) confirmed what Lenin had been thinking for some time, that some compromise with capitalism was necessary until the country was fully ready to accept a communist-planned economy. He did not intend the NEP to be permanent, but it is a measure of his skill and leadership that he persuaded reluctant colleagues to accept it at all.

It was inevitable that a small and privileged ruling élite would need to use force to maintain itself in power. The civil war changed Lenin from a man who dismissed his opponents with contempt to a tyrant who had them eliminated. In his last year, when power was slipping from his grasp, there was some mellowing of his ruthlessness. But by then the machinery of a totalitarian state had been established and could not easily be dismantled. Lenin was becoming concerned about the dangers of abuse of power, when it was concentrated in so few hands. Thus his *Testament* showed a shrewd appraisal of Stalin, and a recognition of some of Trotsky's weaknesses, but his colleagues who had so revered him in life now deserted him in death, and *Testament* was ignored.

It has been argued that, without Lenin, there would have been no Bolshevik revolution, or if one had occurred it would have failed. It could also be argued that Lenin's success in handing on a consolidated communist state to his successors is evidence of Lenin's greatness. Whether it is evidence of his statesmanship depends on whether the seventy years of communism which he initiated in Russia were beneficial or otherwise. Communist historians will continue to give him their adoration; others will scarcely deny him their respect.

10:7

Edward VIII: Was He a Nazi?

The reputation of Edward VIII has been much tarnished by the accusation that he was a Nazi sympathiser, and that during the war he was hoping for a German victory, and for reinstatement as King of England under Nazi protection. The evidence for this is considerable, if largely circumstantial. It is based on Edward's pre-war trip to Germany, his pro-Nazi utterances, his passing of information to German diplomats even in wartime, his reluctance to leave Portugal in 1940 and his private correspondence from the Bahamas. German sources, too, add credence to the view that Edward's antics in 1939–40 amounted to treachery rather than foolishness.

King Edward VIII abdicated in December 1936. Prevented by politicians and public opinion from marrying the twice-divorced woman of his choice, Mrs Wallis Simpson, he preferred to abandon the throne to his brother, the Duke of York, and he and his bride went to France in self-imposed exile. It is probable that he was very bitter against Britain's politicians for the circumstances of his abdication, and against his brother, now King George VI, for the way Edward was treated after it. He was given the title of the Duke of Windsor, but his wife was denied royal status. During the war the Germans, believing that Edward was a Nazi sympathiser, toyed with the idea of restoring Edward to the British throne. They would need to conquer Britain first, but in the meantime they might be able to capture him, and secure propaganda advantage from his pro-German sympathies. Is there any truth in the oft-repeated assertion that Edward would have been a willing participant in this very tentative German scheme?

Edward's political leanings seemed at times more in sympathy with the left than the right, but the Nazis originally claimed to be socialists. Certainly Edward had shown concern for the unemployed, and had astonished and alarmed politicians when, on a visit to South Wales in 1936, he had asserted that 'something must be done'. His outspoken views are said to have made some politicians determined to remove him from the throne, an unproven piece of speculation. But it is a fact that his acquaintance with the Mitfords, some of whom were notorious in their adulation of Hitler, led him to visit Germany where he was shown what the Germans wanted him to see, and where he continued his reputation for making incautious remarks on political matters. The Windsors were ill-advised to go to Germany in the first place, but abdication bitterness made them unreceptive to British advice. They were even more ill-advised to allow themselves to be photographed with Hitler in October 1937; the photographs were a propaganda coup for the Nazis and an embarrassment for the British. Edward certainly admired the way the Nazis were tackling unemployment, and he had no intrinsic repugnance to authoritarian rule. Edward was by no means the only upper-class admirer of pre-war Fascism, but most of these admirers were soon to be found leading the Allies in the war against it.

The outbreak of war brought the Duke's visits to Germany to an abrupt end, and the German invasion of France in 1940 forced the Duke and Duchess to leave their Paris home. They did so with great reluctance; some would allege because they wanted to cooperate with the invaders, but more probably because they were naive enough to think that they would be allowed to continue their private lives and that the Germans would not seek to make political capital out of the Windsors falling into German hands. After a brief spell on the Riviera they moved to Portugal. Here the Windsors continued, despite the war, to entertain and be entertained by German diplomats, and careless talk at the dinner table enabled the Germans to pass useful information about the Allied war effort back to Berlin. Edward wanted a speedy end to the war and a compromise peace and even expressed his opinion that a German bombing campaign against Britain would force Britain to the negotiating table.

The continued presence of the Windsors in Portugal represented a security risk for the British, especially as the Germans were trying to persuade the Windsors to move to Spain. Certainly Edward showed no enthusiasm for being sidelined to the Bahamas, and resisted Churchill's efforts to send him there. That the Windsors eventually agreed to go is attributed by some to Edward's belated patriotic sense of duty, by others to intense pressure by Churchill and the possibility of a court martial since Edward retained his British officer rank. No concrete evidence is forthcoming to support the court-martial theory, although there is no doubt that Edward had been more than once guilty of flagrant disobedience to orders.

The Bahamas was in the comparative safety of the western Atlantic. Even after his arrival there, the Duke, in his private correspondence, revealed his unwitting class prejudices and also made the occasional reference to the benefits that Hitler had brought to the German people. These private remarks do not necessarily make the Duke a Nazi. He was, of course, unaware of the darker side of the Hitler regime: he knew of its political intolerance and its anti-Semitism, though perhaps not of the worst horrors of the concentration camps or the Holocaust. Nor is there any specific evidence that he would willingly have accepted the role of Nazi puppet King of England, even if Hitler had been in a position to turn the scheme into a reality. German sources assume his cooperation, but could well have been excessively optimistic. Churchill, himself, did not think it necessary to protect the Bahamas against the unlikely event of a U-boat attempt to carry off the Duke.

It is one thing to have a naive admiration for some of the Nazi achievements; it is very much another thing to accept Nazism in its entirety, and there is little direct evidence that the Duke ever did. And it is even more fanciful to suppose that the Duke would have been a willing traitor to his country if he had ever fallen into German hands. The Duke may have harboured resentment at his treatment by his country in 1936 and the ostracism afterwards by his brothers and their wives. He may well have felt that being sent to the Bahamas was a continuation of that ostracism and exile. But to elevate this into an intention to commit treason is speculative to say the least, and sympathy for some of the aspects of Nazism did not necessarily make him an out-and-out Nazi. It seems at least that Edward was careless, naive and rebellious. Further than that the evidence remains inconclusive.

10:8

Hitler: Dictator or Dreamer?

It is an error to suppose that from the beginning Hitler had a clear blueprint of the policies he intended to follow in Nazi Germany. The more closely the historian examines this cherished legend the less convincing becomes the evidence for it. For though Hitler claimed to have broad general aims when he came to power in 1933, he had given little thought to actual policies. His preference for broad statements of policy, and the fundamental laziness which prevented him from thinking through his problems, meant that he dismissed details as too

319

boring for him to spend time on; and this meant in effect that he had no policies at all. So what is to be made of the suggestion that Hitler enforced a totalitarian state-controlled dictatorship on the country under the Third Reich?

In fact, Germany was far from being a truly totalitarian state. It is correct that it possessed a frightening apparatus of control and detection – concealed microphones, sophisticated interrogation techniques and so on – but these were only spasmodically applied. The much-vaunted state control was really rather patchy. Vast vested interests went unchallenged by the state, and there were many private empires of control from which Hitler averted his eyes, or even actively encouraged.

The policy vacuum existing in 1933 meant that power rested in the hands of civil service officials, and that in the absence of a clear political lead their policies were essentially debris left over from the Weimar Republic, comprising ideas which Hitler had already unequivocally rejected. Hitler had his mind on other things – hardly on policy at all. The Third Reich did not follow a clear path mapped out by the Führer: its direction depended on the outcome of a series of struggles which, taken together, made up the Nazi state. Least important were the conservative-bourgeois politicians who had been in office in the Weimar Republic, and who were out of harmony with the new ideological order. They were quickly pushed aside. What mattered to Hitler was the power of industry and the military on the one hand, which was going to give the regime its particular authoritarian stamp and, on the other, people mobilised in the National Socialist movement and working for a new society.

To bring about the fusion of the two was something Hitler had no idea how to achieve. He waited for the expected fusion to take place of its own accord, seeing himself as a kind of referee above the contest, and the struggle itself as part of the dialectical character of Nazism. So the dichotomy continued: the military-industrial establishment demanding profits, efficiency and managerial control over the workforce on the one hand, the Nazi movement representing political reorganisation, discipline, employment and social harmony on the other. The meeting-place of the two forces was rearmament, essential for the creation of the Greater Germany, in which the former saw profits and power, the latter work and prosperity. But supremacy in the struggle finally went to the military-industrial complex. National Socialism lost out.

For a self-styled totalitarian dictator Hitler had the curious habit of not interfering. It was part of his underlying belief that the fittest would survive, and that their ideas would (and should) prevail over the effete notions of the defeated. Thus he allowed to grow separate empires of authority, controlled by his party henchmen such as Goering and Himmler. They could do as they liked so long as they did not infringe his own position or contradict party doctrine. Since, however, his own position was undefined and party doctrine studiously imprecise, subordinate leaders found themselves operating within a vague and untested framework – though Hitler's vengeance might fall on their heads at any time, whenever the mood took him. Such a situation did, though, provide him with a cast-iron excuse for protracted idleness, enabling him to devote long hours and spasmodic energy to fringe projects, or simply to watching old movies or day-dreaming. So Nazi controls were a hit-and-miss affair, favouritism and jobbery rampant, and malpractice almost routine.

He also had the unfortunate habit of appointing more than one man for the same job, or two men for very similar jobs, giving neither of them a job-description. For instance, he ignored Foreign Minister von Neurath as a bourgeois diplomat of the old discredited school, and created two Nazi Party bureaux for foreign affairs, headed respectively by von Ribbentrop (a former champagne salesman and a self-styled expert on Britain) and Alfred Rosenberg (party 'theoretician' and a Baltic German mainly interested in eastern Europe). This may have bred healthy competition between the appointees, but it was hardly conducive towards efficient administration.

At the same time the legally constituted form of government of Germany was superseded. During 1933 and 1934, Nazi *Stadthalters* were appointed to supervise the operation of the state governments, and the Nazi Party, replacing all earlier political parties, became the 'state party'. More important, the Gestapo (Secret State Police) under Goering was created to supplement the work of the regular police, with its black-uniformed élite, the SS (*Schutz Staffeln* – security guards) under Himmler, so that the regular work of the civil police was steadily usurped, and the courts bypassed by the party. All guarantees of personal liberty written into the Weimar Constitution were suspended – henceforth no German was safe from arbitrary arrest, torture or imprisonment. With unlimited authority free from proper civil control, the operation of the Nazi government now resembled the seedy machinations of the gangster underworld rather than a constitutionally created regime. Nazi leaders used this system as they saw fit, subject only to Hitler's theoretical veto, so that it was as much the frivolous caprice of the Nazi regime as its brutality that struck terror into the hearts of those who observed it.

10:9

Nazi Foreign Policy, 1933–41: Design or Drift?

Contemporary observers who lived through the successive foreign policy crises of the 1930s were generally agreed on ascribing the coming of the Second World War to Hitler. They saw him as a ruthless, determined leader who deliberately engineered the war so as to gratify his own lust for power, as the first step towards establishing Nazi world conquest. But did he actually embark on a deliberate policy of world domination? Some doubts remain about this.

War was integrally a part of the Nazi world outlook, and Germany would achieve the pinnacle of its national greatness in the service of such an ideal. To those who responded that deliberately to will war and destruction was the action of a madman, they answered that the mental climate of the time was such as to give his exhortations some credence, and that in any case it was quite true that Hitler and his followers had shown that they were all a little unhinged. Hitler planned the war; he worked towards it, and in the end he got what he wanted – the chance to bid for world conquest for himself and his ideology. This view was broadly shared by a number of distinguished writers of the period: the Jewish-American journalist William Shirer who lived through, and reported on, his experiences in his monumental book, *The Rise and Fall of the Third Reich* (1959); and at least two great English historians and scholars, Hugh Trevor-Roper in his book *The Last Days of Hitler* (1950), and Alan Bullock in *Hitler: a Study in Tyranny* (1952, revised 1962). As far as they were concerned it was Hitler's depraved character and his evil machinations that led to the outbreak of the Second World War.

This view achieved striking confirmation at the time of the Nuremberg War Trials by the publication of the so-called Hossbach Memorandum – though little if anything had been heard about it earlier. Much play has been made with this document as revealing Hitler's plans for the conquest of Europe. Even the editors of that most monumental publication, *Documents on German Foreign Policy* say that 'it provides a summary of German foreign policy in 1937'. Its contents were produced against the Nazi leaders in 1945 as evidence of their 'war guilt'. Closer inspection of this Memorandum casts doubt upon its historical usefulness. It was second hand and quite unofficial; it was written after the event and not at the time; it was based on one minor official's recollections; and most important, it did not define with any accuracy what Hitler's plans were, but merely speculated on various possibilities (referred to by Hossbach as 'Cases'). Historian A.J.P. Taylor, in his book *The Origins of the Second World War* (1961), was not slow to dismiss these speculations as 'in a large part day-dreaming', adding: 'His speculations were mistaken. They bear hardly any relation to the actual outbreak of war in 1939. A racing tipster who only reached Hitler's level of accuracy would not do very well for his clients.' That his book should provoke such bitter and acrimonious controversy was partly due to the personal rivalry between Trevor-Roper and Taylor, both of whom were highly esteemed at Oxford University, where they worked. But it was also due to the way that Taylor's theory cut across an interpretation of Hitler and the Nazis that had come to be regarded as authoritative, almost as 'Gospel truth'.

Taylor's view of the Hitler phenomenon was not so heavily centred on the Führer himself, nor on his supposed flaws of character. His analysis took into account the whole background of the 1930s: the feeling, in democratic countries, that the Versailles settlement had been unfair in its treatment of the Germans; the reluctance of the divided Western powers to rearm and to take deterrent action against the Nazis, together with the opinion, as Baldwin put it, that he would prefer, if there were to be a war, to see the 'Bolshies' fighting the 'Nasties'; Chamberlain's hope that underneath all the belligerent bluster Hitler was an honourable man who would finally be prepared to agree terms; hence, the Western powers' preference for 'appeasement' instead of confrontation – all this as well as Hitler's alleged malevolent warmongering was the root explanation of the war. Taylor was rather of the opinion that Hitler was a 'chancer' who struck lucky in a run of opportunities – the Rhineland, the *Anschluss*, Munich – until he came to be convinced of his own infallibility (or 'intuition' as he called it). His followers, too, saw how well he had performed so far and were willing to go on trusting him until he made a mistake. This view of Hitler as a lucky gambler who won so many bets that he thought himself fireproof stressed not the underlying aggressiveness of Hitler but his ability to know and exploit his opponents' weaknesses, and to improvise his successes out of the most unlikely situations. His victories illustrated the virtues of persistence and determination, but they were explained much more by good luck than by good management. Taylor's view appeared more natural than any explanation of Hitler that stressed his demonic features; but in another sense they cut him down to size by showing how human his decisions were, and how ordinary, even how petty, he was. Such a view almost completely discounted his much-vaunted ideology as the basis for his actions. This was merely a smokescreen pumped out in his speeches and writings not because he believed it, or his opponents believed it (indeed, Stalin for one took all the blustering against the Bolsheviks in *Mein Kampf* and his pursuit of *lebensraum* with a generous pinch of salt), but purely for consumption by the German public, hungry for reassurance after their wartime defeat.

Critics of Taylor's interpretation were not slow to point out the fundamental weakness in his case. Perhaps the impact of ideology should not be so lightly written off. One of Taylor's critics, T.W. Mason, in a paper called 'Some Origins of the Second World War' in the journal *Past and Present* in 1964 wrote that: 'the ideology of National Socialism was perhaps the profoundest cause of the war', and that it was highly dangerous to say that no one believed it. Indeed, convinced Nazis all *did* believe it. Besides, Taylor's view that it takes two to make a war goes nowhere in explaining why Hitler *wanted* to take all these risks in the 1930s. If he was not taking steps towards making war, what was he doing? Mason criticised Taylor's limitations when he wrote his book. Taylor, he said, was *par excellence* a diplomatic historian who based his work chiefly on the texts of diplomatic documents; but these were the work of conservative German diplomats who ignored or dismissed the distinctive language of the Nazi ideology and dealt only with the facts that were appropriate to the world of diplomacy. The effect of this self-imposed limitation produced only a partial picture of Nazi Germany in the 1930s. The speeches, the rallies, the propaganda were all of primary importance, and it was they and not the diplomatic documents that really explain Nazi conduct and intentions. Hence Taylor's explanation is only part of the real answer.

Another critic, F.H. Hinsley, in a book *Power and the Pursuit of Peace* published in 1963, offers another criticism of Taylor's methods. He thinks it is logic chopping to say, as Taylor does, that Hitler had no wish for war simply because he had not formulated precise plans for it. The general drift of his policy was in the direction of war, even though (as the Hossbach Memorandum shows) his planning may have still been in the speculative stage. Hitler and his associates took aboard the distinct likelihood that war was in the offing within a matter of years, and instead of working to avoid it, or even postpone it, they set themselves instead the task of winning the war when it occurred. Hinsley takes the view that Hitler was extremely fortunate to pull off his resounding victory at Munich; at that point, any sensible and reasonable man would have stopped. The fact that Hitler persisted first in actions against Czechoslovakia and then against Poland showed not only that he was criminally reckless in his aggrandisement of Germany, but that fundamentally he did not care much whether or not his policies produced war – after all, that was what Nazis had always promised.

The truth seems to be, therefore, that Hitler was a prime mover in the movement that led to war in 1939. He may not have wanted war for itself – indeed he expressed disappointment and dismay when it broke out in 1939 – but he certainly did a lot to bring it about when he took risks, and chanced his arm repeatedly in one coup after another in the 1930s. The other powers made sacrifices and tried their utmost to avoid war; Hitler knew what he wanted and persisted with his demands even when war was imminent. War was the price for his determination to put Germany back on the map, and this was the price he was eventually called on to pay.

10:10

Stalin: Did He Want to Conquer the World?

Divisions between East and West, a few glimpses of which had been seen in the later stages of the Second World War, multiplied as soon as the war ended. By 1946 Churchill was talking about the Iron Curtain, and the Cold War had begun. Stalin has been accused of planning European, if not world, domination as the war ended, and it was certainly Stalin's alleged expansionist ambitions which fuelled the early stages of the Cold War. But this view of Stalin is nothing more than a historical myth.

The Soviet Union had just emerged from a war that had caused tremendous damage and horrific casualties. The Soviet economy was ruined, and rebuilding looked as if it would take decades. Foreign expansionist adventures which would risk alienating the world's only nuclear power would have been madness. Stalin had twenty years earlier rejected the idea of world communism and had adopted the notion of 'socialism in one country'. The war had not changed his mind, but it made him security conscious. So it is not surprising that he made permanent the annexation of the Baltic States, and that his military liberation and occupation of Russia's immediate neighbours led to the establishment of friendly communist governments there.

It is difficult to accuse Stalin of more. Had he wanted to become established in western Europe he would have supported Churchill's plans for an Anglo-American invasion of south-east Europe. This would have given the Russians the opportunity to reach the Rhine and beyond, instead of the Elbe. And Stalin did keep his word. At the Teheran Conference in 1943 the war leaders, Stalin, Roosevelt and Churchill had agreed on the territorial extent of the Soviet Union's sphere of influence. Thus he withdrew Soviet troops from Iran in 1946 as promised, and then, with some justice, complained that the establishment of American influence in Iran was not part of the agreement. While active in Romania and Bulgaria Stalin made no attempt to intervene in the Greek civil war, even though the Greek communists only narrowly failed to overthrow the Greek government. And if Stalin was interested in the spread of communism worldwide he did almost nothing to support the communist side during the civil war in China.

His interests were predominantly security in Europe. He perceived no threat to the Soviet Union through Asia. Stalin is accused of stepping up the Cold War with his blockade of Berlin in 1948, but from Stalin's point of view the existence of the separate western half of Berlin was a threat to the stability of Eastern Germany, and a Western espionage outpost on the eastern side of the Iron Curtain. Stalin called off the blockade when he found that, short of war, he could not prevent the provisioning of West Berlin by air. Perhaps Stalin was paranoid about the need for security, but the expansionist plans of which he has been so often accused would have meant war and a war well beyond the Soviet Union's ability to wage.

So Stalin was not a megalomaniac. His country's postwar weakness, his fear of American nuclear power, and his desire for a *cordon sanitaire* of friendly communist neighbours were what motivated him. He was suspicious of the West certainly: he remembered their intervention against the infant Bolshevik state. But he did not wish to push the West too far, and he stuck by international agreements. The West feared him, but he feared the West more, and his defensive foreign policy was driven by that fear.

10:11

Who Started the Cold War?

Opinions still vary widely about which power or powers started the Cold War, and this remains a question where controversy still continues. Was it the East or was it the West which set it in motion, and how and where did it come into being?

There is little doubt that, by the time of Churchill's Fulton speech in March 1946, the Cold War was under way. It arose out of mutual suspicions and divergent aims, many of which went back a long way.

Stalin was always somewhat wary of a wartime ally whose leader Churchill had been a keen supporter of intervention against the Bolsheviks in 1918 and 1919. Britain, on the other hand, had fought the Germans almost single-handedly for a year in 1940–41, while Soviet-inspired British communists denounced the war and fomented industrial strikes. Stalin's distrust of Britain had led to the 1939 pact with Hitler's Germany, and to his scepticism concerning British information that a German invasion was imminent in June 1941. Both Churchill and Stalin did their best to put past misunderstandings behind them and to wage war as allies, but Stalin's demand for a second front, and his show of public rage when told of the North African landings instead, made him difficult to deal with. Stalin even belittled the value of the convoys which battled their way through the U-boats to Murmansk. The Polish Question caused further dissension, settled only when Churchill and Roosevelt ignored Katyn, virtually abandoned the London Poles, and agreed to Stalin's territorial demands.

Stalin considered that his allies were acting in bad faith when they failed to inform him about the atomic bombs, and when they outmanoeuvred him by turning Iran into an American dependency. Stalin found President Truman less amenable than President Roosevelt. Roosevelt had cultivated Stalin; Truman was abrupt and off-hand with him. Stalin was left feeling frightened, weakened and isolated. This renewal of distrust may have convinced Stalin that the security of his western frontier needed more than friendly states, and he began preparing the ground for communist regimes in the countries liberated by Red armies. The American failure to provide the Soviet Union with a much-needed loan in 1945 angered Stalin, and caused him to exceed the agreed limits in his demand for reparations. While Stalin drained his sector of occupied Germany dry of supplies and machinery, the three western Allies were initiating economic recovery in their sectors and pouring in food and materials. Thus Germany, as early as late 1945, was no longer being prepared for reunification, but was becoming a political battlezone between the occupying powers.

The Cold War was intensified in 1947 and 1948 by Marshall Aid and by the Berlin blockade. But its origins must be looked for earlier. It will no longer do to put the blame on Stalin, accusing only him and his pathological search for security. It could equally well be argued that it was the failure of the Allies to take Stalin fully into their confidence during the war that had sown the seeds of the Cold War. It thus arose from mutual misunderstandings, some of which had their origin in the events of 1918 and 1919. Certainly once it was under way, the statesmen of both sides seemed to go out of their way to intensify it; it gathered its own momentum, and no one had any idea how to stop it.

10:12

Did Gorbachev Cause the Collapse of Communism and the Soviet Union?

After nearly fifty years of Cold War the collapse of communism and the disintegration of the Soviet Union came with dramatic and unexpected suddenness. Since the Soviet leader at the time of the collapse was Mikhail Gorbachev it has been fashionable to blame him for what happened. Russian communists and non-communists alike who look back nostalgically to the 'good old days' of Lenin and Stalin regard Gorbachev as the betrayer, and his political support inside Russia has melted away. This view of Gorbachev has its apologists outside Russia too, but it has not gone unchallenged, and his political record remains the subject of considerable controversy.

The political coup against Gorbachev collapsed on 21 August 1991. The immediate result was the banning of the Communist Party by Boris Yeltsin, the President of Russia, the largest state of the Soviet Union. Gorbachev resigned as Chairman of the party on 24 August. In the following month the Baltic republics renounced their membership of the Soviet Union, having already made unilateral declarations of independence. The Commonwealth of Independent States replaced the Soviet Union in December 1991, and Gorbachev resigned as President of the Soviet Union on 25 December. Thus in a piecemeal kind of way communist rule ended and the Soviet Union was put to rest. Could Gorbachev have prevented this outcome?

The Soviet Union was born out of revolution and maintained by force. It was not a union of consenting states. It was an empire inherited by the Bolsheviks from Tsarist Russia in which the Russians were the dominant nationality and the other nationalities were subject races. Communism was the cement which held it together. Stalin's planned economy was intended to show communism at work, and its superiority to capitalism. On the success or failure of the command economy depended the ultimate success or failure of communism itself. At first the command economy worked because of the comparatively low industrial base from which Russia started; after the Second World War it was boosted by reparations and economically subordinate satellite states. But it could not last. The inherent economic weaknesses were already apparent by the time of Stalin's death. Gorbachev could hardly be held to blame for the failures of Gosplan, and the inability to match the rising living standards of the Western world.

Already in the 1950s serious problems were emerging. Although the Soviet Union sustained its economy by draining its postwar satellites dry, within a few years these satellites became liabilities rather than assets. They required economic sustenance and a heavy and expensive Soviet military presence to keep them loyal to the Soviet empire. And the Soviet economy stagnated. This was inherent in the system. Gosplan decided from above what was needed and how it was to be produced. Market forces were regarded at best as irrelevant, at worst as evil manifestations of capitalism. Monopolies developed within the system. It seemed capitalist and ridiculous to have more than one factory producing spokes for bicycle wheels, or more than one for tractor engines. Needless to say raw material shortages and breakdowns at the sole plant produced national shortages of finished goods. The system was kept going by barter arrangements between primary producers and factory managers. Nor did anyone know how much was being produced. Factory managers inflated both their raw material needs and their finished product output – a relic of Stalin's day when failure to meet targets meant the gulag or worse. Another relic was that targets preferred finished products to spare parts, so broken down machinery could often only be repaired by cannibalising other machinery. Inflation was kept low by rigid price control, but the system was awash with money sitting in bank accounts for lack of anything to buy. It represented a huge inflationary threat in pent-up demand.

Khrushchev knew that urgent action was necessary, if only he knew what. He was well aware that any endeavour to reform communism could end up by destroying it. His attempt to afforest areas unsuitable for afforestation and to grow wheat in areas unsuitable for wheat-growing was typical of the Gosplan approach: 'It will be done because the state says so.' He attempted to boost state farms by penalising private plots. The peasants abandoned their cows and cut their private production. When the mistake was realised and private plots were again given state encouragement it was too late. Peasants now preferred to spend their evenings watching television rather than tending cows or cabbages; during the day they worked perfunctorily on the state farms. Thus demand for agricultural produce multiplied while production languished. His denunciation of Stalin's totalitarian methods in 1956 denied to Khrushchev and his successors the use of force and terror to keep the economy going. Critics both of the regime and of the economic system began to make themselves heard.

Then followed the Brezhnev era. It was imperative, while living standards in the West soared and those in the Soviet Union stagnated, a fact of which Soviet citizens were becoming increasingly aware, that something should be done. The Soviet economy needed to be drastically overhauled, either by a full return to Stalinist policies with political oppression, or by a drastic rethinking of communist economic policy. Brezhnev did neither. His rule was characterised by economic inertia. He was more interested in cutting a bold figure abroad. He added to the Soviet Union's financial burden by invading Afghanistan, and provoked President Reagan into immense defence expenditure which the Soviet Union could not match. Brezhnev's successors Andropov and Chernenko were committed to cautious reform but were so decrepit that the Soviet Union was virtually leaderless, and drifting.

Gorbachev's accession to power in March 1985 gave promise

of better things. He was comparatively young, fit and eager for change. He wanted to liberalise the Soviet Union's autocratic system by introducing an element of popular consent, while recognising the danger that to do so might well undermine the legitimacy of the regime. He was not anti-communist; nor did he envisage the break-up of the Soviet Union. He hoped to reform communism from within, and to preserve the Soviet Union by ending the Cold War, and thus the external threat. He was aware of the dissatisfaction of the satellite states, but he seemed to assume that the Baltic provinces, taken by force in 1940 and annexed in 1945, had no national aspirations of their own. Yet the Russification policies there had been counter-productive and created burning nationalist resentment. So Gorbachev inherited a communist economy which was grinding to a halt, and an empire that was on the verge of disintegration.

The new leader's commitment to *glasnost* meant a more open approach to politics. He began by allowing public criticism of the privileges of the party bosses, and he was prepared to talk to the Soviet people with increasing frankness. His economic policy – one aspect of the politcial and social restructuring, *perestroika* – was to retain a command economy but to combine it with more local control, with some limited concessions to market forces. The more opposition these policies aroused within the party the more Gorbachev relaxed control of the media, so that those opposed to reform found themselves facing mounting public and media support in favour of it.

Abroad Gorbachev had his greatest successes. He withdrew the Soviet Union from the costly and unpopular Afghanistan involvement, and after some hesitancy and false starts he and President Reagan brought the Cold War to an end. Perhaps he went further than he intended when he in effect left the satellite states to fend for themselves. They simply reasserted their lost independence by throwing out their communist rulers. Gorbachev deliberately undermined the East German hardliner, Eric Honecker, and unwittingly paved the way for German reunification. Perhaps this was a price worth paying for ending the Cold War. But it was one thing for the Soviet Union to trim down its expensive satellites, another to be defied by its subject nationalities. When the Baltic peoples saw what was happening in eastern Europe, they too demanded freedom; so did the Ukraine and the Caucasian provinces. This was not what Gorbachev had intended. The military killed civilians in Georgia and Azerbaijan in 1989 and 1990, but the killings in Vilnius and Lithuania in January 1991 spelled the doom of Stalinist imperialism. Gorbachev deplored the killings but did not disown the perpetrators. Most Baltic communist *apparatchiks* hastened to adopt nationalism as the only way to avoid political oblivion. Gorbachev might have tried to preserve the Soviet Union by force; he chose not to do so. He threatened dire consequences on the Baltic separatists, but after Vilnius they felt safe in ignoring him.

This vacillation was Gorbachev's weakness. Glasnost opened the floodgates to widespread denunciation of communism. Gorbachev had merely hoped to reform communism. For perestroika to succeed within a communist framework, glasnost would have to be abandoned. Gorbachev drew back. Hardliners plotted against him; reformers despaired of him and turned to men like Yeltsin. The first free elections in the Soviet Union resulted in the emergence of non-communists and anti-communists. He felt too insecure to seek full power by standing for an executive presidency in a national election. This was left to Yeltsin later. Nor could Gorbachev try to bolster communism and the Soviet Union by using the military. Hard-line generals, appalled by the loss of the satellite states and the defiance of the Balts, planned his overthrow and tried to take advantage of his absence on holiday. But for the most part the armed forces remembered Stalin's military purges in the 1930s, and were keen to avoid becoming involved in politics. Even the KGB could not be relied on; some of them were in secret communication with Yeltsin. So the scene was set for the abortive coup against Gorbachev in August 1991, Gorbachev's eclipse and the emergence of Yeltsin.

The Soviet Union contained from the outset the seeds of its own destruction. It was an imperialist empire clad in communist garb. Lenin and Stalin held it together by force. Once the removal of force was combined with economic collapse it was doomed. Many played a part in its fall: its founders by basing it on force rather than consent; Khrushchev, by making a return to Stalinism out of the question; Brezhnev, by invading Afghanistan; he and his two successors for their inertia; and President Reagan for sanctioning defence expenditure which the Soviet Union could not match. Gorbachev hoped to do what his predecessors signally failed to do – to revitalise a communist Soviet Union. But he lacked both the means and the ability, and he became the unwitting catalyst who helped bring about the Soviet Union's demise.

11

POPULAR MISUNDERSTANDINGS

Did Marie Antoinette Say 'Let them eat cake'?

It is still sometimes said that Marie Antoinette, Queen of France and wife of Louis XVI, when she learned before the Revolution that the French people were suffering from want of bread, told them unkindly to 'eat cake'. What is the truth behind this legend?

Daughter of the Empress Marie Therèse of Austria and sister of the Emperor Leopold II who reigned during the French Revolution, Marie Antoinette was born in 1755 and married the future Louis XVI of France before she was fifteen. Though graceful and attractive, she was pampered and spoilt, and as she got older showed herself prone to petty intrigue. She was intensely unpopular, partly because she was a foreigner (she was known as L'Autrichienne or the 'Austrian woman'), but chiefly because of her legendary extravagance, which was said to have contributed to the bankruptcy of the French government finances – a view for which there is little justification in fact.

Consequently, many unpleasant rumours about her circulated in France, and the 'Let them eat cake' jibe was one. In fact, the whole force of this story rested on a simple mistranslation. The words actually attributed to her were: 'If they have no bread, why do they not eat brioche?' France had numerous different styles of bread, and *brioche* was a rather fancy and more expensive form which to her seemed much the same kind of thing. She ate it all the time instead of the common equivalent. If she was guilty of anything, it was more of stupidity than callousness, since it should have occurred to her that if people could not afford the common type of bread, it was hardly likely that they would be able to afford its luxury counterpart.

There is, however, some doubt whether the episode ever happened at all. The cake story, if not entirely apocryphal, was not attributed to the Austrian Marie Antoinette alone. It was first told about a Spanish princess, Maria Theresa, who had married Louis XIV with great pomp in 1660, and it was repeated about a number of other foreign princesses later, and it mainly illustrates the contempt in which French people held foreigners. Like most clichés, it refused to die even though it was inherently unlikely that such a gaffe would ever be committed, let alone repeated.

11:2

What Did Nelson Really Say to Captain Hardy?

The death of Britain's Admiral Nelson has inspired painters, poets and writers of history and fiction. It has also given rise to an enduring legend.

Nelson won an outstanding victory at Trafalgar on 21 October 1805, but in doing so was mortally wounded. The legend has long persisted that as he lay dying he said to his flag captain 'Kismet, Hardy', an apt comment on the vagaries of Fate. Yet those present at his deathbed are unanimous that he called to the flagship's Captain Hardy to kiss him. In a less inhibited age there was nothing untoward in a dying friend asking this of another. Attempts to bowdlerise Nelson's words into 'Kismet, Hardy' indicate the prudery of the Victorian era and are not supported by tangible evidence; in its absence Nelson's original request still stands.

11:3

What Were the Younger Pitt's Last Words?

Another deathbed legend is that the Younger Pitt's last words were 'My country, how I leave my country.' The Younger Pitt died in office as Prime Minister on 23 January 1806. When great men die their biographers like to attribute to them memorable last words. Thus for Pitt to think of his country as he lay dying was particularly appropriate in that, despite Britain's naval victory at Trafalgar, the disaster to Austria at Ulm and Austerlitz left Britain once again without an ally. This must have saddened Pitt in his last weeks, and he may well have uttered the famous words during one of his more lucid moments. They certainly would have reflected what he must have felt.

However, the truth of his actual last words is probably much more mundane. An aged House of Commons messenger told Disraeli that Pitt's last words were 'I think I could eat one of Bellamy's veal pies', and that he passed away before one could be procured for him. This is bizarre enough to have the ring of truth, and it certainly throws considerable doubt on the authenticity of the 'my country' version.

11:4

The Charge of the Light Brigade: Victory or Catastrophe?

The charge of the Light Brigade, at the battle of Balaclava in 1854 during the Crimean War, is often regarded as an example of supreme courage and brilliant military success, and was immortalised in a stirring ballad by Alfred, later Lord, Tennyson. But this view of the battle was entirely mythical.

In the course of the battle, the British Commander-in-Chief, Lord Raglan, seeing through his glasses that the Russians were about to drag away captured British naval 12-pounder guns, ordered the cavalry to advance and prevent them. Raglan wrote a hasty note in pencil on a scrap of flimsy paper, to be taken by Captain Edward Nolan to Lord Lucan, the commander of the Light Brigade. Nolan was notorious for his previous open criticism of his aristocratic superiors. He scrambled down the precipitous slope to the valley bottom on horseback to deliver his message. From his position 700 feet below Lord Raglan's, Lucan could not see the captured guns. All the same, he read the order meticulously, well aware that Nolan was fuming at his elbow, and asked what guns the general had in mind. Nolan flung his arms vaguely towards the spot at which he remembered the guns were situated, and shouted: 'There, my lord, is your enemy! And there are your guns!'

Looking in the direction Nolan was pointing, the only guns Lucan could see were a battery of Russian 6-pounders at the far end of the long valley, heavily protected by masses of infantry and cavalry. It was clear to him that it would be suicide: any cavalry charging against artillery in such a position must be annihilated. He conveyed the order to his fellow officer, Lord Cardigan. Cardigan pointed out the strength of the enemy position, but Lucan replied that it was Lord Raglan's positive order, and had to be immediately obeyed. Muttering the family name – 'Well, here goes the last of the Brudenells!' – Cardigan gave the order to advance at a slow trot, and dug his spurs into his horse.

It seems clear that Nolan would not have wished to send 600 men to certain death. Suddenly aware that the Light Brigade was not going to wheel to the right as he expected, he galloped after them to correct the error, shouting and waving his arms. Cardigan, perhaps believing that this was another example of Nolan's insolence, ignored him, and shouted to him to get back into line. At that moment, a Russian shell burst a few yards to Lord Cardigan's right, and a fragment tore into Nolan's chest, exposing his heart. His sword fell from his hand, but his right arm was still erect, and his body remained upright in the saddle. With his despairing last shriek, all chance that the tragedy might have been averted disappeared, and the Light Brigade trotted on to certain defeat.

The Russian artillery and riflemen on the Fedioukine Hills and the steep sides of the Causeway Heights north and south of the valley, were astonished at the audacity shown by the Light Brigade as they trotted with parade-ground precision towards the artillery and infantry a mile and a half away. Caught in a murderous crossfire, and with round-shot and grape-shot pouring into their ranks and felling them not singly, but in swathes, they penetrated the length of the valley and captured a number of the guns, fighting hand-to-hand in the blinding smoke. The Russians on the heights fell back in dismay, and Gen Canrobert's Chasseurs were ordered to stage a diversion to relieve the pressure a little, but nothing could be done to avert the disaster. Bosquet, the French general, observed in astonishment: *'C'est magnifique, mais ce n'est pas la guerre!'*

Of the 700 horsemen who had charged down the valley, only 195 returned. The 17th Lancers were reduced to 37 troopers, the 13th Light Dragoons to 2 officers and 8 men; 500 horses were killed. The action entered into legend, but had not the slightest effect on the outcome of the campaign.

11:5

Big Ben: Not the Famous Clock After All?

'Big Ben' is the name by which the clock on the Houses of Parliament in Westminster is commonly known. This, however, is a complete mistake, and is made not only by foreigners but by most English people as well.

After the fire which destroyed parliament in 1834 (a judgment of God on the Parliamentary Reform Act of 1832, according to the Tsar) an ambitious rebuilding scheme was launched, employing the talents, among others, of Charles Barry and Augustus Pugin, two of Britain's most gifted Victorian architects. Attached to the Palace of Westminster there was to be a clock tower, together with the clock whose chimes were later to be broadcast all over the world by the BBC. The name 'Big Ben' is commonly taken to apply to the whole clock, but more correctly should relate only to the massive bell used to sound its hours. This bell weighs 13½ tons, and was named after Sir Benjamin Hall, the Commissioner of Works responsible in 1856 for the bell's installation. His personal dimensions were compared with those of the bell in a parliamentary pleasantry almost as heavy as the Commissioner himself.

11:6

The British Suffragettes: Did They Win Votes for Women?

Although by the beginning of the twentieth century women had made some progress towards the vote in a number of foreign countries, in Britain the case was different. Here the suffragists were as yet in the early stages of their campaign, and attempted to advance their cause by lobbying MPs, and holding meetings. They had high hopes of the new Liberal government of 1906, but the vote was still denied them. By 1910 the suffrage movement became more militant. It adopted methods that fell foul of the law; those who chained themselves to the railings of public buildings or showered MPs in the House of Commons with leaflets did little harm, but arson attacks on public buildings, burning of letterboxes, breaking windows, cutting telephone wires and physical assaults on public figures were more serious. Those who adopted these methods now became widely known as suffragettes. Was their more militant approach any more successful than the peaceful tactics of the suffragists?

In some ways the activities of the suffragettes were counter-productive. As early as the 1890s nearly 200 MPs had supported a motion in favour of women's suffrage. Of these more than 40 were Conservatives. But twenty years later the lawbreaking activities of the suffragettes had alienated many of their would-be supporters. Few Conservatives would now defend women's suffrage in public, and many Liberals, particularly those in government, hardened their attitude against it. The press became increasingly unsympathetic, except when the forcible feeding of suffragette prisoners caused a public outcry. The so-called Cat and Mouse Act of 1913, with its provision for releasing and re-imprisoning suffragette hunger strikers, offended those who believed it undermined civil liberties, and it won the suffragettes some sympathy. Above all, the suffragettes now enjoyed wide publicity for their cause. But to many men their extreme behaviour only seemed to show how unfit women were for the vote, and the suffragettes were no nearer securing it in 1914 than they had been in 1906.

War began in 1914. Suffragette agitation died away as the nation concentrated on defeating the enemy. In 1916 a conference, presided over by the Speaker of the House of Commons, gave majority support to a limited form of women's suffrage. This was not binding, nor was it official government policy. In 1917 the House of Commons debated a Suffrage Bill, the original purpose of which was to remove some of the anomalies in the male franchise. In particular it was clear that if a lengthy residence qualification was required for male voters, most war veterans would be denied the vote. So all soldiers were given the vote without residency requirements. But the war contribution of male munition workers was almost as great as that of soldiers, and they often had to change residence during the war. A proposal to give them the same exemption as soldiers led inevitably to the question of the contribution of female workers in munitions. Thus a Bill originally intended to deal with the male vote ended up by giving the vote to all women over 30 who were either householders or were married to one.

So it was because of their wartime contribution to the national cause rather than because of the pre-war agitation of the suffragettes that women finally won the vote. It is true that the pre-war suffragette campaign raised public awareness of the issue, but it also generated resentment (in the case, for example, of Ramsay MacDonald) and was devoid of immediate results. It seems clear that the war helped to change people's attitudes, and led to public recognition of women's work; but even then the legislation benefited women more by accident than by design. But who can blame the suffragette survivors for taking the credit for the women's vote for which they had so long toiled and suffered?

11:7

Emily Davison: Was it Suicide?

Britain's most prestigious horse race is the Derby, held every year in early June at the famous racecourse at Epsom. The 1913 Derby was on 4 June. As the horses came round the bend at Tattenham Corner, Emily Wilding Davison, an educated woman and a committed suffragette, slipped through the barrier, ran onto the racetrack and was knocked down by the King's horse, Anmer, and trampled by the horses that followed. She died in hospital four days later. This gave rise to the legend put about by suffragettes and by Emily's supporters that she deliberately gave her life for the cause of 'Votes for Women'. There seems, however, to be little truth in this version of events.

An inquest heard a number of witnesses, and concluded that Emily's intention was only to disrupt the race, and not to commit suicide. Nevertheless it was soon put about in the press that she had deliberately thrown herself under the King's horse, thus achieving a premeditated suicide. The hostile press attributed this to an unstable personality rather than commitment to a cause. But the evidence of witnesses and contemporary newsreels does not support this view. In the first place, once she had reached the racetrack she was standing up, not throwing herself in front of a horse. She appeared to be trying to seize Anmer's reins when she was knocked down. Moreover, although her actions are far from clear in the flickering newsreel shots of the time, eyewitnesses asserted that she appeared to have grabbed unsuccessfully at the reins of previous runners, so it seems most unlikely that any specific horse was her target. Character witnesses emphatically denied that Emily was suicidal, nor did she leave a suicide note.

Thus the coroner's verdict seems correct. Emily Davison was an active and militant suffragette. She had planned a bold and spectacular way of gaining publicity for the suffragette movement, and although she knew the risk she was taking she did not intend to throw herself under any horse, nor to commit suicide.

11:8

Was it Belgium that Brought Britain into the First World War?

Many students of history have the idea that a neutral and peace-loving Britain was tipped suddenly and unexpectedly into war in 1914 by the German invasion of Belgium, a country whose independence and neutrality had been internationally agreed under the treaty of 1839. This is at best a misunderstanding of the facts, at worst a downright falsehood.

The First World War had been long expected, but when it came it did so with surprising suddenness. A minor quarrel between Austria-Hungary and Serbia led to war between them on 28 July. Russia mobilised in support of Serbia on the 30th. Germany declared war on Russia on 1 August. On the assumption that the French would support their Russian ally, and needing to get in first to give their predetermined Schlieffen Plan a chance of success, Germany declared war on France on 3 August. As the modified Schlieffen Plan required the passage of German troops through Belgium, the Germans had taken the precaution of asking the Belgians for unobstructed passage on 2 August. The Belgians refused, but the Germans invaded anyway. As the German war plan had no fallback alternative, the Germans were unable to accede to Britain's ultimatum to withdraw their troops from Belgium, and Britain declared war at 11 p.m. on 4 August. Would Britain have gone to war had it not been for the invasion of Belgium?

The essential of Britain's policy of 'splendid isolation' had been to make agreements with other powers to settle specific issues, but not to make binding commitments for the future. Thus the alliance with Japan was not intended to commit Britain to a forward policy in the Far East, but as far as possible to preserve the status quo. Similarly, the Entente with France in 1904 was intended to draw the line under old disputes, rather than commit Britain to take France's side in new ones. Even so the Japanese alliance gave Japan British encouragement in Korea, and the Entente gave France British encouragement in Morocco. Neither Lord Lansdowne, Britain's Foreign Secretary, nor his successor, Sir Edward Grey, wanted to join either of the European alliance systems, and Grey may have deluded himself, but no one else, that by not turning the Entente into an alliance he was both giving Britain freedom of manoeuvre and Germany reassurance of Britain's neutrality. The Entente with Russia in 1907 also settled old differences, but it meant that Britain was now on friendly terms with two countries that were in alliance and which regarded Germany as a potential enemy.

The first Moroccan crisis compelled Britain to choose sides, and it sided with France. Grey's offer of military conversations with France was intended as a warning to Germany not to push too far. Otherwise the conversations, which began in 1908, meant little: Haldane had not yet created the BEF, and the discussions were merely a paper exercise. But to the British public, unaware of the military conversations, Germany was already a potential enemy. The Kruger Telegram, Germany's naval programme, and the press had aroused a general suspicion of Germany. Newspapers speculated not on whether there would be a war against Germany, but when. By 1911, Lloyd George's menacing Mansion House speech was very much in tune with public opinion. It forced a resentful Germany to back down on Morocco, and it aligned Britain firmly on France's side. The naval agreement of 1912 followed. There was no commitment for Britain to take part in a Franco-

German war, but Britain did agree to consult France in the event of war. More importantly, the British navy was to be the only means of defending France's Channel and Atlantic coasts against German attack, while the French navy concentrated on the Mediterranean. Grey may have thought that the agreement did not commit Britain to war, but it is difficult to see how Germany could avoid, in the heat of war, some violation which would bring Britain in. Yet in 1913 and throughout most of 1914 Anglo-German relations actually improved, even if Germany did not take up Churchill's invitation in 1913 for Germany to reduce its naval programme.

Haldane's army reforms, with the creation of a British Expeditionary Force of six divisions to fight on the Continent, seemed to imply that Britain would be drawn in should there be a Continental war. Britain could not allow France to be weakened by another defeat at Germany's hands. This would place the Continent of Europe under the control of a power which was already aiming at control of the oceans, and extending its influence in the Balkans and Turkey. The development of close friendship between Britain and France since 1904, the military conversations and the naval agreement, and the joint stand over Morocco, all suggested that Britain had a moral obligation to support France in the event of war, even if that obligation had not been cemented by an alliance.

But such a war might not be popular with the Labour Party, and would cause dissension in the ranks of the Liberal Party. The Liberal government did not want to enter a war with the nation divided. Belgium would provide the government with a moral crusade. The rigidity of the German war plans made a German attack on Belgium inevitable. Belgian neutrality had been given a collective guarantee by the great powers in the Treaty of London, 1839. Germany was not a party to it, of course, but Prussia was. There was some uncertainty whether Britain was legally bound to defend Belgium, as the guarantee was collective and not individual. But this nicety was not really an issue. Britain would have to join France sooner or later; the Belgian question gave Britain the cast-iron reason for joining them sooner. Of course those in power knew that Britain had to go to war, but the pre-war politicians had by their intricate diplomacy effectively penned themselves into a corner and were faced with the difficulty of selling this war to a general public who seemed at the time totally unprepared for it. Belgium gave them just the chance they wanted to swing the country behind them. Thus the British nation entered the war united against German aggression. Only one Cabinet minister resigned (one had already done so three days earlier); even the Irish nationalists pledged virtually unanimous support. So once Britain had given its moral backing to France, and once Germany was committed to the implementation of the (modified) Schlieffen Plan, Britain's holding aloof from the Alliance System became pointless, and there was no way that Britain could avoid being drawn into the war.

11:9

Was Sinn Fein Behind the Easter Rebellion of 1916?

The Easter Rebellion began on 25 April 1916 and, after four days of fierce fighting, was eventually suppressed by British troops. It was very costly in human life: 128 British soldiers, over 180 Irish civilians, and several hundred armed insurgents were killed. While the fighting raged, and immediately afterwards, Irish opinion had been hostile to the Rebellion, but when the British executed 15 of the leaders, Sinn Fein, supported by much of the American press, proclaimed them as martyrs, and Irish opinion swung behind Sinn Fein. It was not surprising that Sinn Fein was soon taking the credit for having planned and initiated the Rebellion, and this view rapidly gained wide acceptance. But was it true?

In fact it seems doubtful whether Sinn Fein played any part either in the planning or in the execution of the Easter Rebellion. What really happened was that they claimed the credit for what was started by other different, though linked, associations.

Sinn Fein had, unlike other extremist nationalist groups,

opposed violence. Its aim was to set up rival local, and eventually national, bodies which would take over government, and which would bypass the existing official British institutions. It differed from the Irish Nationalist Party in being unprepared to accept any Home Rule compromise which fell short of complete independence, while it denounced men like James Connolly, one of the leaders of the Irish Republican Brotherhood, for his support for violence. But Sinn Fein's patience was exhausted by the time of the Third Home Rule Bill of 1912 in which full independence was again denied. It began to consider that violence might in the last resort be necessary, and its relations with the Irish Republican Brotherhood led by Connolly, and the National Volunteers led by Patrick Pearse, became more cordial.

But it was these organisations, and not Sinn Fein, which planned and started the Rebellion. Of course the three organisations were not mutually exclusive, despite their differences, and there was some Sinn Fein involvement right from the beginning. But Sinn Fein had not had the main responsibility for the Rebellion, yet it gained most of the benefit from it. Its involvement with, and support of, the Rebellion made it the main beneficiary of the collapse of moderate nationalist opinion. In the General Election of 1918 Sinn Fein took 73 out of the 79 parliamentary seats outside the Unionist North, it set up its own Irish parliament, the Dáil, and it subsequently acquired the political responsibility of having to negotiate with the British.

11:10

The Zinoviev Letter: Did it Bring About MacDonald's Defeat in 1924?

It is frequently asserted by supporters of the Labour Party, and also accepted by students of history, that the affair of the Zinoviev Letter lost the Labour Party the election of October 1924, thrusting them from office and restoring the Conservatives to power. How much justification is there for such an assertion?

Ramsay MacDonald was Britain's first Labour Prime Minister. He came to power in January 1924, but did not command a majority of parliamentary seats and held office only with the support of the Liberals. The government was defeated in October when the Liberals withdrew their support. J.R. Campbell, the acting editor of the *Communist Workers' Weekly*, had been charged with inciting soldiers to mutiny by distributing an inflammatory newspaper outside important military establishments. When the charge was dropped the Conservative opposition accused the government of being soft on communists, and of showing weakness towards a real communist threat. Unwilling to be tarred with the same brush the Liberals sided with the opposition against the government, and the government found itself in a minority. But success in the General Election could restore the government's fortunes, and polling day was fixed for 29 October. The Zinoviev Letter was published in the press on 25 October, four days before polling. It purported to be a Comintern document detailing the communist intention of fomenting civil discord in Britain as a prelude to a successful class war. The government lost the election, and the Zinoviev Letter was widely held to be responsible. How far was this true?

The fact that the Zinoviev Letter was a forgery by Russian émigrés in Berlin or Riga who were trying to discredit the Bolsheviks is not in itself significant. It was full of Bolshevik clichés, and was a good and accurate summary of Comintern policy. The British Foreign Office gave credibility to the letter by protesting about it to the Soviet chargé d'affaires in London, and it was therefore widely believed to be genuine. The Campbell Affair had shown that Labour was soft on Bolsheviks; the Zinoviev Letter seemed to confirm it. Liberals believed that they had put Labour in last time; at the polls they deserted their party in droves. Moreover, Baldwin, the Conservative leader, had abandoned his intention to introduce protection tariffs in the summer of 1924, thus removing a main reason for voters to vote Liberal and making the Conservatives more electable. Baldwin was now posing as the Conservative moderate, seeking votes for a common-sense government. It seems likely that most of the electorate had made up their minds before the Zinoviev Letter hit the headlines.

The Conservatives won 415 seats, mostly at the expense of the Liberals who were reduced to 42. Labour secured 152 seats with a net loss of 42. The total poll rose from 71 per cent at the previous election to nearly 77 per cent – a possible Zinoviev effect. Labour put up nearly 100 more candidates and this caused their number of votes to increase from 4.3 million to 5½ million. But in virtually all the seats Labour had contested previously their vote fell. The Liberals lost over 1.2 million votes.

The temporary Liberal reunion for the December 1923 election had not lasted; the old ugly split between Asquith and Lloyd George reappeared, especially since Baldwin's abandonment of the policy of Protection meant they had nothing to unite against. The Liberals looked like a spent force, being riddled with internal acrimony and tainted by their recent alliance with Labour. Baldwin's stance for common-sense government appealed to those voters who were alarmed by MacDonald's rapprochement with Soviet Russia and by the speeches of firebrands on the left of his party. It was convenient for Labour later to claim that the Zinoviev Letter had tricked them out of office, but it is more likely that Labour was overwhelmed by the Conservative revival, the disintegration of the Liberals, and the Campbell case. Zinoviev may have worsened Labour's defeat, but it did not cause it.

11:11

What Was 'The Dole'?

It was a common error in the 1930s to confuse the receipt of unemployment benefit *with the* dole, *and this has created a misunderstanding on the part of students of the period which frequently persists today. Those who wish to paint the 1930s as even blacker than they were use* dole *as a collective word for all out-of-work benefits, and thus falsely convey the impression of universal means testing. The Depression of the 1930s certainly brought hardship and misery to many, and novels such as* Love on the Dole *reinforced the picture of the British living on charities and means-tested handouts. But this picture can be misleading.*

The 1911 Insurance Act provided unemployment benefit to insured male adults for a period of twenty-six weeks. By 1930 most male workers were thus covered for unemployment, and if they became unemployed they were able to draw benefit from the state for six months, the maximum that seemed necessary for them to find alternative employment. This benefit was paid *without regard* to the financial means of the family.

Six months seemed a long time, yet it was inadequate to cope with structural unemployment. Industries such as mining, shipbuilding and cotton textiles were in terminal decline. Unemployment in these industries was not simply a seasonal variation which would soon be rectified by normal market forces. It was long term, and it blighted whole areas, particularly in the north-east and north-west. Its victims often ran out of insurance benefit. The Insurance Act of 1921 provided for additional 'uncovenanted benefit' which was not covered by unemployment insurance. It was intended not for the idle or the unemployable, but for those genuinely seeking work. Amounts were small and grudging, and were said to be 'doled out', thus 'the dole'.

In 1931 specific means testing of the 'dole' was introduced. Total family income was taken into account: wives who took in washing or did some charring, children who took on paper rounds, or earned pennies for running errands, would have such meagre earnings set against the husband's entitlement to the dole. So for twenty-six weeks the unemployment benefit could be supplemented by the earnings of others in the household. After twenty-six weeks families were faced with giving up their extra earnings and being forced to live in penury, or not declaring such earnings and hoping that they would not be found out. Thus for the long-term unemployed the future seemed one of hopelessness and deprivation. Since most British people were in work, or were only unemployed for short periods, the dole came perhaps to have too great a significance in depicting life in Britain in the early 1930s, but it certainly was a degrading experience for those who had to depend on it for subsistence.

11:12

The Spanish Civil War: a Dress Rehearsal for the Second World War?

The more popular type of history textbooks, and therefore a great many students of history who believe what they read in these books, persist in regarding the Civil War in Spain as a major rehearsal for the coming struggle in the Second World War in Europe. The involvement of large foreign contingents in an ideological conflict is said to have foreshadowed the future clash between the forces of Fascism and Bolshevism. But the theory does not hold water.

The two took opposite sides in July 1936, with broad left-wing support for the narrowly elected Popular Front, and right-wing support for the nationalist rebels under General Franco. The signature of the Non-Intervention Agreement in 1936 and the establishment of the Nyon Agreement in 1937 seem to have made little difference to the amount of foreign aid that found its way to Spain. A number of the governments concerned maintained the polite fiction that the arms trade, and other forms of traffic, were difficult to keep in check, and that the participants in the war were civilian volunteers over whom they had little control.

As far as Mussolini was concerned, the whole affair was an embarrassment. Though about 80,000 of his troops went to Spain, they failed to achieve any particular success and were mostly withdrawn by the end of 1937, while sporadic air raids by Italian planes had produced no results. Italian attempts to interfere with republican shipping in the Mediterranean eventually fizzled out after British surface patrols in the area were stepped up. In fact Mussolini had little heart in the struggle, and Italian participation scarcely reflected the glory on the country's arms that the Duce expected.

Hitler, who never allowed his mind to be cluttered with detail, talked in general terms about the strategic reasons for German involvement in the war, and declared roundly 'We must save Spain from Bolshevism!' At the same time, he regarded affairs in Spain as a tiresome distraction from his political mission at home, and preferred to see *Siegfried* at the opera rather than meet with Franco's representatives. When he did meet with them he seemed more concerned with how his forces should be paid rather than with what they would be doing. In the end he sent about 30,000 troops, substantial amounts of armaments, and aircraft, tanks and battleships, but all these produced few results.

France, especially under the Popular Front government of Leon Blum, was keen to intervene actively in support of the Spanish Popular Front, much of whose ideology they shared. Britain successfully prevented this, pointing out that France's ally, the Soviet Union, might well turn out to be more dangerous than France's enemies. France was therefore reduced to making futile gestures from the sidelines of the war.

Stalin, likewise, preferred to concentrate on his domestic problems in the USSR and had little appetite for foreign ventures. 'Socialism in one country' was a policy that seemed to require him to ignore entanglements elsewhere; in addition to which the notion of 'world communism' which seemed to be the issue in Spain had overtones of Trotskyism about it, which Stalin found ideologically distasteful. He was also concerned not to frighten the French by seeming to champion Bolshevism in Spain. In the end, Stalin sent some help, but insisted on being paid for it by the shipment to Russia of the Republic's gold reserves. Much of this gold mysteriously disappeared on its way to the Black Sea port of Odessa, and the rest of it took months to count before it vanished into Stalin's capacious pockets. It was never seen again.

On the Republican side there were a number of so-called International Brigades, containing doctors, nurses, engineers and others as well as soldiers. Among them were French, Poles, Ukrainians, Czechs, representatives of the nations of Scandinavia and the Balkans. The Germans and the Austrians fought both for the republicans and for the nationalist side, contributing together about 5,000 volunteers for the brigades, of whom 2,000 were killed. There were in addition about 2,000 British volunteers and 2,800 from the USA, whose casualties also were quite heavy. There were commonly believed to be about 80,000 serving in Spain. This number was probably an exaggeration. Recent research has shown that the total was more like 35,000, of whom about 18,000 were serving at any one time. The brigades were six in total, and were numbered from Brigade XI to Brigade XVI, probably to foster the idea that the volunteers were more numerous than they really were.

Thus the notion that the Spanish Civil War was little more than a dress rehearsal for the Second World War does not take into account that the contribution made to it by foreign powers was only of limited importance. The war mattered chiefly because of the entangled and deeply bitter divisions existing at the time between the National Front and the Popular Front, which remained far from settled by Franco's victory in 1939 and which in fact continued throughout the period until his death in 1975.

11:13

Did the Wall Street Crash Cause the Great Depression?

Many students of history believe that the Wall Street Crash was the main, if not the only, reason for the coming of the Great Depression. This is a major oversimplification.

The Crash began on 23 October 1929, when millions of shares in common stocks were suddenly put on sale at the New York

Stock Exchange. There was no actual panic that day, although something like $4 billion was lost overall by sales; the panic came later, when selling did not stop, but steadily mounted in volume. The date of 24 October, known as 'Black Thursday', was one of the worst days. The losses of the previous day were more than doubled. Prices fell steeply and did not recover. By the end of the year, paper losses amounted to $40 billion, representing over 60 per cent of the total value of stocks listed on the Exchange. Even then the fall went on. It continued until well into 1933, when the Dow-Jones stood at 32 points, about 10 per cent of its value on the eve of the Crash. It was this catastrophic collapse that is often reckoned to have been the underlying cause of the Great Depression.

But in fact, the causes of the Depression were more fundamental. As the 1920s went on, the US economy showed itself to be basically unstable. As the result of the unequal distribution of income, the richest 1 per cent of the population owned 60 per cent of the nation's wealth, and Republican tax-cuts benefited them as a group disproportionately. Their investment largely kept the economy ticking over, and with their high incomes an increasing proportion of spending went into luxury purchases. At the same time, technological improvements increased the production of goods faster than consumers could absorb them. Though for a time, manufacturers boosted sales by devices such as advertising and hire purchase, the limit eventually was reached, and goods remained unsold. The building construction industry reached its peak as early as 1925; the automobile industry in 1926, and steadily other industries producing consumer durables followed suit until the market was all but saturated.

Meantime, average industrial wages rose by only 10 per cent, while the introduction of new machinery and methods brought more unemployment, until it reached 7 per cent of the workforce by 1928. Unemployment and stagnant wages were a feature of the older staple industries such as textiles, railroads and mines. Furthermore, the closure of mines or mills blighted those areas and communities that depended on them, creating pools of depression and stagnation there. American farmers were also among those who felt the Depression. They suffered from the collapse of commodity prices after the First World War. Initially they had reacted to this fall by stepping up output, hoping to make up in quantity what they were losing in price, borrowing heavily to improve their machinery and increase their acreages. But in the end this remedy made the situation worse and merely aggravated agricultural overproduction. Farmers faced ruin not only because they were overwhelmed by mortgage repayments, but finally because farm produce was so cheap that it was hardly worth growing. Added to this was the phenomenon of the 'dust-bowl'. The soil of the US prairies was often so light that the removal of trees and grasses in the ploughing process reduced it to sand, and it simply blew away. Large areas of the prairie states were thus turned into deserts, and those living there were forced to emigrate.

These problems were exacerbated by faulty policies on the part of the federal government. A creditor state, such as the USA had become, has the obligation to import more than it exports so as to provide for those foreign states that owe it money a chance to pay back what they owe. But instead the United States created even higher tariff barriers to protect its manufacturers and farmers from foreign competition, with the result that the USA ran enormous trade surpluses with its European trading partners throughout the 1920s. This basic error was compounded by Treasury policies of 'easy money', extending credits to European governments on favourable terms; in effect, lending them money with which to make their debt repayments. Even before the Crash occurred, US lenders refused to make further loans, and called in existing ones when they matured. This prevented foreigners from buying American exports, and added further to the problems of oversupply at home. Hence, by 1929, the American market was awash with unsold primary and manufactured produce.

At the same time, it must be acknowledged that the Crash was more than a mere symptom of the oncoming Depression. The machinations of the stock market also helped to cause it.

One of the features of the wildcat boom of the later 1920s was share speculation. Investors borrowed money to invest on the market in anticipation of big profits, enabling them to pay back what they had borrowed and still make a handsome profit. This practice was known as 'buying on the margin'. Even banks did it, speculating with their clients' money. In the autumn of 1929 they got their fingers burned. At the same time, almost 6,000 Middle West banks were caught in a further trap. They had lent heavily to farmers in mortgages against the security of land. The value of this land had catastrophically fallen, so that these banks also failed. This disaster wiped away millions of people's savings overnight, and further reduced liquidity. There was no shortage of goods; only of money. This helps to explain the disastrous price falls that occurred throughout the Depression.

The Crash was therefore important because it signalled a monumental collapse of financial confidence. People were not going to invest money on the Stock Exchange if they thought there was a risk of losing it. Of course, the fixed capital that the shares represented was the same as before, whether the shares were high or low in price; after all, the factories were still physically in existence. The difference was that they were no longer working, and no one had any use for them. And the people who had worked in them were no longer earning. The slump in the Stock Exchange value of the shares simply meant that no one wanted to own the factories these shares represented, because no one thought that the factories would produce enough profit in which to share. The Crash therefore meant not only a reduction in the purchasing power and investing capacity of the wealthy classes, but the entire collapse of the production and trade of the American economy.

11:14

Mein Kampf: *The Nazi Bible?*

Mein Kampf *is often said to be a full statement of the ideals and philosophy of Nazism, and the outline of its aims and intentions; in short the book provided the Bible of the Nazis. In practice, however, the influence it exerted in the Europe of the period, or indeed in Germany itself, is open to serious question.*

The book dates back to the mid-1920s, when Hitler was imprisoned for five years in Landsberg prison for his part in the abortive Munich Putsch of November 1923, a sentence of which he served little more than nine months. During this time, in comfortable quarters, with regular meals and frequent visits from his well-wishers, Hitler, together with his faithful assistant and later Deputy, Rudolf Hess, who took his dictation, produced *Mein Kampf*, the two volumes of which came out in 1925 and 1927. The book is a turgid, rambling, illiterate statement of the Nazi philosophy, spiced up by not always very accurate autobiographical material. Apart from the corrosive vituperation against the Jews with which the book is tainted, *Mein Kampf* is chiefly interesting as a popularisation of the religious and moral thinking of Nietzsche and as a perversion of the ideas of Charles Darwin. Hitler's use of terms such as 'the survival of the fittest' and 'the struggle for existence' – indeed the word 'struggle' even provides the book with its title – are used to point the lesson that the laws of life are those of conflict, and that notions of tolerance, pity and mercy, were no more than snares devised by the weak to inhibit the actions of the strong. In practical terms, the book predicts the extermination of the Jews, a coming cataclysmic world conflict, the overthrow of the Soviet Union, the winning of *Lebensraum* and the assimilation of resources for the new Nazi world order under Germanic domination.

Copies of the book were given to each couple who married in Germany under the Third Reich, and may still be found, their pages unread, on the bookshelves of older German households.

Intellectuals who read *Mein Kampf* regarded it as the lunatic ravings of a fanatic; contemporary politicians did not take Hitler seriously, but dismissed him as a demagogue and a mountebank, some of them later even showing such a catastrophic misreading of his character as to try to use him as a pawn in their own games. Even after he became Führer a large number of them continued to feel certain private reservations about his character and his policies, though it was impolitic to express them publicly. *Mein Kampf*, they felt, was a remnant of early Nazi history that was best forgotten.

Foreign leaders, likewise, ignored his displays of uncontrolled rage and his vulgar personal abuse as part of his act. All of these failed to take in the message that *Mein Kampf* stated so emphatically. Even Stalin dismissed his vitriolic attacks on communism and on the inferior Slavonic peoples as dating back to his former days as a political agitator. He thought they were just designed at that time for winning cheap popularity, and deluded himself that Hitler did not really mean a word of what he wrote.

So in practice no one took the slightest notice of *Mein Kampf*, even though it contained a perfect blueprint of Nazi policies later.

11:15

How Good was Germany's Claim to the Sudetenland?

Hitler laid claim to the Sudetenland area of Czechoslovakia in 1938 on the grounds that the Czech people living there were harassing and browbeating the German minority of the province. He cited numerous examples of this intolerable treatment, and indicated that he was not prepared to countenance it any longer. It was his claim that the Sudetenland should be 'restored' to Germany. Students of history have thereafter taken Hitler at his word, and have supposed that the Sudetenland had formerly been German, but had been stripped from the Fatherland by the terms of the Treaty of Versailles in 1919.

In fact, it was an error to suppose that the Sudetenland had ever been ruled by Germany. Since 1806, when the Holy Roman Empire was abolished, the Sudetenland had formed part of the Austrian Empire, and still was so at the end of the First World War. Indeed, the arrangements for Czechoslovakia (and therefore for the Sudetenland) did not form part of the Treaty of Versailles at all; they were dealt with in the Austrian treaty of St Germain. To speak of the Sudetenland being 'restored' to Germany was therefore quite inaccurate.

The true basis of Hitler's assertion was that he claimed to represent the interests of the German people everywhere, whether they lived within the country's borders or not. This justified him in interfering in the affairs of neighbouring states wherever a German minority existed. His view, and the policy of the Nazi Party, was that his government championed the interests of racially German people as a matter of principle, a principle which he expressed in the slogan: '*Ein Volk, ein Reich, ein Führer*'.

11:16

1940–41: Did Britain Fight Alone?

France signed an armistice with Germany on 22 June 1940. Exactly a year later, on 22 June 1941, Operation Barbarossa, the German invasion of Russia began. It is usual to assert that during the year between these two events Britain and its empire fought alone against the Axis powers. But in fact this was not the case.

Britain did indeed fight alone against its enemies from 22 June until 28 October 1940, and thus was without allies during the Battle of Britain and the period of the greatest danger from invasion. But on 28 October 1940 Italian forces in occupied Albania invaded Greece. Greece thus became an ally of Britain against Fascist Italy, and Britain gave Greece what assistance could be spared from its own meagre resources. Scarce supplies, weapons and vehicles were provided, and British troops helped to garrison some of the Greek islands, especially Crete, as early as January 1941.

In return Greece proved a valuable ally. Its armies tied down sixteen Italian divisions. Its victories in overrunning Italian strongholds in Albania were an important boost to British morale during the darkest days of the war. Italian concentration on the war with Greece prevented effective reinforcement of the Italian troops in Libya, and enabled General Wavell to seize Cyrenaica in January 1941. More than 120,000 Italian troops were taken prisoner during Wavell's campaign, troops which would be sorely missed later.

Greek success against Italy irritated Hitler, and he tried to browbeat the Greeks in February 1941 into coming to terms with Mussolini. But the Greeks could see little point in losing the peace when they were winning the war. Hitler was therefore forced into a Balkan campaign which caused a five-week postponement of his invasion of Russia. On 6 April 1941 German troops crossed the Greek frontier, and Greek resistance collapsed within three weeks, despite British aid. However, the postponement of Barbarossa was a major factor in its ultimate failure. British attempts to assist Greece resulted in heavy British losses both at sea and on land, but on balance the Greek imbroglio deprived Italy of possible success in Egypt, demonstrated the military weakness of Italy in Albania, provided Britain with an ally who could win victories, and forced Germany into expensive involvement in the Balkans. It is, therefore, a historical error to deny Britain any allies from the fall of France until the invasion of Russia.

11:17

What Was the Real Importance of the German Invasion of Crete?

The British decision to defend Crete has been much criticised at the time and since, and remains a controversial episode in the Second World War.

The German invasion of Crete began on 20 May 1941. The defenders lacked heavy artillery, which had been abandoned in Greece, and were short of small arms and ammunition. No attempt was made to defend Crete by air, as most of the defending aircraft had been destroyed on the ground by intense German air attack. Lack of air cover put the British navy at risk, and Admiral Cunningham was forced to withdraw his ships after he had lost three cruisers and six destroyers. General Freyburg's troops on the island put up a heroic defence, but on 27 May he realised that the position was hopeless, and by 2 June as many troops as possible had been evacuated, with 12,000 left behind as prisoners in German hands. At the time it seemed that this was yet another in the long catalogue of war disasters that had begun over a year earlier with the loss of Norway.

The British were well aware of the German intention of invading Crete. Despite the attempt of the Germans to suggest that Malta was the target – from 10 May they subjected it to renewed intensive air attack – the British government knew precise details of the forthcoming attack on Crete from their decoding of the Enigma transcripts. But Crete possessed three vital airfields and a major naval base, and Britain could not afford to lose these if there was any chance that they might be effectively defended. During the first days of the invasion the Germans suffered heavy losses of their paratroopers and airborne gliders. With better radio communication the defenders might well have succeeded, and withdrawals were unnecessarily made when the battle was going considerably better for the defenders than they realised.

Even in defeat the balance sheet was not totally in favour of the Germans. They never did make subsequent effective use of Crete's airfields, neither did they have the naval resources to turn Crete into a successful naval base. They did indeed deprive the British of its use, but Cyprus and later Syria and Lebanon provided good alternative bases. Its loss was not so devastating as it might have been if the Germans had put the island to good use, but lack of naval supremacy, declining air superiority and the activity of Greek partisans made the island an increasing liability to the occupiers. And in the actual invasion, although casualties on both sides were about equal (approximately 4,000 dead and about 2,500 seriously wounded) and the Germans took more prisoners, German losses were more damaging. Not only did they lose a higher proportion of senior officers than the British, Australians and New Zealanders, but their 7th Airborne Division had been decimated. Its highly trained specialist personnel could not easily be replaced. Never again did the Germans use paratroops in a main airborne operation. Moreover, German plans for an airborne and sea invasion of Malta were quietly shelved, and Malta was to prove invaluable to the Allies, both in defending Egypt in 1942 and in providing a base for operations against Italy in 1943.

So the loss of Crete was not such a disaster as has often been supposed, and Britain's decision to defend it was not a sheer act of lunacy of a War Cabinet starved of victories. With the invasion of Russia imminent, German losses in Crete could ill be spared, and the propaganda value of its capture was small. The British could not argue that the loss of Crete was unimportant, but its loss turned out to be far less devastating than many had feared.

11:18

Why Did the League of Nations Never Employ Armed Sanctions?

One of the criticisms – perhaps the main one – that is generally made of the working of the League of Nations is that the Covenant of the League failed to provide within its rules permission for military sanctions to be used against an aggressor state by League members. The result of this was that the whole organisation failed to achieve its main object – the prevention of war. This criticism, however, is entirely without foundation.

It is true that Article 16 of the Covenant laid great stress on those sanctions that fell short of armed intervention. Wilson was not alone in thinking that these lesser sanctions would suffice. Hence Paragraph 1 of Article 16 laid stress on *diplomatic* sanctions, and 'the prevention of all *financial, commercial or personal* intercourse between the nationals of the covenant-breaking state and the nationals of any other state'. Such expressions of international condemnation, it was reckoned, would be enough to bring the offending state back into line. In case not, however, Paragraph 2 of the same Article 16 went on: 'It shall be the duty of the Council in such case to recommend to the several governments concerned what effective *military, naval or air force* the members of the League shall severally contribute to the armed forces to be used to protect the covenants of the League.'

How is it, then, that the League always stopped short of the use of armed sanctions? It was partly owing to the long persistence of the mistaken notion that economic sanctions would be enough – though what happened in the case of the Italian attack on Abyssinia should have been enough to dispel this illusion – but also it was due to the reluctance of member states to use military means even against the most obvious of aggressors. Even the most enthusiastic of members stopped short of using their armed forces at the behest of the Council. In any case, the use of armed forces would bring on the very war which everybody dreaded, and which the League was intended to prevent, in the aftermath of the 'war to end all wars'.

12

PERSISTENT MISREPRESENTATIONS

Paul Revere: Patriot or Troublemaker?

Paul Revere is one of the folk heroes of American history. His epic ride to Concord inspired Longfellow's famous poem, and Revere became immortalised as the reluctant hero who put aside his civilian calling (he was a silversmith by trade) to answer the call of his country. But others have seen Revere differently. One historian described him as 'riding hither and thither as a stirrer up of trouble'. Which is closer to the truth?

Living in Boston, Revere was, of course, on centre stage for the momentous events leading up to the Declaration of Independence. His freemasonry brought him into contact with many of the local Sons of Liberty. He witnessed, and may have taken part in, the anti-Stamp Act riots. He was certainly present when Governor Hutchinson's house was looted. In the late 1760s he began drawing political cartoons, and his famous drawing of the Boston Massacre in 1770 was highly inflammatory.

He began riding for the patriots in 1770 when he became a mounted messenger, liable to be called out at a moment's notice. Thus in the autumn of 1773 he made several trips from Boston to inform the Committees of Correspondence of nearby ports of the arrival of the teaships at Boston. In December he was one of those who, dressed as Mohawk Indians, threw the tea into Boston harbour; whether he was one of those who rendered the watch unconscious is not known.

The year 1774 was a busy one for him. In May he rode to New York and Philadelphia with proposals for a new non-importation agreement in response to the Coercive Acts. In September he was busying himself with carrying messages to and from the First Continental Congress at Philadelphia. In December, hearing that the British garrison at Portsmouth, New Hampshire, was about to be strengthened, he rode there to alert the local militiamen who were in consequence able to break into the fort without casualties and to carry off supplies and ammunition.

His main exploit was in April 1775, when he rode from Boston to Concord to warn the local militiamen that General Gage had sent troops from Boston to seize the arms depot the patriots had assembled there. Gage's intention had been known for several days. Four days earlier Revere had ridden to Lexington to warn the patriot leaders Hancock and Adams of their impending arrest, and sent word on to Concord to remove the ammunition stores. He also planned to use lanterns in a Boston church tower to warn the patriots of British movements by land and sea. Thus his famous ride, four days later, was more to alert the countryside that the British were coming than to alert the patriot leaders who had already been forewarned.

Revere continued as a messenger during the early months of the war. Eventually he became a lieutenant-colonel, and when peace came he returned to silversmithing, in which occupation he became one of America's greatest, and whose work is now keenly sought after.

There seems little doubt that he was a very active patriot, that the ride to Concord was only one of many he undertook for his country, and that if not an active rebel against Britain he certainly incited to rebellion. There was nothing reticent about either his heroism or his patriotism. Perhaps it is not surprising that while his countrymen saw in him the epitome of the patriotic hero, the British regarded him as something of an *agent provocateur*.

12:2

Was Pius IX Ever a Liberal?

Giovanni-Maria Mastai Ferretti was elected to the papacy in June 1846. Within weeks of his accession he had embarked upon a liberal programme that inspired in Italian nationalists, such as Gioberti, the hope that the Pope would become political leader of a united Italy. From Pius much was expected. But he refused to join other Italian states in the war against Austria in 1848. After the murder of his Prime Minister Count Rossi he fled to Gaeta. And thereafter his liberalism, and his willingness to consent even to modest reforming proposals, had so far disappeared that he was soon widely derided as 'Pio No-No'. Thus his liberalism was only skin-deep, and vanished altogether under the stress of the revolutionary events of 1848.

Pius IX's election had been something of a surprise. He was so little known that the Roman crowds were lukewarm in their initial reception of him. He had spent two years in South America and had developed something of a distaste for the worst evils of autocracy. So his release of nearly a thousand political prisoners soon after his accession was a sincere gesture. But it had surprising results. The indifference of the populace gave way to adulation: he was flattered, he revelled in his new-found popularity. Soon he gave greater freedom to the press, set up a council ('*consulta*') to assist in the government of the Papal States, and granted a municipal council to the city of Rome. His popularity burgeoned with each concession. Even so, his moderation of the harsh laws against the Jews was not designed to court popularity, and was effected despite rather than because of it.

Those who wanted the Pope as a political leader of a united Italy were excited by the reforms. But they did not really amount to a great deal. Only some of the political prisoners were released under Pius's amnesty; thousands more, both political and criminal, languished under a barbarous criminal code. Nor was there full press freedom – press censorship had been relaxed, not abolished. The '*consulta*' was merely consultative, and the municipal council was granted only the most limited of powers. Even Pius's genuine concern for the Jews did not extend to giving them full citizenship and absolute freedom of worship. Thus Pius gave some limited liberal freedoms but he did not relax the reins of power, and even then he probably did more than he originally intended, swept along as he was on a wave of public approbation.

When, in March 1848, Metternich fell, and Austria was paralysed by revolution, Pius agreed to allow papal troops and volunteer civilians to join Piedmont, but he would not, as spiritual leader of the Catholics, declare war – especially on Austria, regarded by Pius as one of the main bulwarks of the Faith. When Piedmontese troops were defeated at Custozza and an armistice followed, excited mobs in Rome, angered by the Pope's unwillingness to commit himself and by his recall of papal forces which were on their way to the front, murdered Count Rossi and established a Roman Republic. Pius fled to Gaeta the day after asserting that he would never leave Rome.

It is indeed difficult to see how the Pope could ever really be a democrat or a liberal. Jesus Christ did not take soundings among his disciples before deciding what was in accordance with God's teachings, and the Pope's authority was equally autocratic. It was he alone who ruled on doctrinal matters, and while he might delegate lesser powers to a temporal minister, or committee, this was never anything more than a matter of administrative convenience. Pius had a very clear idea as to what his doctrinal responsibilities were, and here he would brook no discussion. It is not surprising then, that after his bitter exile in 1848–9 Pius's liberalism all but vanished. But he had good reason. After 1849 Italian unification was a purely secular movement. Pius could no more form an alliance with anti-clerical Piedmont than with Mazzini and his republicans. Thus the Pope disapproved of the 1859 war, was alarmed at the union of the Duchies with Piedmont in 1860, and tried to defend papal territory against Piedmontese incursion later that year. His secret correspondence with Victor Emanuel showed his abhorrence of the Piedmontese anti-clerical legislation.

When the kingdom of Italy was proclaimed in 1861 Pius was uncomfortably aware that he was the main obstacle to Italy having Rome as its capital. In the *Quanta Cura* encyclical of 1864 Pius condemned freedom of opinion and of the press, the sovereignty of the people, and the supremacy of the state over the Church. Yet even at this date he thought that there had been some good in the French Revolution, especially such ideas as equality before the law.

In 1870 Pius lost his political power when Italian troops entered Rome. This had been inevitable, and Pius had already in that year (despite some misgivings) issued his doctrine of Papal Infallibility, giving him infallibility on spiritual matters when speaking *ex cathedra* as leader of the Universal Church. Thus Pius strengthened his spiritual authority while losing his political autocracy. His attitude to the new Italian state was one of public hostility, although there was some private cooperation.

Pius, like many autocrats, dispensed his limited liberalism from above. He was certainly more humanitarian than many of his predecessors, and disliked human suffering whether caused by poverty or barbarity. He even had a sense of humour: he captioned a rather poor photograph of himself sent to a nun with 'Fear not, it is I'. But in his first two years his exuberance had carried him along a path that he was later to regret, and after 1848 his main concern was not the advancement of mankind but the protection of the papacy.

12:3

Alexander II: The Tsar 'Liberator'?

History books often give Alexander II of Russia the name he is supposed to have been granted by his grateful people during his reign – the 'Tsar Liberator'. Did he deserve the name?

In 1861, Alexander was responsible for the emancipation of about 45 million serfs, freeing them from feudal servitude and making them into free peasants. This was commonly regarded as a great act of humanitarianism. In fact, it was nothing of the sort. His father, Nicholas I had been faced by a number of serf revolts during his reign, but had got no further than burying the question in commissions of inquiry. Alexander, however, saw his country defeated in the Crimean War, and now felt there was no further excuse for delaying reform. But he was thinking more of modernisation than of liberalism. He wanted to see a free labour force created so that Russia could embark on its industrial revolution, and in particular he wanted to see a healthier and more intelligent class of recruit conscripted into the army if his country was ever to recover its military position. He had the same aims in his other administrative reforms – the introduction of judicial, educational and military reforms, and the reorganising of Russian local government. It was efficiency he had in mind rather than humanitarianism. At heart Alexander remained an autocrat, and this can be seen from his continuing refusal to allow the election of a Russian national parliament.

Nor indeed after emancipation was the condition of the Russian serf much improved. He still required an internal passport to move about the country, and he was still burdened with other restrictions of his freedom. If he moved to the town he was little better off. Even within the village he was generally awarded the poorest land, subjected to the irksome control of the village *mir* and burdened with heavy redemption payments to pay for what he already considered his own. He remained ignorant, uneducated, equipped with nothing but the crudest of tools, and above all desperately poor.

12:4

Cavour: Was He an Italian Nationalist?

Count Camillo Cavour is one of the heroes of Italy, one whose major contribution brought about the unification of the country, and without whom Italy could never have been united. Legends soon grew up around

Cavour after his premature death in 1861. He was soon credited with intentions and aims which he would have hardly recognised: that he was a committed Italian nationalist, that he planned and brought about Italian unification, and that in 1861 he was planning to add Venice and Rome to what he had already achieved. This legendary view of Cavour was consolidated into history by Whiggish historians of high reputation like G.M. Trevelyan. To Trevelyan all that contributed to the progress of mankind was praiseworthy; Italian unification was one of the most praiseworthy examples of nineteenth-century progress, and its two architects were Cavour and Garibaldi. Trevelyan developed his views in his two books Garibaldi and the Thousand *and* Garibaldi and the Making of Italy. *Thus Cavour was credited with aiming at Italian unity, and fashioning his domestic and foreign policies with that single-minded purpose. It was not until the 1950s that Trevelyan's views came under attack, in particular from D. Mack Smith, who, in* The Making of Italy *and other books, undermined the view that Cavour was an Italian nationalist or that his policies and achievements were anything other than pragmatic. But despite Mack Smith the old legend persists, although those who subscribe to it now are very much in error. And so it is still necessary to attempt a balanced assessment of Cavour's limited aims, and to determine how far his achievements were in accordance with these aims.*

Cavour capped a meteoric political career by becoming Prime Minister of Piedmont in 1852. During his nine years of almost unbroken office Cavour strengthened Piedmont's agriculture and army, built up the economy, and undermined the power of the Roman Catholic Church. He sent a contingent of Piedmont's army to fight in the Crimea in 1855; he fought a partially successful war against Austria in 1859, united the Central Duchies with Piedmont in 1860, and added the kingdom of Naples later that year. At the time of his death in 1861 Italy had a national parliament at Turin, and all of Italy except Rome and Venetia owed allegiance to Piedmont's king, Victor Emanuel.

Others, like Garibaldi, are usually credited with a major share in bringing about Italian unity, but the notion that Cavour was its architect dies hard. Yet Cavour was no Italian nationalist, and the Italy of 1861 was very different from the Italy he had envisaged at the outset of his premiership nine years earlier. To Cavour, Italian nationalism was unattractive on several counts. In the first place, he had been appointed to the premiership by Victor Emanuel. His primary duty, therefore, was service to his king, and the preservation and consolidation of the kingdom of Piedmont. Secondly, Italian unity faced the obstacle of the papacy, whose territories straddled central Italy, and any threat to these territories would almost certainly provoke intervention from the major Catholic powers, France and Austria; such intervention could only work to Piedmont's detriment. It was one thing to promote anti-clerical legislation in Piedmont – an attack on the Pope's spiritual power – quite another to threaten his territories in central Italy, an attack on his temporal power. Nor was it feasible to effect a smooth union of north and south. The impoverished kingdom of Naples would be a liability, likely to become a drain on the revenues of the richer north.

But Cavour was Prime Minister of a country where members of parliament were elected on a limited franchise, and where public opinion had to be taken into account. There was a widespread flourishing of Italian nationalism in 1848 and subsequently, and actively to oppose it could have meant electoral disaster. Cavour, therefore, maintained links with the national movement, prepared to use it to nourish Piedmont's ambitions, and to restrain it when it looked like going out of control.

Despite his aristocratic background Cavour had strong Liberal sympathies, which he demonstrated in the newspaper he founded in 1847. His newspaper, *Il Risorgimento* (meaning resurgence or revival), was concerned with the revival and strengthening of Piedmont and the removal of foreign influence from Italy. It soon gave its name to the whole movement for Italian unification, thus crediting Cavour with ambitions for Italy far in excess of his intentions.

The foreign influence Cavour wanted to remove from Italy was that of Austria. While Austria preserved its neutrality during the Crimean War, Cavour was persuaded to demonstrate

Piedmont's strength by joining the war against Russia, with whom Piedmont had no quarrel. Success brought Piedmont to the peace conference table where Cavour, to the horror of the Austrian observers, was able to denounce Austrian rule in Italy unchallenged. But nothing immediately came of it.

It was Orsini's bomb that caused Napoleon III to focus sharply on Italy. He met Cavour secretly at Plombières in 1858. Cavour's aim was to secure French help in expelling the Austrians from northern Italy, and possibly as far south as the Duchies. This would make Piedmont the unrivalled power in the north. In return for French help Cavour agreed to cede to France the predominantly French-speaking areas of Nice and Savoy. No change was to take place in southern or central Italy, although the Pope might be compensated for losing some of the most northern parts of the Papal States by becoming President of a loose federation of the enlarged Piedmont, the Papal States and the kingdom of Naples. This apparent support for Italian unity was marred by the fact that both Napoleon and Cavour knew that the Pope was most unlikely to accept the role thus cast for him.

The war of 1859 was not a total success for Cavour as the Austrians were not driven from northern Italy, and at the peace Piedmont secured only Lombardy and not Venetia. Cavour resigned in disgust at the failure of his plans for northern Italy. Anti-Austrian revolts in the Duchies, however, brought a new situation. It is certain that, as part of his plan to expel the Austrians from northern Italy, Cavour's agents had been active in the Duchies. Their presence during the plebiscites ensured suspiciously overwhelming majorities for the union of the Duchies with Piedmont. Cavour hastily returned to power, incurred the condemnation of Italian nationalists for transferring Nice and Savoy to France, and absorbed the Duchies into Piedmont. Apart from Venetia Cavour's limited aims were now complete. They would have remained so but for Garibaldi.

It was with mixed feelings that Cavour heard of the attempts of Garibaldi to raise volunteers to fight against the King of Naples. Garibaldi was an adventurer, reputedly with republican leanings, who was certainly not concerned to protect the interests of Piedmont. But he had many connections, and was widely admired, both in Italy and abroad. Cavour was under pressure from nationalists both in Piedmont and elsewhere. As Garibaldi's expedition began to gather in the Piedmontese port of Genoa, Cavour was all things to all men. Publicly he denounced Garibaldi; this would please Austria and Naples and was in diplomacy strictly correct. But secretly he gave the expedition his approval; this would please the nationalists and their foreign sympathisers such as the British. Deep down, he wondered how damaging an attack on Sicily and Naples would be? If Austria intervened then Piedmont's cause as well as that of Italy could well be in jeopardy. At least if Garibaldi failed as Cavour half expected him to, and half hoped he would, no blame would be attached to Cavour. It would mean that he was rid of Garibaldi for ever, and that he would no longer have to pander to Italian nationalism, most of the features of which he despised. If on the other hand Garibaldi succeeded, Cavour would have to deal with the inevitable international crisis.

Garibaldi's immediate success took everyone by surprise, and his refusal to hand over his conquests to Victor Emanuel meant to Cavour only one thing – that Garibaldi and Mazzini intended to set up a republic in southern Italy. In such circumstances Austrian intervention would be inevitable, and Garibaldi was only a few miles from the papal frontier which he had every intention of crossing. To do nothing was certain to lead to disaster, so Cavour decided to take action. He sent the Piedmontese army into the Marches and Umbria – the eastern provinces of the Papal States – promising to steer well clear of Rome. This promise satisfied Napoleon III and made isolated action by Austria unlikely. The Piedmontese army easily brushed aside the papal defenders at Castelfidardo and, sweeping round to the south-west of Rome, effectively barred Garibaldi's route to Rome. Garibaldi bowed to the inevitable, handed over his conquests to Piedmont, and the kingdom of Italy was proclaimed in March 1861.

The new kingdom without Venetia and Rome fell well short of nationalist aspirations. But it greatly exceeded those of

Cavour. Far from limiting his aims to driving out the foreigner and making Piedmont the dominant power in northern Italy, Cavour had been carried along by events and achieved for the Italian nationalists what they were incapable of achieving for themselves – the triumph of pragmatism over idealism.

12:5

Disraeli: the Father of Modern Conservatism?

Benjamin Disraeli, Prime Minister of Britain from 1874 to 1880, was the politician whose name is most closely associated with the development of modern Conservatism. He is credited with taking up the cause of social reform for the masses, and restating the old Tory doctrines for a more modern party. He is said to have dreamed at the same time of a great British Empire spreading across the globe, bringing the blessings of civilisation to distant countries while at the same time enhancing the prestige of imperial Britain. This view, like other aspects of his rather overinflated reputation, seems to have been based largely on political and historical legend.

Imperialism. The two great statements of Disraeli's imperial credo were said to have been set out in two of his great public addresses of 1872, those at the Free Trade Hall, Manchester in April and at the Crystal Palace in June. There is no doubt that they were fearsomely long speeches, even in an age accustomed to long public addresses. The former ran to more than three hours. During this time he constantly refreshed himself with draughts of 'white brandy', a colourless spirit looking like tapwater that would have been distinguishable to his hearers only by reason of his undiminished eloquence as time wore on. Nevertheless, in both these speeches, what Disraeli had to say about the empire was disappointingly brief; in both of them not much more than five minutes.

Nor was it very stimulating stuff. For much of this limited time, he was attempting to define home and colonial responsibilities, with the aim of enabling Britain to call on colonial aid if need be – which might have been good news to his hearers, but which would hardly have inspired much confidence in the colonies themselves. The main thrust of his observations was his criticism of the policies of the Liberal Party, which seemed to him to aim at the disruption of the empire. The only forward-looking part of his speeches got away from traditional colonialism, and looked towards an empire with a common tariff policy, greater self-government and a 'central representative council in the metropolis', a view strangely foreshadowing the type of imperialism set out by Joseph Chamberlain. But his juxtaposition of colonial aid for Britain with greater self-government showed that he had not thought through the problem fully, but was simply dreaming on his feet.

Disraeli's imperialism, when put into effect, produced very mixed results. His purchase of the Suez Canal shares had all the bewitching sleight of hand that was the hallmark of later Tory financial operations, but in practice it landed Britain with a continuing headache in Egypt. In Afghanistan in 1879, his efforts at imperial advance produced the murder of the British consul and all his staff; in South Africa, war with the Zulu chief Cetewayo and the annihilation of a small British force at Isandhlwana. Only by his policy of conferring the title of 'Empress of India' on Victoria did he achieve success – in continuing his shameless flattery of the Queen, not in winning the hearts of the Indian people, who were totally unresponsive to the new dignity, most of them never even having heard of it.

In fact, Disraeli had other more important concerns. His primary task, as an utter outsider, was to foist himself on the Tory Party which, as a Jew who converted to Anglicanism and wrote political novels and dabbled in radical causes, it was difficult to do. He achieved success only by leading a discontented group of Tory landowners against their leader Peel in a party rebellion against him in 1846. Lord Derby, who resented the personal ambition of this brazen parvenu, called Disraeli 'that scum'.

Social Reform. Disraeli also made great play with the need for social reform for the masses. It was he who gave many of them the vote in 1867 – though this in point of fact was not his original intention – and in his speeches he outlined plans of social reform in housing, health and conditions of employment. He had, however, no clear mission for social reform. He did not offer specific solutions, nor did his thinking foreshadow collectivism, state funding or egalitarianism. His answer seemed to lie not in social engineering, but in a kind of paternalistic compassion of the upper classes for the lower in an unequal society. He rejected the arithmetical equality and the heartless utilitarianism of the Liberals in favour of sentimental and unspecific talk about 'One Nation'. His government produced social legislation when he came to office in 1874, but by this time he was a tired old man, and his measures were ground-breaking only by accident. Those such as his trade union legislation of 1875–6, which made radical changes to trade union law, created very serious problems later. In any case, most of his legislation was permissive rather than compulsory, so that the application of the new laws was lacking in bite. Furthermore, Disraeli himself played little part in it. He left the drafting of it to Cabinet colleagues, and seemed as indifferent to its details as he was later unconcerned about its parliamentary fate.

So not only was Disraeli the least likely of Tory leaders, but many of his ideas were woolly, idealistic and generalised in content. His knowledge of, and his interest in, the empire was little more than part of his public pose, though he rather fancied himself as a major player in the field of international diplomacy – a view perhaps rather surprisingly shared by the normally shrewd Prince Bismarck, who said admiringly of him at the time of the Berlin Congress in 1878: *'Der alte Jude, dass ist der Mann!'* But, whatever the truth of Bismarck's verdict, Disraeli seemed to have little time for drudgery of domestic reform. Insofar as he had any answers at all to social problems, his belief seemed to be not in dogmatic solutions, but rather in his bland assumption of the unique character and the social cohesion of the nation – which in his own words he saw as 'One Nation'.

12:6

Did Revolution Promote or Hamper Russian Economic Development?

Many students of history persist in regarding pre-revolutionary Russia as a primitive, backward and mainly rural economy, and seeing the communist revolution as the beginning of a process whereby the country was modernised, industrialised and dragged into the twentieth century by Stalin. There are, indeed, school textbooks alleging that 'Stalin found Russia a country with wooden ploughs, and left it one with atomic piles', but do such statements merely restate a grossly oversimplified viewpoint?

In fact, the industrialisation of the country was well under way in the reign of the last Tsar, Nicholas II, and if anything the coming of the Revolution interrupted and set back that process until well into the twentieth century. Even when it took place, industrialisation was on an arbitrary and fragile foundation, often out of touch with economic realities, so that it encountered problems that hampered it for the rest of the century, and from which many would say it never recovered. So the reputation so effortlessly enjoyed by Stalin as the mastermind behind what is sometimes called the 'third Russian revolution' – the modernisation of his country – has to be heavily qualified.

Russia's industrial revolution began in the last quarter of the nineteenth century and was financed largely by foreign capital, and aided by the rapid growth of the urban population in the wake of emancipation in 1861. The growth of railways was one of the most impressive achievements of the later years of the century. Their chief aim was to link the grain-producing areas with the towns, and also with the ports, so as to facilitate the export of grain. Between 1861 and 1880 the track grew from about 1,000 miles to over 14,000. Russia could supply neither the capital for this great expansion, nor the engineering skill, nor even the necessary equipment. Not only did the rails and the locomotives have to be brought in from abroad, but even the screws and bolts. Successive large loans were floated on the Paris Bourse, and later loans were floated also in Berlin and London. This railway boom also helped to encourage the growth of Russian heavy industry. In the later years of the century there was a twentyfold increase in coal production, a tenfold rise in steel, iron and pig iron, and the beginnings of the oil industry. The factory founded by a Welshman called Hughes in the Krivoi Rog basin began to produce coal, iron and steel, while the oil companies in Baku were largely financed by the Nobel brothers. In other industries like cotton spinning and woollen manufacture there was also great expansion. Labour was cheap, machinery was readily imported and management staff could easily be hired abroad. Workers' barracks, exploitation, low wages, child labour, payments in kind, echoed in Russia many of the evils that had characterised early industrialisation in Britain. The government frowned on trade unions, but none the less supplied state labour in the same way it had supplied serf labour before emancipation. This link with the state was connected with the country's failure to develop an industrial and a capitalist bourgeoisie. The few bourgeois who lived in the country tended to be bureaucrats or administrators rather than owners and managers. The state also promoted industrial enterprise through the State Bank, founded in 1860. Note issuing was only a minor function of this bank; its main work was to provide the main prop of the whole credit system. So from the beginning the role of the state loomed large. By the end of the century over 40 per cent of factories in Russia employed more than 1,000 hands; the Putilov munitions factory in St Petersburg employed 12,000.

The spread of industry and the improvement in communications also saw the development of postal and telegraph facilities. At the same time, cheap newspapers in large editions made their appearance: not even the overstaffed censorship could prevent foreign comment or the spread of subversive literature. Travel was easier, quicker and cheaper for

Russians and foreigners alike. European Russia was rapidly being opened up to Western influences.

The effect of the catastrophic defeat in the First World War and of the two Russian revolutions of 1917 was to put a complete stop to this progress, and to throw Russia back on its primitive roots. Industrial activity ground to a halt. The factories produced mass meetings of the labourers, but no output; the railways stopped working, and even where there were peasants who were willing to go on supplying the towns the produce could not be brought in except casually by convoys of lorries. The whole country collapsed in disorder, violence and famine. The Bolshevik leadership found the task of industrial management far beyond its capabilities. It toyed with ever more desperate expedients, such as the abolition of money and its replacement by a system of rationing by 'commodity cards', but all of these came to nothing. Finally they had to call on the expertise of the hated bourgeoisie by enlisting the management skills of 'bourgeois specialists', but this worsened industrial relations further and led to the brink of counter-revolution at the time of the Kronstadt Mutiny. Only the so-called 'New Economic Policy' – which amounted in effect to a major abandonment of communist objectives – managed at the eleventh hour to avert disaster, but by this time the industrial economy had been completely shattered, and could not be salvaged.

The achievement of the NEP was to restore by 1928 much of the output that Russia had produced before the First World War. The output of capital goods stood at about the same figure as it had in 1913, but agricultural output was markedly down and did not recover until the end of the 1930s. Consumer goods, likewise, were expensive and hard to come by. Russia remained a country of grinding poverty throughout the period of Stalin's Five Year Plans. This poverty, coupled with the harsh repression by which Stalin sought to secure his economic objectives, meant that Russia was far from being the workers' paradise that many believed it was. Indeed, Hitler expected in all seriousness that his invasion of the country in 1941 might

Production of Selected Goods in Russia/Soviet Union, 1913–52

Product (and unit)	1913	1921	1928	1933	1940	1945	1952
Industrial							
Electricity, bn kwhs	2.0	0.5	5.0	16.3	48.3	43.2	119.1
Crude Oil, m. tons	9.2	3.8	11.6	21.5	31.1	19.4	47.3
Coal, m. tons	29.1	9.5	35.5	76.3	165.9	149.3	300.9
Steel, m. tons	4.2	0.2	4.2	6.9	18.3	12.2	34.5
Machine tools, 1,000 units	1.8	0.8	2.0	21.0	58.4	38.4	74.6
Locomotives, units	477	78	479	948	928	8	439
Trucks, 1,000 units	–	–	0.7	39.1	136.0	68.5	243.5
Tractors, 1,000 units	–	–	1.3	73.7	31.6	7.7	98.7
Consumer							
Automobiles, 1,000 units	–	–	0.1	10.3	5.5	5.0	59.7
Washing machines, 1,000 units	–	–	–	–	–	–	4.3
Bicycles, 1,000 units	4.9	7.7	10.8	125.6	255.0	23.8	1,650.4
Radio sets, 1,000 units	–	–	–	29.0	160.5	13.8	1,294.5
Television sets, 100 units	–	–	–	–	0.3	–	37.4
Cotton fabrics, bn metres	2.7	1.5	2.7	2.7	3.9	1.6	5.0
Leather shoes, m. pairs	60.0	28.0	58.0	90.3	211.0	63.1	237.7
Canned Foods, bn cans	0.1	0.1	0.1	0.7	1.1	0.6	2.1
Agricultural							
Grain, m. tons		86.0	36.22	73.3	69.1	95.5	75.0	82.5
Cows, m.	28.8	24.8	29.2	19.0	27.8	22.9	24.3
Hogs, m.	23.0	13.1	19.4	9.9	27.5	10.6	28.5
Fish caught, m. tons	1.0	0.3	0.8	1.3	1.4	1.1	2.1

Derived from various Soviet sources in Oxenfeldt and Holubnychy, *Economic Systems in Action* (Holt, Rheinhart & Winston, New York, 1965), quoted in J.P. Nettl.

provide the opportunity for a people who had long groaned under his tyranny to rise against Stalin and flock to his liberating banner. They did not. Nevertheless, after the war things scarcely improved. Soviet Russia remained a country often not able to feed itself by its own output, where corruption, mismanagement and falsification of the figures could not conceal that industry, too, suffered from all the consequences of over-centralisation, jobbery and faulty planning. The privileged few of the *apparat* had reasonably comfortable lives, but the bulk of the people struggled or suffered in silence.

By the year 2000 it became more obvious that the whole communist experiment was an aberration that served only to delay and to pervert Russia's industrial growth. However regretfully older Russians may today look back on the 'good old days' of communist rule, when people had jobs and when quite often there was bread in the shops and something to eat with it, the fact remains that given free development, a proper market and a more liberal government, Russia could have been among Europe's leading nations, instead of struggling along from day to day with the begging bowl, trying to salvage something from the ruins of the Soviet system.

12:7

Did British Living Standards Decline in the 1930s?

The bleakness of British life in the early 1930s has been richly portrayed in literature (e.g. Ellen Wilkinson's The Town that was Murdered) and in film. The picture is one of despairing men on the 'dole', hanging about street corners, and of widespread abject poverty. There are a number of reasons, however, for treating this pessimistic judgment with some caution.

Most of the unemployed received the 'dole' having run out of, or not qualifying for, unemployment benefit. This would mean that, when the men's families are taken into account, probably well in excess of 6 million Britons out of 35 million were dependent on the 'dole'. This provided enough money for only the most basic of necessities. Starvation was avoided, but clothes and even shoes were often luxuries, and many had to clothe themselves with charity handouts. The government cuts of 1931 certainly made things worse, and rising unemployment added to the despair of those who could see no prospect of their own unemployment coming to an end.

But there was one redeeming feature. The cost of living had fallen continuously since the early 1920s and fell even more sharply with the Depression. Thus between 1929 and 1933 the cost of living fell by 15 per cent. In 1934 when prices began very slowly to rise the benefit cuts of 1931 were restored, and the 'dole' was worth more in real terms than it had been in 1929.

For more than 80 per cent of the population where at least one member of the family was in work, even when unemployment was at its height (1933), falling prices, and from 1934 rising wages, brought about modest improvement. Incomes could buy more, and improved living standards could be seen in other ways: the widespread use of electricity, new domestic products, radio and cinema added a new dimension to the lives of most. Improved and more widely available council housing and better houses for rent saw a more rapid disappearance of squalor; a modest house could be rented for 5s a week, or bought for £300 through a low-interest mortgage at 10s a week. Those who were insured qualified for free medical treatment; those who were not could obtain it very cheaply (for children as little as a penny a week) through membership of one of the many Friendly Societies.

The Depression brought hardship to many, and it was concentrated in areas of high unemployment such as the shipbuilding towns of North-East England, of which Jarrow was the best known. But for the vast majority of the population the 1930s was a period of rising living standards, with a notable advance even on the conditions of the 1920s. This improvement was chiefly because of falling consumer prices, which meant that money went further; but it was also due to the increase of available domestic amenities, better housing and sanitation, new services and pastimes, and advanced medical treatment. It was helped also by the low incidence of crime. Folk memory has created this historical error by giving this period a much blacker reputation than it deserves.

12:8

Did Anthony Eden Seek Appeasement?

Anthony Eden resigned as Britain's Foreign Secretary on 20 February 1938. It is widely believed that his resignation marked his dissatisfaction with the appeasement policies of Chamberlain's government. This is erroneous. Eden resigned, not because he disapproved of appeasement, but because he resented Chamberlain's interference in foreign affairs. There is no evidence that, even as late as Munich, Eden was opposed to appeasement in principle.

Eden had become increasingly restless because of Chamberlain's tendency to make initiatives in foreign affairs without consulting the Foreign Secretary. In February 1938 the Italians, anxious to maintain cordial relations with Britain and France to avoid becoming a German satellite, proposed a written agreement which would recognise the Italian possession of Abyssinia and would provide for the withdrawal of Italian forces from the Spanish Civil War. Eden's objections to a written agreement related in part to the unpopularity of the government's handling of the Abyssinian crisis: he did not want to make it even more unpopular by agreeing in writing to the Italian *de facto* possession of Abyssinia. But it also arose in part from the way the proposal was handled. Eden was quite happy to agree informally to the Italian possession of Abyssinia, but jibbed at a formal agreement, at least for the time being. Here he was overruled by Chamberlain, who persuaded the Cabinet to accept a written agreement. Eden therefore resigned.

This did not make Eden an opponent of appeasement. His memoirs speak much of his reservations about Chamberlain's policies. He did not stand and cheer Chamberlain in late September 1938 as nearly all the Conservative MPs did when Chamberlain announced, at the end of a very dramatic debate, that he was flying for the third time to see Hitler. But he did not join Churchill in denouncing the Munich agreement, and there is only second-hand evidence for suggesting that Eden was unhappy with it. It was not appeasement that divided Chamberlain and Eden; it was a personality clash, born of slights real and imagined. Eden had no policy reason for joining forces with Churchill, the pariah of the Conservative Party. To do so would have consigned him to the political wilderness, and Eden was merely sulking in his tent, and waiting to be summoned back to high office. He resigned in a fit of pique, but his resignation looked in retrospect like a resignation over principle. Thus was created the legend of Eden and his opposition to appeasement; Eden was to draw political dividends from this for many years to come.

12:9

The Roaring Twenties: Myth or Reality?

It was a popular illusion, fostered by contemporaries and later enshrined in the history books, that the 1920s in the United States was the time of the 'Roaring Twenties'. This illusion was particularly cherished by countless numbers of immigrants to the USA who were looking forward to a better, fuller life there. Unfortunately, the Roaring Twenties did not roar for everyone. Those either in, or bound for, America who regarded it as being 'the land of opportunity' or 'the land of the free' based this belief on rumour rather than on reality.

It is true that American society permitted its lucky individuals to make good and catered for their needs. There were people of great property, favoured by the tax system, and people of great wealth who used their money to accumulate even bigger fortunes by shrewd management and lucrative investment. But at the bottom of the social pyramid there were hosts of others, many of them first- or second-generation immigrants, who did not share in the bonanza, but who by contrast grubbed away at their dreary tasks silently and uncomplainingly in the hope that good fortune might later smile upon them.

There were those whose parents had been among the

pioneers along the western trails, and who now lived a harsh life in the wilderness-paradise of the prairies or the Rockies, scraping a meagre living from the thin soils of the plains or the mountains. There were the White and Coloured areas of the former plantations or of 'Tobacco Road', who lived in penury and whose Black population lived in constant fear of the Ku Klux Klan. There were the non-unionised wage-slaves of the Northern mills, engaged for a pittance on stupefying, brutalising work that left them drained, deafened, ignorant and on the brink of starvation. One female worker in the service industries, employed in a laundry as late as the 1930s, told of her experiences:

> I worked as a press operator before we were unionised. *Slavery* is the word that would describe the conditions under which we worked. At least fifty-four hours a week it was 'speed up! speed up!', eating lunch on the go, perspiration dripping from every pore, for almost ten hours a day. When I reached home sometimes I was too tired to prepare supper. I would flop across the bed and sleep two or three hours, then get up and cook, and then fall back into bed immediately – you know how unhealthy that was.
>
> The toilet at our place wasn't fit for animals, much less people. There was but the one for men and women. When I complained, the boss said: 'There ain't many places paying ten dollars a week, Evie.' That ended my protests, because I didn't want to get fired.

Many such workers were exploited by their employers and cowed into silence, possibly because they were newly arrived in the USA and did not know what to expect, or possibly because they believed their servitude was no more than temporary and that better times were just around the corner. This faith in their new homeland persuaded many from the older communities of eastern or central Europe to acquiesce in conditions that were scarcely better than those they had fled at home.

Over the period of the 1920s, there was a margin of

improvement. Average hours of labour fell from slightly more than forty-seven per week to slightly less than forty-six, and average wages rose by about 8 per cent. But the increase in rewards for the owners of industry far outstripped any benefit to the workers. Some of this filtered down to the shareholders in industry in the form of higher dividends, but the biggest profits were made by the business and managing class. Furthermore, about 80 per cent of the profits went to only 1 per cent of US citizens. A survey in 1929 showed that the top 5 per cent of the American population were receiving one-third of all the personal income in the United States, while 60 per cent of the population were earning scarcely enough to pay for the bare necessities of life. So, while the decade brought success and prosperity for the few, the remainder felt it left a lot to be desired.

12:10

Is the UN a Great Improvement on the League of Nations?

It is frequently said that the League of Nations was an unfortunate failure, as was shown by its inability to prevent the coming of the Second World War, while the United Nations Organisation is a great success, preventing the outbreak of a Third. As a judgment, however, this verdict is oversimplified in the extreme, and is in need of radical revision.

There is no doubt that the League failed. From the start it placed too much reliance on the effectiveness of merely verbal protest, and overestimated the importance of economic sanctions as a method of restraining an aggressor. It also subscribed to the mechanical view of international relations, operating on the somewhat unrealistic assumption that all nations were equal and should have an equal say in world problems. In addition, the spreading of international responsibility often became a way of avoiding it altogether. Governments seemed to expect the League to take action, while they themselves took none. But the League was only as determined as its members. Membership, too, was limited. There were never more than about fifty members. The USA inflicted what proved to be a fatal blow by refusing to join, and Russia, being communist, was for a long time excluded. The later resignation of Germany (not allowed even to join until 1926), Italy and Japan from the League in the 1930s made it look increasingly like an Anglo-French alliance where, as it was said, 'all the languages of the world were spoken, either in English or in French'.

But the most fundamental reason for the failure of the League was at the same time the most simple: governments existed for the purpose of safeguarding what they saw as their national interests. They were willing to go along with League decisions only for as long as these seemed to be in their interests. No nation was prepared to be overruled merely in order to enforce some international decision with which they might not agree. An effective League of sovereign states remained, at bottom, a contradiction in terms. In practice, the old methods of diplomacy and the traditional states system continued unaltered, with the League of Nations as a kind of moral window-dressing to make them seem respectable.

Efforts were made to remedy some of these weaknesses when the United Nations Organisation was first launched. The membership was wider, and included nearly two hundred states, large and small. Procedure was tightened. Armed sanctions against aggression could be, and were, employed by internationally contributed armies. Decisions no longer had to be endorsed unanimously, but could proceed by majority or by qualified majority. The 'veto' still remained, but was confined to the 'Big Five' in the Security Council. Fanciful efforts were later made to whittle even that away. The competence of the United Nations was much wider by virtue of its additional social, educational, scientific and cultural functions, monitored by large numbers of specialised agencies established for the purpose.

But the fundamental weakness still remains for the United Nations Organisation. It continues to be something of a fiction to represent the member states in UNO equally. For in wealth, size, power and importance they are manifestly unequal. Any world organisation in which Russia, China and the United States can be outvoted by the combined efforts of Uruguay, Luxembourg, Chad and Nauru must be one that no one can take entirely seriously. Even where lesser states try to preserve their neutrality and their voting independence, the number of their votes in the General Assembly gives a grossly exaggerated impression of their true weight. Even their freedom in criticising big-power policies – as Britain's were criticised at the time of the Suez crisis in 1956 – may breed cynicism and irritation on the part of larger powers; worse still there may be resentment of the 'pork-barrel' attitudes of officials from smaller states who exploit their authority, their privileges and their expense accounts in order to make a career out of UN service.

The result is that large and powerful nations continue to do exactly as they like, whatever the world may say. Large powers defy world opinion whenever they think they can get away with it, and gamble, often successfully, on getting their own way. Richer and more powerful nations habitually do the same. Many profess to care for world problems, but offer less than 1 per cent of their wealth to poorer nations struggling to survive, or delay the curtailment of their own environmental pollution while condemning the environmental pollution created by others.

Moreover, the UN claim to impartiality, on which universal respect for its decisions must depend, has often been open to question. The side enjoying the backing of the UN somehow seems to be the side of which the United States approves – the Jews, for instance, or the Kuwaitis, but not the Libyans. And does the United Nations Organisation exist to preserve the 'old order', rather like the French tried to use the League to enforce its demands on the Germans for reparations, or copper-bottom its own military ascendancy in Europe? If it does, it should have supported the Palestinians in their quest for their lost homeland. If not, it should have welcomed the Chinese People's Republic into the UN before 1971, instead of trying to perpetuate the fiction that Jiang Jieshi still ruled China.

On the whole, the United Nations has not achieved much as the result of its interventions. Its repeated attempts to resolve the Arab–Israeli situation have produced few tangible results. Its intervention in Korea was triggered only at the insistence of the USA. Its involvement in the war in the Congo did not sort out the problem, which in the end was left to the Congolese themselves, whose situation speedily degenerated into one of destruction and tyranny. In Cyprus, in Rwanda and in Bosnia UN observers and supervisors have fretted at the problems without producing much in the way of a positive outcome. The overall effect is that the Organisation by the end of the twentieth century has become something of a laughing stock, more famed for its meddling than for its effectiveness.

In fact, to many observers, the United Nations are not united at all. Until 1990 they were divided into two great power blocs – the communist Eastern bloc against what liked to call itself the 'Free World', i.e. the American-led Western bloc. Between the two there was the large and fluid grouping of lesser, or uncommitted, nations known as the 'Third World'. At the end of the century this grouping had foundered. There is now perhaps less to which to be committed. The old ideological distinction between communist and non-communist has broken down and has been replaced more nakedly than before by more nebulous common interests influenced by the almighty dollar. Though in a different fashion, nations are still pursuing as sovereign states what they see as their best interests.

Yet some progress has undoubtedly been made, most notably in non-political matters. Hardship has been relieved more effectively than before. Much has been done over technical matters such as marine navigation, broadcasting frequencies, pest control, postal services, and many others. And while the United Nations has not been able to tackle political problems effectively, or to eliminate conflict, it has at least established channels for discussion. In the General Assembly the exposure of the great powers to the different viewpoints of the Third World acts as some restraint on them, and makes them better informed on the thinking of the rest of the human race. In the last analysis, as Churchill is supposed to have said, 'Jaw-jaw is better than war-war.'

12:11

South African Apartheid: When Did it Start?

The United Party, led by Jan Smuts, ruled South Africa from 1939 to 1948. In the General Election of 1948 the revived Nationalist Party, led by Dr Malan, won a small majority and ousted Smuts. During the election campaign Dr Malan played on the fears of the White minority by stressing the 'Black menace' and proposing 'apartheid' (a term first coined by the nationalists in 1947), or the separation of races, as a means of consolidating White wealth and power. Malan sneered at Smuts who was said to be 'soft on kaffirs', and once in power considerable legislation was passed in the South African parliament to establish and consolidate apartheid. But was this the beginning?

It would be a mistake to assume that 'apartheid' was a new phenomenon in 1948, for not only had the political and social condition of the non-Whites been for a long time greatly inferior to that of the Whites, but their subjection to White control had long been legally enforced through the framework of racist legislation established in the course of the previous forty years.

When the Union of South Africa was set up in 1910 political power was reserved to the Whites. Exclusively White franchises existed in the Transvaal, and the Black vote existed only in the Cape and Natal. The Statute of Westminster 1931 allowed the South African parliament to abolish the Cape Black franchise in 1936. Black members could no longer be directly elected to parliament, even in Natal where a Coloured franchise still existed, but Black voters were allowed to vote for a handful of White representatives to speak for the Blacks in parliament and to defend their interests. Apartheid in the political sense merely meant the removal of remaining Black and Coloured voters from the electoral register, and this was done by 1955.

Socially, separation of races was very much a feature of pre-1948 South Africa, and this was reinforced, at least in part, by legislation. Non-Whites lived in shanty towns well removed from the affluent White areas, and an Act of 1923 specified areas where non-Whites were forbidden to live. Discrimination occurred in public places – baths, toilets, buses, shops, cinemas, etc. Pass laws restricted the movement of non-White males. They were banned by law, as early as 1911, from joining a trade union. An Immorality Act in 1926 banned sexual relations between people of different races.

The economic superiority of White over Coloured was reinforced by law. An Act of 1913 restricted Coloured landholding to less than one-third of the area reserved for Whites, and this one-third was generally land of inferior quality. The Native Land Trust, supposedly set up to encourage native settlement had, by 1948, achieved very little. Another Act prevented non-Whites from holding skilled positions in mines or factories. As Blacks, but not Whites, were banned from organising or taking part in strikes, they had no means and no hope of improving their economic status. By these laws the Whites hoped to keep the non-Whites in non-skilled and poorly paid jobs.

So before 1948 there was a framework of discriminatory laws, political, social and economic, which strengthened the superiority of White over non-White. Before 1948 these laws were random, and racism was to some extent a matter of choice. In 1948 racism, through apartheid, became a system, for which much of the ground had already been prepared.

12:12

The Suez Crisis: Was Nasser Another Hitler?

When Col Gamal Abdul Nasser nationalised the Suez Canal in July 1956, the principal shareholders in the canal, Britain and France, were enraged. Within two months the two countries were secretly negotiating with Israel for combined operations against Egypt, while their political leaders were busily denouncing Nasser in public. If they were going to resort to arms it would be necessary to have public opinion behind them. Not only government ministers, but even Britain's leader of the opposition, Hugh Gaitskell, equated Nasser with Hitler. This view, however, was obsessive and unrealistic.

The imputation of similarity to Hitler was directed against Nasser's international role rather than his domestic one. Nasser was by no stretch of the imagination a National Socialist. He was strongly socialist in sympathy, concerned to increase landholding by breaking up the large estates, to encourage village cooperatives, to improve education and to develop health care and social welfare, and to foster industrial expansion and development. His programme bore a much closer resemblance to Stalin's Five Year Plans than to Hitler's autarchy, especially when, in 1955, he began to buy arms and to secure funding from eastern Europe. Nasser's one-party state had features of all totalitarian regimes, but Nasser was not a mass murderer like Hitler or Stalin. He could be ruthless when Muslim fundamentalists embarked on public outrages and terrorism, but he did not persecute law-abiding religious minorities. When Christians or Jews living in Egypt were attacked by mindless mobs, his security forces came to their assistance, despite the intense national hostility to Jewish Israel. Active opponents of his regime might not sleep easily in their beds, but ordinary citizens who played no part in politics had nothing to fear from him.

Hitler paid cynical lip-service to legality while doing as he pleased; Nasser tried to act legally. When he nationalised the Suez Canal he promised adequate compensation to the shareholders, and freedom of navigation to all, except Israel. He paid fair prices to the owners of confiscated estates. But he had one main obsession, his hatred of Israel. This led him to take an anti-Western stance, as the USA, Britain and France were strongly pro-Israel and were supporting the Jewish state with arms and finance. So Nasser worked hard to destabilise pro-Western Arab states such as Libya, Jordan and Iraq, and he had the vision of a vast union of Arab states with Egypt as its dominant partner. This rather grandiose scheme of Egyptian–Arab supremacy bore some slight resemblance to Hitler's schemes of European and world domination. But when he seized the Suez Canal in 1956 his motive was domestic rather than international. The Aswan Dam was the jewel in the crown of his domestic policy. It would solve the problem of Egypt's unreliable water supply, it would provide power for Egypt's new industries and it would make fertile hundreds of square miles of new land in Nasser's overpopulated and land-hungry country. The canal complemented the dam. Together with the Nile it was Egypt's main thoroughfare. Nasser could not afford to allow its control to remain in the hands of unsympathetic foreigners who might use it to frustrate rather than promote Egypt's economic growth.

Britain and France saw the seizure as a further measure of destabilisation in the Middle East, a further threat to Israel and a prelude to the active involvement of the Soviet Union in the area. By comparing him to Hitler they hoped to make an international leper of him, and to justify whatever forceful action they might take to protect the canal, and possibly to undermine him and his regime. The action they did take closed the canal, rendered the position of pro-Western regimes in Arab countries virtually untenable, and made Israel more isolated than ever in a hostile Arab Middle East. In 1945 Hitler's empire was finally destroyed, but in 1956 Nasser's Egypt survived – once again contrast rather than similarity.

13

UNRESOLVED PROBLEMS

The Darwin Controversy: Apes or Angels?

Among the many scientific advances of the nineteenth century one of the most important in the history of biology, and certainly the most controversial, was the publication in 1859 of On the Origin of Species *by Charles R. Darwin. He was not the first to propound the theory of evolution, but his great merit was that he set out the process by which this evolution in the organic world could be explained. His book caused a sensation. The first edition sold out on the day it was published. Many of the leading scientists of the time supported him, including T.H. Huxley on the zoological side and Charles Lyell on the geological side. Lyell's earlier book* The Principles of Geology *had inspired just as fundamental a reassessment of his own subject when it was published in 1829. Some have sought to diminish the significance of Darwin's work. How important was it?*

Darwin's theory appeared to abolish what had been thought of as the fundamental dividing line between men and animals, and seemed to deny the special creation of man. It is hardly surprising, therefore, that his book generated a heated controversy among churchmen. This has continued to the present day. It was still a matter of heated debate when court action was taken against it at the Scopes trial in Dayton, Tennessee in 1925. An even more recent instance has occurred with the suspension of evolution-based biology teaching in some of the states of the 'Bible belt' in 1999, and with the emergence of just such a 'heresy' at a school on Teesside in 2002.

The reason for controversy was that many of Darwin's researches could not be reconciled with the literal interpretation of the Book of Genesis in the Bible. In treating man as no more than a higher animal, it denied by implication the doctrine of the fall of man and all its theological ramifications. This, when added to the geological theories of Lyell, had the effect of showing that the Scriptures could no longer be accepted as literal statements of fact. The logical conclusion of this line of reasoning was that the Old Testament was no more than a moral fairy tale. The bitter hostility of the Church was therefore only to be expected. Bishop Wilberforce (known to his opponents as 'Soapy Sam' on account of his oily manner) attacked *On the Origin of Species* in the columns of the *Quarterly Review*, and at a meeting of the British Association in Oxford in 1860 enquired of Huxley, who was defending Darwin's position, whether 'it was through his grandfather or his grandmother that he claimed his descent from a monkey'.

Many of the clergymen who attacked Darwin were as ignorant of science as their scientific opponents were ignorant of theology, and this did not sweeten the humour of their exchanges. Nevertheless, some clergy, like Charles Kingsley and Bishop (later Archbishop) Frederick Temple, welcomed the publication of Darwin's book as a contribution to human knowledge, based as it was on scientific observation of the world, fossil evidence of the past and the study of embryology. Dogmatic assurance was shaken, and many scholars felt quietly pleased when Pius IX condemned the doctrine in his *Syllabus of Errors*, since this was taken by them as the final confession of Catholic obscurantism. It is only in the present generation that the Jesuit scientist-theologian Pierre Teilhard de Chardin has squared the circle by arguing that evolution was the engine chosen by God to effect biological change, and that it is therefore possible to believe in science and scripture at the same time.

Darwinism, however, as a theory, had enormous implications and consequences that went far beyond its immediate scientific importance. It affected even economic and social thinking in Britain and the world. Philosophy and metaphysics underwent a change. The struggle for existence in evolutionary teachings was used to support the idea that similar struggles took place even in civilised society. Some 'social Darwinians' felt that humanitarian attempts to interfere between the weak and the strong went against the intentions of Nature. State intervention was resisted on the same grounds, and even Cobden and Bright opposed factory acts because they interfered with the natural rights of men to make wage bargains with their fellows. On the international scene it was not long before Houston Stewart Chamberlain was applying what he thought were Darwinian precepts to notions of racial superiority, and Hitler was using them to buttress his thoughts about the supremacy of the Aryan race. By the twentieth century, the struggle between science and religion was beginning to give way to new debates about the nature and working of human society.

Darwinian theories even at the present time still excite controversy. Those who believe in the need to encourage philanthropic or charitable activity, or who defend and propagate altruistic behaviour instead of personal gain may still find themselves uncomfortable with the teachings of social Darwinism. Even scientists do not wish to see evolutionism accepted with the same kind of blind faith that was earlier bestowed on fundamentalism: many, indeed, concede that there still are questions that have not yet found an answer. Science is a process rather than a final solution.

13:2

The Papacy: Was it Soft on Fascism and Nazism?

The Roman Catholic Church concluded a concordat with Mussolini in 1929 and with Hitler in 1933. The Church continued to cooperate with Mussolini until his downfall in 1943. And although the Church's honeymoon with Nazism was short-lived, the Vatican criticised but never publicly condemned Nazism or excommunicated its leaders, although it was aware of the unspeakable horrors being perpetrated by the Nazis. This has led to some sharp criticism of the Catholic Church's stance during the late 1930s and during the war, not least by some Catholic historians. A recent book on Pius XII by John Cornwell has fanned the flames of this controversy, which still rages without a clear-cut conclusion either way.

Italian Fascism. The three agreements between the Church and the Italian state in 1929 brought to an end more than fifty years of non-cooperation and stalemate. To the Church it meant the restoration (in the small Vatican state) of the Church's temporal power, but even more importantly it made the Roman Catholic Church the state Church of Italy and gave it considerable civil power, especially in various aspects of law and justice. The financial settlement gave the Vatican a vested interest in the Fascist regime because it was given a billion lire in interest-bearing government stock. It seemed that the Church had got the better bargain, even if the Fascist regime seemed to be blessed with clerical approval. It did not mean that the Church had become Fascist, but it certainly preferred Fascism to communism, and Pius XII preferred Fascist autocracy to the uncertainties of the democratic system. To the Vatican the Comintern and Western communist parties represented a threat to the very existence of the Church, and the Spanish Civil War showed that threat coming close to home. Popular Front governments were little better. Yet in some ways the Church exercised a restraining influence on Fascist Italy. It could not prevent political persecution, but it was at least partly responsible for the fact that Fascist Italy never adopted the extremes of racism and anti-Semitism as practised in territories under Nazi rule. Jews lost their service commissions and were driven out of their professions, but that was as far as the harassment went. Aware of the Church's disapproval Mussolini only proceeded against the Jews at all to gratify Hitler, and Mussolini was not pleased to have to change his dentist. Pius XII has been accused of anti-Semitism, but apart from obstructing Jewish attempts to purchase palm hearts in Italy he had not, until 1943–4, been accused of anything more seriously anti-Semitic. Catholics were brought up to believe that Jews were the killers of Christ; Pius XII was almost certainly anti-Protestant and anti-Muslim as well.

Desire for law and order, fear of political anarchy and communism, and the need for the unhindered exercise of the Christian religion made the Catholic Church more tolerant of Fascism than it should have been: Pius XI did not condemn Italian imperialist ventures in Abyssinia, Pius XII had no criticism of the Italian takeover of Albania in April 1939, but he did use all the diplomatic prestige at his disposal to try to keep Italy out of the Second World War.

German Nazism. The criticism of the Church's failure to condemn Nazism is more serious. The success of the 1929 concordat made the Vatican believe that a concordat with Hitler would enable the Church to conduct its work in Germany unhindered. This concordat was engineered by Cardinal Pacelli, later Pius XII, in July 1933. His assessment of the Weimar Republic was that it was weak, and under communist threat. He admired Hitler, and thought that he could save Germany; so did many other high-powered foreign observers. Pacelli's agreement to disband the Catholic Centre Party was intended to strengthen Hitler's apparently insecure hold on power. The accusation that in agreeing to disband it the Church was weakening potential opposition to Hitler is ludicrous. The Centre Party had voted *for* the Enabling Law, trusting in Hitler's promise not to use the Law against the Catholic Church. And a law of November 1933 turned Germany into a one-party state anyway; the Centre Party had but a short time to live even if there had been no concordat.

It did not take the Church long to regret the concordat. The 'With Burning Sorrow' encyclical of 1937 documented the various ways in which the Nazis had broken it. Pius XI learned that Hitler did not keep his promises; he told Chamberlain and Halifax so when he met them in Rome in January 1939. Pius XII, elected in March 1939, could not prevent the coming war;

nor could he prevent Hitler's persecution of the Catholic Church in Germany, nor his policies of anti-Semitism. But he was well aware that if he proceeded to extreme measures he would place Germany's 30 million Catholics in jeopardy: if they defied Hitler they would be in danger from the Gestapo; if they defied the Pope they would risk alienation from the Church. Most men are not born saints; it would not have been reasonable to present Germany's Catholics with such a stark choice. Individual German Catholics spoke out against the Nazi regime, as did other Christians; individual German Catholics out of fear, or misplaced loyalty, took part in the atrocities carried out by the regime, as did other Christians. The true nature and extent of the horrors of Nazism were not fully available to the Vatican until 1943 and 1944, by which time the very survival of the Vatican was in doubt, as Fascist Italy collapsed and the Germans moved into Rome.

By then the Church was behind the scenes encouraging individual Catholics to do what they could to succour those persecuted by the Germans, whether for political or racial reasons. But in public the Church remained cautious. In 1942 Pius XII's Christmas message condemned the inhumanities of war without mentioning Nazis or Jews specifically. But Vatican gold was used to facilitate escapes, and to maintain the thousands of refugees who flocked into the Vatican City. One false move on the part of the papacy and German troops would have entered the Vatican and its usefulness as an Allied listening post and as a refugee camp would have abruptly ended. The Pope's personal safety as a prisoner in Nazi hands might well have been under threat. It was politic for the papacy to tread warily. The alternative was to take a moral stand which would have no practical effect in saving lives, but which might even place more under threat. Hitler could well have echoed Stalin's famous remark, 'And how many divisions does the Pope have?' It has been argued that the practical effect of the Pope's not breaking off relations with the Nazis was that papal intervention was able to save 6,000 out of Rome's 8,000 Jews when the Nazis began a night-time round-up of them. Others have denied that papal intervention saved anyone, arguing that those who escaped owed their good fortune to individuals on the spot rather than intervention from the Vatican. There is even some limited evidence of papal collaboration with some Nazi anti-Semitic policies during the dangerous years of Nazi occupation of much of Italy, so the Church could have been pulling both ways and hedging its bets.

Rome was not clear of the Germans until June 1944. Until then a papal condemnation of the Nazis would have been unwise; after that it would have seemed hypocritical. Not until the war was over did the papacy issue an 'Apologia' for its wartime attitudes and actions.

The papal collaboration with Fascism is understandable: it ended the Pope's virtual imprisonment in St Peter's, and ended the unenviable choice devout Italian Catholics had to make between Church and state. The papacy had helped Nazism, but never given its full support to it; it distanced itself from it in 1937. It was not practical at that stage to undertake measures which would make every German Catholic an enemy of Nazism, although it might have been possible in 1933; it was expedient for the Church to take a soft line. But the Church might have gained in the long term if it had taken a more powerful *moral* stance against Nazism, even at the expense of short-term disadvantages. Pius XII's political sympathies and personal eccentricities may have contributed to the Church's shortcomings in dealing with Nazism, but it is doubtful whether a more vigorous anti-Nazi attitude would have had any effect in limiting Nazism's worst excesses.

13:3

Hiroshima and Nagasaki: Would the Japanese Have Surrendered Anyway?

On 6 and 9 August 1945 the Japanese cities of Hiroshima and Nagasaki were devastated by atomic bombs. Within a few days Japan sued for peace and accepted unconditional surrender after the Allies promised to respect the position, but not the power, of the Emperor. The war was over. Since then generations of historians have argued as to whether the use of the atomic bombs was necessary, and whether Japan was ready to make peace in any case.

Defeat had become virtually inevitable for Japan by late 1944. The American victory at Leyte Gulf in October gave the Americans absolute command of sea and air, and paved the way for the invasion of the Philippine Islands. Success there meant that American aircraft had bases within 500 miles of the Japanese mainland. The chief Japanese supporter of war, Prime Minister Tojo, had already resigned and, as overwhelming Allied forces closed in, Japan faced the shrinking of its empire, the loss of its main sources of overseas supplies, and the destruction of its principal cities by land-based aircraft.

Even so, heavy American casualties were expected when Japan was finally invaded. The Japanese had defended Iwo Jima and Okinawa to the bitter end, and had used *kamikaze* pilots to attack warships and supply ships. The Allies expected Japan to defend itself to the last man, and the war against Japan was predicted to continue to the end of 1946 with at least 2 million casualties on both sides, including large numbers of Japanese civilians.

In late June the Japanese, aware that the Soviet army was committed to joining the war against Japan now that Germany had surrendered, asked the Soviet Union to act as intermediary in peace negotiations. This the Soviet Union was not prepared to do, but the USA and Britain were well-informed of these peace feelers through their successful interceptions of Japanese radio code. Since the Japanese were insisting on a negotiated peace and the Allies were committed to demanding unconditional surrender, the Allies did not think it worthwhile to initiate their own peace negotiations, and contented themselves at the Yalta Conference in July in reiterating their demand for Japan's unconditional surrender.

It has been argued that the reason for this hard line was that the scientists had developed the bomb at great expense, and that both scientists and politicians were anxious to see whether the bomb worked. The test in July showed that it did. Moreover, the USA did not discuss the use of the bomb with its allies; Britain was merely informed in July that it was to be used and asked to approve. Churchill consented without demur. But neither the American scientists nor the American politicians were unanimous in wanting the bomb used in war; had those with reservations pressed their case more strongly they might have prevented or postponed its use. Unconditional surrender was at the time not an issue; it had been demanded of Germany before the bomb had been perfected, and there seemed no reason not to demand it of Japan also, whether the bomb was used or not.

It has also been suggested that the bombs were used to demonstrate US power as a warning to the Soviet Union. There had certainly been arguments and differences between the Allies at the Yalta Conference in July. And as Soviet intervention in the war would only have been effective in north China and Manchuria, the Allies could have used the bomb to make Russian intervention unnecessary. This is a little far-fetched and is pre-dating the beginning of the Cold War. Moreover, it was too late to stop Soviet intervention; the Russians were committed to attack Japan within three months of the ending of the European war, and they actually invaded Manchuria on 8 August, two days after the first atomic bomb was dropped.

A more powerful argument against the use of the bomb was Japan's rapidly deteriorating military and economic situation. War production had been badly hit by air raids, the Japanese were desperately short of raw materials, and the war was inevitably lost. Japan could not prolong the war indefinitely and might have to come to terms even before a mainland invasion. The Japanese knew that a Soviet attack was imminent, and they certainly did not want Manchuria overrun and the northern islands of mainland Japan put at risk. So it is possible that had the Allies abandoned their insistence on unconditional surrender before dropping the bombs, or even been more specific in the warning of the destruction to come, the Japanese might have come to terms. But the possibility was remote. Many of Japan's leaders were prepared, as a matter of honour, to see their country devastated rather than give in. Even after the atomic bombing the Japanese cabinet was equally divided; before it the 'doves' were definitely in a minority. It is likely that the Allies would have had to make more concessions than that concerning the Emperor if peace was to be achieved before Hiroshima. As it was the Emperor had to intervene personally in order to secure peace after Hiroshima and Nagasaki had been destroyed. Those who argue that the same peace could have been secured a week earlier are flying in the face of the evidence, but it could have been worth a try.

13:4

The Conflict in the Holy Land: Why Is it So Intractable?

The controversy in that province of the Near East known as Palestine is not one of long standing, though the parties to the quarrel often claim that it is. Nor is there any obvious reason why it should not be capable of an amicable settlement. Nevertheless it remains a controversy of such magnitude that it can properly be graced with the name of historic, *if not of* historical.

It is not a *racial* conflict, though it is commonly believed to be so. In fact the Jews and the Arabs are of the same Indo-European race, with a similar ethnic and cultural background. As an Arab leader, the Emir Faisal, told the Versailles Peace Conference in 1919: 'The Jews are very close to the Arabs in blood, and there is no conflict of character between the two nations. In principle, we are absolutely as one.' All the same there is no doubt it is certainly a *nationalist* conflict, with each of the two sides in Palestine committed to their own solution of the problem.

Nor is it a *religious* conflict. Indeed, three of the world's greatest religions have their origins in this area. The Muslim, the Jewish and the Christian faiths all acknowledge the same God. But whereas the Christians maintain the divinity of Christ as the Son of God, the Jews reject this, regarding him as an impostor, and continue to await the coming of the real Messiah. The Muslims on the other hand believe that Christ, like Moses, was one of a succession of prophets, the greatest of whom was Mohammed, who through his teachings in the Koran founded a pattern of life based on strict submission to a moral and social code of conduct and the daily routine of prayer, fasting and alms-giving. All three faiths regard Palestine as the 'Holy Land' and Jerusalem as the 'Holy City'. Nevertheless, fundamentalist sects of the Muslim faith in neighbouring countries such as the Egyptian *Jihad* group, advocating the use of terrorist weapons to achieve policy objectives that cannot be achieved by diplomacy, have inspired Palestinian Muslims to turn to hijacking, to suicide bombings and to the other methods of terrorism to secure for themselves an independent homeland and to revenge themselves on Israel for what they see as its imperialist methods. This behaviour the other religious faiths, and even the moderate elements of Islam, cannot condone.

The conflict is certainly *historical*, however, in that it had ancient roots. The ancient kingdom of Israel went back to the reign of David and Solomon in biblical times, though it had been conquered by the Romans in the first century BC, when the diaspora of the Jewish nation began, scattering them all over Europe by soon after 100 AD. Six hundred years after that, Palestine was occupied by the Arabs and became a predominantly Muslim, Arabic-speaking land. There followed eight Christian crusades in the period 1096–1291 when the forces of European Christendom were briefly successful in regaining control of parts of Palestine. But it was not until 1917 that Jerusalem fell into Christian hands again, when General Allenby, at the time of the Arab revolt against the Turks, marched in at the head of British troops towards the end of the First World War. Before that happened, the Jews at the end of the nineteenth century had already embarked on a Zionist movement which dispatched to Palestine about 70,000 settlers from the areas of Europe in which they were subject to persecution, and had begun to build up farming settlements there. After the First World War, a minority of Jews coexisted uneasily with Arabs; while Britain, now the *mandatory power* after the peace settlement, struggled vainly to maintain peace between the two. Both were convinced that the British had betrayed them: the Jews blaming Britain for failing to honour the promises made in the Balfour Declaration, the Arabs for having denied them independence in spite of the promises implied in the MacMahon letters. Eventually Britain, exhausted by its efforts in the Second World War and tormented to distraction by the continuance of pressures from the Arab League and a number of Jewish guerrilla organisations, handed over Palestine to the newly formed United Nations Organisation, and ignominiously pulled out of the country. Seizing the chance, the new state of Israel declared its independence.

Hence in May 1947 the Arab states surrounding Israel determined to crush the infant state that had sprung up in their midst. They failed. Wars recurred in 1956, 1967 and 1973, but all the Arabs succeeded in doing was to give the Israelis the opportunity to consolidate and expand their original fragile frontiers, and so to create a massive Arab refugee problem. It also drew into the conflict the Western and the Soviet blocs, thus ensuring that it became an international problem, simultaneously entrenching Arab–Israeli hostility and turning it into an intractable obstacle to peace.

The first steps towards a settlement of the problem were taken by President Sadat of Egypt and Prime Minister Menachem Begin of Israel in 1977. Since then progress has been slow and faltering. The 1998 negotiations between the parties only narrowly averted collapse, and in any case dealt only with comparatively minor issues. The main stumbling block of Palestinian autonomy still awaits solution, and extremist organisations on both sides seem determined to thwart a peaceful settlement. It is Palestinian autonomy particularly that has produced such formidable difficulties. Why this unreasoning extremism?

From the Israeli point of view: Arab hostility is unjustified. When the Jews arrived in Israel it was a poverty-stricken land, sparsely inhabited by Arabs who scratched a meagre living from the soil and tended scraggy flocks of sheep and goats. The Jews established thriving settlements, cultivated the soil, made the country's output immeasurably greater and brought in generous supplies of foreign capital, making massive investments that have benefited the whole community. They suspect that Arab hostility is due to a peevish jealousy, and fear that it constitutes the main threat to the country's future. They believe that Arab determination to oust them completely from the country still persists, and regard this as the justification for their heavy arms expenditure, and for the retention of arms by Jews in scattered rural areas.

Many Israelis were born in Israel, and regard Arab national aspirations as being not only threatening, but at the same time archaic. In their attitudes the Israelis have the sympathy and support of the Jewish lobbies in Washington, and hence also the support of the United States; while Muslims generally see US interference with the affairs of the area in terms of old-fashioned global imperialism.

The security problem is not merely the excuse for Jewish intransigence. Outlying settlements have found themselves subject to attack by Palestinian terrorists, and repeated bomb outrages in Israeli towns such as Tel Aviv have caused heavy loss of life. Extremist Islamic groups such as *Hamas* seem determined to destroy Israel regardless of official Palestinian opinion. Until Israel has internal security and viable frontiers recognised by all its Arab neighbours, the country will not be able to rest easy. But Israel's Arab neighbours are not politically stable. Egypt's President Sadat was gunned down in 1981, and his successor has difficulties in restraining Muslim fundamentalists who wish to make war on Israel. Syria and Libya are in the hands of unpredictable dictators who may be replaced at any time by others even less reliable. Lebanon, artificially created in the first place, has been a battleground for the past twenty years. Not so far away the Iraqi leader Saddam Hussein has been threatening Israel and has in recent years launched missile attacks on it. One of the few remaining factors for moderation in the area was removed with the death of the Jordanian King Hussein in 1999.

Hostility also comes from fundamentalist Muslim groups in Iran, Pakistan and Afghanistan. It is small wonder that many Israelis regard making a deal with the Arabs as a very dangerous policy. The right-wing Likud Party is generally reluctant to reach such a settlement, while the Israeli Labour Party concedes to it only with ill grace. Israel's most conservative and orthodox Jews, whose influence is growing, resolutely oppose any concessions at all. What unites all political groups is the question of Jerusalem, regarded since 1980 as Israel's historic capital. The Labour Party alone seems willing to consider some sort of partition or power-sharing there, while remaining aware that either of these courses could well involve political suicide. It has the same difficulties over restricting new Israeli settlements on the West Bank, where Likud will not raise a finger against them and every step the Labour Party takes to disown them transfers votes to their political opponents.

Above all looms the question of 700,000 Palestinian refugees. These abandoned their homes and settlements, some in 1947 and others in 1967. Jews and Arabs dispute whether the refugees were forced out by some form of ethnic cleansing, or whether they fled of their own accord to escape the war or to hold aloof from the Jews. Living in cramped and squalid conditions, the refugees present enormous problems. Their present camps are hotbeds of extremist violence, the lands and homes they abandoned left in Jewish hands for nearly half a century. Are the refugees now to return? Will such an influx swamp the electoral registers and undermine Israeli democracy? After all that has happened since 1947 can Jew and Arab be trusted to live side by side in peace and harmony?

From the Arab viewpoint: the Jewish claim to Palestine, dating back 2,000 years, is quite unacceptable. On such a basis Italy could claim ownership of all the lands of the Roman Empire, or Saxony the ownership of much of Britain. The Arabs resent not only the numbers of the massive Jewish immigration, but the manner in which it took place. Many Arabs accepted Jewish money when they sold out to the immigrants. Poor land that was bought cheaply has been transformed by hard work, skill and foreign capital into wealth beyond their imagining, leaving them feeling cheated as they see the capital value of their former holdings increase. Landless Arabs resent this, however legally it was brought about, and organisations dedicated to Arab solidarity and Muslim fundamentalism continue to foster this resentment. Though a number of Arab neighbours of Israel have come in the course of the last few years to accept Israel's existence, more populist Arab attitudes remain basically hostile to any reconciliation.

To the Arabs the most pressing problem is that of the Palestinian refugees. The Palestinians aim for a state far larger than the Gaza Strip and a few towns like Hebron. They want the return of the whole West Bank and with it Jerusalem; and they want the restoration of the refugees to their homes and the expulsion of the present Jewish occupants. Even if full possession of Jerusalem is denied them, the Palestinians expect to play a proper part in the affairs of the city.

But the Arabs have other concerns as well. The end of communism in the Soviet Union released a new flood of immigrants into Israel, many of whom settled on the West Bank, establishing illegal settlements. Although these settlements have been condemned by the United Nations, no serious steps have been taken by Israel, nor any serious pressure brought to bear by the US, to remove them. Indeed the ground is being cleared and new areas planted with each year that passes. In the light of this continuing provocation many Arabs feel disinclined to restrain the more militant extremists among them from continuing with their campaigns of rioting and violence. Thus Arab opinion is increasingly split between the official leadership under Yasser Arafat, prepared to negotiate with the Israelis, and more extremist groups who distrust Israeli promises and want no more truck with idle promises of future self-government. In these circumstances, extremist factions proliferate and Arafat is under pressure from his supporters and has increasing difficulty in responding to Israeli criticisms that he has lost control over his own followers and no longer represents them.

In the autumn of 2001 the forces of international terrorism, having in the previous year launched bomb attacks on a number of US embassies sited in African capitals, again prepared their weapons, and with the tacit approval of Muslim fundamentalists in a number of Asian countries began to threaten the stability of a diplomatic order they saw as dominated by Israeli and US imperialism. A number of organisations of extremists, one of which was *al-Qa'eda*, controlled and financed by Osama bin Laden from his secret headquarters in Afghanistan, organised the training of select armies of fanatical Muslim volunteers in terrorist suicide tactics and in biological and chemical warfare techniques. They struck at Israel's powerful ally in September 2001 when they brought off daring and catastrophically successful suicide bombings of the Pentagon in Washington and of the heart of the world money market in New York. It would not be an exaggeration to say that the shock waves generated by this formidable coup shook not only the United States, but the whole capitalist world to its foundations, revealing how fragile and exposed were their institutions, and foreshadowing the mounting of a systematic effort on the part of the major powers to defend themselves and their traditional world position against a wholly new type of threat – systematic and world-scale terrorism.

So, the prolonged existence of the controversy is seen to be due to the influence of irreconcilable extremism on both sides: orthodox Israeli conservatives on the one hand and militant Palestinian activists on the other, and behind them the faceless threat of anarchy and nihilism on a world scale. The Arabs want Israel to revert to its pre-1967 frontiers, and to set up a Palestinian state incorporating all the territory taken by Israel since 1948, further requiring that all those refugees ousted from these lands should be allowed to return there. Such demands are as unacceptable to the Israeli nation as were the earlier Arab demands for the utter extinction of Israel.

Orthodox Jews regard Palestine as their Zion, given to them by God, and so believe they have a God-given right to develop it and to people it for ever, whatever the obstacles. Neither side is willing to compromise. Compromise to orthodox Israelis means undermining Israel's existence as a nation; to the extremist Palestinians it means abandoning their just claims to their homeland and accepting the invading foreigner. Whatever moderate opinion on both sides may say, extreme opinions on both sides at present enjoy the more receptive audience; it is political suicide for any moderate to suggest otherwise. So hatred and suspicion cannot be swept away in a few days of peace talks, however well intentioned. A final settlement will be dependent on the rise of moderate wisdom; hence it will be difficult to achieve and long in coming.

The bigger and perhaps even more urgent threat arising from global Arab resentment is world terrorism. We have, at the beginning of the new millennium, just sat through the era of the nation state, a historical episode enduring for upwards of the 500 years since the end of the fifteenth century, with its very public features of legally controlled civil government, ordered society, regular armed forces using agreed methods of operation, international alliance systems and conventional diplomacy; and most established governments are now determined if they can to preserve this order, and to prevent the world sliding into the bottomless black hole of anarchy. The alternative is increasing globalisation in a borderless world dominated by large corporations and highly mobile labour forces.

13:5

Why Does the Irish Question Remain Unresolved?

Sellar and Yeatman, in their famous book 1066 And All That, *said with uncommon perception that the main reason why the Irish Question had never been solved was that whenever the English found the right answer the Irish very unsportingly changed the question!*

Unresolved Problems

Indeed, the Irish Question which has for so long plagued England has never remained the same question for very long, and this factor gives it its historic *if not its* historical *character.*

It was originally a *tribal* and even a *national* conflict between the Gaelic Irish chieftains and the conquering Norman knights from England. Norman knights were encouraged by Pope Hadrian IV (born Nicholas Breakspear, the only English Pope) who was indignant at the insubordination of the Irish bishops, and issued his Bull *Laudabiliter* with the aim of bringing them to heel. The Norman English set about a military conquest of Ireland in the reign of Henry II. Disunity between the Irish kings aided Henry's task. The dispute between the O'Connors and the MacMurroughs, kings respectively of Connaught and Leinster, provided him with an excuse, especially when Diarmuid MacMurrough fled to England and pledged feudal allegiance to Henry. The King therefore in 1170 sent a strong force of Norman knights under Richard FitzGilbert, known as Strongbow, to impose Norman order on Ireland. Landing on the Wexford coast, Strongbow besieged Waterford and captured Dublin without too much difficulty, and in due course Henry II received the homage and fealty of most of the Irish kings in a ceremony at the Rock of Cashel, County Tipperary. Though the Irish were subdued they were far from pacified. The building of Dublin castle and the fortifications surrounding other Irish towns and cities became symbols of an English predominance that has poisoned relations to this day. When Henry VIII dissolved the monasteries in 1547, the Irish, far removed from English influence, remained loyal to their Catholic roots.

So in the seventeenth century the Irish Question became principally a *religious* one. Elizabeth's wars in Ireland failed to quell disorder in the country, and under James I a systematic plantation of Ulster in 1611 took place by Scottish Presbyterian landlords in place of quarrelsome Catholic clan chieftains such as Tyrone and Tyrconnell. Their lands were declared forfeit after a rising in 1607. The new settlers showed themselves men of great energy, and in their hands Ulster, which had been the poorest and wildest, became the most prosperous province in Ireland, but a Presbyterian one, and the wrongs suffered by the dispossessed chieftains were never forgotten. This resentment was the basic cause of the Irish rebellion of 1641, on behalf of the crypto-Catholic Charles I of England against his Puritan opponents. Continuing Royalist disaffection in Ireland led to the appointment of Cromwell as Governor and Commander-in-Chief in 1649, from which there stemmed the bloody massacres at Drogheda and Wexford and the completion of the Cromwellian conquest. Though Cromwell and his Puritan lieutenants were driven by the purest and most sincere of Protestant beliefs, their conduct was brutal and merciless, and their memory is hated to this day by the bulk of Irish Catholic. The later years of the century witnessed no improvement in the lot of the Irish Catholics. In 1690 the Catholic James II, gathering the support of his loyal Irish followers, marched to defeat at the battle of the Boyne, vanquished by the Protestant William of Orange, recently made King William III of England.

Although it was in violation of the generous promises made under the Treaty of Limerick in 1691, the subjugation of Irish Catholics was carried even further by the imposition of a savage Penal Code in the eighteenth century, discriminating against the continued practice of their faith. Irish Catholics were forbidden to enter the learned professions, to carry arms, to educate their children as Catholics or to purchase or to inherit land. No Catholic was allowed to own a horse worth more than a hundred shillings (£5), and Catholic chapels were not to have steeples lest their bells be used to call for men to rebel. Dean Swift, himself a Protestant, observed in 1724 that: 'The Catholics are become hewers of wood and drawers of water to their conquerors.' The end of the century brought the final abolition of the Irish parliament and the enforced union of the two countries in 1800.

Conscientious efforts were made by Ireland's English masters in the nineteenth century to remedy the grievances of the Catholics. They were politically emancipated in 1829, and thereafter Catholic schools and colleges were set up and grants increased to Ireland's leading seminary. In 1869 Ireland's Protestant Church was disestablished and much of the money from its endowments devoted to the relief of poverty. Unfortunately these concessions could not conceal the fact that Ireland was a backward and poverty-stricken country. In the middle 1840s it went through the trauma of the Potato Famine, which reduced its population by getting on for 50 per cent. England did what it could to bring in improvements such as railway-building to facilitate the marketing of Irish produce, but much of the country remained sunk in lethargy and want, and leading Irish figures such as C.S. Parnell believed that what the government did was always too little and too late. The question now became a party political one. The British government made three serious efforts to grant Home Rule to the Irish, but this succeeded only in hopelessly splitting the main English political parties and preventing an agreed solution. Hence a movement began to grow pressing for full independence for Ireland under the leadership of Sinn Fein, the 'Ourselves Alone' party. The conflict culminated in the Dublin Rising of 1916 and of an Irish civil war when the First World War ended. By this time, the Fourth Home Rule Bill has been passed into law, and a Northern Irish state still linked with Britain had been set up in accordance with most of its inhabitants' wishes.

Thus was ushered in what might broadly be described as the Northern Ireland Question, the most recent phase of the Irish Question. There was no doubt that Northern Ireland was, and still is, an artificial British creation. The resistance of the Ulstermen to Home Rule had begun at the time of the Third Home Rule Bill when, as Unionists, they declared their determination to remain under British rule. They were in alliance with the British Conservative Party, and this led to near civil war in the north. Lloyd George, the British Prime Minister, attempting after the war to honour Britain's commitment to Irish self-government, found himself opposed by the Conservative majority in his coalition government. The only way he could overcome their entrenched opposition was to allow the Northern Irish Protestants to break away and remain under the British Crown. So the six counties of Ulster with the largest Protestant populations were detached from the remainder of Ireland. They remained British, with their own parliament at Stormont, while the rest of Ireland achieved virtual independence, the last vestiges of British sovereignty being swept away by 1939.

This situation was never fully accepted by the Irish nationalists. They wanted a united Ireland. The Irish Republican Army, while only a minority within the nationalist community, could see no hope of winning Northern Ireland by democratic means, and had resorted to terrorist violence even before the Second World War. The Northern Ireland Protestants developed an even stronger sense of community, using the Orange Order to safeguard its position by discriminating against Catholics in housing and jobs, by fraudulent voting and by gerrymandering local government boundaries.

It was hardly surprising that the Civil Rights movements that sprang up in the later 1960s in so many parts of the world should have a strong appeal for Northern Ireland's Catholic minority. In 1968 Civil Rights protests began. They were not, at first, exclusively Catholic and Protestant. But what began as peaceful protest soon turned violent, and led to the breakdown of law and order. Sectarianism reared its head: mixed communities became subject to sectarian cleansing, where the minority of one faith was subjected to such intimidation that houses and in some cases whole streets were abandoned. Districts where Protestants and Catholics had lived side by side in comparative harmony became exclusively Protestant or Roman Catholic. British troops were sent to maintain order. They soon came to be regarded by the nationalist community as an occupying force, and IRA murders of British troops began. The IRA also targeted prominent Protestants and members of the Northern Irish Constabulary. Explosions and bombings killed indiscriminately. Protestant extremists organised themselves into paramilitary groups and began revenge killings of Catholics. Stormont was divided and helpless; it was replaced by direct British rule in 1972.

Since then the number of deaths in the province has exceeded 4,000. Some tragedies, such as 'Bloody Sunday' (Londonderry, 1972) embittered the Roman Catholics; others, such as Enniskillen (1987), embittered the Protestants. The IRA extended its terrorist campaign beyond Northern Ireland, as for example when it killed Lord Mountbatten in the Irish Republic in 1979, and tried to wipe out Margaret Thatcher's whole Cabinet at the Conservative Party Conference in Brighton in 1984.

Various attempts have been made since 1972 to bring peace to Northern Ireland, some involving close cooperation between the London and the Dublin governments. So far they have had limited success. Violence breeds entrenched positions. Most Northern Irishmen yearn for peace. But a substantial minority of Catholics support the IRA and Sinn Fein who will accept nothing short of a united Ireland in the long term. So the IRA spurned democratic initiatives and, until 1998, continued its campaign of violence, supported and largely financed from overseas by those who mistakenly believed that there was in Northern Ireland a large Catholic majority brutally held down by force by the British government. Its political wing, Sinn Fein, does not condemn terrorism, though it does on occasions find it politically expedient to distance itself from it. The Protestants can afford, because of their majority, to flourish their democratic credentials – yet are determined to remain British and will accept no solution which appears to place them under the rule of Dublin. In the meantime, their paramilitaries continue their tit-for-tat murders, and Orangemen insisted on their traditional marching routes celebrating the 300-year-old victories of William III, even when these take them through areas which were formerly Protestant but no longer so. The British government has declared that it is committed to keeping Northern Ireland British, unless and until a majority of the population wills it otherwise.

Finally, on Good Friday 1998 the politicians arrived at a compromise that would retain British sovereignty but would allow Dublin some say in the affairs of Northern Ireland through cross-border bodies. The Protestant political parties were prepared reluctantly to accept this, thinking that the agreement guaranteed the continuance of British rule in the province; while the nationalists also accepted it, seeing it as a major step along the inevitable road to a united Ireland. Extremists on both sides continued terrorism for some time after the agreement, but the Omagh bombing, in August 1998, when twenty-nine people were killed and hundreds injured, caused such revulsion that most – even of the extremists – renounced violence.

The chief remaining difficulty seemed on the face of things capable of solution, but in practice proved quite intractable. The elections held in Northern Ireland in June 1998 produced a result much as was expected: the Unionists had a solid majority (though somewhat smaller than originally predicted) and the nationalists held a minority of seats. One of the conditions for the Good Friday agreement had been the military disarmament of both sides: the Unionists said *before* a joint executive was formed, it being a point of principle that parties committed to democratic procedures should demonstrate their good faith by abandoning their weapons; while the nationalists, even at this late date suspecting sharp practice on the part of their adversaries, refused to disarm until *after* the joint executive came into being. They succeeded in securing the release of large numbers of terrorist detainees, but could not get agreement on the disarmament issue. Various attempts were made to run the two processes in parallel, but without success. The best the nationalists could offer was disarmament to be completed about Easter 2000, but the Unionists were deeply sceptical of this offer. Proposals, likewise, after the Patten Report, to rename and reform the Ulster Constabulary met with resistance from both sides. Meantime, the joint executive promised for Easter 2000 was established, suspended and re-established again by the middle of the year 2000.

The year 2001 saw the continuance of extremism and bigotry on both sides, with the provincial Northern Ireland parliament teetering on the brink of collapse. The stalemate continued, with sporadic assassinations and bomb outrages perpetrated by both sides in turn, and with the Catholics blocking Protestant marching routes in the Orange ceremonies because they passed along 'their' roads, and Protestants blocking the route of Catholic schoolgirls to primary school because they were walking along 'their' streets to school. The Unionist parties demanded the exclusion of Sinn Fein deputies from the assembly unless they embarked immediately on public and effective disarmament, while Sinn Fein accused the Unionists of trying to sabotage the agreement, and offered if not to disarm, at least to put its armaments 'verifiably beyond use'. Each side argued that the deadlock was due to the equivocations and to the bad faith of the other. Both remained intransigent.

So it remains to be seen whether the Good Friday agreement can be the foundation of a permanent settlement in Northern Ireland. The auguries are not good. The demand of the nationalists for a united Ireland brooks no compromise: if they revive the struggle because progress towards their objective is too slow, their opponents would have every reason to fight back, since they have never really believed what the nationalists have been saying. If, on the other hand, the Unionists suspect that the nationalists are merely feigning disarmament and are not sincere in their profession of democratic principles, the Unionists may renounce the whole peace process. The two sides have adopted irreconcilable positions. What each finds acceptable and necessary the other finds absolutely out of the question. The temptation to the British government – sometimes articulated by outside observers – to abdicate its responsibilities for this troubled corner of the United Kingdom and leave the two sides to fight out an answer for themselves is resolutely resisted. It is not only deeply immoral and offensive to civilised opinion, but would increase violence rather than resolve it. The government of the Irish Republic also has responsibilities towards the whole Irish nation and feels obliged to offer its participation. However much Britain and Ireland may regret it, and however much the moderates of both sides may sicken of the killing and yearn for the restoration of peace and order, the declared attitudes of both Unionists and nationalists are not amenable to further compromise. The wishes of the majority are thus of no account and, until something changes, a solution to this phase of the Irish Question remains beyond human devising.

13:6

Did Tony Blair Betray British Socialism?

It is sometimes said that, in the course of the 1990s, Tony Blair emasculated or else totally destroyed the British Labour movement, removing its whole raison d'être *by perverting the purposes it was designed to serve, and redefining its aims to the point of extinguishing them. Such criticisms come not only from his opponents but also – even more vociferously – from his supporters. How far is it justified to lay the blame for the decline of traditional British socialism at the door of Tony Blair?*

In spite of many protestations to the contrary, historically it is doubtful whether the British Labour Party was ever truly socialist. Evolving in the late nineteenth century as a loose coalition of disparate groups engaged in improving the condition of the working classes, its roots were mainly planted in the ideas of the English radical movement, of the Chartists, and of the gradualist movement headed by the Fabian Society. There was also a strong religious influence from the Nonconformist Church – Methodism was always far more important than Marxism. Nevertheless, under the influence of thinkers such as G.D.H. Cole, who stressed the need for worker control of industry, R.H. Tawney, who demanded greater class equality, and later Harold Laski, who endorsed public ownership as a means of diminishing class tensions, the Labour Party, anxious in part to give itself a distinctive definition setting it apart from the Liberal Party, moved towards dogmatic socialism in its 1918 Constitution. In Clause IV of the document it stated its aim: 'To secure for the producers by hand and by brain the full fruits of their industry, and the most equitable distribution thereof that may be possible, upon the basis of the common ownership of the means of production and the best obtainable system of popular administration and control of each industry and service.'

For such a party, capitalism represented an evil system based on wasteful and destructive competition. A truly socialist system could not be established until cooperation replaced competition, and private ownership became public. Labour's election manifesto in 1945 set out a 'shopping list' of industries to be nationalised – coal, steel, the railways and other basic industries – as the first step towards the peaceful, democratic creation of a planned socialist state.

The idea of the planned society never worked. After 1960, when Clause IV was effectively abandoned by all except a few traditionalists and intellectuals, little more was heard of it. Why was this? Partly it was because the system of public ownership that it brought was in practice little different from the former system of private ownership and management. The workers were now employed by different bosses who continued to operate the industries in the old way and, since many of them – like coal and transport – were in terminal decline, came to be chiefly engaged in running them down and finally dismantling them, contrary to the workers' wishes. A second reason was that, at bottom, the trade unions, the Labour Party's main supporters, did not genuinely believe in planning, but in a modified form of private enterprise, which left them free to pursue their own wage objectives and to resist direction of labour, price controls and the other paraphernalia of planning. So at an early date the Attlee government was obliged to abandon the notion of physical planning in favour of economic management, using instead as its main tools instruments of the fiscal kind – tinkering with the bank rate, using export incentives and import quotas – and attempting freezes on prices and wages in order to achieve their broad objectives. Hence the whole apparatus of the Wilson era in the 1960s – the Ministry of Technology (Mintech), the Prices and

Incomes Board, the Monopolies and Mergers Commission, the Department of Economic Affairs, and all that went to make up the statutory enforcement of George Brown's 'National Plan' – were little more than window-dressing, and there was no real effort to impose a planned, socialist economy on Britain.

But the final reason for this steady loss of faith in planning was that, by 1990, the whole system of a command economy and publicly operated industry was shown to be completely bankrupt. Even the Soviet Union crumbled and finally collapsed. At that point, the inability of a 'command economy' to bear all the strains that political expectation imposed on it suddenly became glaringly obvious. People stopped believing in socialism for the simple and sufficient reason that it did not work.

How did the decay of socialism affect the fortunes of the Labour Party? One of the results was that the party, in its election manifestos, began to lay less importance on policies leading to the creation of a command economy. Even as early as 1970, for example, the party had begun to stress the importance of a 'mixed economy' rather than one completely directed by the state: 'It is our purpose to develop a new relationship with both sides of industry, in which the forward plans of both Government and industry can be increasingly harmonised in the interests of economic growth. In the public and private sectors, industrial enterprises are paying increasing attention to medium- and long-term planning.'

The party also reverted to its former traditions by spending less time on such Marxist notions, and reverting to its earlier ideology of equality and social justice, both of them rather loosely defined. Hugh Gaitskell had stressed this aspect of the party's work in a speech in 1958, when he said: 'The central socialist ideal is equality. By this I do not mean identical incomes or uniform habits and tastes. But I do mean a classless society . . . one in which, though people develop differently, there is equal opportunity for all to develop.'

In practice, the policy of equal opportunity implied the provision of a state system of benefits to eliminate the most obvious forms of poverty and social inequality, together with a system of universal state-provided education to replace the various distinct forms of private education existing at that time. Hence welfare policies were at the centre of their work. As the 1970 election manifesto put it, the party aimed to take care of 'the widowed mother with children, the chronically sick, the unemployed, and the millions of old age pensioners without adequate superannuation'. At the same time, Labour's education policy was seen as 'the best way to develop a society based on tolerance, cooperation and greater social equality'.

Hence the idea of a *caring*, and even a *classless* society tended to replace policies which envisaged a *planned* society. However, circumstances forced a retreat even from these objectives. Social engineering as a means of achieving equality and justice began steadily to fade. On the one hand, the prohibitive cost of providing universal benefits was so great that Labour found itself forced to adopt in power in 1997 the same economy measures that it had deplored while in opposition; on the other hand it found itself compelled to concede in the name of 'freedom of choice' for parents the continuance of private schooling, and an added lease of life for selective education instead of comprehensive. The other measures, which they had resisted in opposition, e.g. streamlining and improving the National Health Service, they also took over from the Conservatives, sometimes changing them by title only, sometimes not at all, but merely suggesting that they would carry them into effect more efficiently than their predecessors. In their anxiety to capture and retain middle-class support they had to acquiesce in the preservation of those middle-class 'perks' – such as private health insurance and private schooling – that argued the continuance of social inequalities based largely on wealth. For this and similar reasons, trade unionists and other traditional labour supporters began to question the direction in which they now seemed to be moving, and began to wonder what had induced them to give their votes and their support to Blair's 'New Labour'.

Even Labour intellectuals began to feel disillusioned with the new government. 'New Labour' ministers either turned against – or worse still completely ignored – their cherished theories.

They turned their backs on 'child-centred' education, but instead proposed to publish exam results, to lay stress on reading and writing, and to ensure that children did their homework. They refused to accept that children's homes are preferable to adoption by parents whose colour, class or principles are not exactly in accord with the accepted view. They began to talk about punishments and penalties for wrongdoers instead of blaming society for crime. Such lack of proper conviction was hard for militant trade unionists, progressive teachers or politically correct social workers to accept. Life had been bad enough for the intellectuals when the Tories told them to use their common sense; but the thought that the Labour Party were now telling them the very same thing was particularly galling to their self-esteem.

One of Blair's critics, writing in the left-wing magazine *Marxism Today*, took him to task for being too interested in capturing the admiration of the *glitterati*, and for being essentially superficial in his attitudes. He was accused of setting out the case for and against a suggested reform, using the highest of moral language, but then failing to give a lead on it. Instead he was said to slip into the easy suggestion that he was looking for a third way 'towards politics without adversaries'. So Blair was dismissed as the 'Nowhere Man', without deep ideological roots, given to posing, generalising and evading the uncomfortable issue; a man who was essentially a post-Thatcherite figure, of whom it is said that 'his experience of Thatcherism was his main formative political experience'.* Even those less critical of Blair's leadership sometimes admit that as a leader he tends to be stronger on strategy than on tactics: better, that is, on making broad policy statements than on the day-to-day details of political management. He seems often to have a clear vision of where his policies are leading, but hesitates and equivocates over the practical steps for reaching his goal. Perhaps his popularity means too much to him.

---

* Indeed, a quote attributed to his former Northern Ireland Secretary, Peter Mandelson, held that 'We are all Thatcherites now.' (June 2002)

Some of this criticism seems to be justified. The fact that Blair won a second election in 2001 almost as emphatically as he won his first in 1997 was much more due to the errors and the divisions of the Conservative Party than it was to the strength of Labour. In fact those who had believed that, being split over Europe, only the Tories were an obstacle in the way of the country's future, found to their dismay that the Labour Party hedged its bets in just the same way. Radicals who looked for a firmer, clearer lead on the common currency or on closer integration with Europe found exactly the same hesitancy that they had deplored under John Major's divided Cabinet. The same ignorance of the issues, or the same vested interest on the outcome of the decision, divided the Labour Party as it had divided the Conservatives. At the same time, those less favourably inclined to European solutions found themselves fobbed off with Gordon Brown's insistence on the fulfilment of the 'five necessary conditions of membership' before Britain joined, when they would have much preferred him to give a straight 'no'. Other policy issues, such as health spending, education and social welfare, supposedly so much closer to the hearts of British voters, are in fact also contingent on a clear sense of political direction, and on Britain's being in a position to afford them, and hence are not separate from the question of Europe, but linked with that same economic prosperity and international status.

It is perhaps not too much to say that the European issue is of such importance that it overshadows all the others and demands a much more central position in public debate. Other more exclusively political policies fade almost into insignificance. The abolition of the House of Lords, that venerable banner around which the forces of Labour can unhesitatingly unite, is almost as anachronistic as that House itself; while proportional representation, which some left-wingers have come to support as a means of recovering something of their former position as a unified socialist parliamentary grouping, and political devolution, giving power to Scottish or Welsh assemblies and restoring a parliament to Northern Ireland, are both arguments about political *means* rather than political *ends*. These seem to be the distinguishing marks of a party that does not know where it is going, but is marking time, offering instead only vague ideals for a future utopia; worse still, of a party with a completely open mind that is merely biding its time to see the way the wind is blowing.

Tony Blair has to confront, and to respond to, these criticisms. Of course, he is not personally responsible for the decline of socialist ideals, any more than he is for world economic trends or for recent international developments, but his current position at the centre of power thrusts on him the responsibility for devising new policies to deal with all these things. No one begrudges him his obvious love of the limelight; all that is required of him is that he performs in it with greater and more permanent effect.

13.7

Was Prime Minister Blair naïve or dishonest over his War in Iraq?

The problem created by the Anglo-American invasion of Iraq, and the consequences of this effort at a 'régime change' there, have created more international controversy than its originators ever intended. It is the continuing rumbling of this problem which gives this Near Eastern episode its historic if not its historical character.

When Britain and the USA invaded Iraq in March 2003 Prime Minister Blair secured the support of a large majority in the House of Commons by insisting that the war was to enforce the Resolutions of the United Nations and to remove Iraq's threat both to its neighbours and to the world in general. There were protests from a small minority of the Labour members, and the Liberal Democrats refused to support the government on the grounds that the war lacked a mandate from the United Nations. But within weeks of the invasion the good faith of the government was called into question. It was alleged that the government had secured the vote for war by 'sexing up'(i.e.

exaggerating the importance of) the intelligence dossier of September 2002 which provided the main evidence against Iraq. The inquiry by Lord Hutton found the government innocent, and laid the blame for the unfounded allegation firmly at the door of the media, in particular the BBC. Lord Hutton had not considered it his brief to enquire into the accuracy of the intelligence information, only whether the government had distorted it. It was Lord Butler's inquiry reporting in July 2004 which tackled that second question, criticising the unreliability of the intelligence, but absolving both the intelligence services and the government of any responsibility for its inaccuracy and misuse. Both inquiries and reports left unanswered the major questions: if the government was unaware of the unreliability of the intelligence, then the Joint Intelligence Committee should have made it aware, so the government was incompetent in not probing the J.I.C more searchingly. And if the government was aware of its unreliability then the government was dishonest in its use of the evidence.

By almost universal consent Saddam Hussein would be ranked high on the list of the most vile and revolting dictators. On coming to power he disposed of many of his opponents by judicial murder, and did not hesitate to subject rivals within the Ba'ath party to the same treatment. He was not unique in suppressing dissident nationalities, but his use of cyanide and mustard gas against the Kurds in Helabjeh in 1988 was only surpassed in depravity by Hitler; others, like Stalin and Pol Pot may have exceeded him in numbers killed but he had the edge over them in method. His unprovoked attack on Kuwait in 1990 brought universal condemnation, even from Arab neighbours professing friendship, and the public executions in Kuwait City were broadcast to the world on television and aroused widespread horror. Coalition forces with United Nations' backing liberated Kuwait in 1991. Saddam was forced to agree to 'no-fly' zones over Northern Iraq, policed by American and British planes, and he was to give up biological weapons and abandon his attempts to become a nuclear power. Nor was he to manufacture or stockpile long-range missiles. Inspection teams were to have free access to all of Iraq, and to seek out and destroy any weapons or raw materials that contravened these terms. United Nations' sanctions were imposed to bring Saddam to heel, and to prevent him interfering with the free access of the weapons inspection teams. Saddam co-operated only desultorily; sometimes he was positively obstructive. Eventually the arms inspectors were expelled altogether. The sanctions bit hard, and although Iraqi oil could be exported in exchange for medical supplies and other limited essentials the quality of life in Iraq sharply declined and corruption at the top ensured that Iraqi hospitals were desperately short of essential medical supplies. Meanwhile the weapons' inspection teams found no great quantity of any of the banned weapons and materials, and it was widely assumed that Saddam had hidden them well. Nevertheless there was no specific intelligence to this effect.

The al Qa'eda attack on the New York Trade Centre on September 11, 2001, precipitated President Bush's crusade against international terrorism. He was angry with Saddam for his half-crazed plotting to assassinate former President George Bush (senior), who had been President at the time of 'Operation Desert Storm' in 1991. Such schemes were not unique to rogue states; the CIA had long plotted the extermination of Fidel Castro. But in his 'axis of evil' speech President Bush (junior) seemed to be implying a link between terrorists such as al Qa'eda and Saddam Hussein; it was not stated explicitly, but many were convinced by it. Why Saddam, leader of a secular Iraq, should want to encourage a militant Islamic fundamentalism that would undermine his own régime was never explained.

Saddam's expulsion of the United Nations' weapons inspectors in 1998 had convinced the world that Saddam had something to hide. Saddam's denials that Iraq possessed weapons of mass destruction were treated with contempt and disbelief, and although the weapons inspectors were eventually allowed back into Iraq their failure to find such weapons was generally attributed both to the skill of the Iraqis in concealing them, and to the difficulties under which the inspectors worked. On September 24, 2002 Britain's Joint Intelligence

Committee (J.I.C.) submitted a report to the Cabinet in which generalisations were made about Iraq's aims and capabilities, and in which it was specifically stated that Iraq was ready and able to use weapons of mass destruction within 45 minutes of the decision taken to use them. On the day of publication Tony Blair told M.Ps that the contribution of the intelligence agencies was *extensive, detailed and authoritative,* an assertion which Lord Butler's Report was later to question. This September JIC dossier was to form the intelligence basis upon which Britain was to go to war six months later. In the meantime the weapons inspectors, finding nothing but convinced there was something to find, became exasperated by Iraq's attitude, which varied from lukewarm co-operation to deliberate obstruction. The chief inspector, Dr. Hans Blix, asked for more time. But even the United Nations Security Council felt that too much extra time would merely encourage Saddam to continue to prevaricate. In Resolution No. 1441, agreed by the Security Council in November 2002, it

recognises the threat that Iraq's non-compliance with Council resolutions and the proliferation of weapons of mass destruction and long-range missiles poses to international peace

and proceeded to threaten *serious consequences* if its resolutions continued to be ignored. Whatever was meant by *serious consequences,* on the basis of this resolution the USA and Britain threatened Saddam with war if he did not at once produce for inspection and disposal the said weapons. For four months there was much sabre-rattling as Britain and the USA attempted to garner support for their intended war. With the failure of Germany and France to support them it was impossible to obtain a Security Council resolution for war, and this failure made the war illegal to those individuals and to the several countries which would not support it. Unable to win the support of the United Nations, Britain and the USA decided to act on their own. Blair's decision to give Bush (junior) unqualified support for the war has been attributed to various motives. 'Greed for oil' has been among the more fanciful. But far more probable was Blair's desire to stand shoulder to shoulder with Britain's most powerful ally, and to share in the international kudos accruing from a joint stand, far better than playing second fiddle to Germany and France from within the EU. Both Labour and Conservative politicians have long shared the great delusion that, despite the loss of Empire, Britain still has a great role to play on the international stage. Blair's righteous conviction that UN resolutions must not be defied with impunity seems a rather hollow explanation of his stand in view of *Israel*'s notorious defiance of UN resolutions and the UN's own reluctance to enforce them. But he probably had a genuine belief – derived from faulty intelligence information – that Saddam constituted a threat not only to the stability of the Middle East but also to the wider world. Whatever his motives it was difficult for Blair to avoid being depicted in parts of the media as 'President Bush's poodle'. The vote in the British House of Commons for war was boosted by Conservative support. The Conservative leader Ian Duncan Smith had a private interview with Tony Blair at 10 Downing Street which appeared to convince him of the necessity and justice of the war. Many people felt that Blair had made Duncan Smith privy to secret intelligence information not contained in the September dossier and which it would not be prudent to reveal to the public. The Liberal Democrats, however, and a number of Labour M.P.s, refused to support the war so Conservative support was vital. The war began in March 2003 and formal military operations were over by May.

The invading armies faced little resistance and found no weapons of mass destruction. It was widely rumoured that two Iraqi ships had left Basra two or three days before the invasion laden to the gunwales with heavy but concealed cargoes bound probably for Pakistan. Did they contain the banned weaponry? We shall never know: the story of the ships passed into mythology, and they certainly never made an Asian port. So since the Iraqis had not deployed their WMDs (weapons of mass destruction) within the 45 minutes mentioned in JIC dossier, and indeed had not deployed them at all, voices began to be raised about the origin and accuracy of the 45-minute claim. At the end of May Andrew Gilligan, a BBC defence reporter, began alleging that the September dossier had been 'sexed up' in order to convince doubting politicians and a doubting public of the justification for war. Gilligan repeated his allegation in June, this time asserting that the Prime Minister's press secretary, Alastair Campbell, had been responsible for inserting the 45-minute claim. Gilligan repeated before the foreign affairs Select Committee this assertion which Campbell, appearing before the same committee a week later, vigorously denied. Gilligan refused to reveal his source but hinted that it came from high up in the intelligence services. But the media were given enough clues by the Ministry of Defence to identify Dr. David Kelly , a former weapons inspector, as the source from whom Gilligan obtained his material. Since Dr. Kelly was not in the intelligence services but a minor official in the Defence Ministry without an office or even a desk of his own, it was presumed that a higher source must have been involved. The foreign affairs Select Committee of the House of Commons summoned Dr. Kelly before it and subjected him to a gruelling cross-examination. Labour M.Ps in particular gave Dr. Kelly a roasting; they must have felt that to protect Blair they must humiliate Kelly. On the day of his last appearance before the committee Dr.Kelly committed suicide.

Dr. Kelly's death was an embarrassment to the government, which a few days later set up an inquiry under Lord Hutton, a former Lord of Appeal, to look into the circumstances of his death. In the meantime the BBC and Alastair Campbell engaged in a war of words, and Campbell, now the subject of intense press hostility resigned while still protesting his innocence of Gilligan's charges. Lord Hutton reported at the end of January 2004. Lord Hutton agreed that some minor changes were made to the intelligence dossier at Alastair Campbell's suggestion; nevertheless Campbell was absolved of the charge of adding the 45-minute reference. This, Hutton said, was inserted before Campbell had made any changes to the dossier. Lord Hutton did not blame any individual for Dr. Kelly's death, but he did criticise the BBC for its attack on the *integrity of the government and the Joint Intelligence Committee*, and for its uncritical backing of Gilligan. On the issue of Dr. Kelly Hutton had no doubt that he had expressed reservations to Gilligan about the content of the September dossier and that Gilligan had put his own slant on his conversations with Kelly. It is most likely that Kelly queried some of the dossier's general conclusions. It was unlikely he did more, since he had no access to information that would have allowed him to challenge any specific evidence it contained. On the day the Hutton Report was issued the BBC chairman, Gavyn Davies, resigned, and on the following day Greg Dyke, the BBC Director-General followed suit. Gilligan managed to hang on for only a few more days. As Hutton absolved the government of responsibility for the 45 minute reference it must have been inserted while the dossier was still in the hands of the Joint Intelligence Committee and before it was submitted to the Cabinet. Lord Hutton declared that his terms of reference related specifically to the circumstances of Dr.Kelly's death and the allegations against the government made by Gilligan and the BBC. It was not his brief to cover the issue of the reliability of the September dossier for how the government built up the case for war.

So the government faced increasing media and political clamour for a separate investigation into the reliability of the intelligence information contained in the dossier. Iraq is a large country and the WMDs could well be waiting to be discovered. But by the summer of 2004 even those politicians in Britain and America who had favoured the war most strongly were now not expecting any WMDs to be found and were saying so publicly. It was with considerable reluctance that the British government established a new inquiry headed by Lord Butler, a respected establishment figure and former Cabinet Secretary. He was to judge the reliability of the evidence contained in the September dossier, but as an establishment figure he was not expected (by the media at any rate) to be too censorious of those in high places. He reported surprisingly quickly in late July 2004. The

Butler Report was highly critical of the methods of MI6. It had had no agents in Iraq, yet it relied on information from sources hostile to Saddam, and this information had not been cross-checked for accuracy or reliability. In the original dossier the JIC had expressed doubts about the reliability of the evidence upon which the judgments of the dossier was based, but when the dossier reached the Cabinet the 'caveats' had been removed. Blair was to claim that the removal of the 'caveats' did not materially alter the judgments of the JIC's report (that Saddam was a bad lot?), and anyway the 'caveats' had been removed in the preparation stage before the government became involved. As for the 45-minute claim, this referred not to long-range but to short-range missiles, and this was not made clear at the time either to parliament or the public. So who neglected to clarify the 45-minute claim? Butler does not say; presumably he could not find out. And did the dossier lose its 'caveats' in order to please the politicians? The culpability can rest only lightly on the shoulders of the JIC, since Butler specifically recommended that the promotion of John Scarlett, chairman of the JIC, to be Head of MI6 should still go ahead. But there seems to have been some crucial failure of duty in all this; Butler accepted Blair's good faith, and in so doing seems to suggest that on the crucial issue of whether or not to go to war he was served by incompetents.

The complicity of the Attorney-General, Lord Goldsmith (himself a Blair appointee), whose advice was sought on the matter of the legality of the war, has also been blamed for Britain's error in going to war 'on a faulty prospectus'. In fact, being a lawyer, he was careful to offer advice – opaque, and in any case later completely revised – to the Prime Minister, advice which finished by suggesting that the legality of the war did not finally depend on the passing of a second UN resolution in favour of it. He also asserted that the 'serious consequences' threatened by the Security Council in Resolution 1441 could be interpreted as including those consequences which involved the British and American 'police action'. If his advice was as reliable as Blair said he believed, the doctrine it enshrined certainly rewrote the meaning of Article 51 of the UN Charter, which clearly limited 'the inherent right of self-defence' to the occurrence of 'an armed attack against a member of the United Nations' – and, even then, only until 'the Security Council has taken measures necessary to maintain international peace and security.' No amount of judicial word-play could ever have suggested that Saddam Hussein had attacked (or indeed *could* attack) Britain and the United States; or that the Security Council was willing to undertake armed action against his 'acts of aggression'. Prime Minister Blair scarcely needed legal advice to tell him something so obvious.

So Britain seems to have been bounced into war on faulty judicial advice and inaccurate intelligence information. To what extent was the government aware of this, and how far was it prepared to gloss over the shaky intelligence in order to please Bush? Butler said that intelligence played only a *limited* role in determining the legality of the war. But its legality was not at the time satisfactorily determined; indeed, Prime Minister Blair did not reveal the nature of the Attorney-General's advice until the eve of the 2005 General Election. And, in spite of what Lord Goldsmith said, Security Council Resolution 1441 could *not* be extended to provide an adequate pretext for war.

And then there is the question of 'sexing up'. Hutton absolved the government of this charge. But if removing the 'caveats' is not 'sexing up' it is difficult to know what is, even if those who removed them failed to appreciate the significance of their removal. Dr. Kelly's death was a regrettable side effect of a conscientious man's efforts to provide the press with the truth, even if Gilligan's attempt to blame Blair for the 'sexing up' was his own gloss on Dr. Kelly's information. Who and for what reasons omitted the 'caveats'? It seems to have been the JIC, and if so why did it not report the doubts concerning those aspects of the dossier to the Cabinet? And since it seems that the Conservatives were persuaded to vote for the government on the basis of evidence that was faulty, their new leader Michael Howard's statement that had he known he would not have supported the government hardly deserved the fury of some Labour M.P.s, at least one of whom described Howard's statement as 'cynical political opportunism'. The weakness of Howard's assault on the Prime Minister in the Butler debate seems to reinforce the air of mystery that hangs over Ian Duncan Smith's pre-war visit to Downing Street.

Saddam Hussein will have had cause, in his prison cell, to regret how ineffective allied intelligence was. His probable game of bluff - denial of the existence of WMDs to be disbelieved in Iraq to bolster the régime, and believed by the UN in order to stave off a war he had no resources to fight - backfired in a way he could not have anticipated. Better intelligence would have meant no war. If, after all, Blair was involved in sharpening up the September dossier by omitting the 'caveats' and then using it to obtain a favourable parliamentary vote for war – an allegation he continues to deny – then the whole episode is a clear abuse of the democratic process and a monstrous (but an entirely characteristic) miscalculation on the part of the Prime Minister. If, on the other hand, government and opposition alike were misled by doctored intelligence information, doctored by person or persons unknown within the JIC, and if the government relied on faulty, and reluctantly divulged, judicial advice from its own Attorney-General, then the whole episode betrays more naivety, more contempt for international law, more scorn for the British democratic process, and more bungling incompetence than the Prime Minister would ever admit. Neither option reflects much credit on the probity or the principles of New Labour.

BIBLIOGRAPHY

There follow two booklists: the first a General List for the student and more serious general reader, the second a Reference List, which comprises references to some of the many texts used by the authors in the compilation of this book.

General Booklist

British History

Gash, Norman, *Aristocracy and People: Britain 1815–1865* (Edward Arnold, London, 1979)

Gregg, Pauline, *A Social and Economic History of Britain, 1760–1972* (Harrap, London, 1973)

James, R.R., *The British Revolution: British Politics 1890–1939* (Methuen, London 1977)

Langford, Paul, *England, 1727–1783*, (OUP, 1989)

Mowat, Charles Loch, *Britain between the Wars, 1918–1940* (Methuen, London, 1959)

Oxford series:

Steven Watson, J., *The Reign of George III* (Clarendon Press, Oxford, 1960)

Woodward, E.L., *The Age of Reform, 1815–1870* (Clarendon Press, Oxford, 1954)

Ensor, R.C.K., *England, 1870–1914* (Clarendon Press, Oxford, 1952)

Taylor, A.J.P., *English History, 1914–1945* (Clarendon Press, Oxford, 1965)

Read, Donald, *England, 1868–1914, The Age of Urban Democracy* (Longman, London, 1979)

Seaman, L.C.B., *Victorian England: Aspects of English and Imperial History, 1837–1901* (Methuen, London, 1973)

Seaman, L.C.B., *Post-Victorian Britain, 1902–1951* (Methuen, London, 1966)

Bibliography

Empire and Commonwealth
McIntyre, W.D., *Colonies Into Commonwealth* (Blandford, London, 1966)
Miller, J.D.B., *The Commonwealth and the World* (Duckworth, London, 1965)
Watson, Jack, *Empire to Commonwealth, 1919–1970* (Dent, London, 1970)

European History
Blandford History series:
    Leslie, R.F., *The Age of Transformation, 1789–1871* (London, 1975)
    Western, J.W., *The End of the European Primacy, 1871–1945* (London, 1965)
Bullock, Alan, *Hitler and Stalin: Parallel Lives* (HarperCollins, London and Alfred A. Knopf, New York, 1991)
Collins, Irene, *The Age of Progress: A Survey of European History between 1789 and 1871* (Arnold, London, 1964)
McCauley, Martin, *The Soviet Union, 1917–1991* (Longman, London, 1993)
Schama, Simon, *Citizens: A Chronicle of the French Revolution* (Penguin, London and New York, 1989)
Seton-Watson, Hugh, *The Russian Empire, 1801–1917* (Clarendon Press, Oxford, 1967)
Shirer, William L., *The Rise and Fall of the Third Reich* (Pan Books, London, 1964)
Taylor A.J.P., *The Struggle for Mastery in Europe, 1848–1914* (OUP, Oxford, reprinted 1965)
Tulard, J., *Napoleon* (Methuen, London, 1985)
Westwood, J.N., *Russia, 1917–1964* (Batsford, London, 1966)

US History
Morison, S.E., Commager, W.E., and Leuchtenburg, H.S., *Growth of the American Republic* (two volumes, OUP, Oxford, London and New York, 7th edition, 1980)
Moss, George, *America in the Twentieth Century* (Prentice Hall, New Jersey, 1989)
Snowman, Daniel, *America Since 1920* (Heinemann, London, 1968)

World History
Ambrose, Stephen E., *The Rise to Globalism* (Allen Lane, New York, 5th Ed., 1972)
Gilbert, Martin, *A History of the Twentieth Century* (three volumes, HarperCollins, London, 1999)

———, *The Second World War* (Guild Publishing, London, 1989)

Johnson, Paul, *A History of the Modern World, 1917 to the 1980s* (Wiedenfeld & Nicolson, London, 1983)

Watson, Jack (ed. O'Leary, Brendan), *World History Since 1945* (Murray, London, 1989)

Reference List

British History

Becket, J.C., *A Short History of Ireland* (Hutchinson, London, 5th edn., 1973)

Blake, Lord Robert, *Disraeli* (Eyre & Spottiswoode, London, 1966)

Curtis, R., *A History of Ireland* (Methuen, London, 6th edn., 1973)

Dangerfield, George, *The Strange Death of Liberal England* (Paladin, London, reprinted 1970)

David, Saul, *The Homicidal Earl* (Little, Brown, London, 1997)

Evans, Eric, *The Forging of the Modern State: Early Industrial Britain, 1783–1870* (Longman, London and New York, 1983)

Fussell, Paul, *The Great War and Modern Memory* (OUP, Oxford, 1975)

Gash, N., *Peel* (Longman, London and New York, 1972)

Grigg, J., *Lloyd George, the People's Champion, 1902–1911* (Eyre Methuen, London, 1978)

Hammond, J.L. and Barbara, *The Bleak Age* (Pelican, London and New York, 1947)

James, Robert Rhodes, *Albert, Prince Consort: A Biography* (Hamish Hamilton, London, 1983)

James, Robert Rhodes, *Anthony Eden* (Wiedenfeld & Nicolson, London, 1986)

Letwin, S.R., *The Anatomy of Thatcherism* (Fontana, London, 1982)

Lewis, M., *The History of the British Navy* (Penguin, London and Baltimore, 1957)

Magnus, Philip, *Gladstone* (Murray, London, 1954)

Paxman, Jeremy, *The English, The Portrait of a People* (Penguin, London, 1999)

Reilly, Robin, *Pitt the Younger* (Cassell, London, 1978)

Sawyer, Roger, *Roger Casement's Diaries: The Black and the White* (Pimlico, London, 1997)

Simpson, C., *Lusitania* (Longman, London, 1972)

Skidelsky, Robert, *Politicians and the Slump: The Labour Government of 1929–1931* (Pelican, London, 1967)

Strachey, Lytton, 'Florence Nightingale' in *Eminent Victorians* (Penguin, London, 1948)

Bibliography

Taylor, A.J.P., *The First World War* (Hamish Hamilton, London, 1963)

Turner, E.S., *Roads to Ruin: The Shocking History of Social Reform* (Michael Joseph, London, 1950)

Empire and Commonwealth

Cross, Colin, *The Fall of the British Empire, 1918–1968* (Hodder & Stoughton, London, 1968)

Grierson, Edward, *The Imperial Dream, British Commonwealth and Empire, 1775–1969* (William Collins, London, 1972)

Jeffries, Sir Charles, *The Transfer of Power, Problems of the Passage to Self-Government* (Pall Mall Press, London, 1960)

Macmillan, W.M., *The Road to Self-Rule: A Study in Colonial Evolution* (Faber, London, 1959)

European History

Almedigen, E.M., *Emperor Alexander II* (Bodley Head, London, 1962)

Glorney Bolton, J.R., *Roman Century, 1870–1970* (Hamish Hamilton, London, 1970)

Bower, Tom, *Blind Eye to Murder: Britain, America and the Purging of Nazi Germany: A Pledge Betrayed* (André Deutsch, London, 1981)

Conquest, Robert, *Lenin* (Fontana/Collins, London, 1972)

Cooper, Duff, *Talleyrand* (Jonathan Cape, London, reprinted 1958)

De Jonge, A., *Stalin* (Fontana/Collins, Glasgow, 1986)

Farquharson, John, *Explaining Hitler's Germany: Historians and the Third Reich* (Croom Helm, London, 1983)

Fest, Joachim, *The Face of the Third Reich* (Wiedenfeld & Nicolson, London, 1970)

Harris, Robert, *Selling Hitler: The Story of the Hitler Diaries* (Faber & Faber, London and Boston, 1986)

Koch, H.W., *In the Name of the Volk: Political Justice in Hitler's Germany* (Tauris, London, 1989)

Lewis, Gwyn, *The French Revolution: Rethinking the Debate* (Routledge, London and New York, 1993)

Loomis, Stanley, *Paris in the Terror* (Jonathan Cape, London, 1964)

Mack Smith, D., *The Making of Italy, 1796–1970* (Macmillan, London, 1968)

Mansergh, Nicholas, *The Coming of the First World War: A Study in European Balance* (Longmans, London and New York, 1949)

Rudé, George, *The Crowd in the French Revolution* (OUP, Oxford and London, 1959)

Taylor, A.J.P., *The Course of German History* (Hamish Hamilton, London, 1945)

Thomas, Hugh, *The Spanish Civil War* (Hamish Hamilton, London, 1977)

Thorne, C., *The Approach of War* (Macmillan, London and New York, 1967)

Vovelle, Michel, *The Fall of the French Monarchy* (CUP, London, 1974)

Williamson, D.G., *The Third Reich* (Longman, Studies in History series, London, 1982)

US History

Banks, Ann, *Third Person America* (Vintage Books, New York, 1981)

Boromé, Joseph A., 'The Evolutionary Controversy' in *Essays in American Historiography* (Sheehan & Syrett, Colombia, New York and London, 1960)

Boyer, Richard O., *The Legend of John Brown: A Legacy and a History* (Alfred A. Knopf, New York, 1972)

Brogan, D.W., *Abraham Lincoln* (Duckworth, London, 1974)

Cannon, Lou, *Reagan* (Putnam/Perigee, New York, 1982)

Graebner, Norman A., *A Manifest Destiny* (Bobbs-Merrill, Indianapolis, Indiana, 1968)

Jonas, Manfred, *Isolationism in America, 1935–1941* (Imprint Publications, Chicago, 1990)

Leuchtenburg, W.E., *Franklin Roosevelt and the New Deal* (in New American Nation series, Harper & Row, London and Glasgow, 1986)

Manchester, William, *The Death of a President* (World Books, London, 1968)

Monaghan, J., *Custer: The Life of General George Armstrong Custer* (University of Nebraska Press, Lincoln and London, 1971)

Parish, Peter J., *The American Civil War* (Eyre Methuen, London, 1975)

Prange, Gordon W., *Pearl Harbour: The Verdict of History* (Penguin, London, 1991)

Tefertiller, Casey, *Wyatt Earp, the Life Behind the Legend* (Wiley, London, 1997)

White, Theo H., *Breach of Faith: The Fall of Richard Nixon* (Cape, London, 1975)

World History

Brody, Richard L., *Strategical Defence in NATO Strategy* (National Institute for Strategical Studies, London, 1987)

Higgins, Hugh, *The Cold War* (Heinemann Educational, in Studies in Modern History series, London, 1983)

Marquand, Leo, *The Peoples and Policies of South Africa* (OUP, London, 1966)

Bibliography

Rayner, E.G., *The Cold War* (Hodder & Stoughton, in History at Source series, London, 1992)

Watson, Jack (ed. O'Leary, Brendan), *World History since 1945* (Murray, London 1989)

White, Stephen, *Gorbachev and After* (CUP, London and New York, 1996)

INDEX

N.B. Entries highlighted in **Bold** refer to topics which have separate listing in the table of contents.

Index

Index